PUBLICATIONS OF THE

ARMY RECORDS SOCIETY

VOL. 35

The Diary of Corporal Vince Schürhoff 1914–1918

198145 Corporal Vince Schürhoff MM, 11 May 1918.

The Diary of Corporal Vince Schürhoff 1914–1918

Edited by

Jim Beach

Published by

THE HISTORY PRESS
for the
ARMY RECORDS SOCIETY
2015

First published in the United Kingdom in 2015 by
The History Press · The Mill · Brimscombe Port · Stroud ·
Gloucestershire · GL5 2QG

British Library Cataloguing in Publication Data
A catalogue record for this book is available from the British Library.

ISBN 978-0-7509-6600-9

Typeset in Ehrhardt.
Typesetting and origination by
The History Press.
Printed and bound in England.

The Army Records Society was founded in 1984 in order to publish original records describing the development, organisation, administration and activities of the British Army from early times.

Any person wishing to become a Member of the Society should consult our website for details of the procedure. Members receive at least one volume per annum and are entitled to purchase back volumes at reduced prices.

The Society's website can be found at
www.armyrecordssociety.org.uk

Contents

List of Figures	viii
Acknowledgements	ix
Abbreviations	xi
Maps	xiii
Introduction	1
1 Infantry	9
2 Intelligence	79
Appendix	301
Bibliography	317
Index	323

List of figures

Frontispiece 198145 Corporal Vince Schürhoff MM, 11 May 1918

1 No. 13 Section at Moseley, January 1915 22

2 Lance Corporal Vince Schürhoff and Private Linder Robinson in France, 1916 43

3 Lance Corporal Vince Schürhoff with Sappers Bill Auckenthaler and Cecil Stallworthy, 1917 139

4 British troops delivering German prisoners to Arras Prison, April 1917 168

5 Wounded British troops at 43rd Casualty Clearing Station, Frévent, 7 April 1918 249

Acknowledgements

I must begin by thanking Joyce Hutton, archivist at the Military Intelligence Museum. By showing me a copy of the typescript diary she set in motion the process that has resulted in this volume. Throughout the project she has been consistently helpful and enthusiastic regarding its progress towards publication. I am similarly grateful to the museum's trustees for their interest and encouragement. I must also thank the following librarians, volunteers and archivists for their cheerful help in answering my queries: Martin Killeen, Ivana Frlan, and Helen Fisher (Cadbury Research Library, University of Birmingham); Dr Simon Robbins (Imperial War Museum); Ann Backhouse (Malvern Museum of Local History); William Spencer (National Archives); and Stuart Wheeler (Tank Museum).

I am deeply grateful to Annie Jackson, the society's copy-editor, for again helping to bring my manuscript up to a publishable standard. She intends this to be her final volume for the society and so, as Secretary, I wish to thank her for the excellent work performed throughout my tenure. I know that her patience, professionalism and good humour have consistently eased the paths of our volume editors.

Thanks are due to Professor Ian Beckett and Dr John Bourne who, early on, gave up their time to look at my unedited transcript of the diary. Their encouragement to get it published in book form was instrumental in moving things along. I wish to thank the Council of the Army Records Society for selecting it when an unexpected vacancy occurred in their publication schedule. In this regard I offer thanks to the anonymous referee for their comments and to Dr Tim Bowman for assuming Secretary's duties for the proposal and draft. A particular thank you to Barbara Taylor for her work in producing the maps. I must also thank Tim Halstead, the society's Treasurer, for suggesting sources on the Royal Warwickshire Regiment.

Drs Paul Fox, Dan Lomas and Alaric Searle all helped with advice and/or references for which I am thankful. Dr Bruce Cherry provided a copy of his thesis, which was much appreciated. A special mention is warranted for Dr Brian Hall who inadvertently directed me to the Australian War Memorial (AWM) file containing a copy of SS.165. I must also offer thanks to the Australian Army History Unit for their permission to reproduce that document (see Appendix).

Thank you to Susan and Roger King for sometimes putting a roof over my head while en route to Kew. Thanks also to my mother, Christine, for an unsolicited proofreading of the edited diary and to my brother, John, for helping to transport me to Canberra. A special thank you is needed for my old friend Jock Bruce who, unimpressed by my lack of persistence in tracking down hard-to-find soldiers, deployed his formidable research skills to that task. Some of the footnotes are therefore more his work than mine. In the past he has also discussed his own work on a First World War infantry battalion and some of his ideas have, I strongly suspect, been reflected in my own analysis. So, yet again, I am in his debt.

Finally, I must offer my greatest thank you to Rodney Shirley, Vince's son and the copyright holder of the diaries. As well as giving consent to publication of the diaries, he offered me a most friendly welcome to his home and since then has been very patient in awaiting this volume's appearance. I sincerely hope that what I have added and subtracted makes it a fair and useful presentation of his father's wartime thoughts, emotions and observations.

Abbreviations

16/Warwicks	16th (Service) Battalion, Royal Warwickshire Regiment
AD	Assistant Director
AF	Army Form
ANZAC	Australian and New Zealand Army Corps
APM	Assistant Provost Marshal
ASC	Army Service Corps
AWM	Australian War Memorial
BEF	British Expeditionary Force
CB	Companion, Order of the Bath
CCS	Casualty Clearing Station
CMG	Companion, Order of St Michael and St George
CO	commanding officer
DSO	Distinguished Service Order
EF	Expeditionary Force
GHQ	General Headquarters
GOC	General Officer Commanding
GSO	General Staff Officer
HQ	headquarters
i/c	in command
IP	Intelligence Police
IT	intelligence telephone
IWM	Imperial War Museum
MC	Military Cross
MIM	Military Intelligence Museum
MM	Military Medal
MP	Military Police
MVO	Member, Royal Victorian Order
NCO	non-commissioned officer
OC	officer commanding
OTC	Officer Training Corps
POW	prisoner of war

QM	Quartermaster
QMS	Quartermaster Sergeant
RAF	Royal Air Force
RAMC	Royal Army Medical Corps
RE	Royal Engineers
RFA	Royal Field Artillery
RFC	Royal Flying Corps
RMLI	Royal Marines Light Infantry
RNAS	Royal Naval Air Service
RSM	Regimental Sergeant-Major
SS	Stationery Service
TNA	National Archives
VAD	Voluntary Aid Detachment
WAAC	Women's Auxiliary Army Corps
WO	War Office
YMCA	Young Men's Christian Association

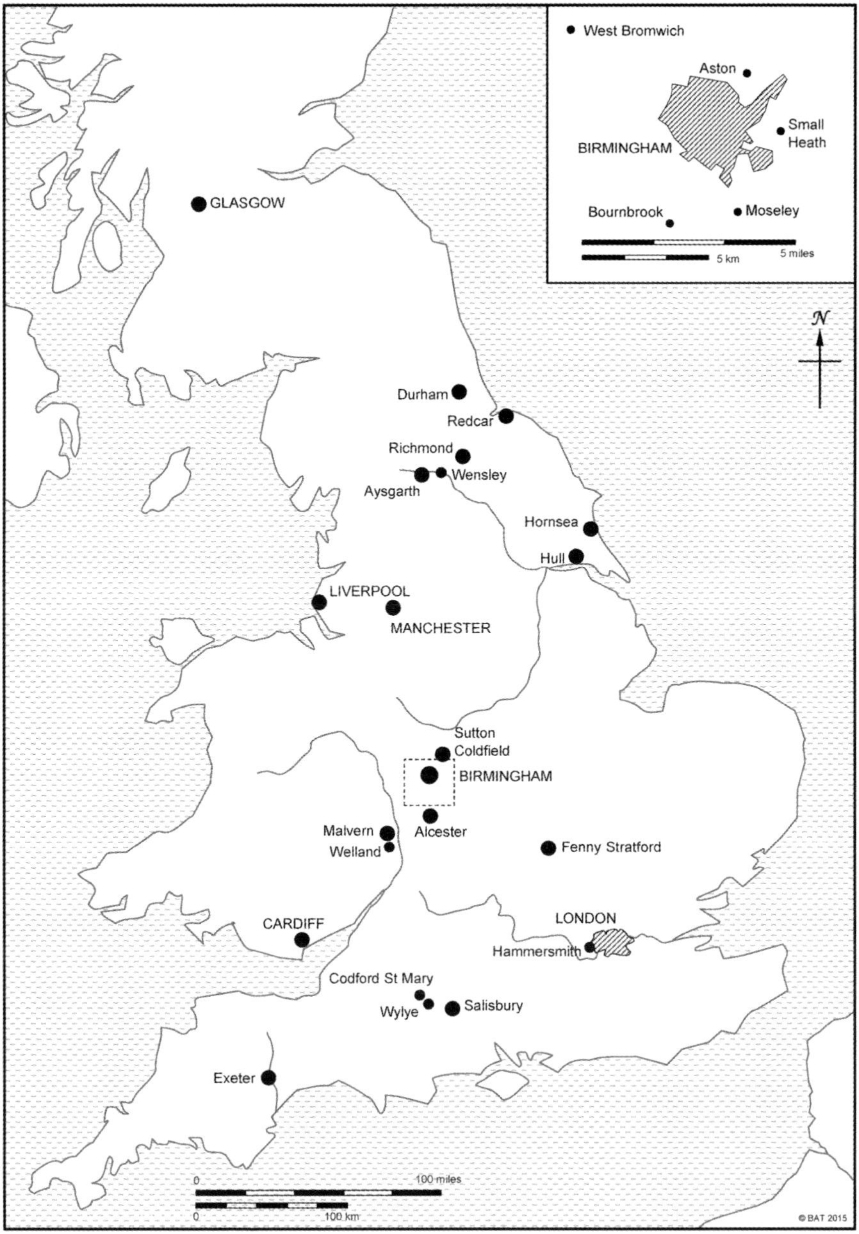
West Bromwich
Aston
Small
Heath
BIRMINGHAM
Bournbrook
Moseley
5 km
5 miles
GLASGOW
Durham
Redcar
Richmond
Wensley
Aysgarth
Hornsea
Hull
LIVERPOOL
MANCHESTER
Sutton
Coldfield
BIRMINGHAM
Malvern
Welland
Alcester
Fenny Stratford
CARDIFF
LONDON
Hammersmith
Codford St Mary
Wylye
Salisbury
Exeter
0
100 miles
0
100 km
© BAT 2015

Britain

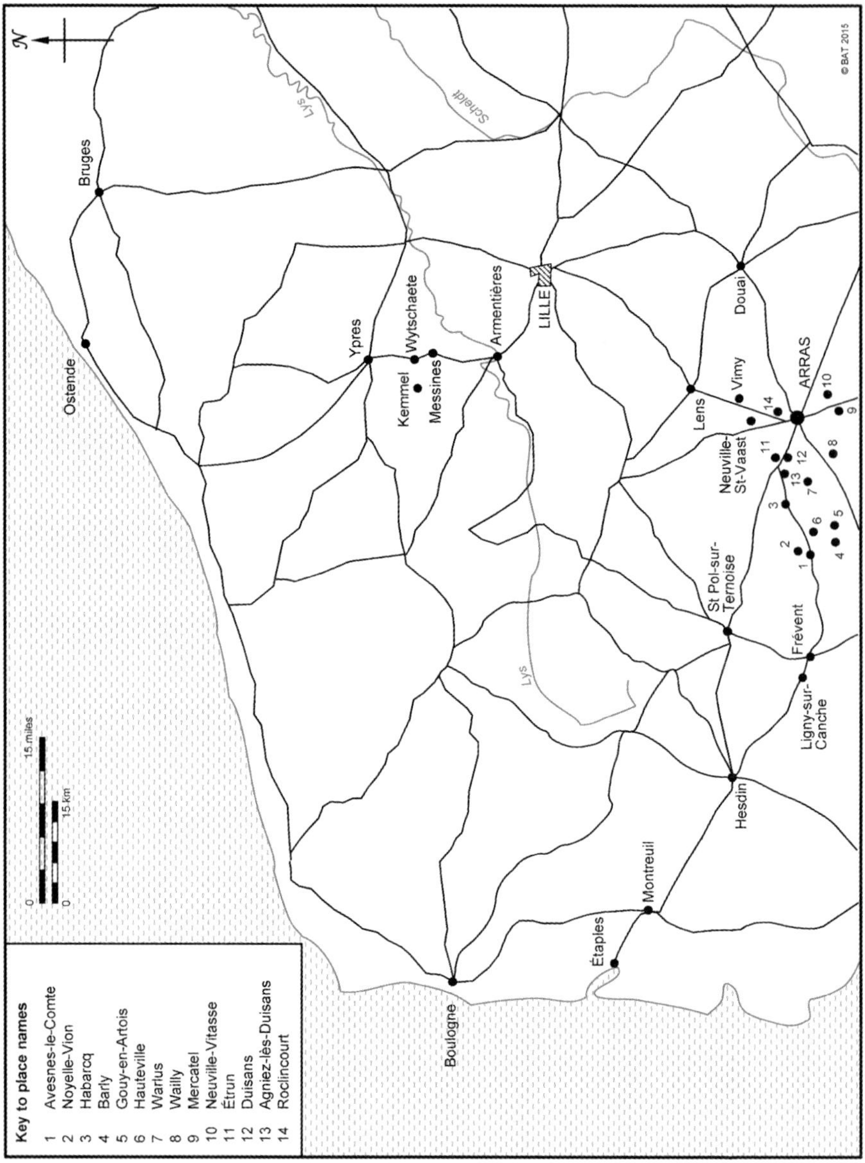

Flanders *(above)* and Somme *(right)*

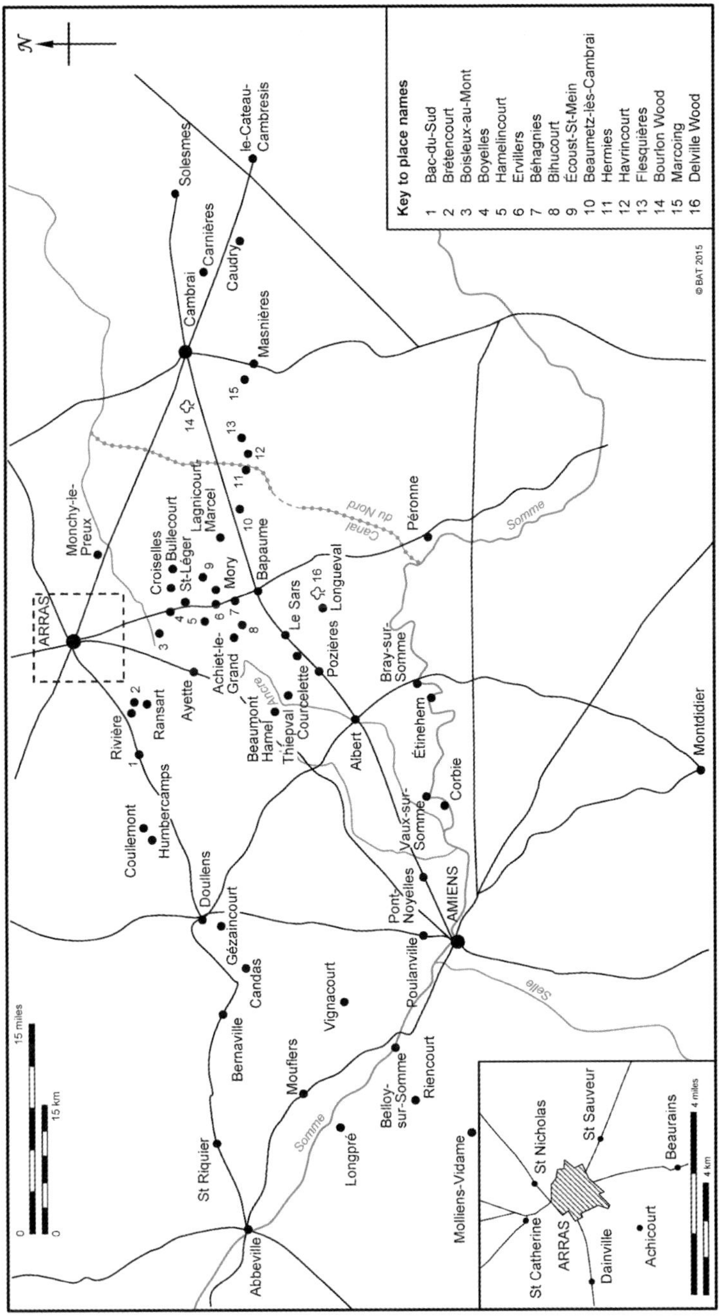

Key to place names
1 Bac-du-Sud
2 Brétencourt
3 Boisleux-au-Mont
4 Boyelles
5 Hamelincourt
6 Ervillers
7 Béhagnies
8 Bihucourt
9 Écoust-St-Mein
10 Beaumetz-lès-Cambrai
11 Hermies
12 Havrincourt
13 Flesquières
14 Bourlon Wood
15 Marcoing
16 Delville Wood
N
Solesmes
le-Cateau-Cambresis
Carnières
Caudry
Cambrai
Masnières
Monchy-le-Preux
Croiselles
Bullecourt
St-Léger
Lagnicourt
Marcel
Mory
Bapaume
Canal du Nord
Péronne
Somme
ARRAS
Ayette
Achiet-le-Grand
Le Sars
Longueval
Pozières
Courcelette
Bray-sur-Somme
Ransart
Rivière
Beaumont Hamel
Thiepval
Ancre
Albert
Étinehem
Montdidier
Humbercamps
Coullemont
Corbie
Vaux-sur-Somme
Doullens
Pont-Noyelles
AMIENS
Gézaincourt
Candas
Poulanville
Selle
Vignacourt
Bernaville
Riencourt
Belloy-sur-Somme
Domart
Flers
Longpré
St Riquier
Abbeville
Molliens-Vidame
15 miles
15 km
0
St Catherine
St Nicholas
St Sauveur
Dainville
Achicourt
Beaurains
4 miles
4 km
© BAT 2015

Introduction

Vince Schürhoff

In September 1914, aged twenty-three, Fritz Vincent Schürhoff enlisted in the British army as an infantryman. After training in Britain, he was deployed to France at the end of 1915. Following service in the trenches, he transferred to intelligence work in June 1916 and was later promoted to corporal in the Royal Engineers (Signal Service). For his conduct in March 1918 he received the Military Medal (MM). Demobilised in January 1919, he returned to the family business. The enterprise ran into difficulties and, after a period of unemployment in the 1930s, Vince worked in sales for an aluminium company. During the Second World War he served in the Home Guard. He married in 1926 and the couple had a son. Vince died in 1974.[1]

Before the First World War Vince lived in Birmingham and his family was German on his father's side. In 1918 they changed their surname to Shirley,[2] but throughout his military service Vince had to use his original surname of Schürhoff. Therefore, for consistency and authenticity, this volume has adopted that nomenclature along with his preferred first name.[3] Vince's father, Walter, was born in Westphalia in 1855 and came to Britain when he was twenty, becoming naturalised six years later.[4] In 1890 he married a British woman and Vince was born in West Bromwich the following year.[5] Vince received at least part of his secondary education

1 Rodney Shirley, [typescript memoir] (2010), 5–9; Oxfordshire Home Guard certificate (28 May 1940 to 31 December 1944) held by the Shirley family.

2 *London Gazette*, 2 July 1918.

3 His use of Vince rather than Fritz began in 1914: Foreword to Vince Shirley typescript diary, Vol. 5, Military Intelligence Museum (MIM).

4 Walter came to Birmingham in April 1875 and was naturalised in September 1881: HO144/87/A8619, National Archives (TNA). The law required him to have been resident for five years prior to naturalisation: Panikos Panayi, *The Enemy in Our Midst: Germans in Britain during the First World War* (Oxford: Berg, 1991), 61.

5 Alice Bayley. His German first wife had died, probably in childbirth; information supplied by Rodney Shirley, January 2013. Corroborated by the number of Walter's children in the 1911 Census. Vince had a younger sister, Millicent.

in Germany, attending a school in Hildesheim.[6] This gave him fluency in the German language and he also spoke French. By the age of twenty Vince was working as a clerk in Gotscher & Company, a manufacturing business run by his father and his uncle Gustav.[7] The company produced mostly decorative tableware for export. They had business connections with Latin America and in 1893 Walter became the Colombian consul for Birmingham, with his brother undertaking the same role for Mexico.[8] Vince had experienced foreign travel before the war, visiting Cuba with his parents in 1910.[9] From the passing references to home life in Vince's diary, and the fact that the 1911 Census notes three female servants in their household, his background was clearly that of the commercial middle class.

However, from June 1916 it was his status as the son of a German-born immigrant that had the greater effect upon his wartime experiences; his geographic and social position led him into a locally raised infantry battalion in 1914 but his German language skills prompted the transfer to intelligence. Although there is no suggestion of divided loyalties on the part of Vince or his family, they became part of a much-maligned wartime minority. In the last quarter of the nineteenth century the number of Germans in the West Midlands had grown from around 300 to almost 1,500. But this was a small community in comparison to the much greater concentrations of Germans in London, the south-east, Yorkshire and Lancashire. Before 1914 Germans were subject to some prejudice, which was directed particularly against recent and poorer migrants. These feelings were, of course, heightened during periods of Anglo-German tension on the international stage.[10] As a naturalised British subject Walter was not subject to wartime internment,[11] but along with 6,000 others of German birth he was viewed as a potential threat.[12]

On the outbreak of war Vince's family had a brush with the popular outburst of feelings against Germany. A crowd of 'excited young people' gathered outside his uncle Gustav's house and began shouting and booing.

6 Diary entry, 25 January 1917.

7 1911 Census online, accessed 27 November 2012.

8 *London Gazette*, 21 February 1893; 'Disorderly Scene: Mexican Consul Mistaken for German', *Birmingham Gazette*, 5 August 1914, 5.

9 Disembarked 2 May 1910, from the *Fürst Bismarck* at Plymouth: UK Incoming Passenger Lists, 1878–1960 on ancestry.co.uk, accessed 27 November 2012. Diary entry, 12 October 1918, Vince Shirley typescript diary, Vol. 6, MIM.

10 Panikos Panayi, *German Immigrants in Britain during the Nineteenth Century, 1815–1914* (Oxford: Berg, 1995), 92–3, 202–3.

11 For internment of Germans in Britain, see Panikos Panayi, *Prisoners of Britain: German Civilian and Combatant Internees during the First World War* (Manchester: Manchester University Press, 2012).

12 Panayi, *Enemy in Our Midst*, 62.

Apparently they had mistaken his residence for that of the German consul. No damage was done but the crowd moved on and attacked another residence nearby, smashing the windows with stones.[13] This event was less serious than attacks happening elsewhere in the country,[14] but it presumably caused the family much concern. The next wave of widespread anti-German violence occurred after the sinking of the *Lusitania* in May 1915. These attacks occurred predominantly in Liverpool, Manchester, Yorkshire and London.[15] In Birmingham, Walter and Gustav Schürhoff made a publicly declared contribution to the *Lusitania* Relief Fund, writing to the Lord Mayor to state their 'feelings of detestation' and 'emphatic abhorrence' towards the German government's 'barbarous methods'.[16] A week later, with anti-German handbills circulating locally, both men joined other 'naturalised British subjects of German … birth' in signing an open letter protesting against Germany's 'inhuman methods' of war.[17] Later, in early 1918, a tenacious campaign against naturalised Germans was waged by parts of the right-wing press.[18] With the tide of war apparently running against the Allies, they called their loyalty into question and the phrase 'once a German, always a German' gained currency. Suspicion fell upon those who had adopted Anglicised names and conspiracy theories suggested that a pro-German 'hidden hand' was hampering Britain's war effort.[19] The nationalist publication *John Bull* even demanded that naturalised Germans should be 'compelled to wear a distinctive badge'. The Cabinet responded with legislation to regulate name changes and imposed restrictions upon employing those of German birth in government service. It was this general context that presumably prompted the Schürhoffs' surname change. In this regard, Vince's receipt of an MM was rather timely as a public indication of the family's loyalty to Britain.[20]

---

13 'Disorderly Scene: Mexican Consul Mistaken for German', *Birmingham Gazette*, 5 August 1914, 5.

14 Panayi, *Enemy in Our Midst*, 223–4.

15 *Ibid.*, 229–53.

16 'Birmingham Consuls Protest', *Birmingham Mail*, 13 May 1915, 3.

17 'True to Their Oath: German Loyalists' Protest in Birmingham', *Birmingham Gazette*, 21 May 1915, 8.

18 Panayi, *Enemy in Our Midst*, 64–9, 218–19, 234.

19 Panikos Panayi, '"The Hidden Hand": British Myths about German Control of Britain during the First World War', *Immigrants and Minorities*, 7 (1988), 253–72.

20 'Malvern Officer Wins Military Cross', *Birmingham Post*, 13 May 1918, 6; *London Gazette*, 6 August 1918; 'More MM Awards: Midland Men to Receive the Decoration', *Birmingham Gazette*, 9 August 1918, 3; 'Local Honours', *Birmingham Mail*, 14 August 1918, 2; 'Birmingham Military Medallists', *Birmingham Post*, 14 August 1918, 6.

Diaries

In 1915 Vince and his friend, Linder Robinson, decided to record their impressions of military training. His later recollection was that they had been written up primarily 'with the object of killing boredom'.[21] Once in France, Vince kept his own conventional diary, recording short entries within the daily spaces. After moving to intelligence work he continued in the same manner before switching to notebooks in January 1917 and in this format made lengthier entries.[22] Vince stated that the books were then 'smuggled out of France under my kit every time I came home on leave'.[23] Prompted by his wife, between Christmas 1967 and the summer of 1968 Vince typed up his writings, added some comments, and then grouped them with personal photographs and ephemera in a set of ring-binders.[24] In November 1969 he showed the typescript diaries to the Imperial War Museum's librarian and, a few months later, loaned them for microfilming.[25] In 1981 the diaries were lent by his family to the Intelligence Corps Museum, Ashford.[26] That museum later became the Military Intelligence Museum, Chicksands, and in 2008 they again borrowed the typescript and a photocopy was deposited in their archives.[27]

Vince's motives for keeping his diaries seem fairly conventional; to make a record of his adventure and, later, as a 'safety valve' for expressing discontent. It also seems to have become an embedded habit during the war. Contrary to popular belief, diaries were allowed in operational theatres, but could not be posted home and were not supposed to record

21 Vince said they were 'largely written up during the autumn of 1915 from memory': Foreword to Vince Shirley typescript diary, Vol. 1, MIM. The Wensleydale section suggests that they had started the project during the summer.

22 The Shirley family still have the originals of the 1915 and 1916 diaries but the later notebooks are missing, although they are still thought to be somewhere in their possession.

23 Foreword to Vince Shirley typescript diary, Vol. 1, MIM.

24 Vince said they had 'lain unread for 50 years' and that retirement had made 'time available' to 'decipher the close script': Foreword to Vince Shirley typescript diary, Vol. 2. MIM. For the 1960s phenomenon of recently retired veterans returning to their First World War experiences, see Dan Todman, *The Great War: Myth and Memory* (London: Hambledon, 2005), 192–3. From the captions on some of the photographs with the diary, it is clear that Vince revisited the battlefields in the summer of 1921. For the context of this type of visit, see David Lloyd, *Battlefield Tourism: Pilgrimage and the Commemoration of the Great War in Britain, Australia and Canada, 1919–1939* (Oxford: Berg, 1998), 100–30.

25 'Shirley, Cpl Vince', Microfilm PBS No. 125 (April 1970), IWM. Interaction with librarian taken from information in IWM correspondence file for Vince Shirley papers supplied by Dr Simon Robbins, June 2014.

26 Robson/Shirley correspondence, 17 September, 6 and 24 October 1981, 12 March 1982 held by Shirley family.

27 To produce this volume, a duplicate photocopy was made and loaned by the museum to the editor. The text was later compared with the 1915 and 1916 manuscript diaries and the IWM microfilm.

anything that was militarily significant. Middle-class diaries, especially officers' ones, are fairly common, particularly amongst those whose military employment allowed them the time to write.[28] On a practical level, from mid-1916 Vince's record-keeping was helped by his consistent access to writing materials, light and some form of table. Also, the long and often uneventful night shifts presumably gave him the space to reflect upon events and compose his thoughts. That said, some entries, like that of 6 January 1917, were clearly recorded in the heat of the moment. The obvious question is whether it was appropriate for someone engaged in sensitive intelligence work to be keeping a diary at all. Although he is reticent in commenting directly about his work, there are many indirect statements that could have been useful to the enemy had he been captured. As this volume shows, when triangulated with other sources the diary is quite revealing about British intelligence techniques. But Vince and his comrades were not closely supervised by commissioned officers and so his diary writing was most likely concealed from anyone who might have been concerned by it.

As an infantry diarist, Vince is far from unique. Indeed, up to mid-1916 his work is directly comparable to the recently published diary of Harry Drinkwater who, like Vince, served in a Birmingham battalion.[29] Comparing the two, Vince gives a much fuller account of pre-deployment training, but once in France his entries are shorter, albeit with similar detail overall. However, it is as an intelligence diarist that Vince is historically significant. He was later quite modest about his writings, reflecting that he had been just 'an average youth, quite fond of life and adventure, [but] with little regard to the more scientific aspects of [intelligence work]'.[30] Such contemporaneous personal records of intelligence work are rare and, as an 'other rank' at the front end of the intelligence system, his is even rarer. This is especially true with regard to tactical signals intelligence. Therefore, taking into account the longevity of the record-keeping and the richness of his observations, Vince's diaries may be unique. Beyond the core of his military work, Vince also provides a fascinating window into the physical and mental worlds of the British soldier on the Western Front. Serving in a variety

28 Jessica Meyer, *Men of War: Masculinity and the First World War in Britain* (Basingstoke: Palgrave Macmillan, 2009), 47–9.

29 Jon Cooksey and David Griffith (eds), *Harry's War: The Great War Diary of Harry Drinkwater* (London: Ebury Press, 2013). Another possible comparison is with the very detailed memoir of Geoffrey Husbands: John Bourne and Bob Bushaway (eds), *Joffrey's War: A Sherwood Forester in the Great War* (Nottingham: Salient Books, 2011).

30 Shirley to Director, IWM, 1 February 1970; information from IWM correspondence file for Vince Shirley papers supplied by Dr Simon Robbins, June 2014.

of roles and with varying proximity to the frontline, he observes and records a wide range of day-to-day activities. In this regard, he is an excellent chronicler of the nuances of 'everyday life' in the British army; a dimension of history that can sometimes be overlooked.[31] Furthermore, his language skills allowed him to easily transcend the boundary between the British army and the local French population. Therefore, within those environments, the subsequent introductions seek to contextualise Vince's status, his motivation, and the variety of settings that he found himself within. Anticipating the details provided in the diary itself, comments will be made about his everyday life, especially his work, the dangers experienced, as well as food and leisure.

Editorial Method

The 1968 typescript contains over 200,000 words.[32] This was transcribed and then edited down by half through the removal of repetitive or very mundane entries. Minor slips have been corrected silently, but where Vince made an obvious error in recording a location or an individual, the adjustment has been made clear. Similarly, where necessary, geographical information has been inserted using the relevant unit war diaries.[33] Where additional details of military events could be ascertained, they have been added. For Vince's recreational reading, only the first date of a book's publication has been listed because in some cases it is impossible to know which edition he actually read. Similarly, the films he watched are noted with their original release dates.

Attempts have been made to trace every serviceman mentioned by Vince. This has been more successful for the period of his infantry service. During his time in intelligence, the prevalence of common family names and their affiliation to a large corps have sometimes made the task

31 'The history of everyday life' is centred upon 'the actions and sufferings of those who are frequently labelled "everyday, ordinary people", a term as suggestive as it is imprecise. What is foregrounded is their world of work and non-work. Descriptions detail housing and homelessness, clothing and nakedness, eating habits and hunger, people's loves and hates, their quarrels and co-operation, memories, anxieties, hopes for the future … Central to the thrust of everyday historical analysis is the life and survival of those who have remained largely anonymous in history.' Alf Lüdtke, 'What Is the History of Everyday Life and Who Are Its Practitioners?' in Alf Lüdtke (ed.), *The History of Everyday Life: Reconstructing Historical Experiences and Ways of Life* (Princeton, NJ: Princeton University Press, 1995), 3–4.

32 It also contains over 100 photographs, postcards, sketches, manuscript letters, and ephemera. Unless otherwise indicated, this volume's photographs have been reproduced from the diaries.

33 'For security reasons, no village or town was spelt out in full in the original entries, but, memory permitting, I have endeavoured to give them their full names when typing.' Foreword to Vince Shirley typescript diary, Vol. 1, MIM.

impossible. Unless otherwise specified, where only the first given name of a soldier has been listed this has been taken from the National Archives' online medal roll index cards. Any additional biographical information has, unless explained, been taken from an individual's service record where it survives. Basic information on the men in his infantry battalion has been drawn from their *Book of Honour* which lists personnel on deployment to France.[34] Although a certain amount of 'churn' would have occurred during the subsequent six months, reliance has been placed upon the platoon or company affiliations within that text. Officers' details have been taken from the monthly and quarterly *Army Lists*. Where an individual is known to have died, information has been taken from *Soldiers Died in the Great War* and/or the Commonwealth War Graves Commission website.[35] Where no positive identification could be made, individuals have been left without annotation.

34 William Bowater (ed.), *Birmingham City Battalions: Book of Honour* (London: Sherratt & Hughes, 1920). Digitised by Midlands Historical Data, 2005.

35 War Office, *Soldiers Died in the Great War, 1914–19* (London: HMSO, 1921).

1

Infantry

In late September 1914 Vince enlisted in the 3rd Birmingham City Battalion of the New Armies, becoming number 219 Private Schürhoff.[1] Later designated as the 16th (Service) Battalion of the Royal Warwickshire Regiment (16/Warwicks), they assembled in mid-October and spent their first winter of the war near Birmingham. In April 1915 they concentrated with other battalions at Malvern and two months later went to Wensleydale to become part of the newly formed 32nd Division. In August, after some musketry on the Yorkshire coast, they moved to Salisbury Plain. The unit deployed to France in late November and, after re-subordination to 5th Division, they were employed on the Somme for three months before moving north to Arras. Vince left the battalion in June 1916.

Status

During his time with the infantry, there were two main phases in the evolution of Vince's military status; from civilian to soldier, then to junior non-commissioned officer (NCO) and specialisation as a 'Gas NCO'. Because of Britain's difficulties in providing materiel resources for its rapidly raised mass army, the first phase was unavoidably prolonged. Although Vince was notionally a soldier as soon as he enlisted in September,[2] the army was unable to house its flood of recruits. So, like others across Britain, he became officially a member of the army's reserve and would have stayed at home on a modest subsistence allowance.[3]

1 The wartime service of the city's three battalions has been chronicled in Terry Carter, *Birmingham Pals: 14th, 15th & 16th (Service) Battalions of the Royal Warwickshire Regiment* (Barnsley: Pen & Sword, 2011).

2 Battalion nominal roll: '"City" Battalions', *Birmingham Post*, 2 October 1914, 3.

3 'Training Depot at Moseley', *Birmingham Post*, 14 September 1914, 8; Peter Simkins, *Kitchener's Army: The Raising of the New Armies, 1914–16* (Manchester: Manchester University Press, 1988), 73–4.

Summoned to a disused theological college on 19 October 1914, he then became physically part of a military unit. But without proper uniforms, his battalion seems to have remained, at least mentally, in a transitory stage, with Vince noting that discipline was initially 'very slack'. The arrival of uniforms and rifles in January 1915 seems to have been the watershed in giving the men a sense of military purpose. Interestingly, unlike other sources which stress their unpopularity, Vince and Linder did not complain too bitterly about their blue rather than khaki uniforms up to mid-1915.[4] However, they did clearly resent their subordination to the 'erstwhile theatre-door attendants, commissionaires, park-keepers, [and] railway guards' who served as their NCOs. These men were presumably former soldiers and, across the New Armies, this inversion of the normal social hierarchy was galling for middle-class recruits.[5] For Vince and Linder it seems to have been domestic duties in the Sergeants' Mess rather than interaction at work that put the new relationship into sharp relief.

In February 1915 Vince was promoted to lance corporal. His employment as a scout during manoeuvres also suggests he was perceived as an above average soldier. Later, in Wensleydale, we see him transferred to take charge of a notoriously difficult section of soldiers. By his own account, he adopted a calm approach which was a mixture of encouragement and coercion. It is likely that his previous exposure to personnel management in the context of a small manufacturing firm influenced this approach.[6] Once the battalion was in France, Vince appears to have performed effectively but not remarkably as a junior NCO. Like his peers, he seems to have struggled initially with the hard winter conditions, but he undertook the normal range of low-level command tasks such as the leading of working or carrying parties. Furthermore, his French language skills – which appear to have been unique within his company – made him more useful in the rear areas than the average lance corporal.[7] Presumably perceived as intelligent and generally competent,

4 Simkins, *Kitchener's Army*, 263. The 1st and 2nd Battalions received khaki uniforms while in Wensleydale, so presumably the 3rd Battalion did too: Carter, *Birmingham Pals*, 114.

5 Simkins, *Kitchener's Army*, 225, 227. For the imitation of an 'Old Army' culture within the New Armies, see David Englander, 'Discipline and Morale in the British Army, 1917–1918', in John Horne (ed.), *State, Society and Mobilization in Europe during the First World War* (Cambridge: Cambridge University Press, 1997), 127.

6 For the New Armies' junior leadership, see Simkins, *Kitchener's Army*, 228.

7 For the numbers of French-speaking soldiers, especially within the New Armies, see Craig Gibson, 'Relations between the British Army and the Civilian Populations on the Western Front, 1914–18' (PhD thesis, University of Leeds, 1998), 80, 82; Craig Gibson, *Behind the Front: British Soldiers and French Civilians, 1914–1918* (Cambridge: Cambridge University Press, 2014), 147.

Vince was therefore a sensible choice to be trained as the company's Gas NCO in March 1916.[8] This role required semi-independent work and gave him much greater freedom of movement around the frontlines than he had experienced beforehand.

Had he stayed in the infantry, it is highly likely that Vince would have progressed beyond lance corporal. However, an attempt to obtain a commission at the beginning of 1916 was thwarted. At an earlier stage, presumably while still in Britain, he had been unsuccessful in applying.[9] That first failure is unsurprising, as New Army units initially sought to follow the army's social norms when appointing their officers.[10] Being young, without a public school or university Officer Training Corps certificate, and lacking any personal connections within his unit's hierarchy, Vince would have had no obvious route for overcoming the prevailing convention.[11] And without casualties to thin the officers' mess, there would have been little demand once the establishment had been filled. But, taking a longer view, Vince was reasonably well educated and from the 'commercial and clerical' class that provided most of the war's temporary officers.[12] The catalyst for his second attempt was the news that a close friend had been successful in his own application. After an interview with the brigade commander and a month-long wait, Vince was turned down with no explanation. In later years he would suggest to his family that his German family background had been 'a handicap to him getting a commission'.[13] This would have been a very significant factor after he had left the infantry, as there were definite barriers to intelligence officers having German parentage.[14] But in February 1916, Vince's application may just have been premature in both his readiness

8 For the early German development of chemical warfare and the Allies' response, see L.F. Haber, *The Poisonous Cloud: Chemical Warfare in the First World War* (Oxford: Clarendon Press, 1986), 22–82; Donald Richter, *Chemical Soldiers: British Gas Warfare in World War I* (Lawrence: University Press of Kansas, 1992), 6–21; Albert Palazzo, *Seeking Victory on the Western Front: The British Army and Chemical Warfare in World War I* (Lincoln: University of Nebraska Press, 2000), 41–77.

9 Had he applied in November/December 1915, one would have expected it to appear in the diary.

10 Gary Sheffield, *Leadership in the Trenches: Officer–Man Relations, Morale and Discipline in the British Army in the Era of the First World War* (London: Macmillan, 2000), 38.

11 For the sufficiency of OTC trained candidates and the importance of personal connections, see Simkins, *Kitchener's Army*, 221, 223. In the case of Vince's regiment, this is corroborated by research indicating that, across all battalions, 63 per cent of those commissioned between August and December 1914 had OTC experience: Changboo Kang, 'The British Infantry Officer on the Western Front in the First World War with special reference to the Royal Warwickshire Regiment', PhD thesis, University of Birmingham (2007), 107.

12 Sheffield, *Leadership*, 31.

13 Rodney Shirley, [typescript memoir] (2010), 4.

14 Jim Beach, *Haig's Intelligence: GHQ and the German Army, 1916–1918* (Cambridge: Cambridge University Press, 2013), 77.

and its timing. On a mundane level, before and after his commissioning interview, he had attracted negative attention from both his company commander and second-in-command. Also, by his own admission, during this period he did not perform well when given an opportunity to drill the platoon. This may have been an unofficial test and, within a 'subjective system of personal recommendations',[15] such a minor slip-up may have carried undue weight. Also he had only seen a couple of months' active service, during part of which he had been on the sick list. But more significant may have been the general timing. Relative to later periods, in early 1916, the British army was not sustaining large numbers of casualties and so the need to replace junior officers was not as pressing. Spurred on by his friend's success, Vince might have been successful in obtaining a commission if he had waited a little longer.

Motivation

In seeking to understand Vince's military motivation, two key questions arise. First, why did he join the army in September 1914? Second, what kept him going once he was confronted with the difficulties and dangers of trench warfare? In addressing the former, the general context of recruitment in Britain as well as specific conditions in Birmingham must be understood.[16] Prompted by bad news from the Western Front, the national wave of recruitment peaked in early September with men responding patriotically to Lord Kitchener's call for volunteers.[17] The army was overwhelmed by the weight of numbers seeking to enlist so local government stepped in to help manage the process. In Birmingham over 15,000 men joined up in the first half of September.[18] Within that surge, the city raised three infantry battalions that would, in theory, be drawn from the 'non-manual' workers of the middle class.[19] These men

---

15 Sheffield, *Leadership*, 39.

16 For general introductions to recruitment in this period, see Peter Simkins, 'The Four Armies, 1914–1918', in David Chandler and Ian Beckett (eds), *The Oxford Illustrated History of the British Army* (Oxford: Oxford University Press, 1994), 241–54; Clive Hughes, 'The New Armies', in Ian Beckett and Keith Simpson (eds), *A Nation in Arms: A Social Study of the British Army in the First World War* (London: Tom Donovan, 1990), 99–125.

17 Catriona Pennell, *A Kingdom United: Popular Responses to the Outbreak of the First World War in Britain and Ireland* (Oxford: Oxford University Press, 2012), 145; Simkins, *Kitchener's Army*, 59, 64–5.

18 John Hartigan, 'Volunteering in the First World War: The Birmingham Experience, August 1914–May 1915', *Midland History*, 24 (1999), 167.

19 Editorial, *Birmingham Post*, 28 August 1916 cited in Carter, *Birmingham Pals*, 48–9 and Hartigan, 'Volunteering', 176.

were recruited primarily through a newspaper campaign, with the names of volunteers printed in the *Birmingham Post*. The 1st and 2nd City Battalions were quickly filled, but the 3rd took slightly longer to bring up to strength.[20] Because of this later start, there is a strong sense that the 3rd Battalion lost out in the subsequent local competition for resources such as accommodation.[21] It is also interesting to note that, unlike its siblings, the 3rd Battalion had no public parade to mark its founding.[22]

Vince's membership of the 3rd Battalion tells us immediately that he was not at the very front of Birmingham's queue, suggesting a considered rather than spur of the moment decision to join the army. Lack of haste is also indicated by the fact that, unlike many others, he did not join another part of the army after growing impatient at the delays in assembling the Birmingham battalions.[23] Given his age, he may have also been driven by an underlying desire for adventure. The likelihood is that the family's export business was disrupted by the war, so any economic restraints upon his departure would have been lifted. It is also fair to assume that Vince was influenced by the national mood of doing one's duty in response to German aggression.[24] This would have been complicated by his father's German birth and so a familial duty to demonstrate national loyalty may have been an unspoken assumption. The opportunity to join a local, class-conscious unit was perhaps also significant in being seen locally to fulfil this dual duty.[25] However, from his apparent loneliness on the first day at Moseley, he did not join up with any 'pals' and so peer pressure can probably be ruled out.

During his time in the infantry, Vince's diaries do not discuss the wider war and are silent upon his attitude towards the enemy. Once he arrives in France the Germans are, of course, mentioned frequently as the source of violence directed towards him and his comrades, but these instances are couched in fairly neutral terms. For example, on 31 January 1916, the retaliation against the German sniper is portrayed as exciting rather than overtly vengeful. The Germans are referred to as 'Bosch' but, in the absence of any direct contact, they are a faceless, almost abstract threat. Like other soldiers, Vince's mood fluctuated according to the physical

20 Simkins, *Kitchener's Army*, 86–7; Hartigan, 'Volunteering', 175; Carter, *Birmingham Pals*, 59.

21 'The raising of a third battalion was not so easy, owing to the increased competition of other units and doubts as to whether suitable quarters could be found for training': Bowater (ed.), *Birmingham City Battalions*, 3.

22 Carter, *Birmingham Pals*, 84.

23 Simkins, *Kitchener's Army*, 87; Hartigan, 'Volunteering', 176.

24 Simkins, *Kitchener's Army*, 165, 168–9, 172; Pennell, *Kingdom United*, 156–7, 159.

25 Hartigan, 'Volunteering', 176.

conditions that he found himself in as well as the psychological influences of his human surroundings.[26] From his diary, it appears that his motivation was tested most severely on two occasions in December 1915. His first night in the trenches was described as 'a nightmare'. Clearly inexperienced, his section was berated by the battalion commander responsible for their induction, necessitating the drawing of lots to sacrifice a shirt for cleaning their rifles. Then, during his second stint in the trenches, on Christmas Eve he experienced another 'nightmarish' low point when he was broken down physically by the extremely muddy conditions. Barefoot and possibly hypothermic, he stumbled into a dug-out and was revived by his comrades. This latter incident neatly illustrates the core importance of small or 'primary' groups in providing order and mutual support in combat environments.[27] That said, from this point until his departure from the battalion in June 1916, Vince's motivation was never again placed under such severe strain. His rotations through the trenches were short compared to his later experiences, and their regularity allowed time for recovery. The battalion was not involved in any offensive actions and their experience of shelling was of the 'routine [and] short-range' variety, rather than intense and large-calibre.[28] Also, although the battalion and company were taking casualties consistently, the absolute numbers were not yet excessive and, importantly, did not include any of Vince's close comrades. Had he remained with 16/Warwicks and gone with them back to the Somme, it seems likely that further and much deeper low points would have tested him.

Settings

During his time as an infantryman the physical and mental settings within which Vince operated changed considerably. The physical environment of the improvised barracks at Moseley was fairly Spartan, but once much of the battalion had been billeted out, it provided a reasonable base compared to those used by many New Army units in the winter of 1914.[29] Although Vince and Linder chafed against the cramped conditions and

26 Helen McCartney, *Citizen Soldiers: The Liverpool Territorials in the First World War* (Cambridge: Cambridge University Press, 2005), 240.

27 Alexander Watson, *Enduring the Great War: Combat, Morale and Collapse in the German and British Armies, 1914–1918* (Cambridge: Cambridge University Press, 2008), 66–7.

28 Edward Madigan, '"Sticking to a Hateful Task": Resilience, Humour, and British Understandings of Combatant Courage, 1914–1918', *War in History*, 20 (2013), 85.

29 Simkins, *Kitchener's Army*, 207, 243–4, 250.

lack of privacy, it was a necessary part of their military socialisation. As they observed, the battalion's time under canvas at Malvern in the spring and early summer of 1915 was a more invigorating environment. It was also fairly close to Birmingham, and so maintaining direct contact with family and friends was still possible. Wensleydale was similar but less popular due to its remoteness and, initially at least, a limited water supply. However, Vince's battalion seem to have coped better with the conditions than the other Birmingham battalions who had much less experience under canvas.[30] Although the practice trenches were uncomfortable, the huts at Codford St Mary, on Salisbury Plain, seem to have provided a useful context for off-duty bonding within platoons. Once they were in France, conditions were harsh. Obviously forward and reserve trenches in winter were extremely challenging, but even when they were out of the line, the collective billeting in farm outbuildings was very austere.[31] That said, by the spring of 1916 there is a clear sense that Vince and his comrades had become hardened to their itinerant rural lifestyle.

Important within these environments was the presence of civilians. While the battalion was in England, the various local communities, and particularly the Young Men's Christian Association (YMCA),[32] provided them with welfare support. On a more personal level, 'Mrs L' in Moseley and Mrs Robinson in Wensleydale welcomed Vince and Linder into their homes. And, from their account, the village of Codford St Mary resembled a 'country fair' with its facilities for the transient population of soldiers. In France the battalion also interacted continually with the civilian population and, even early on, Vince's account reinforces the argument that the presence of a friendly population was important in sustaining British army morale.[33] For example, at the end of February, merely staying in houses and reaching a fair-sized town generated a noticeable surge in his spirit. And, being able to converse with the locals, Vince clearly enjoyed non-military human contact with the women and children they were billeted upon. Initially some things were surprising to him, such as the woman who chatted with him while he was washing, but he seems to have quickly adapted to the surrounding rural culture. However, the battalion's oscillations through the trenches and then its

30 Carter, *Birmingham Pals*, 110–12.

31 'In rural areas … men were normally sheltered in barns, most of which could hold a company … or at least a platoon.' Gibson, *Behind the Front*, 130–1.

32 For the YMCA's work during the First World War, see Michael Snape (ed.), *The Back Parts of War: The YMCA Memoirs and Letters of Barclay Baron, 1915 to 1919* (Woodbridge: Boydell Press for the Church of England Record Society, 2009), 17–88.

33 Gibson, *Behind the Front*, 12, 382.

movement from the Somme to Arras meant that contact with individual civilians was curtailed. In this regard, and in comparison to Vince's later interactions, it is notable that he does not often record women's names during this period.

During his infantry service we can also follow the evolution of Vince's military relationships. As well as having a clear local identity, most men of the battalion had been recruited simultaneously. This meant that, while in England, the unit's composition was very stable and presumably quite cohesive. As Vince noted, his platoon 'had remained practically unaltered since [its] formation'. This is corroborated by the fact that, when they deployed to France, 85 per cent of them had a service number lower than 250.[34] However, it is interesting to note that Vince and his immediate circle of friends maintained some distance from the rest of their section. This may have been due to underlying class-consciousness and the remnants of pre-war formalities. But it is clear that Vince formed two very close friendships, with Linder Robinson and Philip Titterton. Before deployment, the relationship with Linder was stronger, as indicated by their decision to seek a billet together at Moseley and their joint authorship of the first section of this diary. But, after struggling with respiratory difficulties on the battalion's first march in France, Linder was transferred to a logistics role and his contact with Vince became episodic. The friendship with Philip then came to the fore, with the two men in close proximity in and out of the line. Their closeness is illustrated by Vince's diary entry of 4 January 1916 which describes Philip '[showing] his affection for me by linking arms with me and clasping hands' while they slept.[35] Once Philip had been commissioned in March 1916, the diary does not indicate that another strong friendship was formed. This is perhaps significant because, when the process of recruitment into intelligence commenced, there were no close bonds to hold Vince back from embracing the opportunity that it presented.

Everyday Life

Although Vince's diary paints in a great deal more about his daily life, at its core is his military work. This is quite normal. Whereas letters home

34 Bowater (ed.), *Birmingham City Battalions*, 126.

35 The modern reader might view such physical contact as odd or vaguely sexual. But in the context of harsh weather conditions, the close physical proximity of barn billets, and their recent exposure to life-threatening danger for the first time, it seems more a subconscious and platonic expression of middle-class male friendship.

would have constituted an interaction with a civilian environment, the diary is focused upon his army life and that was, of course, underpinned by his military function.[36] During his battalion's initial thirteen-month odyssey around Britain, Vince and Linder recounted, and reflected upon, the various stages of their training. In theory their transition from civilian to battle-ready soldier should have taken six months; encompassing basic recruit training, platoon training, musketry, company training, further musketry, and then large-scale exercises.[37] Although these stages were generally followed, the timeline was greatly extended as the army wrestled with its insufficient training infrastructure. The first period at Moseley consisted mostly of 'monotonous drilling'. In January the arrival of uniforms and rifles facilitated weapons training and tactical exercises which continued at Malvern. In Wensleydale, the battalion became properly part the 32nd Division and Vince and Linder highlight the mental shift in self-perception from a standalone 3rd Birmingham City Battalion to 16/Warwicks within a larger military system.[38] At this point the physical demands increased, with longer and night marches occurring. Once on Salisbury Plain there was a definite shift in the emphasis of tactical training. Whereas the battalion had previously scampered around the countryside rehearsing 'open warfare', they now conducted exercises in trenches, practising handovers and holding routines. Vince and Linder mention mock trench attacks, but the lack of detail perhaps suggests these were not particularly sophisticated.[39]

The question therefore arises as to how well prepared the battalion was for conditions in France. It is fairly clear from Vince's account that the reality of war on the Western Front was a shock to the unit. The combination of harsh weather conditions, the rough sleeping out of the line, and a very difficult first period in the trenches clearly took its toll.[40] Furthermore, Vince's interaction with the Cheshires' commanding

36 Meyer, *Men of War*, 48–9.

37 Simkins, *Kitchener's Army*, 296.

38 32nd Division. Formed in mid-1915 with infantry units of the New Army drawn from Birmingham, Bristol, Salford, Lonsdale and Glasgow. The three Birmingham battalions were subordinated to 95th Infantry Brigade: A.F. Becke, *Order of Battle of Divisions: Part 3a, New Army Divisions (9–26)* (Historical Section, Committee of Imperial Defence, 1938, reprinted Uckfield: Naval & Military Press, 2007), Part 3b, 27–32.

39 For the 'unreality and amateurishness' of field training and the belated incorporation of lessons from the Western Front, see Simkins, *Kitchener's Army*, 305–7. Their testimony is significant because it was recorded before their exposure to real trench warfare and so cannot have been tainted by the subsequent contrast.

40 It is hard to reconcile Vince's account with the recent assessment of 'a cushy start to their war', even with the caveat of a 'miserable first Christmas' for his battalion: Carter, *Birmingham Pals*, 139, 165.

officer in the trenches a week before Christmas suggests that their mentors were unimpressed with their standard of soldiering. This would help to explain the decision, enacted on 26 December, to separate the Birmingham battalions and re-subordinate them to 5th Division, a 'regular' formation. Their divisional history noted the unpopularity of the move but deemed it to be a 'sound policy' given the severe 'ordeal' that they had experienced initially.[41] The military authorities also diagnosed a leadership problem with 16/Warwicks. Upon its formation the battalion had been commanded by Colonel David Lewis, a regular infantry officer who had been brought back from retirement.[42] Lewis departed in March 1915 due to ill health and was replaced by another 'dug out', Lieutenant-Colonel Thomas Diver.[43] But Diver did not take the battalion to France. That task fell to a younger man; Lieutenant-Colonel Alan de Trafford, a forty-five-year-old whose seven years of militia service had concluded twenty years earlier.[44] In October 1914 he had been recommissioned and took command of Vince's 'A' Company before becoming the battalion second-in-command in April 1915.[45] According to later testimony, de Trafford had accepted command of the battalion 'under protest, as he did not feel justified in holding it'. In January 1916 his brigadier requested his removal, but was overruled and instead a regular officer was appointed as second-in-command 'to assist' de Trafford.[46] However, in the eyes of his superiors, things did not improve and in June he was relieved of command.[47]

Once Vince's battalion had settled on the Western Front, it slipped into the normal cycle of rotations through the front line, reserve trenches, then back into rest. Vince's work was similar to any other infantry NCO, although the heavy manual labour involved in maintaining trenches and during working parties was perhaps an unexpected dimension for him. Furthermore, when in or near the trenches, exposure to life-threatening danger became a part of Vince's everyday existence. He learnt of the

41 A.H. Hussey and D.S. Inman, *The Fifth Division in the Great War* (London: Nisbet, 1921), 90–2.

42 For the difficulties in obtaining commanding officers for the New Armies, see Simkins, *Kitchener's Army*, 217–18. Lewis was fifty-nine: Carter, *Birmingham Pals*, 85.

43 'Boys of the New Brigade', *Birmingham Post*, 15 March 1915, 4. Diver was fifty-four and had retired from the regiment in 1908.

44 He was promoted to lieutenant-colonel a week before the battalion departed for France.

45 Application for Commission, 18 October 1914, WO339/21805, TNA; captioned photograph of Major de Trafford, Vince Shirley typescript diary, Vol. 1, [no page number], MIM.

46 15th Infantry Brigade to 5th Division, 24 May 1916, WO339/21805, TNA. Major Robert Dudgeon, Cameron Highlanders.

47 GOC 5th Division to VI Corps, 30 May 1916; GHQ to War Office, 5 June 1916. He was sent back to England to command a reserve battalion: War Office to GHQ, 17 June 1916, WO339/21805, TNA.

steady trickle of the battalion's casualties, either by word-of-mouth or as a witness. Those that occurred beyond his company do not seem to have had a significant effect but, in January, the loss of 'A' Company's second-in-command did have a personal impact. Vince himself had plenty of exposure to routine shelling and sniping, but only three close calls. In his first visit to the trenches he was 'covered with a shower of earth, mud and loose stones' when a shell landed nearby. Then, in March, he heard a rifle shot pass close to his head. But the most serious was his 'miraculous escape from death' on 19 May 1915, when a shell exploded just above where he was sitting. Although unharmed, he and a comrade were clearly very shaken.

Another significant aspect of Vince's daily life was food. His infantry diary provides an interesting window into the army's food culture,[48] especially as he chronicles the erosion of his middle-class sensibilities regarding meals. Like others in the New Armies,[49] Vince and Linder's initial exposure to military catering was deeply disconcerting and is therefore given prominence when recording their memories of the first day at Moseley. Also troubling were their first experiences of food preparation which, in the case of the Sergeants' Mess, underlined their sudden change in social status. Once they were under canvas, meals were still produced centrally but their consumption was decentralised to section-level, often in the open air. At Codford St Mary, each hut had a stove, and so normal meals could be supplemented with warmed snacks and suppers. Unsurprisingly, conditions in France were more challenging and required further adjustment. This is graphically illustrated by the 'epidemic of diarrhoea' in early December, caused apparently by the consumption of tinned meat and vegetables. However, it is possible that poor hygiene was also a factor.[50] Initially there seems to have been difficulty in obtaining bread but, once the battalion settled in, the food supply appears to have stabilised. At this stage, Vince's accounts of frontline meals are not particularly detailed and, apart from occasional references to making their own hot beverages, he and his comrades seem to have relied upon the normal ration being brought forward. As his experience at the end of March suggests, such supply work was

48 For the significance of the army's food culture during the First World War, see Rachel Duffett, *The Stomach for Fighting: Food and the Soldiers of the Great War* (Manchester: Manchester University Press, 2012), 69, 83, 147–8.

49 For similar experiences, see Simkins, *Kitchener's Army*, 198; Duffett, *Stomach for Fighting*, 82, 85–7.

50 Duffett, *Stomach for Fighting*, 164.

problematic given the food-carrying equipment then available.[51] That said, taking his trench menu over Christmas 1915, Vince seems to have no complaints about the consumption of sardines, bread, butter, jam, cheese and cakes. Out of the line, we see the importance of parcels from home, but more significant was recourse to the local economy for supplementary meals. With money in their pockets and Vince's command of the French language, he and his comrades availed themselves when opportunities arose. For example, the hare suppers consumed in early December were considered to be 'ridiculous' in their low pricing. Another option was to prevail upon local women to cook army rations for them, such as on 19 January.

Like other soldiers on the Western Front, Vince's off-duty activities can be assessed under the headings of religion, culture, games, alcohol/tobacco and sex; or at least, during this period of Vince's life, the cultivation of romantic relationships with women. In the infantry, Vince's religious observance was limited but consistent. His faith was Protestant so he attended the army's mainstream church parades.[52] At the start of the war, he and Linder were not impressed by the services at St Christopher's in Moseley, where the ministers seem to have made stereotypical assumptions about the soldiers' morals. Churches had a strong welfare presence during the rest of their time in England, but the diary does not pass comment upon their religious ministry. Once in France and just before his first visit to the trenches, Vince provides an emotive description of an open-air service with accompanying artillery fire, aircraft and hailstorm. In February, after some frontline service, Vince notes his attendance at voluntary church services and also a 'good talk' with Linder about 'war and religion and the influence of prayer'. However, he recorded no religious references with regard with his 'miraculous' escape from death in May.

Culturally, Vince's time with 16/Warwicks provokes little comment. He makes only one reference to seeing the divisional concert party and offers no review of their performance. However, in this period we can discern the development of his literary habits, particularly from the spring of 1916 when he records a good deal of reading while in the trenches; for example, on 29 April, when he climbed out of his trench and lay in the grass reading a novel. Similarly, Vince makes only passing comments

---

51 For the development of better devices, see *ibid.*, 161.

52 For religion in the British army during the First World War, see Michael Snape, *God and the British Soldier: Religion and the British Army in the First and Second World Wars* (Abingdon: Routledge, 2006), 87–116.

about games and sport.[53] He played tennis at Malvern and makes several references to seeing football matches but not his participation.[54] He did, however, record his winning of the 100 yards sprint at a company sports day in early May.

Easier to track is Vince's use of stimulants. From a handful of references, his consumption of tobacco appears to have been mainly through a pipe, although he also notes with some relish the cigars sent by his family. Alcohol is mentioned more frequently and includes observations on the conduct of his comrades. Although the canteen at Moseley is depicted as a social hub from day one, there are no other references to consumption in England. In France, Vince's daily record gives us some insight into his unit's alcohol culture. Importantly, he makes no mention of drinking in the trenches, with consumption occurring while in rest and, unsurprisingly, purchased from the civilian population. There is no apparent pattern to their preferences, with rum, cider and a variety of wines being consumed. Twice Vince refers to his friends being drunk and, after failing to obtain a commission, he notes his own downing of eight glasses of wine. But, apart from a sergeant who was apparently drunk en route to the trenches, their habits do not seem to have impinged greatly upon their military duties or resulted in disciplinary action. In February, for the first time, we see Vince being rewarded with free drinks in exchange for translation work in a hostelry.

The infantry diary provides limited evidence regarding Vince's love life. This is to be expected for the period in England, as the text was produced jointly with Linder. The only possible exception is the reference to the unit's apparent attractiveness to women at the seaside in August. In France, Vince's personal diary is also reticent and must be treated very carefully. In the early twentieth century, discussion of sexuality was repressed and it is therefore extremely difficult to analyse the sexual behaviour of British soldiers on the Western Front.[55] That said, from the absence of any references to a Birmingham sweetheart, we can begin by

53 For sport in the British army during the First World War, see J.G. Fuller, *Troop Morale and Popular Culture in the British and Dominion Armies, 1914–1918* (Oxford: Clarendon Press, 1990), 85–94; Tony Mason and Eliza Riedi, *Sport and the Military: The British Armed Forces, 1880–1960* (Cambridge: Cambridge University Press, 2010), 80–111.

54 In Moseley he had played as a forward for the battalion's football team, scoring a goal in their victory over the 1st City Battalion: cutting from *Evening Despatch*, 26 November 1914, Vince Shirley diary, Vol. 1, 5, MIM.

55 For the methodological challenges, see David Cherry, 'Sex and Morale: The Sexual Life of the British Soldier on the Western Front, 1914–1918' (PhD thesis, University of Reading, 2012), vii, 6–7, 14–15, 35–6, 40, 48; Gibson, *Behind the Front*, 320. For the general context of the First World War accelerating change in sexual behaviour, see Dagmar Herzog, *Sexuality in Europe: A Twentieth-Century History* (Cambridge: Cambridge University Press, 2011), 45–61.

No. 13 Section at Moseley, January 1915. Privates Vince Schürhoff (centre), Philip Titterton (rear right) and Linder Robinson (front right).

assuming that Vince was unattached back home. This part of the diary records only a 'mild flirtation' in a café with Madeleine in late November and, in January, a talk with a pretty barber's daughter. In February he visited the 'bad' part of Amiens, but only 'out of curiosity'. The phrasing suggests this was a collective activity with his comrades and this may have acted as a mutual restraint upon them. They were, after all, from a locally recruited unit and therefore rumours about one's behaviour might easily reach the ears of family and friends at home. So, in the absence of any obvious relationships, his time with the infantry is primarily important in establishing a datum for Vince's subsequent romantic exploits.

* * *

In summary, Vince comes across as a quite ordinary infantryman of the New Armies. His prolonged training in Britain did not fully prepare him for the arduous life of the trenches, but his youth, intelligence and good health allowed him to quickly adapt.[56] Apparently having joined up for fairly conventional reasons, it was his immediate circle of close comrades that were most important in sustaining him during the difficult first months in France. During this period he retained some of his middle-class sensibilities, but these were gradually eroded through prolonged exposure to the rough-and-ready lifestyle. However, as late as March 1916, he remained conscious of the difference in the 5th Division between his unit and the regulars with their 'awful' language. Although his time in the infantry was mostly unremarkable, it gave him some hard-earned frontline experience which would set him in good stead for the rest of the war.

56 For the resilience of the New Armies' middle-class soldiers, see Watson, *Enduring the Great War*, 149.

Moseley

Monday 19 October 1914 found me at 9 am at Moseley College, one of 250 odd lined up in two ranks in front of the main entrance.[57] Originally a theological college, the last twenty years saw it inhabited by a caretaker only. At the outbreak of war, it became government property and was converted into barracks … At length we tramped inside and took possession of our rooms. To each of these rooms or cubicles, 9 foot square, four men were allotted. Plain, tightly drawn wire mattresses with wooden frames were placed on the floor. Our luggage we dumped on these mattresses and then each man had a look at his room mates and his quarters … Our room boasted of a fireplace and a window; otherwise nothing but the bare walls. Having absorbed these details, I decided to stroll around the building. Everywhere the same, groups of men chatting, laughing, smoking, lazing around. Some looked as if they had not touched soap for weeks, others were 'knuts' personified.[58] Some had found their quarters and were either playing cards or looking about as I was, others were still searching for a spot to squat and one or two had actually already lost their baggage.

By degrees a most insistent Babel of voices became audible and I found it came from the canteen. I here scanned one face after the other hoping to discover an acquaintance, but in vain. To me it seemed everybody knew each other. I began to feel somewhat lonely and slightly depressed. I called myself a fool and ordered a drink … By 1.30 pm I began to feel hungry … I remember a bugle call and … there followed a wild scramble to the dining hall and I next remember a mad crowd rushing about with plates, knives and forks trying to reach some cooks, apparently serving out meat and potatoes. Next I suddenly found myself in a large queue, awaiting my turn … At last, after half-an-hour's waiting, I reached the cooks. A fork was dug into a slice of meat and a greasy thumb and forefinger pushed the slice of meat off the fork onto the plate. I was told to move on and found myself confronted by another cook who quite unconcernedly scooped a couple of potatoes out of a pot with his dirty hands and dropped them on my plate. Quite suddenly my appetite had vanished. I next remember sitting on a wooden form at a long wooden table, with plate and meat in front of me, considering myself lucky at having steered through the crowd

57 The battalion had taken over the buildings three days earlier and it was known initially as the 'Military Training Depot, Moseley': Carter, *Birmingham Pals*, 85; [notepaper] October 1914, WO339/21800, TNA. Later it was referred to as 'Springfield Barracks, Moseley': 'Boys of the New Brigade', *Birmingham Post*, 15 March 1915, 4.

58 Fashionable young men.

without mishap. The crush reminded me of handing round tea cups and saucers at our tennis club and I could not help smiling at the contrast. There everything refined and clean, here boards on trestles, pieces of bread on the table, forms and floor. Fat, grease and gristle lying about everywhere and I thought of the clean tablecloth at home, the flower vases filled with fresh flowers and the whole feeling of happiness that reigned at our meal times …

We were left to ourselves the remainder of the day and I joined a game of soccer of about twenty a side. Tea was a repetition of dinner on a smaller scale and at 5.30 pm we were dismissed with orders to be in barracks by 9.30 pm. That time found us, or most of us, in our rooms in comparative darkness, groping about for our odds and ends out of our bags or cases. A very dim light in the corridor outside just enabled us to see the difference between a pair of pants and pyjamas, but was not enough to prevent us from continually colliding and bumping into each other … At 10.15 pm 'Lights out' sounded, but of course, bar the corridor lights, there were none to put out. By degrees the up till then never ending chatter ceased …

Reveille [was] at 6 am, but it was a very heavy and sleepy lot of men who turned out at the 7 am parade. A brisk run woke us up a little and for breakfast we had our first taste of bully beef. 9 am found us drawn up again, ready to learn how to right and left turn and form fours; the first movements raw recruits are taught … On the whole, it cannot be said that we took to our work seriously; most men seemed to look at it as a big lark, as a chance of having a good time. Had strict army discipline been imposed on us from the beginning instead of about six months later, all fooling would have quickly ceased and our progress in proportion more rapid … Parades were fixed for a certain time, however it was no uncommon thing for men to be five or even ten minutes late … So the first weeks passed, squad drilling and marching, with an atmosphere of slackness pervading our work which caused some few a certain sense of disappointment …

The interior of Moseley Barracks was bare and forbidding with its dark walls and draughty corridors connected by narrow winding passages with everywhere a feeling of gloom … Continual rain, damp and cold did not improve matters, in fact only added to our discomforts. As already shown, at the commencement there existed a great state of confusion, but it was not until the whole battalion, some 1,200 strong, had been in training several weeks, that this was remedied, especially in regard to meals. Each company paraded separately and had its separate table. Unfortunately the quantity and quality did not improve and caused a great feeling of dissatisfaction … It was a peculiar and regrettable fact how soon one lost the little mannerisms of decent upbringing. Instead of passing the salt or enquiring whether bread was wanted, on entering the dining hall one's first act was to grab hold of whatever food one could lay one's hands on and altogether live up to the saying 'Each man for himself', not caring a snap of the hand for one's neighbour …

During the formation of the City Battalions, as of any other battalion, plenty of stress was laid on the importance and glory of serving one's country and of the benefit derived from drill and so forth, but never a word was mentioned of fatigue work. So naturally it came as both a surprise and shock to be told on one's second day that "You are on Sergeants' Mess" … I was taken to a small, stuffy, overheated kitchen with four or five other men and, as if I had been used to the job since infancy, told off to wash up plates, cups and saucers, knives, spoons and forks … off came the coat, up went the shirt sleeves and moments later I was enveloped in a cloud of steam, washing up and drying … At length finished and carried the breakfast things to the Sergeants' Mess. This I had hurriedly to tidy up and then lay the table for thirty. By degrees the various Sergeants strolled in, the breakfast was brought up and I had to wait on these erstwhile theatre-door attendants, commissionaires, park-keepers, railway guards and so on. Nor were they slow at asking for whatever they wanted. The meal over, some fatigue men cleared the breakfast things away, whilst others swept the room. In the kitchen, the process of washing up was gone through again. Others had to clean knives, carry away the breakfast refuse, peel potatoes, wash out saucepans and dishes. Towards midday the table was laid again, then followed the waiting on and serving round, and ending by the washing up. Tea over, we were detailed off to scrub the kitchen floor and the tables. The gas stove had to be cleaned and polished, the range and grate well brushed and blackened. At 8 pm, after all this had been done and the cook had ceased calling us a lazy lot of devils, we were dismissed. It is no exaggeration to say that on the first occasion this Sergeants' Mess fatigue upset about half the men detailed for the job; the stuffy kitchen air, the smell of raw meat, kitchen refuse, seeing how the meals are prepared, the dirty and messy work, all combined to have an internal eruptive effect on one, especially, as in most cases, like mine, it was the first experience of working in a kitchen …

The Officers' Quarters were in a large house close by the Barracks. Spacious dining room, a billiard room and smoke-room with comfortable bedrooms, decent beds and two bathrooms, these men basked in the lap of luxury on a scale some of them had never known before; and possibly would never know again even if they came safely out of this war. This [fatigue] entailed a lot of menial work as described above, added to which the fatigue men had to clean out rooms, beat carpets, dust the banisters and polish the candelabra. This polishing of the candelabra was a piece of work that went slightly against the grain as one would muse and reflect on the absurdity of such a luxury in an Officers' Mess during war time. Each officer had his batman or orderly, but the duties of these men were confined to their officer's bedroom and to the care of their uniforms …

Another fatigue was 'Dining Hall' where eight men had to wash up 1,200 plates three times a day and cut bread and butter for the same number of men for tea. Then 'Cookhouse' was a most unpopular fatigue. It consisted of hacking up raw meat and carrying it to the kitchen, of cleaning out 'dixies' or large stew pans, keeping certain boilers or fires going and doing any odd jobs such as cleaning knives, washing or scrubbing tables in the kitchen. To pick up dirty paper, peel, cigarettes ends and all bits of rubbish lying about and to keep in order all sanitary arrangements was the work of the 'Pioneer' fatigue. This fatigue was not much sought after and its only advantage lay in the chance of being dismissed early. 'Quarter-Master's Stores' was very much liked. It gave a glimpse behind the scenes of what was in store for us to have on some future day. QMS fatigue men were always much sought after for information. As early as April 1915 the first sun helmets had arrived "so Egypt and the Dardanelles was a cert" …

Section drill soon became platoon drill and this in turn company drill, but it took weeks and weeks of monotonous drilling to advance from one stage to the next. The actual drill was wearisome enough, but what annoyed us almost more was being told to 'Fall in', then to be ordered to 'Dismiss', to be followed a moment later to 'Fall in' again, again to be dismissed, all for no apparent reason whatsoever. This happened not once or twice but scores of times, in fact one rarely expected an order to be given out without its being cancelled directly after. Windermere Fields, our parade ground, was the scene of many trials and hard though they were, occasional humorous incidents served to break the monotony … We shall not easily forget the day when the company was drawn up stiffly to attention and … a cow calmly strolled up and began licking the faces of the front rank men …

It was not until January 1915 that the mysteries of a rifle were explained to us, how to load, aim and press the trigger. After several weeks, during which we had obtained a certain amount of proficiency, certain NCOs were sent to [the Musketry School], and returned giving us quite a new version of rifle drill and all had to be learnt again.[59] This happened whenever a batch returned from their course of instruction and soon everybody knew exactly what was the right thing to do …

Although very slack to begin with, after some months we began to feel the iron grip of discipline. It was first felt in connection with fatigues. A man would be having tea when a tap on the shoulder and "You're wanted for a fatigue" would put an end to any hopes of going out that evening or of keeping an engagement. Nothing loath, tea had to be left behind and without a word of protest the victim would be kept at work until it pleased the NCO in charge to dismiss him. The continual changing of orders indirectly promoted discipline. On leaving barracks, the Battalion Police Sergeant would pull you up for having a button undone, for having your hands in your overcoat pockets, for not having two crosses in your puttees or for not having the boots correctly laced. Of course, any day the winding of puttees or lacing of boots might have been changed to suit somebody's fancy or whim … We discovered discipline to be a peculiar force, a mixture of fear and respect, that compelled one automatically to obey a command, to march until one felt inclined to drop and unconsciously to add "Sir" to any commissioned officer when addressed, although perhaps conscious of the officer's inferior social standing during civilian days, before the war.

Church Parades. These were held at St Christopher's, Moseley, and by the majority were looked upon as a great bore and means of having a quiet doze. Very few went in the proper spirit. Unfortunately, the clergy were not of the right type of men to grasp the situation. They seemed only capable of condemning us as lustful, drunken and lost men fit for everlasting damnation. Rarely was a really encouraging and helpful address given to us.

Inspections. Everybody regarded these as a great nuisance. Had we been given an example of how our mattresses were to be laid, the proper way to fold blankets and to lay out our equipment, the correct positions of our tunics and accessories and how to fold them and this example adhered to for always, nobody would have grumbled. But many a time the Sergeant Major would show us how to arrange things prior to an inspection and five minutes later the Orderly Officer would come round and alter, with a great air of importance, the folding of the blankets, adding that the hat must be on the overcoat and *not* on the tunic …

---

59 For NCOs with outdated military knowledge, see Simkins, *Kitchener's Army*, 226.

Canteen. A room filled with tobacco smoke, a ceaseless chatter of voices intermingled with the clink of coin and the ring of the cash register, with an occasional loud guffaw of laughter, this gives an idea of the inside of a canteen. It takes the place of the public house. Men meet and over a glass of beer discuss the events of the day. The Canteen, however, differs from the ordinary public house inasmuch that everything for a soldier's use is supplied and that on the whole a greater state of order is observed. One more difference; in a public house the beer is always served in a clean glass. In the Canteen, owing to a lack of staff and time, such a minor matter as washing up glasses is considered unnecessary. One glass might be used by fifty men in one evening before being washed ...
Punishments. The usual punishment was so many days CB or 'confinement to barracks'. During off-duty hours the defaulters' call would sound every half hour when the miscreant would have to report at the Guard Room. His name would appear on the Defaulters' List in the Canteen and YMCA and entrance to these latter would be forbidden him. A very hard punishment was pack-drill. After the usual day's work, with full pack and rifle, the offender would have to march up and down a certain spot for an hour without ceasing. This monotony, the exhaustion and the weight on the back of the pack cured many a fellow of the inclination towards missing parades, coming in after 'Last Post'. For bad offences, under the name 'Detention', men were locked in cells and fed on bread and water.
Red Letter Days. The monotony of everyday life was broken by occasional bathing parades at the Moseley Baths. But either the baths could not be filled in time (we sometimes found only 4 or 5 inches of water on our arrival at 7 am) or the whole affair was too much trouble, in any case later these bath parades were discontinued; much to our disappointment ... An outstanding day was [13 March 1915] when we had our first official inspection by [Lieutenant-General] Pitcairn Campbell in Calthorpe Park,[60] in conjunction with the 1st and 2nd Battalions. A march past through Birmingham followed, everybody seemingly turning out to see us. The *Birmingham Post*, next day, after the usual words of praise, pointed out the contrast between the smiling and excited faces of the spectators and the 'smile less, set and serious faces of the men'.[61] And somehow this march, for the first time, seemed to make us realise that

60 Lieutenant-General W.P. Campbell, GOC Southern Command. Carter, *Birmingham Pals*, 95.

61 'The troops ... went past with soldierly bearing; they looked workmanlike and adequate; but they did not waste time on careless grinning.' 'Boys of the New Brigade', *Birmingham Post*, 15 March 1915, 4.

what serious work we were engaged on, that it meant leaving home some day, leaving Birmingham, with all the familiar scenes and smells and street noises behind us; and for how long?

Better Days. As the months went by, letters in local papers and insistent rumours of the conditions under which we lived and worked were mainly instrumental in bringing improvements about. Drain pipes were laid down, the barracks were fitted with gas, we were given good bolster mattresses with sheets and pillows, though living up to army standard, these latter were taken from us after a month or two … Men began to take a pride in their rooms, they adorned walls with pictures, postcards, cigarette cards, photos etc., some even adding pieces of furniture such as small cupboards and shelves.

Then, the YMCA erected a tent and it is impossible to express how much Mr Williams helped through his never-flagging enthusiasm, cheerfulness and personal magnetism to make life easier for us. Neither do we forget the kindness of his fellow-workers. To all, the YMCA came just at the right time, as to have a decent place to read in, a place to write in, a place in which to have a quiet chat, were advantages unknown to us. Many an otherwise miserable evening was turned into one of cheerfulness by the concerts arranged and in fact it can be safely stated that the YMCA was the one bright spot of Moseley Barracks.

Then one day [the] Lord Mayor of Birmingham, made an inspection accompanied by local sanitary authorities. As a result, by degree 900 men were billeted out, leaving only 300 in barracks. Having our suspicions before the order to make arrangements was given, my friend [Linder] Robinson and I one evening visited all the neighbouring houses with a plausible story of a likelihood of men being billeted out, asking whether we could be taken in should the order be confirmed. Each home visited was minutely examined with a view to future comfort; condition of armchairs, sofas and other furniture, appearance of landlady, conclusions drawn from photographs, etc. If not to our liking, excuses were easily made and the next house tried. Eventually, after a most exciting and humorous search, Mrs L we found 'met our requirements' in every way. Keeping in touch with her as the days went by, at last, one Monday in January 1915 we were able to inform her that we had received orders to quit barracks. Piling our belongings on wheelbarrows borrowed from the Pioneers, we moved in, amidst the jokes and jests of all we passed …

About this time, early in 1915, we received our uniforms. They were blue and it was a toss-up whether they resembled most a Salvation Army member or a picture house attendant …

As a most pleasant interlude, 'A' Company were marched in February 1915 to Alcester, a town some 17 miles from barracks for a week's company training ... Our training ground was in Ragley Park, the residence of the Marquis of Hertford and there for the first time we indulged in proper field days, nobody at the beginning of the day knowing the whereabouts of the other platoons of the company. Having just received my first stripe,[62] as a Lance-Corporal I acted as one of the Company Scouts and, with others, was entrusted with the mission of discovering the 'enemy' before the real operations could commence ...

A great disappointment awaited us on our return. New billeting arrangements had been made ... We were sent to Mrs D who welcomed us with the statements that she wished us to keep our equipment downstairs, to always change our boots before going upstairs and she hoped we would always be in by 10 pm. Objecting to the front door being used, the back door and entrance were shown as 'short cuts'.[63] A little diplomatic pressure, however, moderated these somewhat severe restrictions ... All were delighted to move [to Malvern]. The march through Birmingham was exciting, the streets being quite crowded and to casual observers, the final farewells, as the train steamed out of Snow Hill Station to the strains of *Auld Lang Syne* must have been quite touching. To the majority of us, however, this move meant the first rung on the ladder towards the ultimate goal.

Malvern

The Camp. What struck us most as we alighted from the train at Malvern [on 17 April 1915] was the sunshine, the pure air and the fresh spring green.[64] An advance party had pitched camp and we moved straight into our tents, 12 in a tent ... Boards and bolster mattresses were handed out and the afternoon spent putting them down, arranging our belongings and digging a trench round the tent as an outflow for rainwater. Our camp occupied part of the Malvern Golf Club course, the Golf Club House being the Officers' Quarters ... Camp discipline brought about several changes in our work. Each tent provided an orderly and assistant orderly, roughly speaking, to fetch rations, the latter to clean up. Every Saturday

62 Date of promotion corroborated by photograph of 'A' Company at Alcester: Vince Shirley typescript diary, Vol. 1, 14, MIM.

63 For unfriendly reactions and problems with billeting, see Simkins, *Kitchener's Army*, 245–9.

64 Carter, *Birmingham Pals*, 105.

the lines were cleaned, the boards taken up and scrubbed down, blankets shaken, mattresses beaten, followed by the special weekly inspection, arranging of equipment, immediate altering of same, usual complaint by the CO over some minor detail; perhaps a match seen lying about.
Camp Life. Our meals were much better than those at Moseley and thanks to the glorious weather prevailing, we were nearly always able to enjoy them in the open. The Corporal in charge served the meat. In the fine weather all went well. In rainy weather it sometimes happened that the wet plate would slip from beneath the meat or the meat from off the plate and go skidding across the muddy boards. The mud would be scraped off with a knife and the meat returned to the plate when perhaps the same thing would happen over again. At first this and similar incidents disgusted us, but soon we grew used to them and they actually caused us a certain amount of amusement. It may be mentioned at this point that feelings of refinement and decency had long since disappeared. Our 'pantry' was a large basin and in it bread, jam, butter, salt, fruit, knives, tin-openers, etc. were all mixed up together and nothing was thought of cutting bread with a rusty knife, hastily wiped over with a towel which had just been used after a wash. What a rush for clean plates there would be when the orderly came in with tinned fruit as a treat after dinner. Those unable to obtain them would use newspapers and vigorously scrape, rub and wipe off the meat and grease remaining and the fruit never tasted any the worse. Paper was always invaluable. We used it for cleaning plates, knives, forks and spoons, for shaving soap, wrapping up rations on field days, as 'table cloth' when the knees, kitbag or valise served as table or as a means of removing mud off our boots.

The meals themselves were conducted in a very free and easy style, each man pleasing himself as regards both accommodation and dress. Anything from the bare ground to a mattress served as a table, meals were taken in and outside the tent and as a rule with tunic off and shirt sleeves rolled up. In wet weather with all twelve occupants in the tent, space being limited, there was a little difficulty in placing both plates and legs and we eat with remarkable disregard to lumps of mud falling off our boots on to the meat or to tea slopping over to the bread and jam, or to one's mug of tea being accidentally kicked over by one's neighbour, thereby trickling under and wetting the kit, equipment and anything that may have been in the way. The meal over, the knives and forks would be dug into the ground, the sand removing the grease, then a drop of water poured over and wipe over with the towel or a piece of paper and they would be ready for the next meal.

The sanitary arrangements were very crude, the 'washhouse' being a long trough with pipes and taps out in the open, no roof and passers-by derived considerable amusement at watching us perform our ablutions after a day's work, in full view. We had four baths for 1,200 men and he was indeed a lucky man who managed to get one. The bathroom consisted of canvas tightly drawn round stakes 10 foot high; the roof was corrugated iron, the door a strip of canvas with a piece of wood attached to the bottom to prevent it from being blown about … Shaving took place under many conditions – standing, sitting, kneeling, even lying – with the mirror hung up on the tent pole, or balanced on kitbag, mattress, blanket pile or basin. Most men used cold water in their mugs, a few obtained hot water from the kitchens but it was always greasy with many strange objects floating round. Some even made use of hot tea remaining after breakfast. All this tended towards hardening us. At the same time it was a great means for teaching us self control, for making light of hardships and finally it taught us to be adaptable, resourceful and always to keep smiling …

Our Work. Here at Malvern the wearisome platoon and company drill came to an end. More and more frequently we had rations and spent the day out … Companies 'fighting' [each other] … Scouts would be sent out and according to their information, the respective dispositions made. Generally Welland village would be defended and the excitement of the inhabitants and children when street fighting took place was great. Often the 'British Camp' would be the objective and the tiring marches … will never be forgotten. On those days it always seemed as if No. 13 Section had the hardest work to do, the furthest distance to march, was always blamed for being late or last and was always last to get its grub. Sometimes the Colonel was present on these field-days.[65] At the conclusion he indulged in 15 minutes criticism during which all NCOs were present. Without any mercy or feeling each officer's faults were brought up and exposed, usually accompanied by a remark that in the presence of NCOs might well have been left unsaid. His absolute outspokenness caused much ill feeling and more than one officer has departed 'on sick leave' or 'transfer' without returning …

I acted as one of the Company Scouts [and] enjoyed more independence than the average man on these field-days. True, until the enemy was found the work was hard, but then followed a true period of freedom. Whilst the Company would be resting, either on a roadside or in a field,

65 Lieutenant Colonel Thomas Diver.

with two fellow scouts ... we would be creeping up to hedges, crawling slowly over exposed ground, climbing trees, examining footprints, always on the lookout for a sign of the 'enemy' ... Great alertness was required, every resource brought into play to obtain intelligence of the enemy, such as drawing conclusions at the sudden flight of birds or from the nervous movement of cattle, from recent footprints on sand or in mud, to the crude method of simply asking passers-by ... At night, one man holding on to the back of another, both stooping, with overcoat covering both and a rifle stuck out in rear, at 50 yards anybody would have taken us as some animal slowly walking and many a time we tricked the enemy's outposts and got within their lines by this dodge.

Off Duty. At night Malvern streets would be packed with our men and special mention must be made of the Soldiers' Clubs which enabled us to while away many an evening. Our most popular retreat was a Club organised and run by the Reverend and Mrs P.[66] They always made us very welcome and I shall not easily forget the many long chats and discussions, on all kinds of topics, held in the clubroom ... Most evenings of the week we were able to play tennis at the Manor Park. Some games were very close, there being little to choose between us. Then what a treat to be in flannels again, to walk through the town, boldly staring at each officer without having to salute, on our way to the Café Royal for tea – and what fun we had over tea. Those were days when we could rely on evenings off duty; we squeezed every ounce of enjoyment out of them that we could and really felt and behaved like schoolboys.

On Whit Sunday of 1915, the Battalion Sports took place, with the usual running, jumping, hurdles and obstacle race, but one of the most interesting and novel competitions was between the various Company Lines. Which were the best kept lines? 'A' Company, beyond laying out a bed of geraniums facing the road bordering the Quartermaster's hut, decided to do nothing except just to clean up their lines in the usual manner. The other companies ordered in a large quantity of flowers, 'B' Company actually erecting an archway, ornamenting it with hanging flower pots and creepers and each tent had its own 'garden'. They were absolutely confident of the prize, a large shield with an engraving of the camp stamped on. The eventful day came, the Colonel of the 13th Gloucesters,[67] stationed at Malvern inspected each company's lines, not a

66 Either Reverend E.M. Poole of Holly Mount Congregationalist Church or Reverend W.J. Povey of the Baptist Church; information supplied by Malvern Museum.

67 Lieutenant-Colonel H. Webb. This battalion had three privates charged with inciting mutiny while at Malvern: Julian Putkowski, *British Army Mutineers, 1914–1922* (London: Francis Boutle, 1998), 22, 129.

muscle in his face indicating his thoughts. Eventually he gave his decision and to [our] huge delight … awarded the prize to 'A' Company as having the neatest, cleanest and most 'business-like' lines …

The two months spent at Malvern will always be remembered more in the form of a summer holiday than as a period of military training. Our work was not over-heavy, camp life suited us splendidly, the inhabitants of Malvern were extremely kind, the weather was ideal and these good points, coupled with visits from the folks at home, combined to make us leave Malvern [in late June][68] with great regret …

Wensley

We discovered Wensley to be a small village lying between a range of hills … Looking at the panorama from the summit of one of the hills, the endless rows and rows of white tents seemed to fill the valley, the ant-like figures moving to and fro, in and out, to be the only signs of life, but at the same time the whole struck the observer as being hopelessly out-of-place, as if the hundreds of white tents were put purposely to destroy the natural beauty of the scene and one longed for them to be conjured away by some invisible hand, to let the light green fields they blotted out once more harmonise with the dark green trees and mountains in the background …

Here in Wensley, a general feeling of activity seems apparent everywhere. Close by our tent [are transport lines] with men brushing down horses, washing wagons. A little further away are the Army Service Corps and before long their heavy wagons pulled by powerful horses became a familiar sight. Opposite, the Gloster bugle band might be playing the tattoo, marching from one end of their camp to the other, the usual crowd of half-dressed men looking on. Here a party of dirty men, black from head to foot, are returning from a day's cookhouse fatigue, whilst yonder others are kicking a football. Here a man is hammering a tent peg, there a man sitting on a basin, with a glass resting on a washbowl upside down, is shaving, at the same time keeping up an animated conversation with another man cleaning his buttons, his cap balanced on back of head, sleeves turned up, pipe in his mouth. And above all is a hum of talking, whistling, singing, [and] shouting … The never-ending numbers of soldiers present everywhere somewhat bewilders one and it

---

68 Carter, *Birmingham Pals*, 107–8.

is a relief to get away to the hills to escape the noise and dust. Then one reflects that here, at last, are visible signs of the Army, not a mere 1,000 odd, but [the] whole [32nd] Division, 15 to 16,000.[69] We begin to realise that 'business' was meant, that the 3rd Birmingham City Battalion was a thing of the past, and that now we must take our allotted place with the rest, without murmuring, without expecting any favouritism through being a non-manual City Battalion and be looked upon and consider ourselves simply as the '16th Warwicks'.

Discipline became more severe, work became harder, opportunities for amusement fewer and far between. Our work took us over bad roads in to the wilds of the Yorkshire Moors … It always meant a very, very stiff climb of over an hour up a steep hill, the road being covered with loose stones. Of an average ½ dozen men fell out and the first time two had to be carried back to camp. It must not be forgotten that we always marched with full pack and rifles and that it was midsummer. A rest at the top, then we practised extended order drill to become used to the uneven, bushy and broken ground, thereby causing many a sprained ankle or knee … On the whole, tiring as they were, we enjoyed these field-days, the hopeless muddles certain officers got us into according us great amusement.

Then we had long night marches. We soon got used to them although at first they tired us out. No warning was given except that no man was to leave camp or undress. At 11 pm we would start off and the first six miles would be alright. By degrees feeling of drowsiness would creep over one, one's step became less steady. One man would lurch and bump into his neighbour who the next moment would unconsciously return the compliment. The eyelids seemed to weigh a ton and it became a physical effort to keep them open. More and more began marching as if drunk, lurching forward here, stumbling there. Vague memories of march discipline entered the mind and one would repeat "left, right, left, right" but the monotony of it only increased the drowsiness. One's sole thought soon became a longing for the next halt, anything to be able to close one's eyes. Yet on one would have to go. At last, when it seemed as if consciousness had disappeared, as if the body had been transformed into an automatic machine, the long wished for 'Halt' would be given. 'Fall out' would be passed down the column and at once, without troubling to look where you were or about taking off the pack, you would fall down like a log, sound asleep. Ten minutes later, the command 'Fall in' and the

---

69 At this point only two of the division's brigades were in Wensleydale; another was at Richmond: Becke, *New Army Divisions*, 27.

noise of movements round you, heard as if far away in the distance, would rouse you. Up you would get, marching off a moment later, when after a time the whole process repeats itself and so on until camp is regained.

Then night marches soon became night operations. A certain spot had to be reached at a certain time which in the dark is no easy matter. Scouts would be sent out and according to their information the opposing forces would meet, the sharp reports of blank cartridges being audible for miles around …

The water supply was very poor. Eventually large cisterns holding reserve water were installed, thus improving matters. At the commencement, the supply gave up 5 minutes after being used in the morning when there was always a rush and with luck there was a short run during the afternoon though usually the water started with great gusto, then quickly became less and finally fizzled out with a few irritating drops, all within a few seconds. At night the supply seemed to regain strength, enabling us to fill our buckets and basins for the following morning, should the water give out. This had the great advantage of getting fellows out early as it was not over pleasant washing in a basin wherein 6, 8 or 10 men had washed themselves previously.

The food was not as good as at Malvern, no doubt owing to transport difficulties and had it not been for parcels from home and from friends, we should have fared badly. We had to spend a lot in the canteen, but to add to our misfortunes, twice it was blown to the ground during violent storms, burying everything, destroying a lot and days passed before business was resumed.

Towards the latter half of our stay we struck luck. One Sunday, passing through Preston-under-Scar, we were informed that a Mrs Robinson made tea for soldiers. We entered and found ourselves in a charming old fashioned room, containing grand old furniture. [She] welcomed us most warmly and her tea, consisting of home baked bread, homemade jam, homemade buns and homemade cakes, seemed to us to be luxurious. She herself was a typical elderly hardworking village dame, full of gossip, full of kindness, always busy, but always bright and with a cheery word to say. In the village everybody knew her and she knew everybody. She spoke with a broad Yorkshire accent which sometimes was difficult to understand … We got very chummy and popped in several evenings for a chat and finished with some of her delicious eggs, ham and cheese. These visits did away to a large extent with the dreadful monotony after a day's work. At the commencement, the evenings used to drag terribly; then [Linder Robinson] and

I decided to write this diary and this occupation filled up many an otherwise tedious evening …

We had some good walks [and went to Aysgarth] to see the falls … one Sunday immediately after Church Parade. [They] were beautiful; well worth a visit. We then went to the only hotel but found it full of officers, so leaving it, we hit on a public house for dinner. Imagine our surprise and astonishment when we were told "You can have what you want until 1 pm (it was then 12.40 pm), but after that we cannot serve you with anything and you will not be allowed on the premises". The injustice of not being able to serve us because we were soldiers struck us very keenly as we had so looked forward to a good meal. Civilians could have all they asked for, but, oh no, not soldiers. We remonstrated, but were told that they were police orders and that all public houses would suffer as they were doing, as soldiers were their best customers. There was no help for it, we had to abide by the regulations, eat what we could in the time allowed, and leave.

It was during the last weeks at Wensley that I was ordered to take charge of another tent. This was a great disappointment as it meant leaving my old friends and section and having to mix with a set of men whose reputation of being 'The Devil's Own' will convey to the reader what class they represented. Their three great faults were uncleanliness, untidiness and laziness. It soon became apparent to me that owing to diversity of character and temperament, my task was not going to be an easy one. There was not one among the eleven who possessed traits of a gentleman, of refinement or ordinary courtesy and it was obvious that the majority would kick at any interference in their mode of life … By a lot of patience, tact and showing each man individually, the first thing was every morning to get the kit and equipment stowed symmetrically, blankets shaken and folded, tent flaps tied up and the ground swept out. Slowly but surely, mixing 'soft soap' with sharp words, but always leading, never pushing, I managed to inculcate a feeling of order in the men and the bits of paper, waste food etc., once so prevalent lying about here, there and everywhere became conspicuous by their absence. Getting the men out of 'bed' in the morning was hard work. Usually I had my wash first and found the men fast asleep on my return. So at last I warned them that after my wash, in future I would squeeze the water out of my sponge on any man found asleep. I did so and never was a man sworn and cursed at by a more astonished set of men. But by mercilessly repeating this operation every morning, it soon became quite amusing to see them jump up and scramble into their togs as soon as my head appeared through the tent flaps with the usual "Now then, my lads, out you get". By degrees all opposition ceased and although such habits as swearing, drunkenness and rowdyism occasionally cropped up, yet their violence decreased more and more ...

Hornsea

We left Wensley on 5 August 1915 and it was with great relief that we did so.[70] The awful solitude, isolation and hard work, no weekends, the monotony and scanty food, made us all stale and long for a change and a bit of excitement. All this we found at Hornsea, a little seaside resort north-east of Hull ... It was a very merry lot of fellows who marched through the town en route to their camp, some 2 miles outside, and a girl's voice calling "Good old Brum" cheered us up still more. Seeing people, houses, traffic and the sea air acted as tonic on us. The evening off enabled us to 'do' the town. Wherever we went, our men were to be seen all with beaming faces. The holiday spirit soon gripped us and parties of holidaymakers and our men soon became acquainted, pairing off, leaving the men in mufti standing. The concerts were a great attraction and the music uncommonly good. Enough will be said by stating that the two hours' freedom, from 7 to 9 pm can rank as some of the brightest hours of our training, all the more sweet after our enforced confinement at Wensley.

From early morn until dusk we spent at the rifle range, firing. Certain men were detailed to work at the 'butts' or targets, as markers. Their work consisted of signalling hits and changing targets ... Shooting began at 100 yards, grouping and application, then came the 200 yards application, snap and rapid fire after which followed the 300 yards, 400, 500 and 600 yards. All this took the Battalion a week to work through. It was an easy time, as until detailed to shoot, we could read and write, in fact, do as we liked, as long as we remained on the range.

The great event at Hornsea, however, was the Zeppelin raid.[71] Linder and I were strolling along the prom, round 8.30 pm, just thinking about

70 Carter suggests that the Birmingham battalions left Wensley on 28 July and arrived at Codford St Mary's on 5 August. However, Vince's account indicates that his battalion was at Hornsea until at least 9 August: Carter, *Birmingham Pals*, 119–20.

71 On 9 August, shortly before Vince saw it, Zeppelin *L9* made landfall to the north before proceeding along the coastline. The British aircraft he saw were from the local aerodrome. *L9* passed again over Hornsea after dark to bomb Goole, returning by the same route around midnight: No. 23 Provisional Battalion to Northern Command, 10 August 1915; RNAS Redcar to Northern Command, 11 August 1915, AIR1/564/16/15/78, TNA; Wilbur Cross, *Zeppelins of World War I* (London: I.B. Tauris, 1991), 28–9.

returning to camp, when the hum of engines made us look skywards where, to our blank amazement, a Zeppelin airship was in full view, flying fairly low, quite visible, just veering round towards the sea. Long, straight, rounding to a point at both ends, what struck us most was the cool, unconcerned and easy manner the vessel sailed and was manoeuvred. We watched her turn round and make out to sea at full speed ahead, until, from a quarter of an hour after first sighting her, the grey, silken body was no longer visible. Curiosity seemed to be the dominating feeling; there was no panic or excitement. The prom became chock full of people, all gazing upwards and there seemed to be a sensation of disappointment when the vessel disappeared. A few minutes later three biplanes circled overhead. On our way to camp, an anti-airgun unit on a lorry manned by coastguards rumbled past, preceded by a motorcyclist and followed by another lorry filled with more coastguards, the rear being brought up by a Red Cross car. The news had already reached camp and all lights were out and no talking was the order. At 10.30 pm the hum of engines became audible again, also at 2.30 am when some men swore the Zeppelin was discernible flying over the camp; however, that might have been imagination …

Codford St Mary

On 12 August 1915, we once more entrained, this time for Codford St Mary, Salisbury Plain … On our arrival, we found we were to be housed in hutments. Each hut had electric light, straw palliasses on boards, tables and forms, coat hooks and shelves and space for 30 men. In camp, we had hot and cold showerbaths, clothes drying rooms, a Salvation Army Hut, Church Institute and Corporals' Room. At that time, Codford St Mary itself, not a mile away, resembled a country fair with many shops, booths, coffee houses on all sides, the majority only hastily erected to cater for troops on a space of waste ground bordering the road. Here also, the YMCA had a large hut and the Wesleyan and Baptist Churches also had one each. Excellent concerts took place, artistes coming to sing and recite from as far away as London. A picture house, showing alternatively pictures and variety turns passed away many an evening, the variety turns sometimes bordering on the ludicrous in the attempts to be humorous …

Work. This took a new turn. The greater part of our time we spent in some trenches dug by the Canadians. At the beginning we continued these and also dug trenches of our own. In every respect these resembled those in France. We would leave camp in the early morning and after a few miles, branch off from the road and after passing a few dug-outs, enter a gulley. The path then became narrower and we formed up in single file. At length we found ourselves in an actual trench, piles of white chalky stones heaped up on either side beyond which only the sky was visible. The trench was barely wide enough for a man to pass and soon our tunics and equipment were covered with white chalk. After stumbling along some 100 yards, we reached the 'first line of supports', crossing the communication trench we came up on at right angles. Half of the platoon was detailed to occupy certain sections or bays to the left of the 'crossroads', the other half occupied the right. Close by the crossroads or meeting of communication trench and support trench, was a dug-out, the officers' quarters. The support trenches were slightly wider, allowing for one man to pass the other. With the entrenching tools, seats were dug out of the side and at intervals rests were made for the rifles on the parapet. Each section had its lookout man and each section had to keep in touch with the other for passing down messages. Sections had their respective frontages to observe and in case of need to fire at and defend. These rules were cast iron in the firing line trench, where the lookout men were doubled or trebled and they could only peep over the trenches. All trenches in the vicinity of the firing line were much deeper and more elaborate. The firing line trench itself was equipped with sandbags covered by turf. It zigzagged alternatively to the left and right, in curves or in straight lines. Dug-outs, skilfully hidden from view, used by officers, were in telephonic communication with the rear. A kind of platform, 2 foot wide, allowed men to stand up and fire over the parapet. Later on, when we began sleeping in the trenches, this platform served as our bed.

Although there is nothing comfortable about sleeping in the trenches, yet nights spent in them have a peculiar attraction, hard to define. Whilst passing through the base en route for the trenches, the camp fires, men squatting round them, shadows of men hovering about, huddled up figures of men asleep, the subdued talk, the ring of hoof striking stone, the neighing of a horse, the darkness all around together with the knowledge that there are hundreds of men sleeping, lying talking and walking quite close, yet nearly all invisible, cannot but help make an impression. Gradually this scene fades away, the shadows become fewer, the camp fires are left behind, nothing but our tramping feet is heard. Then comes a hoarse whisper "Single file". A few halts, and we enter the communication trench. The shuffling and scraping noise of tunic and equipment rubbing against the trench sides, the metallic ring of a rifle or mug hitting a stone, suppressed whispers, those are the only noises. At length we reach our objective; a firing or support trench. Lookouts are posted, an hour at a time, the remainder fish out their mufflers, cap comforters, mittens etc. and we soon resemble Arctic explorers. Each man chooses a spot, lays down his waterproof sheet and then settles himself, as best he can, to sleep – until called for his turn as lookout. When on this, the absolute silence strikes one. The abrupt challenge of a lookout in a section further along is quite startling. One strains one's eyes to pierce the darkness and all sorts of inky objects, conjured up by the imagination, seem to resemble men crawling along … A feeling of drowsiness soon creeps over. One tries to throw it off and for a time steadily continues looking ahead into the darkness. A faint light in the east and one dreamily realizes that it is the first sign of dawn. Slowly, the light increases, one can already see some distance ahead. One discovers that what looked like crawling enemies are earth mounds. A glance at the watch, one's time is up. The next man, the relief takes over. One curls up and has a short sleep, then the order comes down "Stand to and man the parapet". One wakes up and finds it is broad daylight and thus passes a night in the trenches at Salisbury Plain.

A day in the trenches is a very tame affair, consisting of wishing breakfast would come, then when it has come and gone, one can have a smoke, at the same time read, or write a letter, sitting on the platform or in one of the scooped-out holes. Perhaps my turn as lookout follows and, when over, I feel hungry. The Corporal-in-charge at last whistles 'Cookhouse' and the rations are passed down in mess tins. The afternoon is very similar, possibly enlivened by a so-called 'enemy' attack or we are called upon to be the attackers. Then follows tea and, as a rule, at dusk the relief force comes up and we once more scramble down the narrow communication trench … and with 'trench' chalked over us from head to foot, we march back to camp.

Hut Life. Quite a feature of our life at Codford was the hut life. We lived like a lot of schoolboys in a dormitory. No. 13 and 14 Sections of our Platoon had remained practically unaltered since their formation … so each man knew the other well, but hut life brought us still closer together. True, owing to diversity of characters and interests, [Linder], 'Titty'[72]

72 224 Private Philip Titterton. Twenty-year-old bank clerk, commissioned into 14/Warwicks in April 1916: WO339/60265, TNA.

Lance Corporal Vince Schürhoff and Private Linder Robinson in France, 1916.

and Clive[73] and I never became intimate with the remainder, but always kept on a friendly 'how do' footing, even to using Christian names …

But it was in the evening that the real hut life atmosphere influenced one. After a tiring day's work, with the tea things still lying about, everybody dressed anyhow, a feeling of relaxation, of abandon overcame one. With a sigh of relief one would lie on a blanket and just doze or read. Or blankets would be laid over the trestle tables and soon two or three card parties would be at play. Forms would be drawn up to the stove and … the yarning spirit would grip us and one man after another would relate his past experiences. Here a man would be doing some sewing, there another would be polishing his buttons, whilst another, lying flat on his back, passed the time playing a mouth organ, looking sublimely contented. During all this, there would be a ceaseless hum of conversation … or the mouth organ. But the whole time there was an undercurrent of peace and happiness unconscious to all, perhaps, rarely interrupted by any outburst of temper, very different from the old Moseley days. No thought was given to the future, we lived completely in the present. As supper time approached, one by one, men would get up, cut a slice of bread and toast it, and with a layer of jam or cheese, make it serve as supper. Towards 9.30 pm the beds would be put down and men who had been in Codford for the evening would be coming in and their arrival would mean a livening up of the hut inmates …

21 November 1915

We were awakened by the hut door being burst open, an excited voice exclaiming "You ought to have been up half-an-hour ago" and I became aware of Mr Greenwood[74] executing a *pas seul* on the doorstep, wildly waving his cane. As we dressed, the unspoken but dominant thought was "Today we leave for France" … We had our last Roll Call and with the band at the head of the column playing *Warwickshire Lads and Lassies*, we marched off at 11.15 am … We left Wylye at 12.30 pm, several people, friends of officers, waving us off … It was an uneventful journey, nobody seeming to realise that we were leaving for the Front, we might have been moving to another training camp in England. There was slightly more excitement when we embarked at 7.15 pm. Accompanied by destroyers, we had a quiet crossing. We lay huddled together in the hold like cattle … [At Boulogne] we marched through the town whistling the *Marseillaise*

73 158 Private Neville Harrison.

74 Second Lieutenant Bertram Greenwood. Thirty-five-year-old schoolmaster, commissioned from within 16/Warwicks in March 1915: WO339/24484, TNA.

and *Till the Boys Come Home.* We reached [Ostrohove Camp] after a hard pull up a hill.

22 November 1915

Paraded at 10.45 pm and entrained. We were told we ought to consider ourselves lucky at having 3rd Class carriages and not cattle trucks. Train crept along at snails' pace. Had some biscuits, an apple and a bar of chocolate for supper and started to smoke Dad's last cigar to me which Linder, turning over in his seat opposite in his sleep, knocked out of my hand. It fell in some mud off our boots and I very reluctantly had to stamp it out.

23 November 1915

Got out of train at a place called Longpré. Were told that a 4 mile march lay in front of us. At first passed through a district with lakes and ponds bordering the tree-lined road. Then came a devilish hill ... Our packs began to weigh very heavy. Besides ordinary kit, had extra pair of boots, blankets and waterproof cape ... After many hours of marching, men began to fall out fast and frequent halts had to be called for them to catch up. Poor Linder was very plucky, refusing all offers to carry his rifle though he gasped in a way that frightened me ... A transport driver encouraged us by saying that our destination [Saint Riquier] was only a mile away. We reached it at last, a rather sorry looking lot, I'm afraid, round 10.30 am, having marched 14 miles since 4.30 am on an empty stomach ... My section, No. 13, were in a barn ... For first time my French came in useful as owner of house and barns rattled away to Captain Heaven[75] about his well and "the care to be taken of the cord", Captain Heaven understanding nothing, so was able to act as interpreter. Had a good wash, the first since leaving Codford ... Discovered that a *café et rhum* for 4 sous (2 pence) was the fashionable drink, so we had some together. We then returned to our billet and in soft straw had a very restful sleep.

24 November 1915

We ought to have had kit and feet inspection but both were cancelled through the late breakfast. Spent a lot of time looking up and warning men for afternoon parade ... At 4 pm men marched off and I returned to café

---

75 Captain George Heaven, 'A' Company second-in-command. Twenty-three-year-old motor engineer, University of Birmingham OTC, commissioned from 15/Warwicks, October 1914: WO339/21800, TNA.

and talked nonsense about language of eyes with a girl called Madeleine … Linder Robinson joined the Army Service Corps [detachment] attached to the Battalion … Although it means he will be safe from the firing line, I have lost my only real pal and am very disappointed.

25 November 1915

Had a *café et rhum* at a café where had my first warm water wash … Whilst washing in kitchen, bare to waist, Madame came in, combing her hair and kept up a running chatter as if her curling and combing her hair and my washing together were quite everyday occurrences.[76] Meals are rather messy and a farm barn is not an ideal dining hall, dust getting into everything; besides, our barn is not very light. Luckily the cafés supply some passable meals. QMS Staples[77] seems to find me useful and has no hesitation in asking me to inform the owner of this place that one of our men has lost his [well] bucket … [We borrow] a long cord with an anchor at one end. With this we fish up the bucket, the wire rope and the [bucket] … Had supper of nice mashed potatoes and steak, wrote home and carried on mild flirtation with Madeleine. Her beauty is somewhat marred by two front teeth missing, otherwise, quite a decent looking girl.

26 November 1915

We had our first Pay Roll Call. Rather funny seeing Captain Heaven in lounge chair and Staples sitting on three bully beef tin boxes, one on top of the other, paying out … Bitterly cold night and after falling asleep, woke up at 10.45 pm and to get warm started tramping the streets. Then managed to snatch a wink until 12.30 am when cold woke me again. We had had to hand in blankets the night before, thus we had no cover … Up again at 3.30 am and had half-hour's tramp in village then managed to sleep until 6 am out of sheer exhaustion.

27 November 1915

Most monotonous march … Passed through some villages, all rather tumbling down, very dirty, inhabited by old men and women, the latter wrinkled and filthy. They stand with their hands tucked into their skirts, as if they contained pockets, pulling the skirt up to the knee. They wear clogs often and have a coloured handkerchief over head. Eventually reach Mouflers and had another barn billet.

76 For soldiers' initial discomfort at such informality, see Cherry, 'Sex and Morale', 165.

77 Company Quartermaster Sergeant W. Staples. Served as a corporal with 2/Warwicks in South Africa: WO100/170, TNA.

28 November 1915

Biting cold. Perspiration in my socks from previous evening frozen hard and had to put on clean ones. Boots also frozen hard and had to hit them against rafters to make them more pliable. Water frozen in several water bottles ... We [made] a bit of a fire over which we cooked our bacon. Shortly after, we had to "Fall in" and in due course marched off ... [Our destination] Vignacourt composed of the usual varied types of houses, cafés, *epiceries* and shops with few people about, no girls, only old men and women.

29 November 1915

Broke ice in duck pond opposite and had wash. Filthy water! Later began to thaw, weather becoming much warmer ... A foot inspection and the rest of the morning was spent trying to find a barber and to buy bread. Obtaining same is becoming a fine art, the best way being to keep in touch with a *boulangerie* as if it were a Stock Exchange.

30 November 1915

After brekker [breakfast], Titty and I got some hot water and washed our socks and handkerchiefs, our first experience of washing personal belongings. Then had lecture [from Third Army's Chemical Advisor] and gas helmet inspection, going into gas-filled chamber and out into the open again.

2 December 1915

Started the day well by straining or spraining my left ankle ... Found I could not march, so Captain Richardson[78] told me I could go by lorry ... At 1 pm four Red Cross vans took us to Pont Noyelles. Fearful roads and cars rolled about like ships, but quite enjoyed ride ... The Battalion arrived at 5 pm, tired out. Never had had such a march before. Had been misled and came several miles out of their way.

3 December 1915

At 7.15 am went to Medical Officer and after waiting some time the Regimental Sergeant-Major bawled out "All men riding, to parade in front of Headquarters" ... At length found wagons for sick men. Terribly crowded when settled in, quite unable to move. When journey three-quarters done, pain really beastly. Held out somehow and then several

78 Captain H. Richardson, 'A' Company commander.

had to clear out to let a man who was 'done in'. This man was on the point of crying when we halted at [Vaux-sur-Somme].

4 December 1915

Twelve men absent from Roll-Call, mostly men who had dropped out during march and not turned up. Depressing day, with occasional sharp showers and drizzle ... Ankle improving ... There is a general feeling of "Thank Heaven we are here". The men have got somewhat knocked about by the recent marching and a rest is needed. Just now a few were singing in a very mournful tone of voice *My Little Grey Home in the West*, but now, beyond a low murmur of voices, there is comparative silence, most men trying to sleep. Later [we] had a beautiful supper of hare, potatoes, salad, wine and cider, all for the ridiculous sum of 1 franc. People would not accept more, so promised to bring them some bully beef and corned beef tins.

6 December 1915

Spent greater part of day in billet until I got sick of the sight of it. On the floor; straw, littered with pieces of equipment, blankets, boots, socks etc. The walls are partly bare boards, partly plaster and opposite me the walls are plastered with newspapers. On a piece of string tied from one end of the barn to the other, hangs our washing and on a portion of the wall is a drawing of 'Codford Liz', together with other inscriptions, mainly the work of previous occupants, men from Glasgow.

7 December 1915

Had a hare supper over the way, but the conversation was not exactly brilliant. When came back, Walters[79] was brought in dead drunk and with two men holding him up, he sang *The Trail of the Lonesome Pine*. Could not decide whether the scene was extremely pathetic or screamingly funny, but judging from the roars of laughter, it was regarded as screamingly funny. In fact, I could not help laughing myself. The moment the candles were out, a biscuit throwing fight ... It was great fun in the dark. This is the way the dog biscuits issued to us are used.

8 December 1915

The MO gave me 'two days no marching' ... Had dinner of Macconachie's tinned mixed meat and vegetables. As a result, we all later began to suffer

79 727 Private G.E. Walters.

from diarrhoea ... Got a book from Mme Ivonne opposite called *Fettered Lives* and read it the greater part of the day.[80]

9 December 1915

Epidemic of diarrhoea still raging and it is quite amusing how time after time men meet at the 'bog' and discuss their condition ... Played bridge, lying on straw, waterproof sheet as table, candles stuck into bottle mouth giving light.

10 December 1915

News that the 1st Battalion had been in trenches for four days and that one man had been killed. Rumour said he was either a sniper, or a signaller or a scout. Before dinner got a plum pudding from home. Huge delight.

11 December 1915

My orders were to report to the RSM at 10 am. Did so at 9.55 am and was shouted at for being 5 minutes too early ... Shortly after, the Adjutant, Mr Martin,[81] told me to guard the blankets at 'B' Company lines ... [Later] our wagon pushed off whilst I was putting on my overcoat etc. and so had ½ hour's walk before I overtook them ... Soon it began to rain cats and dogs. Verey lights from the trenches became visible and often there were 6 or more up at the same time. One wagon stuck in the mud ascending a hill, so our horses, who had managed to reach the top, were unharnessed and they brought the wagon up. Linder and I during that time, sat on the box seat, huddled in our overcoats, the rain pelting down ... watching the glares reflected in the sky over the trenches, talking of our people at home. After a cold and wet ride, we at last reached Étinehem. Found no accommodation for wagons or for horses or for blankets or for us and it was by then early morning. In pouring rain left to find 'A' Company billets.

12 December 1915

The sound of guns is close and we can hear each report distinctly. Met fellow of 1st City Battalion who had been in trenches and who had been sent to hospital owing to "his circulation stopping" he said. Was covered in mud and looked a nice mess. Brought him in to dinner when he told us of his life in the trenches. Mud, cold and monotony predominating features. Church Parade ... beneath the old windmill, a landmark

80 Henry Farmer, *Fettered Lives: A Story of Prison and the Stage* (1912).

81 Lieutenant M.J. Martin.

overlooking the rolling country towards the trenches, the 'voluntary service' was held. Owing to the cold and boisterous weather, only a few were present. But just a few miles away, throughout the whole service, could be heard the thunder of guns, overhead an aeroplane was flying around and at the end, whilst singing *Abide With Me*, a hailstorm swished down. It was the most remarkable Church Service I have ever attended. Later strolled about and entering a café, found it was a gambling den. Played for an hour and lost 2 francs.

15 December 1915

It struck me how very monotonous yet how fascinatingly interesting this country is ... Although there is rarely anything to see, there are always men standing there, looking in one direction – towards the trenches. One cannot suppress pictures appearing in the mind's eye, of standing inches deep in snow and mud, bitterly cold and the chances of no sleep. I hope the stories we have heard have been exaggerated, as here in the billet even, with chances to move about, the cold is intense. The latest rumour is that tomorrow we move – and I am glad as sooner it is over and I know what to expect, the more shall I be pleased.

16 December 1915

Greased feet, rolled blanket, packed valises and soon marched to Bray-sur-Somme where we were crammed into a train which dropped somewhere midst rolling plains. By this time it was dark. A short wait for gumboots which eventually turned up but which we hadn't time to put on and so had to sling over our shoulders; and we entered the trenches for the first time, at once splashing through water nearly knee deep. We slid along and at length stumbled down into a dark, muddy and slippery dug-out, where, heaven knows how, we put our waders or gumboots on, at the same time dropping off the heavy valise.

17 and 18 December 1915

The trenches are awful, wringing wet, usually over ankle deep sometimes knee deep, with occasional holes into which one sinks lower still. One keeps one's balance by digging the elbows into the trench sides, but before ¼ hour we were all covered with mud. I was in charge of a sentry post in the firing line from midnight Thursday [16 December] until 4 am Friday from 7 am until 12 noon, 2.30 pm to 6 pm and 10 pm to 2 am Saturday and 7.30 am Saturday to 11 am. In the afternoon we went to the support trenches, spending the night to Sunday and until Sunday afternoon in a dug-out where the candles Father sent me proved to be a blessing. In the firing line, the Cheshires,[82] with many Old Contemptibles amongst them, were with us, instructing us and they were a grand lot of men, very cheerful, very confident and doing all they could to make things easy for us. I cannot praise these men highly enough. If the whole of our line is like these men, we have nothing to fear as far as 'morale' is concerned.

Apart from occasional pot shots, the line was quiet, though the first evening several 'sausages'[83] came across, one covering the stored valises of No. 1 Platoon with mud and dirt. The German trenches appear like mounds of earth and barbed wire entanglements, here 30 yards away, there more, up to 100 yards or more. At night Verey lights are sent up illuminating the whole area. At early morning we 'Stand to' and as soon as light breaks, we start to clean rifles on which occupation the whole time is passed as the mud and rain play havoc with the bolts. The CO of the Cheshires,[84] on his rounds first thing Friday, kicked up a terrible row at the state of our rifles. "Christ Almighty, can't you men realise that the safeguarding of this sector lies in your hands? What's the damned good of a rifle in that bloody condition?" When I mentioned that all our cleaning rags had been saturated with mud, he roared out "Never mind, damn it, you've got a shirt on your back, rip it up and for God's sake get these bolts working. The smooth working of your rifle bolt is more important than a shirt on your back" – and we drew lots after he had gone as to whose shirt should be ripped up. Thank heaven it wasn't mine. X went mad and tried to clamber over the parapet. This first night a nightmare, I shall never forget it.

The dug-outs to which we proceed when off duty are caves supported by poles and candles are either stuck to them or into recesses in the walls. Most dug-outs are very small, smell of mud, are usually overcrowded, each man trying to squeeze in, sitting on his valise or just in the mud, in which position we try to sleep. Being tired out, sleep, however uncomfortable and cramped the position, generally comes, even if only in snatches and I slept three nights, wet through, caked in mud, in this position without feeling any the worse. The trenches themselves are a maze and one can easily lose one's way. One soon gets one's trench feet though, and falls into the way of sliding and slipping along, stopping to pull out a leg that has sunk in here, jumping over a hole there. The trenches are not so bad

82 Only 'A' Company was attached and they were broken up and instructed by platoons: 1/Cheshires war diary, 15–18 December 1915, WO95/1571, TNA. For a summation of the battalion's trench induction, see Kang, 'British Infantry Officer', 196–7.

83 German trench mortar shells.

84 Lieutenant-Colonel Richard Oldman.

when dry, as was the case the last day of our first spell in. Luckily, when in the trenches we are protected from the wind.

[Relieved] and after forming up, we marched through Bray-sur-Somme to Étinehem, to our old billets. As we were taking off our gum boots or waders, we had our first experience of being under shell fire and once I was covered with a shower of earth, mud and loose stones. The shell exploded just the other side of the parapet.

19 December 1915

We left the trenches, a happy though muddy set of men and soon were singing. The only 'casualty' was a man who accidentally shot and lost two fingers. Lucky devil, he should be in Blighty by now.

20 December 1915

The day consisted of a rifle inspection (the cleaning took up the whole morning), dinner of bully beef and all afternoon we spent scraping the mud off overcoats, tunics, trousers and equipment.

21 December 1915

Spent morning cleaning equipment which was a tedious job owing to rain ceaselessly falling. Had shave in house of old woman opposite who said it was pitiful to see us sleeping in barns in the cold although I assured her that as long as rain did not fall through the roof, sleeping in barns on clean straw was quite comfy. Eventually, at dusk, we moved off to Bray-sur-Somme … Wrote letters in a club, afterwards being compelled to leave a café owing to a 'Crown and Anchor' game starting up beside us and the crowd becoming intolerable. Had a touch of indigestion and had to sit up a lot, retching and feeling far from well.

22 December 1915

Woke up feeling like 'the bottom of a birdcage', but brekker brought a bit of life into me. Were marched into a field where each man had a shot at throwing a live bomb. Threw mine very badly … Strolled into another club and read a little during which the band played in the square outside in front of the Church. Was struck by cleaned boots of conductor and bandsmen.

23 December 1915

We left round about 12.30 pm en route for trenches on this sapping job … Passed several graves with wooden crosses, some very well and neatly finished, with names etc. painted on. I noticed amongst several of the Duke of Wellington's men one grave of a Bavarian soldier ... The Norfolk's[85] Sergeant Major showed us the [trench] stores and took us round the trenches after [we] spent time in his dug-out, talking and having tea until the Company arrived. Had barely settled down in dug-out with No. 13 Section when was called out for fatigue which consisted of filling sandbags with mud and piling them to fill a gap caused by an enemy's 'sausage'. Rain poured down incessantly. The German trenches were only 50 yards away and the Jerries kept on potting at us and when fixing the bags, we were quite exposed. Worst of all, the shovels were useless, the mud sticking to the blade and refusing to drop into the sack and so we had to claw the mud off with our bare hands and drop it in. We finished after two hours of beastly work, the dirtiest fatigue I have ever done. In our dug-out, thanks to Titty's help, I managed to get a dry pair of boots, I put on dry socks and got warm over a brazier we had in the dug-out.

24 December 1915

Captain Richardson woke me at 5 am saying that the parapet had fallen in where I had been at work and that I was to repair it at once. So there followed another two hours mud clawing, but by getting to the other side into No Man's Land and hauling up a number of bags which had fallen down, we managed to finish before dawn in spite of pouring rain, much mud, much cursing and sudden outbursts of enemy machine-gun fire ... 'D' Company should have relieved us at 2 pm but did not turn up until 4.30 pm. I had no waders or gum boots so stayed behind to borrow a pair from one of the 'D' Company men. I got a pair but the journey down was appalling, sticking in the mud and having to be helped out, then not being able to put on my boots. At last I managed to do so thanks to [some] help ... but midway [to] No. 13 Section's dug-out, I got stuck again and was on the point of collapsing, when Sergeant Harvey[86] and Bayliss[87] came along. The only means of getting free was by pulling feet out of boots, which had stuck fast. Somehow or other they hauled me up, leaving the two boots standing in the trench. These, by combined efforts we got loose and lacing them together and slinging them over my back, I went on. Eventually I had to take socks off as my feet would not grip and so I reached No. 13 dug-out, dead beat, no socks and myself a walking mass of mud.

---

85 1/Norfolk Regiment. On 26 December 16/Warwicks were re-subordinated to 15th Infantry Brigade (5th Division).

86 36 Sergeant H. Harvey.

87 121 Private E. Bayliss.

Titty, Witty[88] and Woodward[89] and Weaver,[90] who shared the small dug-out with me, behaved like absolute bricks. I had had as good as no breakfast, absolutely no dinner and therefore felt very weak, but they stuffed me up with bread and jam, cakes, sardines etc. and soon I felt very much better. After tea, Titty scraped the mud off my feet with my clasp knife as there were no means of washing them and Witty rubbed some anti-frostbite cream on them. We then had a smoke and chat and soon I fell asleep. This Christmas Eve will always stand out in my mind as one of the most nightmarish I am ever likely to experience, tramping heavily through the clinging thick mud, without boots or socks, bitterly cold, in the last stage of exhaustion, ending with the warm welcome given me by my pals in the small dug-out.

25 December 1915

The Germans started shelling us and we obtained our first casualties – 4 dead, 3 wounded including RSM Morgan.[91] Luckily they were all 'B' Company men and nobody we knew, but the news cast quite a gloom over us … During the afternoon [we] procured a brazier. A chat with [a Company cook] got us some coke and charcoal and after dark we had a cheerful fire and with some of Mother's tea tablets, bread, butter, jam and cheese, we had a good feed, though at 9 pm we had to turn out and dig at the trench leading to the headquarters until midnight when we had five full table spoonfuls of rum.

26 December 1915

Whilst digging at '71' trench, our artillery started up and kept more or less continuously at it until afternoon. The Germans soon answered and our shovelling was punctuated by rushes to shelters. Two new dug-outs, built by REs were very popular. Our men stuck the nerve strain well but we were not sorry when the time came to pack up … [During the relief] two shells were sent after us and had either exploded, several men would have been laid out, but both were 'duds'. With several pounds extra of mud sticking to us, we reached Étinehem after a gruelling march.

---

88 243 Private A.E. Whittingham.

89 225 Private H.T. Woodward.

90 236 Private H.J. Weaver.

91 Regimental Sergeant-Major Peter Morgan. Subsequently died of wounds: 16/Warwicks war diary, 31 December 1915, WO95/1574, TNA.

27 December 1915

Although far from ideal, it is a tremendous relief to be in billets again, out of danger, no chance of being hurt and without dirty work to do. After subconsciously tightening the muscles for three days, one falls back on one's pack with a great sigh of relief, not only the relief from physical fatigue, but also from danger.

28 December 1915

We marched to Bray where we had a bath – tubs, into which hot water dropped through holes punched into a large pipe crossing the ceiling.

29 December 1915

Was ordered to take party for laying cable … [At] a spot ¾ on the way to the trenches. There dug hole for cable, laying same and filled in other holes. Sounds simple, but was back-aching work.

30 December 1915

Busy morning preparing to move back to trenches. The many still remaining Xmas puddings take up such a lot of room … Witty has got a job with a Brigade Major, lucky dog … We marched to the station with waders on and there entrained for the trenches. Once there, it was not long before [we] were called out for fatigue and from 11 pm to 6 am were on guard with No. 5 Platoon. Nothing happened, except one sniper's bullet which whizzed quite close.

31 December 1915

Had hardly finished breakfast when was put in charge of four men to clean trench. This is very hard work, very tiring, the thick mud sticking to the shovel and the weight, when throwing it on to the parapet is considerable. In the trenches there is no rest, just one continual period of guard, fatigues, digging and water pumping, until work resembles more a navvie's life than that of a soldier. It is tremendous physical strain and men are complaining on all sides of ruptures … At 9 pm had to turn out and with a fatigue party of six men, started work on a trench. It was pitch dark and work was a farce. Suddenly, at 11.15 pm two 'sausages' came over, a moment later the sky was lit up with Verey lights from all sides, the artillery, ours and the Germans', began thundering until the noise was deafening. It was all so sudden our feelings were those of men bereft of thought for the moment. I had enough voice left to yell to the men to make for the nearest dug-out and to keep well apart. On our way, the shells kept exploding … For 15 minutes the roaring continued, the machine-guns popping away, the big guns booming, the whistling of the shells coupled with the flashing up of sky lights making a most weird effect, almost one could have imagined oneself in a different world. Then, by degrees, the noise decreased until I gathered it was safe enough for us to continue work, but it was with a great sense of relief when at midnight, with the passing of the Old Year, we were relieved and able to have a well deserved rest.

1 January 1916
Spent night in dug-out, bombproof and of steel and luckily had a good sleep out … During afternoon, moved up to firing line and had a good view of the Bosch trenches.

2 January 1916
Miserable day, spent in pouring rain, in firing line trench. After tedious wait, relieved … and on our way to rear, sprained ankle and was brought to dressing station on a stretcher where spent night.

3 January 1916
MO gave me three days off duty and Linder and Titty brought me to our billet where the remainder of No. 13 [Section] were. Again they showed me their good feeling by looking after me. Philip had reserved a corner for me and he gave me more grub of which I was in want. Had a coke fire and felt nice and warm, as billet itself was not very attractive.

4 January 1916
Philip and I slept together in straw and during night he showed his affection for me by linking arms with me and clasping hands. Next morning he had no recollection of this. Got parcels … and the tins are beginning to accumulate at our feet.

5 January 1916
Hurried preparations to get clean owing to inspection by Brigadier.[92] A runner says he was dissatisfied with state of cleanliness of our tunics. Wish he could spend four days in trenches as we do and then try to clean his own stuff. Felt off-colour … Philip excited about his Commission application and everything looks as if it will come off. If it does, I shall

92 Brigadier-General M.N. Turner.

be left quite alone and thoughts of my applying again come into my mind. Wrote more letters but could not shake off feeling of 'off colour'. Later had a bad attack of diarrhoea.

6 January 1916
Went to MO who, without looking at ankle, gave me 'excused trenches' … Decided to apply again for a Commission and to take necessary steps when Battalion returns from trenches.

7 January 1916
A fellow of No. 3 Platoon, Moore,[93] under age and claimed by his mother, left at 8 am for England.

9 January 1916
This 'sick man' time is very slack. We simply lounge about; write, smoke, drink and do as we like … I still feel very far from myself, no vitality or energy. This trench life or something is affecting me but am counting on this rest to buck me up.

11 January 1916
Before we had barely finished breakfast, Sergeant Harvey came and told us a wagon could take 'A' Company's blankets to old billets, so we worked [hard] until 1.30 pm lifting and unloading blankets. These are in heavy rolls and take two men at least to lift them. During the afternoon we had to carry them down and were hard at it until the Battalion came in.

13 January 1916
Up at 5 am and in the dark went to trenches and started sapping. Had easy time, pulling up sacks by means of a windlass and throwing them on to a chalk heap … Were shelled during work but not enough to frighten us away … Back again, had wash in river, bought cutlets, also chips and then went to barber's who between bouts of spitting, cut hair very badly. Stayed and had chat whilst drinking coffee, talking with daughter who, had she been clean, might have been pretty.

14 January 1916
Usual feeling of excitement in air when just before going up into trenches. Blankets rolled, packing in all odds and ends not wanted, inside them.

93 1191 Private G. Moore. For underage enlistment, see Simkins, *Kitchener's Army*, 180–3.

Eventually moved off at usual time, took the train, packed like sardines and reached the disentrainment spot. On way down, walked over those hateful railway line sleepers and some shells exploded that from a distance looked very awful. For once, trenches dry. Was detailed to take on post duty first. Soon discovered there was a German sniper just opposite us.

15 January 1916
Had breakfast on post … Were relieved peacefully and got a spot in a dug-out at bottom of steps. Very draughty. Rigged up some macks as protection and, in spite of men passing, managed to sleep although not soundly.

16 January 1916
Moved up to firing line. Put on fatigue again but was called away with Philip [and] went out on patrol to within 20 yards of German trenches. Was glad to return safely.

17 January 1916
Out on fatigue but having nothing to do, returned to dug-out. Then Sergeant Lewis[94] found us laying 'in bed' at 1 am and started shouting at us, asking why we had come off duty and so kept us busy doing nothing really useful until 3 am, when we were dismissed. All feeling very bitter. Up again at 5 am, but were dismissed until 9 am, then went on working cleaning trench until 11.30 am … Captain Heaven angry because some men had knocked off before their time. Ordered me to take their names.

18 January 1916
Sergeant Lewis has certainly got his knife into me and I have been working and running about … Spent afternoon running about supervising [gum] boots being carried to dump. Moved out of trenches at usual time … Back at billet [in Bray-sur-Somme] got three parcels, also my papers [regarding] commission.

19 January 1916
Captain Richardson surprised us by inspecting bayonets. Told him we had no special orders to clean them so grunted and passed on. Had no time to shave and at end of inspection Captain Richardson said "For this afternoon I want every man to have his bayonet cleaned and to be well

94 183 Sergeant J.W. Lewis.

shaved", looking very pointedly at me as he said this. Took food tins into old woman's house and she made me some pea soup, boiled the steak and kidney pie and judging by her grunts and smacking lips, quite enjoyed her share of the repast. Finished with pineapple chunks and some wine.

20 January 1916

Popped question to Captain Richardson about commission … [Told] our papers had been signed by the CO and that we have to appear before the Brigadier tomorrow morning at 9.30 am.

21 January 1916

Shaved before breakfast by candlelight, but by 9 am were at the Orderly Room, then were moved to Brigade Office. Saw Brigadier, who asked questions about education etc. Very non-committal. Then back to earth again, joining working party at river to unload hay and oats from barge.

22 January 1916

On way to trenches, usual ordeal of slithering through mud and over the railway lines to the by now well-known entrance. Went straight into the firing line where we were at once subjected to 'sausages', four exploding quite close. One 'dud' landed nearby which became the object of great interest … Made cocoa, but methylated spirit stove gave out, so boiled water with cut up candle, later adding a piece of 4 x 2 [inch flannelette] … Went into reserves. Was cramped and crushed in dug-out, so pathetic it became humorous. Actually having quiet evening for once but a 'sausage' burst on No. 2 Platoon dug-out, killing three … and putting nine others *hors de combat.*

23 January 1916

Yesterday's tragedy to No. 2 Platoon caused a cloud to settle on us and again showed up the uncertainty of our life. Another fellow called Jones went off his head.[95] Didn't envy the men engaged on digging out the casualties and burying them who had to go on working at this gruesome job until early morning.

---

95 Probably 176 Private D.E. Jones or 177 Private J.S. Jones. Beyond Vince's platoon, 'A' Company had three more Joneses.

24 January 1916

Moved into firing line during afternoon … Sergeant Borham[96] gave us an easy sandbag carrying job after guard duty and we got to dug-out to sleep about midnight.

25 January 1916

Somehow lost rifle and spent time looking for it … [found] it had been moved in dug-out from where I had put it. Went to steel dug-out in reserves. At 4.30 am moved out and had to wait until 6.30 am, every moment expecting mines to go up.[97] We all felt very nervy … Had three narrow escapes from 'sausages'. The trench I was in was partly blown in and blocked. Was only 20 yards away when explosion happened. Whilst on second shift carrying sandbags, news came through that Captain Heaven had been shot and later saw him being carried past on a stretcher.[98] This was another blow to us and I felt it very much indeed … This time we are getting it thick and no mistake.

26 January 1916

Slept well – I needed it. Just heard that Routledge,[99] the Navy man, was shot through the neck and killed instantly last night. What scientific murder war is … Into Bray-sur-Somme where turned in at the old familiar billet.

27 January 1916

Volunteered to take a fatigue and with six men caught the little train which 500 yards from station collided with and upset lorry … Reported at Waterloo Junction and had to push trolley to dump. Fearful mud, most disgusting work. Returned on engine footplate.

28 January 1916

Had to have a quick dinner and turn out again for sapping fatigue … Lively artillery fire whilst we were working. Returned on limber wagon … Orders to "Stand to" and we have to sleep ready dressed to move at a moment's notice.

---

96 116 Sergeant Frederick Borham. Twenty-four-year-old brewer, commissioned September 1916 into 16/Warwicks: WO339/73927, TNA.

97 The battalion was involved in a sustained engagement of the German trenches using artillery, small mines, and Lewis guns: 16/Warwicks war diary, 25 January 1916, WO95/1574, TNA.

98 Heaven died later that day.

99 1270 Private Edgar Routledge.

29 January 1916
Violent bombardment going on close by and report hath it that French have lost ground.

30 January 1916
Usual bustle before leaving for trenches. Sergeant Broomhall drunk and nearly fell several times en route. Spent quiet night in blown-in dug-out.

31 January 1916
Worked at laying floorboards in trenches and really took interest in job sawing pieces to fit in gaps. A 'D' Company man killed, shot through eye. Went up to firing line and discovered sniper's post through periscope. Great excitement at this. We tried one or two shots. Incidentally, it was a German working behind the post who first drew our attention. He is the first German I have seen … Slept little during night owing to itching.

1 February 1916
Men drifted up to relieve us and we left at 6.45 pm.

2 February 1916
Marched off at dusk … Booming of guns becoming fainter and fainter until they died away. Great feeling of cheerfulness … Arrived at [Corbie] about midnight. Local villagers gave us a hearty welcome.

4 February 1916
Lovely warm wash and shave. It is a very peaceful feeling, being in comfortable billets like this one. We had some Swedish drill and physical jerks, also bayonet fighting practice, this after the usual rifle and equipment parade. We spend a lot of time in tea room, eating cakes and drinking coffee … Went to the Church [with Linder] and had a good talk there over war and religion and influence of prayer.

5 February 1916
Orders to clean equipment from 9.30 am to 12 noon. Whilst I was washing at 10 am, Lieutenant Greenwood danced down the yard and jumped at me saying two men were playing cards instead of working. Calmed him down but had to appear before Captain Richardson who let us off with a caution, somewhat to Lieutenant Greenwood's disgust.

6 February 1916

Hurry and bustle with blankets prior to marching off. Madame gave me 'prayer' before leaving. Marched to [Poulanville]. Felt tired at one stage but some bread and cheese put me right.

7 February 1916

If billet is uncomfortable, the straw bed is a treat and I have not slept so well for weeks.

8 February 1916

Very cold early morning parade, the first since we left Codford St Mary. Several men had to fall out. Later had Platoon drill and I had a shot at drilling the men, but got a bit boxed up.

9 February 1916

Early morning parade consisted of running up and down road, practising saluting and turning. It snowed hard all morning and prevented us from going for a march … Took a bit of notice of our billet. Adjoining is a cowshed with accompanying noises and smells and fowls constantly parade up and down beams and rafters, cackling away and [we] watch with great interest if any men opposite should receive a visiting card from any of them.

10 February 1916

Up at 5.30 am as Orderly Corporal and was soon busy getting sick reports etc. Passes also took up time and what with attending to this and that, have only mealtimes to myself. Orderly Corporal's job is to be always smiling and unruffled, never to lose temper and to be always *au fait* – no easy thing.

11 February 1916

Up early, all bustle for the march. Usual bother with sick, blankets, packs etc. Eventually marched off in pouring rain, along miserable road, often only pools of mud, passed through villages and through suburbs of [Amiens] where we saw a tram, the first since we left England. Rain kept on. 1½ hours continuous marching at dinner time when we expected dinner after 40 minutes did a lot of men in … We reached Molliens-Vidame dead beat.

15 February 1916

Had pleasure of sleeping out, my Orderly Corporal job being over now … Woman in the Café Central said I could have free drinks if I acted as interpreter in the evenings.

16 February 1916

Philip and Witty [unwell] and they were sent to the apology of a hospital – a bare room, a bit of straw on the floor, a hole in the wall covered with canvas being the window. Altogether a most miserable place. Brought them bread and other odds and ends in an effort to make them more comfortable.

18 February 1916

Were supposed to go for a Brigade march but just after we had started, it came on to rain and so we turned back and had orders to clean mess tins and test gas helmets … It became my turn to have a bout of the 'flu. Felt decidedly queer so went to bed early, had no supper and tried to sleep.

19 February 1916

Had fairly good night and felt well enough to go to [Amiens] by the slow train … Had good dinner, saw the Cathedral, discovered the Rue St Geoffroy,[100] visited the 'bad' quarters out of curiosity, had coffee and cakes in a very nice café during which English nurses came in.

20 February 1916

Voluntary church service during which the Brigadier read the lessons. Then was ordered to Orderly Room where Mr Martin told me my Commission application had been turned down. No reason given so tried to console myself by drinking 8 glasses of wine and spent rest of evening in house.

21 February 1916

Had miniature 'extended order' attack in field overlooking village. Our attention was somewhat drawn away by a football match going on nearby. Later was put in charge of a patrol and because I sent a message "Road crossed wood", Lieutenant Dingley[101] said "Excellent". What for, I don't know. He is a bit of a gas-bag but I prefer him to Richardson.

---

100 Bishop of Amiens in the twelfth century.

101 Lieutenant F. Dingley. Thirty-six-year-old brass founder, commissioned January 1915 from 13/Warwicks. WO 339/18323, TNA.

22 February 1916

Paraded for baths. Jolly cold waiting for one's turn and even then we only had 2 or 3 inches of water.

24 to 26 February 1916

Up early and a general feeling of expectancy about. After a period of uncertainty, we fell in and marched off … Reached [Belloy-sur-Somme] at night. This sudden move mystifies us; it certainly means our rest has come to an end. We are absolutely in the dark as to what is going to happen. Rumour has it that the French line has been broken.[102]

Left [Belloy-sur-Somme] in a heavy snow storm and soon were held up owing to transport sticking in snow. Eventually went a roundabout way. Marching appallingly bad. Fell six times. Icicles formed on lips. Cap straps froze on march. Snow only stopped for one short period. March discipline soon disappeared and we got on as best we could. At last arrived here at [Candas] and thanks to woman in billet, were able to thaw ourselves in front of her fire. No blankets and so had wretched night in my wet things. Found boots had frozen hard but at last managed to get them on.

27 February 1916

Went to voluntary church service in Girls' School. Walls hung with sentences warning against alcohol.

28 February 1916

A lovely wash and shave after which I joined others round the stove, reading, chatting and drinking *vin rouge chaud* and cider … The warmth, comfort and feeling of being in a house made me feel very fit indeed and during evening was in high spirits.

29 February 1916

Orders for moving again. Packed up and then … fell in, waited the usual ½ hour and off we marched. On the whole, rather a pleasant march. The snow has thawed but has not left the roads in as muddy a state as I would have thought. Got an attic billet at [Doullens]. Felt jolly at being in a town again. Had some real tea and cakes followed by a beef, mashed potatoes and beans supper with bottle of wine.

102 The German offensive at Verdun had commenced on 21 February and four days afterwards Fort Douaumont had fallen.

1 March 1916
Our hopes of staying in [Doullens] for some days shattered by orders to roll blankets. I borrowed a bucket from people living in basement and [we] performed our ablutions in the street. Had time for a hurried cup of tea and then off we moved. The shoulder straps of my pack hurt me, but otherwise felt none the worse for the march. Close to [Coullemont] the road was like quicksand, whole yards being covered with ice, moving up and down with our marching steps … Whole company billeted in a gigantic loft.

2 March 1916
Although there was little straw, I slept fairly well on the concrete floor … Managed to ingratiate myself into lady of house's graces and round her stove managed to keep warm … This is a miserable village with only one café but have discovered that a Banyuls is quite a good drink.

3 March 1916
To our delight, no orders for moving yet, so had an iron ration inspection, each man having to throw away his old biscuits and replace them by 4 dog biscuits instead.

5 March 1916
At last we moved off. Was put in charge of two pack mules. Still cold with plenty of snow. Actually quartered in huts [at Hauteville]. Had to burn straw left by French. Walters and Witty drunk and later were sick. Awful mess and noise.

6 March 1916
Philip and I put up some very natty shelves, pinching the nails from an adjoining unfinished hut. We were very proud of our achievement. Later snow came down very fast, penetrating the roof, so we rigged up a waterproof sheet and thus managed to sit in peace.

7 March 1916
Lieutenant Dingley took us to the next village, gave us a few rifle exercises, we had a snowball fight, he talked about the Fokker aeroplane and marched us back again. During afternoon, new draft came in.[103] All looked rather miserable. Got a magnificent parcel … Supper 'in bed' with cake, sweets etc. and a cigar thrown in for good measure.

---

103 Ninety-nine men: 16/Warwicks war diary, 7 March 1916, WO95/1574, TNA.

9 March 1916
Had three new men from [the] draft to No. 13 Section and then came news that we were to be transferred ... What a topsy-turvy life this is. Marched off at last. The boom of guns became louder, but kept pecker up by whistling the waltz *Destiny* and *Pueppchen* ... Eventually arrive at Arras and leaving the remainder of the Battalion, we of the newly formed No. 1 Section sleep in barracks on the bare floor.

10 March 1916
Called up at 6.30 am and marched through Arras to new billet, the cellars of the museum. Town like a dead city, hardly a house undamaged. The museum, a most magnificent and impressive building larger than Birmingham Town Hall, now a mass of gaping holes, ceiling-less rooms and distorted archways and walls ... Spent day on sapping, tiring and exhausting work. Trenches in a bad state.

12 March 1916
Went [sapping] and had a rather 'cushy' time, doing little work. Wrote letters sitting on a log ready to jump into nearby dug-out should 'sausages' or 'whizzbangs' start coming over. Had to make three flying leaps.

13 March 1916
Sapping in three shifts of 10 men ... Had another soft job as orders are that no infantry must work in saps ... Heard a sniper's shot whizz very close past my ear and later during the afternoon a piece of shrapnel from an anti-aircraft gun fell close.

14 March 1916
Philip and I had last wash together and we said goodbye in one of the courtyards of that bleak, ruined and desolate museum. He is leaving to take up his commission ... We went [sapping] and had a very easy time, hardly shifting 50 sandbags ... Returned to dug-outs where we slept the sleep of the just.

15 March 1916
Soon after dinner moved off to fire trench ... [which] being dry and the sun warm made the conditions very favourable as one is as well off sitting or standing in the open as in a stuffy dug-out. Was on post until 9 pm and was impressed by the mysterious quiet that always seems to come at sunset. No cannon are heard, just the occasional rifle shot, followed by

dead silence again. It seems incredible that within a few hundred yards are thousands of men facing each other, yet quite invisible.

16 March 1916

On sentry go from 3 am to 5 am and felt very tired. Could hardly keep my eyes open ... Mr Hadley[104] of No. 2 Platoon seems to enjoy a little chat when I am on duty. Otherwise time passed uneventfully though I fired a few rounds just to show the Germans we were awake and to break the monotony.

17 March 1916

Our dug-out, though long, is very narrow where my place is and unfortunately, damp, drops of water dripping at short intervals; furthermore, I cannot lie down, there being no room and so have to sleep in a sitting posture. It is pitch dark down below and candles are in great demand. Life is monotonous, consisting of being on sentry go at night, sucking peppermints or Horlicks tablets, then trying to sleep under the dripping water – and eating.

18 March 1916

Actually had a wash and shave 10 yards behind the firing line, my mess tin being my basin ... Though the nights are long, it is quite nice having nothing to do during the day except read, write and smoke. Unfortunately there is a dearth of matches and I am restricted to one pipe a day.

19 March 1916

Tried to realise it was Sunday but these days in the trenches are so monotonously alike one's proportion of time and date becomes stunted.

20 March 1916

Existence still consists of going on post at "Stand to", exchanging some bantering joke with dug-out sentry on way, peering into the darkness, looking at the moon and stars, chatting occasionally with ... a new draft man, then, after two hours, stumbling back to dug-out, knocking head against beam, cussing, entering a subterranean passage full of snores, lighting a candle after some fumbling about, hanging up one's equipment, then sitting on waterproof sheet and then trying to fall asleep. This is repeated until "Stand down" in the early morning after which the day passes sleeping and eating, cleaning rifle and writing.

---

104 Lieutenant G.H. Hadley.

22 March 1916

We left the trenches at 10 pm last night and were marching practically through the night, reaching [Harbarcq] at 4 am this morning. Everybody tired out, Lieutenant Dingley saying "It's only 5 miles" with the distance turning out to be nearer 10 doing us all in.

23 March 1916

Told to parade at Orderly Room in Marching Order. Found I was to attend the Gas School with three other men ... We reached [Agniez lès Duisans] by a very roundabout way ... Had lecture in afternoon by good old Lieutenant Greenwood, who gave us rations and behaved very decently. Our billets ... were rotten, so ... we got settled in village school and sticking a candle on a form we had supper of bread, butter, jam, cheese and sardines and then went to sleep on floor.

24 March 1916

Morning's course on tear shells, later going through a room filled with tear gas fumes which simply made our eyes stream.

25 March 1916

Morning lecture followed by practice of changing and putting on helmets. Have had occasion to notice the Bedfords – very rough and ready crowd but good humoured. Their language awful. Several of the 'old soldier' type. We bought a bottle of Malaga wine and had feast in the schoolroom, all getting slightly lively.

26 March 1916

Were told our 'routine for gas drill in the trenches'. After tea we returned to Habarcq and just caught 'A' Company before leaving ... Marched to Arras and got billets in barracks.

27 March 1916

Lieutenant Dingley detailed me to accompany some men up to trenches to act later as guide to our sector. Went up through Saint Nicholas, a [northern] suburb of Arras, but then branched off and after a long tramp up a communication trench, reached a village, razed to the ground. The trenches run through the village, through roads, houses, rooms and gardens alike.

28 March 1916

This dug-out is quite luxurious. One enters by a door into the 'sitting room' which possesses a stove, several more or less rickety chairs, a marble slab table, a box cupboard and it has windows and curtains. The stoves, chairs and other odds and ends must have been looted by the French who built this dug-out. But it is a great improvement on any others we have been in. A passage leads to where several bunks are constructed, one on top of the other, some in quite good condition, others decidedly lousy.

29 March 1916

Our work consists of carrying rations up to the Norfolks in the firing line, a fearful jaunt, the journey there and back taking two hours. The tea is carried in dixies, with wooden handles balanced on one's shoulders but the front man usually gets tea down his back, legs and puttees and the rear man down his legs on to his boots, thus both arrive fairly wet through. This is caused by the tea slopping from under the cover or lid which very rarely fits properly. We then rush back as fast as possible reaching the dug-out more or less dry, in two senses.

30 March 1916

Felt rather 'chatty' and spent time looking for [lice] … I am now going to read *Ailsa Page* by Robert Chambers,[105] … a book picked up heaven knows where and with a pipe and a bar of chocolate, enjoy a quiet evening, the last for several days, perhaps, as tomorrow we move into the firing line.

31 March 1916

During breakfast, the Bosches started bombarding the gun emplacements 500 yards away. Shells fell singly at first, then in pairs. Wonderful scene. A whistle or whine, vision of a sudden upheaval of earth, stones and debris, then a tremendous roar. A white house, some red outhouses or barns and a red wall surrounding the lot, just razed to the ground. As shells flew over us and exploded, men began betting on whether "the tree would be hit or the church spire". Showed how very callous we had become. I moved up with tea party, then took over our post for look-out.

1 April 1916

Our post is supposed to be unknown to the Germans and is called a 'listening post'. It is in an advanced position and is surrounded on three

---

105 Robert Chambers, *Ailsa Page* (1910).

sides by Bosch trenches. All we do is to keep quiet, listen and watch. So far we have not heard any talking in the German trenches.

3 April 1916

Heard that an RE officer who failed to answer a challenge had been shot through the head by one of No. 4 Platoon's men … Conditions much livelier, the Bosch trenches being strafed. The Gloucesters sent over some rifle grenades which fell short and I had to send a message telling them to stop. Round 8 pm the Lewis gun started off close by our post and the next ¼ hour we had a brisk time dodging 'sausages', rifle grenades, etc. One fell on a machine gun team wounding a man who had a leg broken, four pieces of shrapnel in each leg and two in the back of his head. It was harrowing hearing the poor fellow's groans. [We] did our best to help him until the stretcher bearers turned up and removed him after an hour's waiting.

4 April 1916

We were told that the man who was wounded last night, had died, as also the officer in charge of the machine gun team. When the relief came up, we were glad. Our dug-outs are not comfortable, being dirty, draughty and smelly. Brought up tea … no joke in the pitch dark. Upset tea and rum out of mess tin on to jerkin and oil sheet and thoroughly lost temper.

5 April 1916

Down to Saint Nicholas. There had wash out of well close by our old dug-out. My services as 'gas expert' first required and during morning did nothing but examine helmets. After dinner … looked at Vermorel Sprayers[106] and made out report … On the whole, I am having a very cushy time. In this dug-out, holding 20 men of No. 1 Platoon, I am the only NCO and have a bit of a job dishing out rations.

6 April 1916

The usual 3 tins of honey for 20 men and 2 tins of butter for 31 and so many loaves for 27 men … Very large rats round here and I've just heard the dug-out sentry say "I'm getting the wind up, these bloody 'rabbits' have started running about the parapet". Being the 'Gas NCO' exempts me from fatigues so down in the dug-out I can [rest] without fear of being awakened or called out.

106 'Similar to insect sprayers [containing] a solution of thio to absorb chlorine. Worn on the back like a knapsack, the sprayer proved capable of decontaminating dug-outs and trenches in a remarkably short time.' Richter, *Chemical Soldiers*, 13–14.

7 April 1916

Made a search for 'chats', a word coined by us for [lice]. Nobody really knows the origin of the word. [Lice] are damnable; they lay eggs in seams and in all hidden corners of underclothing. We find them crawling on fabric and kill them by squeezing between nails. Nobody seems to escape and most men take them as a matter of course. Just when falling asleep, a mine went up and next moment we seemed to be the centre of a furious bombardment. Except one, I had all candles out and then we could only wait and hope. I found … myself putting my boots on and off, the whole time trembling violently. Luckily nobody hurt, though this bombardment furnished theme for brekker conversation.

8 April 1916

Went into Arras to see about gas solution and to draw new boots … Back in our lines in the trenches, found we had been bombarded more than last night, the signallers' dug-out having been blown in and the fellows in a rather nervy state. Nothing happened during the remainder of the day but we were quite glad to move up to the 'immediate supports'.

10 April 1916

Life in our dug-out is very cramped and jam and butter is getting over my trousers and mess tins with tea are continually being spilt over me.

11 April 1916

During the day another mine went up, close to No. 2 Post, adjoining ours when we were in the firing line. Result, 5 men killed, 5 gassed, 3 wounded. The stretcher bearers sleeping in our dug-out kept very busy … Had a very slack time, spending all day reading *The Idol of the Town.*[107]

12 April 1916

Told to report at Battalion HQ at 10 am [and] went to Habarcq … In pouring rain, reported, found Town Major and took over our billets, the huts … Battalion came in at 3 am. After the usual cursing, they settled down and at 4.30 am just when daylight appeared, we fell asleep.

13 April 1916

[Told] to report at the Orderly Room at 10 am tomorrow about my knowledge of German.

---

107 William Le Quex, *Idol of the Town* (1903).

14 April 1916
Interviewed by a [General Staff Officer], a Lieutenant who spoke to me in German and French. Except that I could not speak Bavarian German dialect, think I made a favourable impression.

15 April 1916
Measles broke out … The Battalion is in quarantine, only two cafés and one shop open to us.

17 April 1916
Captain Richardson, following a message received, asked me whether I would like to join the Divisional Police. "Yes, sir", said I but very much doubt anything will come of it.

19 April 1916
During morning, with four other men, detailed to dig grave in local cemetery. Thought it a cheerful occupation for one's birthday. Noticed graves of several English soldiers, though most were French, all with wooden or improvised crosses. One was made of empty shell cases, soldered cross-fashion, with two French bayonets … Marched to Arras in pouring rain. My birthday dainties added to weight of pack.

21 April 1916
Called at 2.15 am for sapping and at dump made first acquaintance of New Zealand engineers … very decent men.

22 April 1916
After recent rains, trenches in an appalling condition and on arrival at sap squeezed mud and water out of socks, then put them on again. In turns, wound up sandbags on winch, then carried them to old crater and on an apparatus similar to a 'rowing exercise' contraption, pumped air into sap.

24 April 1916
Returned to trenches at dusk, this time to a new sector … Sergeant Reeves put me on post and by the time I was relieved, had no dug-out to go to.

25 April 1916
On patrol during the night and towards dawn, Bosches sent over a lot of 'sausages' over the marshy ground on our right. Could see them sailing

over, then the explosion lit up the whole surroundings and a second later a rending and crashing roar was heard. Looked at gas sprayers and later moved into stretcher bearers' dug-out, a little beauty. Then had to leave as some 'Listening Post' men … came in instead … Managed to stick to my bed in spite of strong hints to oust me out.

26 April 1916

A new officer for our Platoon, a Mr Dills.[108] Seems to be a good sort.

27 April 1916

In our dug-out there is a large mirror and at every opportunity we have, look at ourselves. We may be vain, but this is the first decent mirror we have had since we left Blighty. One fellow actually brushed his teeth in front of it. Usual exclamation is "Blimey, how I've aged!"

28 April 1916

At night we moved to the reserves … After had fallen asleep was awakened at 11.30 pm by Sergeant Reeves who said I was in charge of gas sentries. Swore badly, turned over and went to sleep.

29 April 1916

Slept with night socks on, a welcome change after several days and nights with boots on. After inspecting Vermorel Sprayers, took things easy, got over parapet and on a nice spot with long grass, read and went to sleep … I am reading *Don Orsino* … a story of youth in the transition stage, a story well worth reading.[109]

1 May 1916

Had rifle inspection, also of gas helmets. Thought the latter rather unnecessary as almost every helmet I had seen myself previously … Then lay in sun and wrote letters and later finishing *Dr Nikola*.[110] Just when I began to feel horribly fed up and bored, even wishing the Bosches would bombard us for a bit of excitement, a gas alarm was given. Went

---

108 Probably Second Lieutenant J.D. Dell. Thirty-eight-year-old solicitor who subsequently came to the attention of the authorities for his politics: Metropolitan Police Special Branch to War Office, 18 January 1937, WO339/44861, TNA. Dell was secretary of the Britons Publishing Society, an organisation dedicated to dissemination of anti-Semitic literature: Gisela Lebzelter, 'Henry Hamilton Beamish and the Britons: Champions of Anti-Semitism', in Kenneth Lunn and Richard Thurlow (eds), *British Fascism: Essays on the Radical Right in Interwar Britain* (London: Croom Helm, 1980), 48.

109 Marion Crawford, *Don Orsino* (1901).

110 Guy Boothby, *Dr Nikola* (1896).

round and found all correct. Posted gas sentries … [but] alarm proved to be false. Post from home consisted of anti-[lice] belts and cards.

3 May 1916

We had to 'Stand to' at 3 am until 3.30 am. We sleep on trench-boards but layers of sandbags do away with hardness. Actually had jam ration, the first for months … [Told] I was amongst the first 50 men for leave.

4 May 1916

Was twice awakened through frogs jumping about my face. When woke up at breakfast, felt as if I had been drugged. We all feel more tired than last night. This damp, close and stuffy cellar is the cause. Had a wash in the marsh in a spot of clean water, also washed handkerchiefs. Rumours that we stay here 12 days more … Sewed new sandbag cover to my 'jelly mould' helmet.

5 May 1916

We were relieved. Very thankful to leave this hole. After a short rest … we marched back to [Agniez lès Duisans] and got quite a good billet in a barn with straw and a fair amount of room.

6 May 1916

Went to the school where we were billeted during our Gas Course to enquire after having photos taken. All blanket rolls have been undone, the 'spare kit' taken out and the blankets re-rolled in rolls of 10. Those who had spare kit inside to be punished.

7 May 1916

Shrapnel helmet fell off nail on to my head during night, bruising and cutting cheek. Gave me a fearful fright, thought at first a bomb had exploded.

8 May 1916

The Company sports were held and rather to my surprise, won the 100 yards and long jump. Philip turned up in his new officer's uniform and looked like a 'dear, dinky, kissable' sub[altern]. Linder came for tea and later we saw the last half of the 'Whizzbangs', the divisional pierrot troupe.[111]

111 Formed in the autumn of 1915: Hussey and Inman, *Fifth Division*, 96.

9 May 1916

Had a windfall of 25 francs prize money.[112] After dinner, had sports in pouring rain, most dismal and disappointing affair. Ran rottenly, my best being 3rd in three-legged race.

11 May 1916

Marched off and found marching very hot and at first halt was wet with perspiration ... Took overcoat off and felt cooler. Very hard work, exhausting and tiring coming up to trenches.

13 May 1916

Dingley came in at 'Stand to' and found some men lying down. Soon had them up. Rainy weather for a change and trenches soon ankle deep.

14 May 1916

Usual sentry post at night, but Dingley, who seems to have wind up, has given out several new orders.

15 May 1916

We have a black cat that walks about the trenches. It also visits the Germans, we think. This cat and a dog the Germans have and which we hear barking at times gives quite an additional touch of interest to this dull life.

17 May 1916

At 2.45 pm had miraculous escape from death. A 'whizzbang' burst on top of traverse where I was sitting, making a hole 2½ foot square just over me. Was covered with earth etc. Remember giving a shriek and bolting to dug-out, then trying to collect senses and returning to traverse, finding Weaver hurt.[113] Accompanied him to dressing station ... and after being painted with iodine, returned to dug-out. Am sure I shall never be closer to death than I have been this afternoon. Only feel slightly bruised and shaken. News of my escape soon spread and the lads kept coming to congratulate me on my good luck. Left for Arras.

18 May 1916

In museum cellars, but have a very good spot. Went sick and saw doctor who gave me 'light duties'. Came back and had a downright good wash,

---

112 For officers giving cash prizes on unit sports days, see Gibson, *Behind the Front*, 250.

113 Weaver was recorded as shell-shocked: 16/Warwicks war diary, 17 May 1916, WO95/1574, TNA.

head and feet included, shave, teeth etc. and felt ever so much better. Really, of yesterday's awful experience I feel nothing beyond a stiffness and a bruised feeling between the legs.

19 May 1916

Although I pose as a bit knocked about, in reality I'm feeling as fit as a fiddle. It has been the means of getting me off the detestable sapping and I spend the day receiving the congratulations of all and sundry on having escaped so well. Have to tell the story over heaps of times. Reminds me of when I was hurt at soccer.

22 May 1916

Just come up from sapping again. Hard work, i.e. carrying sandbags full of chalk, in spells … These New Zealanders are very decent men and we get on very well with them. They are a very big and tough lot. I am now sitting at entrance to sap, feet against one beam, coat, equipment and rifle against the entrance beam … A few 'whizzbangs' and rifle grenades came over but we jumped back safely to cover. Won another 3 francs at 'Crown & Anchor' … Felt rather tired and so after a fish paste supper, started *The Amateur Gentleman*[114] which had been sent me and then slept.

23 May 1916

Sergeant Major Staples warned me that I was to come up with him … Did so, taking over Sprayers and testing them, also some gas sample tubes, a new thing.

24 May 1916

[My relief] didn't turn up until 'Stand to', so got no sleep until 4 am. Looked at some gas helmets and feeling very sleepy, went to sleep before and after dinner … It started raining during the afternoon, so I thought "Damn work" and lay down on my oilsheet and so-called pillow, smoked some … 'baccy and read *The Amateur Gentleman* until I was quite glad to have to turn out on post.

25 May 1916

Sergeant-Major Staples told me to build emplacement for Gas Sample Tubes and at this job spent whole morning. Then … told Mr Dingley about using sprayers for disinfecting dug-outs. Said he would see into it.

---

114 John Farnol, *The Amateur Gentleman: A Romance* (1913).

Drew water … and on return was told about sprayer having been knocked about from [the] traverse under which I was nearly killed.

27 May 1916

Dingley surprised us by appearing in dug-out at 'Stand to'. Must have been waiting to pounce upon us. Toss up who is most unpopular, he or Captain Richardson.

29 May 1916

After tea was given message to return to Agniez and tomorrow report to Divisional HQ. So packed up things, met [Lieutenant] Colonel de Trafford[115] en route who again told me how sorry he was my Commission application had not been accepted and that he had done his best to help.

30 May 1916

To [Divisional HQ] where saw a Major with whom had interview in German. Told me confidentially what I was expected to do and this makes me think I shall be taken. Spent day knocking about, though at night [we] had a very jolly meal in house here: sausages, peas, chips, eggs and pears, finishing a bottle of Malaga and champagne. Rather pretty girls, specially little kiddie of about 12. Felt very much the merrier and acted the fool a bit at night.

31 May 1916

[Told] that Sergeant-Major Harvey wanted me. Felt rather annoyed at this wakening, so to pay him out took no pains to carry out what he wanted, namely to get a woman to lend him her stove for a roast. Had a very imposing inspection during afternoon when a Private Newey … [was] given the Military Medal for gallantry in field. Newey is the first of our men to be decorated.[116]

2 June 1916

Met Linder and then saw officers horse racing, Major Dudgeon[117] winning the competition or race we saw.

---

115 The battalion's commanding officer.

116 957 Private F.A. Newey, of 'D' Company, had gone 'to the assistance of a comrade who had been wounded by an enemy sniper and lay in a shell hole, and rendered first aid under a heavy and concentrated rifle fire': 16/Warwicks war diary, 31 May 1916, WO95/1574, TNA. He was seventeen years old: Carter, *Birmingham Pals*, 219.

117 The battalion's second-in-command.

3 June 1916
Washed handkerchiefs and sewed buttons on overcoat, then watched 'A' Company play 'B' Company at cricket.

4 June 1916
Attended Church Parade in orchard … On Arras road saw five mines go up. Awful sight. Later artillery so active we had to take shelter behind farmhouses. Limbers, horses, odd men passed, all bolting for cover. Saw one man being dragged, head downwards by riderless limber, one leg caught in stirrup, head bobbing up and down on road surface, horse bolting, terrified. Most fearful thing I've seen so far. Poor fellow, must have been killed at once, but battered beyond recognition … Eventually moved on and took position in trenches, very much relieved. Owing to shortage of men, difficulty in detailing posts.

2

Intelligence

In April 1916 Vince's French and German language skills were tested. Two days later he was asked if he wanted join the divisional police. Given that both languages were examined and a policing role mentioned, it seems likely that he was being lined up for the Intelligence Police, the organisation that was responsible for counter-espionage work within the BEF. Six weeks later he was interviewed again, but this time only his German was assessed. Reporting to the 'Intelligence Department' in Arras on 8 June, Vince was tasked with some counter-espionage work but, before the day was out, he was moved on. The double interview and initial confusion suggests two branches of intelligence were interested in employing him. However, assuming a rational process, the higher quality of his German channelled him into signals intelligence. He joined the wireless section of VI Corps' signal company and although he would later be detached to other intelligence duties, his administrative subordination to that organisation would persist until almost the end of the war. Vince was employed initially as an interpreter of German communications at No. 22 IT Station in the southern part of Arras. In December 1916 he was sent to GHQ at Hesdin for retraining, after which he took command of No. 26 IT Station. During the Arras offensive in April 1917 he was sent to VI Corps HQ for work with German prisoners. This detachment persisted until August when he joined No. 24 IT Station at Croiselles. Vince then remained mostly with that station until the German offensive in March 1918. After that, he spent much of the summer and autumn interrogating prisoners within the medical system. In late October he was withdrawn abruptly from his duties and sent to the signals depot at Abbeville where his war ended.

IT apparently stood for 'Intelligence Telephone' and was often referred to as 'I Toc'.[1] In the most straightforward circumstances, IT stations picked up messages when they were transmitted using the ground as a

1 Oswald Croft interview (1979), IWM Sound Archive 4440, Reel 2.

bearer. Alternatively, they were successful because either signal wires had become inadvertently earthed, or they were poorly insulated and leaked their current. Two means of interception were used. The most straightforward were sets of carefully placed 'earths', the other being roughly rectangular 'loops' of wire, several hundred yards long, that were laid parallel to the enemy's trenches. The earths and loops were connected to the 'instrument' at the station which amplified the signals. Although Vince's later recollection was that intercepts could be made up to 'a couple of miles', success was dependent upon many factors especially the local geology.[2] A full explanation of how the system operated in 1917 can be found in this volume's Appendix. But when Vince was seconded in June 1916, for the British this type of intelligence collection was still in its infancy.[3] The Germans had started intercepting Allied messages in late 1915 with the French following suit. Vince was led to believe that French efforts had been prompted by the capture of a German listening device during a raid north of Arras.[4] The British then became increasingly suspicious of the threat from German interception and in March began to organise their own response, with their initial focus being upon security measures to reduce the leakage of information. In July the capture of German intelligence materials revealed more fully the extent of their success and some British failures of the first day on the Somme were attributed to it. By 1917 the IT systems had matured and, as discussed below, it appears that there was less success on both sides of the front. In 1918 the resurgence of mobile warfare overtook a system that usually needed a good length of time and a stable front to yield results.

Status

While undertaking intelligence work, Vince's formal military status changed three times. First, he was an infantry lance corporal attached to corps signals. He was then transferred to the Royal Engineers (Signal Service) in October 1916 and, in November 1917, was promoted to corporal. It might be argued that the award of an MM in May 1918 also enhanced his informal standing within the army. After receiving

2 This is generally consistent with Croft's later recollection of ranges up to 2,000m in 1916 before the amplifier was upgraded.

3 For additional details of its development, see John Ferris (ed.), *The British Army and Signals Intelligence during the First World War* (Stroud: Alan Sutton for the Army Records Society, 1992), 26–52, 321–2; Beach, *Haig's Intelligence*, 157–9.

4 Vince Shirley typescript diary, Vol. 2, 37, MIM.

his medal he came under pressure from his family to reapply for a commission. He obtained the papers but does not appear to have pursued the matter.

In 1916 Vince's intelligence duties were unrelated to his rank. With another linguist he was required to interpret German messages from the IT apparatus while a small team of signallers, led by a corporal, managed the technical aspects of the collection. This structure and division of labour was similar to another station at the time and was presumably due to a limited number of interpreters and their lack of technological expertise.[5] The shortage of linguists is best illustrated by the seven weeks Vince had to spend in the line during his first stint. At the end of the year, after transfer to the Signal Service, he and the other interpreters were retrained as signallers and also given job-specific instruction on the IT system. In 1917 this allowed a more equitable sharing of the teams' technical work. In Vince's case he was also appointed to a leadership role, taking command of his own station. Although he had infantry and IT experience, and was already wearing a stripe, we cannot assume that the assumption of this role was automatic. But from his account of 1916, especially of his time out of the line, it seems that Vince had made a positive impression upon his employing officer who then sought to reacquire his services. Furthermore, he seems to have shown an aptitude for signalling, something that was not shared by all of his comrades.

Between January 1917 and March 1918, Vince's diary provides us with a fascinating account of leadership in a small team of specialist soldiers. It is an important source because discussions of British leadership in the First World War tend to focus on the role of commissioned officers and combat units, although it has been noted that small units perceiving themselves to be 'elite' had to be handled less formally.[6] We can see this in the approach adopted by some of Vince's employing officers, but their direct supervision was limited once the teams were deployed in the trenches. On taking over No. 26 IT Station, Vince immediately established his leadership style. He led the dirty and difficult work of repairing the loops and also adopted a consensual approach with his men, often noting that he consciously sought to speak calmly to them in difficult situations. He refers a couple of times to the group holding 'councils of war' to determine the way they would deal with new challenges. As an indication of the unit's early cohesion, when a controversial task came up

5 The shortage is demonstrated further by one station having only a single interpreter: Oswald Croft interview (1979), IWM Sound Archive 4440, Reel 2.

6 Sheffield, *Leadership in the Trenches*, 184.

on 19 February his men were unanimous in volunteering for it. We can also see Vince seeking to manage the rotation system to reduce contact between men who were known to have poor relationships. In April the team was broken up, with the interpreters joining those of other stations for general intelligence duties. Although being out of the frontline made the leadership challenge less demanding, the group dynamics became more complicated through the more consistent presence of problematic individuals. However, for much of this period they were working closely with one of the corps' intelligence officers, so Vince could look to him for leadership, tasking, and disciplinary back-up. By mid-July Vince was rather bored with this rear-area existence but, out of a sense of obligation to his men, held back from volunteering for trench duty. His time back in the IT stations from August onwards was more fragmented as he was sometimes deployed to another team. But even when acting as a second-in-command he instituted consensual rota systems for day-to-day jobs. In this period he had to deal with some challenging personnel but was acutely conscious that the 'cramped life [was] very conducive to periods of snappiness' and so deliberately moderated his approach. That said, in mid-October he formally reported one of his men for disobeying orders. Overall, Vince's effectiveness as a junior leader in 1917 seems to have been above average at the very least. By contrast, in mid-September, when commanded by another junior NCO, his team complained about that man's 'meek' approach. Therefore, in dealing with his group of intelligent and often independently minded soldiers, Vince seems to have blended the manufacturing of consensus with some command direction.

Part of Vince's success appears to have stemmed from his considered approach to the commissioned officers who supervised their work. Unlike his time in the infantry, Vince's contact with his employing officers was mediated much less by senior NCOs. Some of the officers, like Lieutenant Bury in April 1917, were clearly rather poor at basic man-management.[7] In that instance the relatively benign circumstances and temporary nature of their task probably led to Vince's stoic acceptance of the situation. But in the case of Lieutenant Marsh, the officer's perceived incompetence caused inconvenience and danger to the IT team over a lengthy period. With his men apparently 'within an ace of semi-mutiny', Vince confronted Marsh with his shortcomings and this seems to have had a positive effect. Vince had a much better relationship with two other officers, Captains Redgrave and Bowle-Evans. The latter was an eccentric

7 For soldiers' attitudes to incompetent officers, see Englander, 'Discipline and Morale', 129–30.

corps intelligence officer to whom the team was temporarily detached in 1917. Vince found him very engaging and in June noted that he had 'treated us better than any other officer I have known'. More important in the long term was his relationship with Redgrave, the officer commanding the corps' wireless section. Redgrave had a relaxed management style and in July 1917 was apparently admonished for treating the interpreters 'as equals' because of their 'superior education'. He and Vince developed a rapport and sometimes had 'confidential' chats regarding IT work and personnel. After Redgrave had recommended him successfully for the MM, he wrote to Vince's father telling him that:

> A pluckier, cheerfuller & more conscientious & good worker one could never have wished for. With the work he was on, one had to place great confidence in the NCO in charge, and never once did he let me down, but seemed to do more than was expected on every occasion ... [His] sound judgement & common sense make him most valuable.[8]

The MM was awarded for Vince's actions on 21 March 1918, with that day constituting his greatest test as a junior leader when he found himself on the northern edge of the German spring offensive.[9] Under a heavy bombardment the IT station stuck to their post and, delivering the messages under fire himself, Vince fulfilled their intelligence function by passing reports to the local battalion HQ. In the absence of orders from Redgrave,[10] he demonstrated tactical awareness by taking a decision to pull out in mid-afternoon, guiding his men to safety through the bombardment and an air attack. It was the most dramatic episode of his war and we are fortunate that Vince also recorded his later recollections. These provide additional details as well as telling us that, in later years, his sleep was interrupted by dreams of its recurrence. In the summer months that followed the German offensive Vince experienced something of a sabbatical. Working mainly in the medical system, he had no leadership responsibilities and, as in 1916, his employment was unrelated to his rank.

On 21 October 1918 Vince's status changed suddenly. He was removed from frontline duty and banished to the signals depot where he supervised

8 Redgrave to Walter Schürhoff, 12 May 1918, Vince Shirley typescript diary, Vol. 5, 25, MIM.

9 For the German planning and execution of the offensive, see David Zabecki, *The German 1918 Offensives: A Case Study in the Operational Level of War* (London: Routledge, 2006), 97–173.

10 Redgrave had attempted to reach the station but was halted a mile short by German fire: Redgrave to Walter Schürhoff, 12 May 1918, Vince Shirley typescript diary, Vol. 5, 25, MIM.

the mundane work of prisoners. The diary does not provide a reason and neither did he comment upon it fifty years later, so we can only guess at it from the circumstances. Vince tells us that it was related to an 'enquiry' he had attended a few days earlier, that another colleague was similarly treated, but his employing officers were satisfied with his work and the order had come 'from Base'. The enquiry is stated to be 'private' and presumably too sensitive militarily or personally to be recorded in the diary. Also, Vince made arrangements with his close friend 'to inform him of what should befall us' and was subsequently in 'fear … of the unknown future'. Ten days later they were joined at Abbeville by two other men who were 'marked' in the same way as themselves. In trying to draw a conclusion, the fact that three of the four men had Germanic surnames seems pertinent.[11] Therefore it is conceivable that Vince and his colleagues fell under suspicion in some way, were considered a security risk, and so were removed to the coast pending further enquiries. This conclusion is supported by the fact that earlier, in July 1917, the interpreters had been 'watched' and investigated because one from a neighbouring corps had tried to help a German prisoner to escape. But before Vince's situation could be resolved the war ended for him on what was clearly quite a sour note.

Motivation

Although still not wholly forthcoming, during his time in intelligence Vince is a little more revealing about his attitude towards the enemy. After April 1917 his work brought him into regular contact with German soldiers, but we can detect some curiosity before then. When out of the line in August 1916, he took a close interest in a group of prisoners held close by, but curtailed his discussion with them when an officer approached. In this regard, perhaps from fear of prejudice, Vince seems to have been quite reticent about declaring his German language skills in general military contexts. For example, in August 1917 he intervened when a colleague showed off his linguistic prowess at meal times in corps HQ. Vince's initial impressions of large batches of German prisoners were fairly negative. On three occasions he refers to them having simian features, but this is linked with their poor physical condition, having just left the battlefield. Later, when the flow of captives was weaker, he was able to engage in meaningful discussions. We can see here a more

11 Schürhoff, Lederer, and Nienhaus.

nuanced perception of his enemies; recording some names, showing respect for one who made an honourable refusal to answer questions, and debating the ethics of the blockade with another. In July 1918 he met German airmen and again his attitude varies. One is a 'regular boasting Hun' and so Vince took 'diabolical delight' in snubbing him; but with others he found it 'very difficult ... to imagine these men deliberately bombing hospitals'. From comments made in June 1917, Vince was in favour of treating prisoners well to encourage others to surrender. A year later we see him putting this into action when he intervened to get a prisoner's valuables returned from a camp guard. Overall, he seems to have had a rather neutral curiosity about the enemy. On a professional level this was admirable and on a personal one, perhaps self-conscious of his German heritage, Vince had decided to steer a middle course between condemnation and sympathy.

In the intelligence diaries Vince records a much greater interest in the events of the wider war. Primarily this is because, being within the intelligence system, he had regular access to information of higher quality and the time to absorb it. He noted that the IT stations were well supplied with newspapers and when detached to the corps intelligence officer they had near-daily access to intelligence products. In early November 1917 the collapse of the Italian army seems to have set off some current affairs discussions within the dug-out, causing Vince to reflect that they were becoming 'quite a debating society'. General intelligence work also gave Vince access to the enemy's perspective on the war. In March 1917 he was rather cynical about official propaganda when the British communiqué incorrectly reported an incident in his locale. Three months later, some work on German newspapers caused him to reflect upon their different content. Furthermore, the reading of German soldiers' letters gave him an even deeper insight. For example, in late November 1917 he observed that the recent success in Italy had had little effect upon the tone of their letters and concluded that 'the German people would welcome peace at any price, even to the giving of Alsace-Lorraine to France'. Also interesting is his reading of a U-boat commander's book and 'seeing us spoken of in about the same fashion we speak of the Germans'. The implication here is that although Vince saw himself as British, he was sufficiently intelligent to look at the world from his enemy's perspective. Again, a useful characteristic for an intelligence soldier.

After June 1916 Vince's frontline experiences were rather different to those which he had experienced in the infantry. The most obvious contrast was the summers of 1917 and 1918 which he spent away from the trenches. That said, when he was in the line it could be for many weeks and on some occasions he was subjected to much heavier bombardments than those he had experienced in 16/Warwicks. Whereas in the infantry he could sometimes seek better cover, in an IT station he was forced to remain static. Such circumstances were always highly stressful because frontline soldiers naturally felt disempowered, while also having to cope with the limited vision and claustrophobic effect of prolonged sheltering.[12] Putting aside 21 March 1918, which has already been discussed, Vince gives us detailed descriptions of his responses to heavy bombardments in January and March 1917. During the first he was under a German counter-bombardment for much of the day. Vince admits that his hands trembled and, fearing they would be trapped underground, he made a dash outside to obtain digging implements. However, the 'calmness and apparent unconcern' of the local infantry caused him to settle down. On 10 March his attitude to a similar situation is more stoical, noting that all they could do was to 'grin and bear it and hope for the best' and that 'chewing a match [was] a great nerve soother'. Five days later their sector was raided and subjected to a short, intense bombardment. On this occasion a neighbouring building was hit and his team were 'speechless with the shock' until Vince made an impromptu joke about it. However, he noted later that they were all jumpy and 'screwed up to a pitch of nervous strain'. In these examples Vince seems fairly normal in giving a 'candid voice' to his fears, while putting a brave face upon the situation, and then employing humour to defuse tension.[13]

But much of Vince's later wartime experiences were not spent under the threat of German artillery. In the absence of immediate danger, boredom and war-weariness were the main threats to soldiers' effectiveness.[14] In this regard, the diaries provide some insight into Vince's coping mechanisms for both short- and long-term fatigue. At the core is the relationship with his intelligence work. Put simply, he and his comrades usually had a meaningful military role which used their talents to good effect. For example, twice in February and once in September 1917 Vince noted that the working of the IT instrument was a 'barometer' for the spirit of his team. The obvious conclusion is that they were prepared to work hard and endure discomfort if they saw it was for a good purpose. On an individual level, Vince comes across as a person who fundamentally liked to work. Indeed, on several occasions he became restless in the

12 Watson, *Enduring the Great War*, 28–30.

13 Madigan, 'Sticking to a Hateful Task', 93.

14 Watson, *Enduring the Great War*, 74.

absence of military tasking. Another important factor is variety. Although in 1916 and in subsequent winters he spent weeks on end in IT stations, these were followed by significant blocks of time on other intelligence duties in a range of settings. Overall, we see a soldier who, unlike many on the Western Front,[15] had a high degree of personal agency within his work and this seems to have underpinned his normally strong motivation. There were, however, some periods when Vince's enthusiasm clearly flagged. The first came in July 1916 during the initial seven weeks at the IT station without relief. Later on, his cheerful endurance seems to have run out after about a month. Once sufficient interpreters were available, the obvious solution of regular rotations was enacted by the signals officers. However, it was also important that their rest periods were properly managed. In September 1916 Vince and his colleagues had to work in a quarry, a task they clearly considered beneath them. Their 'unspeakable disgust' carried forward when, on returning to the trenches, they decided to cease IT work as a silent gesture against their treatment. Another significant low-point for Vince came immediately after his leave in January 1918.[16] This contrasts with unexpectedly positive feelings when making the transition back to the Western Front in February 1917. Although general war-weariness may have been a factor, it is important to note that after his first leave he went straight to the trenches and the companionship of his comrades, but following the second he returned to a more impersonal rear-area camp.

Settings

While in intelligence, mostly around Arras, Vince worked in a multitude of physical settings; frontline IT stations in the trenches, at rest with the signals company, a training course, prisoner 'cages', a corps headquarters, hospitals both static and mobile, a logistics base, and finally the main signals depot. Of course these differed geographically and in terms of the people with whom Vince interacted. But, more importantly, the military environment varied greatly, especially with regard to formality and discipline.

During the second half of 1916, the autumn/winter of 1917 and 1918, and August 1918, Vince oscillated between IT stations in the trenches

15 Madigan, 'Sticking to a Hateful Task', 87, 97.

16 'British soldiers received ten days or, after November 1917, two weeks at home every fifteen months': Watson, *Enduring the Great War*, 101.

and the corps signals company in the rear area. Although they were located within the trench systems, the stations were usually towards the rear, in either a cellar or a deep dug-out. From Vince's accounts, the living conditions were tolerable rather than comfortable, with the teams continually seeking to improve their surroundings through the acquisition of additional stores, furniture, and equipment. The most consistent logistic challenge was the resupply of batteries which had to be manhandled from vehicle drop-off points usually some distance from the station. Initially, the secrecy of their work meant that there was a strict policy regarding admission to the station, but later co-location and interaction with frontline medical personnel indicate a relaxation of this regime. When in the line, the station personnel enjoyed considerable freedom of movement both within the trench system and outside of it. Early on, while still wearing an infantry uniform, Vince was accosted by the Military Police for wandering into Arras but official passes were soon issued.[17] Because they operated a shift system and were rarely under the direct supervision of commissioned officers, the stations were able to regularly spend evenings at cafés and *estaminets* close behind the lines. When in rest at the signals company, the team members were involved in resupply runs to the stations, but otherwise appear to have had considerable latitude to move around on foot in pursuit of leisure activities. Lifts on motor transport, either official or unofficial, further enhanced their radius of potential entertainment. The general atmosphere seems to have been quite relaxed, perhaps reflecting both the management style of Captain Redgrave and the general context of signals units operating independently in small detachments. Throughout December 1916 Vince attended a training course at GHQ (Second Echelon) near the town of Hesdin. Ostensibly this was more regimented, with early parades, marches and inspections, but once they had settled in, the atmosphere became more congenial. Vince and his colleagues did not work particularly long hours and were able to socialise consistently in the town.

From April until early July 1917 Vince was based primarily at VI Corps' prisoner 'cages'; initially at Dainville but then mostly at Arras Prison. He returned to this type of setting in November 1917 and again, at Third Army's cage, in June and July 1918. In the second half of the war, forward corps cages were improvised facilities for processing up to

17 For the work of the Military Police in France, see Gary Sheffield, *The Redcaps: A History of the Royal Military Police and Its Antecedents from the Middle Ages to the Gulf War* (London: Brassey's, 1994), 49–83.

1,000 German captives per day. Usually incorporating existing buildings, they were a series of barbed wire enclosures configured to allow basic searching and initial questioning.[18] As Vince's account of Dainville makes clear, they could be unpleasant places for both staff and their temporary inmates. Therefore once offensive operations had eased, VI Corps shifted its prisoner handling to the still-intact Arras Prison on the western edge of the city. Here Vince and his team were able to make themselves comfortable while dealing with an ongoing trickle of prisoners. In 1918 the Army cage at Candas fulfilled a slightly different purpose. Here, a long way from the front, captives could be processed at a more leisurely pace before their despatch, as full-blown prisoners-of-war, to camps in Britain or labour companies in France. Enemy soldiers from specialist functions could be subjected to detailed interrogations, while clothing and equipment were examined to ascertain developments in the German war economy. While working at the Army cage, Vince was accommodated within a logistics base. His account of this camp is intriguing. It was populated by an ill-disciplined collection of 'old soldiers', so Vince temporarily befriended a sensible Quartermaster Corporal and enjoyed the mostly tranquil surroundings. In July 1917 Vince worked at VI Corps HQ. His diary captured the general atmosphere of idleness in what they called 'the desert'; the area evacuated and desolated by the Germans in early 1917. In a place almost devoid of civilians the surroundings presented significant leisure challenges, with the main solution appearing to lie in frequent journeys to populated areas.

From the spring of 1918 onwards Vince also spent lengthy periods working within the medical system.[19] In April and May he was based at 43rd Casualty Clearing Station in Frévent, and from August to October he served with VI Corps, Guards and 3rd Divisional Dressing Stations. These units were normally tented, but also established themselves in buildings during the latter stages of the advance. This was a good period for him in that he generally got on well with the medical staff, but his diary also records many difficult sights amongst the wounded. In early September he was particularly affected by the fate of a soldier with an abdominal wound. Vince's war then ended on a low at the signals depot in Abbeville. This was apparently 'one of the most … well-disciplined centres in France' and the picture he paints is of some comfort in terms of

18 Beach, *Haig's Intelligence*, 100–1.

19 For developments in the BEF's medical system in 1918, see Mark Harrison, *The Medical War: British Military Medicine in the First World War* (Oxford: Oxford University Press, 2010), 85, 87–8, 91.

food, accommodation, entertainment, and access to the town. But it was also an impersonal and highly regimented environment where his unusual status as an interpreter was then held against him. Further humiliated by the work of supervising prisoners untangling cables, Vince's sudden lack of freedom underlined the army's loss of trust in him.

Within intelligence, Vince's military relationships were more complex than those he had experienced within 16/Warwicks. He was working within small teams of specialists that fell into two employment categories; signallers from the wireless section, and interpreters who, from January 1917, were also expected to have technical knowledge of signalling and the IT system. When in the IT stations the two groups were merged, but when the interpreters were used for wider intelligence work the signallers were reassigned to general communications duties. Furthermore, both groups rotated in and out of the stations either singly or in pairs. So, unlike the infantry where his immediate circle of comrades was fairly static, Vince's trench companions changed on an almost weekly basis. That said, the pool from which they were drawn was not a large one and so there was some continuity which allowed the development of small-group cohesion. Although they had frequent contact with other troops in their sector, the constant battalion rotations did not allow the build-up of much rapport. An exception to this is the relationship with the Intelligence Police, who were based permanently in Arras until the advance. Vince and his colleagues socialised with them frequently and it seems likely that the congruence and official secrecy of their work helped the interaction. Put simply, they could relax and even 'talk shop' with one another in a way that they could not do with other soldiers.

Relationships within the IT teams were often strained and Vince records many low-level disputes as well as individuals who became renowned as difficult colleagues. The rancour ebbed and flowed, but occasionally Vince was surprised to find erstwhile troublemakers starting to pull their weight. Within this context, Richard Lederer stands out because of an additional layer of prejudice directed towards him because he was Jewish. Nicknamed 'Dirty Dick', in June 1917 Vince first described him as 'the bête noir of our crowd'. Three months later he noted that he was 'detested' and his departure from the trenches for Yom Kippur was considered to be 'swinging the lead'. Although from Vince's descriptions of his earlier behaviour it is hard to warm to Lederer's character, the casual anti-Semitic insults jar with the modern reader. But they are indicative of wider attitudes at the time. Although anti-Semitism was less vicious in Britain than in some other countries, the First World War reinforced existing hostilities and in some cases it was heightened by the Jewish community's connections to Germany.[20] In 1918 Vince and Dick came back into professional proximity and seem to have established a reasonable working relationship, particularly in October when they were both despatched under a cloud to Abbeville.

In contrast, Vince's relationship with Bill Auckenthaler[21] stands out as especially close and it later blossomed into a life-long friendship. They met in December 1916 at Hesdin and established an immediate rapport which was cemented during their first stint in the trenches together. Vince's understanding was that Bill, the son of a French winegrower,[22] had been working in a Glasgow shipping office on the outbreak of war and had enlisted in the 5th Lancers.[23] According to this account, Bill then served with the French Foreign Legion in 1915 before transferring back to British IT work because of his fluency in German. Bill was certainly a character; wearing brown boots and carrying an unauthorised revolver, he excelled at cooking in the trenches. His personality seems to have been quite mercurial with his speech accompanied by strong gesticulations. Vince found his personality to be 'invigorating', but also noted immaturity, bluster, mood swings, and the alienation of colleagues through unnecessary arguments. After the war Bill settled in south-west France and the two men remained in contact, occasionally spending holidays together.

Everyday Life

In 1968 Vince noted that his move to intelligence meant that he had been 'able to lead a far freer and independent life'.[24] This is reflected in a much greater range of activities both on and off duty. Even when officially 'in the line' he and his comrades were able to avail themselves of some leisure. Furthermore, his increased mobility when 'in rest' or living with rear-area units exposed him to further opportunities, sometimes

20 For British anti-Semitism at this time, see Colin Holmes, *Anti-Semitism in British Society, 1876–1939* (New York: Holmes and Meier, 1979), 112–15, 122; David Cesarani, 'An Embattled Minority: The Jews in Britain during the First World War', *Immigrants and Minorities*, special issue (1989), 61–81; Todd Endelman, *The Jews of Britain, 1656 to 2000* (Berkeley: University of California Press, 2002), 127, 150, 153, 162, 184.

21 206938 Sapper William Auckenthaler.

22 From details of marriage recorded in the Register of Servicemen's Marriages: RG34/9, TNA.

23 Photograph annotation, Vince Shirley typescript diary, Vol. 2, 88, MIM. The regimental affiliation is corroborated by his medal roll index card.

24 Vince Shirley typescript diary, Vol. 2, 37, MIM.

on a near daily basis. This variety makes him a much better witness to the 'everyday life' of the British army than if he had remained within the infantry. Had he stayed with 16/Warwicks, he might have seen more of the Western Front overall, but the depth of engagement with his surroundings would have likely been curtailed by the more restrictive and repetitive context of an infantry battalion.

While at work, Vince's primary role was as an IT translator and later operator. Given the secrecy surrounding the electrical technology, he was understandably reluctant to record any specific details in his diary. However, the snippets that he offers do allow some sense of how the system worked and, importantly, its utility over time.[25] In 1916 the impression gained is that collection was good, particularly after the station had been redeployed to a better position. The interpreters were busy during their four- or five-hour shifts and, by 27 June, the expectation was that their results would make the staff officer responsible for intelligence 'sit up in his chair'. They were also engaged in monitoring British communications and in September one of the station members had to testify at a court martial of, presumably, a careless signaller. However, their work faced several challenges; interference from bombardments and friendly messages, the lines breaking, and their batteries running out. The technical difficulties persisted but, according to Vince's later recollections and the documentary evidence about the British Mark II amplifier contained in this volume's Appendix, the 'instrument' was significantly upgraded in the winter of 1916/1917, copying a French design, and the collection distances were enhanced and interference reduced. There was also a noticeable shift in the reporting system. Instead of going only to a higher level, Vince's stations were also sending information of tactical significance directly to local battalions. That said, IT appears to have been considered useful only in static conditions as the interpreters were reassigned to general intelligence duties during the Arras offensive of April 1917. Following successful tests in July, the stations were redeployed and afterwards the picture is mixed. In early September the intelligence authorities were apparently pleased with their work but by the end of the month, albeit in a different station, 'no results [were] obtainable'. The suggestion of a significant dip is also indicated by Vince's narrative of 17–18 October which 'after weeks of

25 Although we have some insight from official documents, the number of contemporaneous personal accounts are very limited. An exception is that of an American IT translator/operator in late 1918, but he is even more reticent than Vince: Ernest Hinrichs (ed.), *Listening In: Intercepting German Trench Communications in World War I* (Shippenburg, PA: White Mane Books, 1996), 4–7, 14–15, 31, 54–5, 65–6.

silence' suddenly became 'reminiscent of the IT at its best'. Apart from some activity on 23 December, he is then quiet about their output during the winter of 1917/1918. For the German offensive on 21 March Vince's contemporaneous account, supplemented by his reminiscences half a century later, state very clearly that he was intercepting German messages in clear. But, apart from a fortnight in August, this was the last IT work he conducted. This suggests very strongly that diminishing returns meant such collection was no longer deemed a good use of specialist manpower, especially once the British army started moving forward with increasing rapidity.

Beyond his IT work, Vince was employed on other intelligence duties including prisoner handling, interrogations, and document analysis. In October 1917 he also offered his services to the local infantry battalion for tactical questioning after a raid. When detached initially to VI Corps HQ in April 1917, Vince and the other interpreters were used to corral and document large batches of German prisoners. Their employment in this role stemmed from the army's experience on the Somme in 1916, when it was realised that prisoners needed to be screened properly before some could be chosen for interrogation by Intelligence Corps officers.[26] Having gained experience during this initial period, Vince was then able to carry out his own prisoner interrogations. As had become the norm by then, he tended to adopt a friendly, conversational approach to questioning. In this regard, his personal knowledge of Germany seems sometimes to have helped to break the ice. Additionally, Vince was used to process the huge amounts of documentary material that was either taken from prisoners or found during searches of captured positions.[27] In 1918 Vince was attached to medical units to document and, if necessary, interrogate wounded German prisoners. In June he provides us with a contemporaneous, and probably unique, first-hand account of the use of a decoy prisoner to elicit unwitting testimony from a wounded captive.[28]

As already discussed, Vince was in most danger on 21 March 1918. But during his intelligence service, when in and around the trenches, he was under a near-daily threat from German fire. When inside the IT station the team was fairly well protected. As Vince explained on 17 March 1917:

> Experience has shown us to be just out of reach of trench mortars, 'whizzbangs' are not strong enough to hurt us and what gave us

26 Beach, *Haig's Intelligence*, 101–3.

27 *Ibid.*, 108–12.

28 On his own initiative Vince had earlier used a decoy prisoner in June 1917.

> some big frights in the shape of loud bangs we found was shrapnel so there only remains real heavy stuff falling directly on us that could do us any harm.

This fear of direct hits from large-calibre shells caused the team to be very wary of highlighting their position through cooking smoke or unguarded light, and they also became concerned when troops clustered close by. However, in the same diary entry, Vince noted that shelling had become 'an everyday occurrence, [and] we are getting quite used to it'. As was normal for experienced soldiers,[29] when moving around the trench system Vince became adept at recognising the types of German fire and thereby took precautionary action. His team were also fortunate in that their semi-independent existence allowed them to dictate when they carried out many of their tasks. Therefore we see them, for example, delaying repairs to the loops until shelling had subsided. But using this 'weather eye' for bombardments was not always possible when meeting their resupply drops and this, in part, explains the tensions with Lieutenant Marsh regarding their timing and location. Vince records a number of close calls from shells landing very close, but on three occasions it was German rifle and machine-gun rounds that brought him close to death or serious injury. In July 1916 a single round passed between him and a colleague; in February 1917 what was presumably indirect fire from German machine-guns splashed near the road on which they were walking; and in September he had what was very nearly a 'Blighty touch' when a round hit his boot. By 1918 a new threat dimension had also emerged with the advent of German aircraft bombing the British rear areas. This seems to have been initially quite disconcerting. As Vince put it in May, 'one expects danger in the trenches, but when out resting, to have to expect the same thing goes very much against the grain'. In October 1918 he experienced a near-miss from a German bomb which slightly wounded a comrade sleeping nearby.

Vince was certainly better fed during his time in intelligence than he had been in the infantry. The underlying reason seems to have been the greater degree of personal agency. As a small group he and his comrades took responsibility for their own food preparation and, when in and out of the line, they had good access to the civilian economy. Initially, the IT stations were supplied by the local infantry unit, but the system was frequently disrupted by battalion rotations. Vince was often involved in

29 Watson, *Enduring the Great War*, 105.

resolving these supply problems, noting in March 1917 the importance of 'putting on the usual professional beggar's wail and semi-starved facial expression'. During the team's period in Arras Prison he gained further insight into the rationing system when he had to fetch food from a centralised source. Later he did the same task while on rest from the IT station. His description of 'dropping raw meat, bacon, [and] loaves of bread' into sandbags is not an appetising one. When in the trenches, we can see the evolution of Vince's culinary skills.[30] In October 1916 the team acquired their own stove and when establishing later stations, this item was always high on their 'scrounging' list. Sometimes they did their cooking underground, but even with an improvised chimney there were problems with fumes. Learning from his comrades, Vince's repertoire of meals improved and by October 1917 he was particularly proud of his steak and chips. However, his diary does note difficulties with food perishing before it could be consumed and, when the supply system is disrupted, the need to fall back upon biscuits and bully beef. Treats sent from home also feature. When in the rear areas Vince made full use of cafés and *estaminets* and there is a strong sense that his language skills allowed him to establish an excellent rapport with some hosts.[31] For example, whenever possible he visited Mme Pruvost's café, giving us in June 1917 a delightful description of French mealtime customs. When living in more remote army camps he also established good relations with the cooks, giving them German postcards and other souvenirs in exchange for special treatment.

Vince's religious activity is better documented than when he was in the infantry. With more freedom of movement and greater leisure time, he was able to attend religious services, especially at the YMCA. There appears to be obvious connection between his frequent non-religious visits to the YMCA's huts and attendance at their services. In September 1916 and January 1918 Vince tells us that he went to a service with the express purpose of raising his spirits. These occasions are noted because they were not successful, so it seems fair to assume that other observances were undertaken for similar reasons and had the desired effect. During moments of stress Vince's faith seems to have been important. While under heavy bombardment in January 1917 he and Bill had a discussion about 'the nearness of a Higher Power'. He also records 'half trying to pray' during the moment of crisis on 21 March 1918. Finally, at the Armistice he highlighted the Abbeville chaplain's assertion that a 'visible

30 For trench cooking, see Duffett, *Stomach for Fighting*, 172.

31 For the importance of civilian food outlets, see *ibid.*, 215–19; Gibson, *Behind the Front*, 135.

act of God' had caused the British army to reach Mons, where its fighting had commenced in 1914.

As with religion, Vince's intelligence diary provides a great deal more detail about his engagement with popular culture than did his infantry one. In this regard he is an important source because he provides some commentary on collective entertainments.[32] Vince's attendance at concert parties was fairly consistent from the winter of 1916/1917 through to the end of the war. They varied considerably in their quality, ranging from the 'Light Blues' in March 1917 who had some 'painful' acts to 'The Stars' in April 1918 who, after a poor start, launched a new and 'first class' programme. The venues included locations fairly close to the frontline, such as the theatre in Arras, so Vince seems to have always had access to this type of performance. This contrasted with his access to cinemas which usually required him to be further back from the trenches. His first visit to a cinema occurred in August 1916 and his attendance later peaked while working at a static hospital in 1918. His commentaries on the films are more restrained and they seem to have had less impact upon him. Vince also highlights a number of musical concerts. When recording these he drew direct parallels with similar experiences at the British seaside, suggesting that for him this type of collective entertainment was a more powerful 'imaginative space'.[33] But his most consistent cultural pleasure was the reading of novels. Although his documenting of their titles is erratic, his reading is consistent throughout his time in intelligence and by 1918 it had become an almost non-negotiable part of his daily routine. Indeed, in September he went to some lengths to ensure that his sleeping quarters complied with the black-out requirements against bombing so that he could indulge this habit. We can perhaps see here a thoroughly middle-class form of escapism from the war.

During his off-duty time Vince also indulged in games. Unsurprisingly, given the cramped conditions, when in an IT station cards were a popular pastime amongst his group. In the summer and autumn of 1916, games of whist were the norm. But a year later this was superseded by pontoon played for money, with Vince recording a comrade's record loss of 30 francs in one session. The games became part of the daily routine and, in October 1917, Vince noted his suggestion of one as a method

32 For the methodological difficulties in researching this subject, see Fuller, *Troop Morale*, 98, 111.

33 'Entertainment, as a form of popular culture, allowed soldiers to find an imaginative space away from the realities of military life and war, and provided a much-needed escape that contributed to their ability to endure': Amanda Laugesen, 'More than a Luxury: Australian Soldiers as Entertainers and Audiences in the First World War', *Journal of War and Culture Studies*, 6:3 (2013), 236.

of defusing tension in the dug-out. When out of the line Vince did not engage consistently with any sports. There was a bit of desultory physical training while at Arras Prison, some swimming in a reservoir, and the occasional football kick-about. In 1918 he even tried his hand at fishing. In July 1917 he and Bill took advantage of a slack period at corps HQ to renovate a tennis court and engaged in several hard-fought matches before the breaking of one of their racquets brought proceedings to an abrupt halt. The circumstances are interesting in that a few weeks earlier Vince had observed officers playing tennis and experienced what he called an 'abnormal' spasm which caused him to clench his fists and 'yearn … to meet [them] on an equal footing and play'. The reference to inequality in this outburst suggests some resentment at his military status in comparison to his pre-war life with its membership of the local tennis club. There is another instance where games offered both an escape and a link to civilian life. In October 1916 Vince recorded his enjoyment of playing hide-and-seek with some French children, noting the contrast between this and his 'rough and ready life, always in men's company'.

Alcoholically, Vince's infantry service seems fairly abstemious in comparison to his time in intelligence. The tone was set when, two days after joining his first IT station, he left it temporarily to spend an evening drinking a bottle of wine in a local village.[34] Reflecting his increased engagement with French civilians and their culture, the rest of the diary records fairly consistent alcohol consumption with meals and in the evenings. This intake seems moderate and unremarkable given the historical and social context. However, during the autumn of 1916 Vince highlighted several bouts of quite heavy drinking both in and out of the line. In late August and early September he noted two instances when this had at least some effect on his ability to man the IT instrument. In 1917 the outbreaks of binge drinking are less frequent and the picture is similar in 1918. That said, after promotion to full corporal put him into social contact with sergeants in the rear areas, he did experience an increase in intake of whisky and also of hangovers. Overall, Vince does not appear to have had an alcohol problem and its use was clearly an important social lubricant and safety valve within the group. With regard to the latter, an example would be the large bottle of beer given to him by Captain Redgrave late on 21 March 1918.

From mid-1916 Vince's love life also becomes more interesting. This is primarily because he sometimes spent reasonable stretches of time in single

34 For the BEF's regulations on the sale of alcohol to soldiers, see Gibson, 'Relations', 178; Gibson, *Behind the Front*, 136.

localities and could therefore build up more meaningful relationships with French women.[35] Around Arras in 1916 his rest periods were fairly short and so he recorded only brief flirtations. There is nothing to indicate any significant romantic connections in this period. In December, while on his training course at Hesdin, there was another visit to a red-light district 'out of curiosity' but, as before, no indication of engagement with the services on offer. In 1917 women feature less prominently in the diary, but Vince is more forthcoming about his personal thoughts. In April he had a lengthy discussion with a colleague about sexual morality and, a few months later, commented upon novels that addressed 'sexual questions'. Just before returning to the trenches in early August, Vince made a visit to Amiens during which he clearly wrestled with his urges in a city that he saw as being 'soaked with loose women and temptations'. In several cafés Vince declined what he perceived as opportunities for sexual encounters, but eventually made his way to the 'lowest quarters'. Here he 'strolled up' but was ultimately repulsed by the 'disgusting' ambience. In opting for restraint when confronted by the realities of commercialised sex, Vince was not alone. Although peer pressure, alcohol and a fear of impending death may have accelerated many British soldiers towards the services of prostitutes, there were others for whom pre-war morality and/or the risk of sexually transmitted diseases acted as a brake.[36] More significantly, when at Candas in 1918, he began what was initially a 'mild flirtation' with Lucile, a married woman from Lens. Taking into account her marital status,[37] their relationship is probably the most intriguing of Vince's war. He was impressed by her youth, charm, intelligence and 'chic', describing her as 'the easiest person to talk to I've met out here'. With her sister as a highly embarrassing chaperone, they shared an awkward lunch at an officers' dining room in Doullens. When he had to leave a few days later, he noted a 'most affectionate farewell'; returning the following day because 'the temptation to see her again was too strong to resist'. On that second occasion he was rewarded with her photograph. Three months later, en route to the coast, Vince returned. Finding Lucile 'as delicious as before', they had a 'wild evening' that would 'long remain in [his] mind'. To a modern reader the implication might be that their relationship had become a physical one, but this would take the written

35 In this regard, Vince was unusual: Craig Gibson, 'Sex and Soldiering in France and Flanders: The British Expeditionary Force along the Western Front', *International History Review*, 23 (2001), 572.

36 Cherry, 'Sex and Morale', 79, 121, 139, 140, 143.

37 For the complexities of British soldiers' relationships with married French women, see Cherry, 'Sex and Morale', 160, 173; Gibson, *Behind the Front*, 331.

evidence too far and would project backwards later social mores. All that we can say for certain is that, aided considerably by his language skills,[38] Vince greatly enjoyed the company of French women throughout the war. He may have struggled personally with the ambiguous moral climate of wartime France, but we can definitely discern a maturing of his interactions with women. Within his fairly conventional approach to courtship, we can detect a shift from mild and short-lived flirtations based on perceived physical attractiveness towards more intense relationships driven by personality.

* * *

Two incidents in July 1917 help to capture the fundamental change in Vince's military life that occurred after he left the infantry. At the beginning of that month, when looking for their assigned billets, he noted that a French woman mistook him and his comrades for 'common or garden Tommies'. Of course, by then he had ceased to be an ordinary soldier but was, instead, a trained specialist who carried out technologically complex work. This gave him much greater responsibilities, but the army also rewarded him with higher pay and, more importantly, much greater freedom. A couple of weeks later, while serving at VI Corps HQ, Vince was taken aback by the polite table manners of the 'draughtsmen, surveyors, chemists, [and] engineers' who served with him in the intelligence section. In part this illustrates the fact that Vince still saw himself as a trench soldier despite some lengthy periods behind the lines. Although his headquarters colleagues came from a similar social class, his experiences had roughened him considerably and the change had stuck. In this regard, one of the most interesting aspects of Vince's intelligence diary is the way in which he transits back and forth between the frontline and rear area environments, observing their characteristics.

Overall, Vince's service with intelligence seems to have been a positive experience. He found himself in a role that exploited his intellect and language skills and, the last few weeks of the war aside, he seems to have been very satisfied with his contribution to Britain's war effort. The popular image of the British soldier on the Western Front is a miserable one, with soldiers often depicted as the passive victims of relentless, grinding attrition.[39] To be fair, there were some dark periods in Vince's

38 For the significance of this factor, see Cherry, 'Sex and Morale', 175.

39 McCartney, *Citizen Soldiers*, 1–3; Helen McCartney, 'The First World War Soldier and His Contemporary Image in Britain', *International Affairs*, 90 (2014), 299–315.

trench service, but the overwhelming narrative is of a proactive and normally optimistic individual who always adapted fairly successfully to his circumstances. And it is this personal agency that seems to have been most important in sustaining him. Of course it helped that the army gave his small group considerable latitude to achieve their tasks, but nevertheless they were usually operating in the same hostile environment as other trench-dwellers. In his diary, Vince three times gave voice to underlying feelings about his intelligence service. In April 1917 he reflected upon his first command of an IT station, noting the 'excitement, comfort, danger and homeliness, an atmosphere of independence and a feeling of Bohemianism never felt before', before going on to stress the 'feeling of comradeship with real fine fellows, equally fine in sharing danger as well as pleasure'. Later that month he succinctly summarised life in intelligence as 'cushy and yet interesting' compared to the infantry. Then, in October 1918, when confronting exile at the signals depot, he articulated his anger at being wrenched from 'all the scenes so familiar, the faces so well known, both of which one has almost learnt to love, in spite of the many hard times'. So, for Vince, despite its many horrors it became quite a good war and perhaps something of an adventure, both militarily and personally.

8 June 1916
At 'Stand down' ... the Orderly Corporal told me I had to report to the Town Major, Arras ... Was interviewed by an Intelligence Department Captain and actually told to trace the whereabouts of a suspicious character this very afternoon. Read secret reports which were given to me ... and altogether was welcomed most warmly by the Intelligence Department NCOs and men. During dinner, however, a note was brought saying I had to leave, a mistake had been made, so was brought here, Achicourt, by motor and on foot. Men welcomed me in and in due course they told me that this was a cushy job.

Vince had joined No. 22 IT Station, later subordinated to VI Corps Signal Company's Wireless Section.

9 June 1916
Of my work I am bound to secrecy ... Saw prospective new home and we are all pleased with it. It is the skeleton of a farmhouse, has a sleeping room, work and living room and, above, another living room. The men I find are very decent indeed. The Corporal in charge is 'Jock' [Robertson], a Scotchman, has been all over the world ... Jack Gilkes, a Londoner, was at Suvla Bay and wounded. 'Taffy' is a Welshman, quiet, but can play the organ a treat ... George Lillis completes the group. He is an Irishman, a survivor of the 'Old Contemptibles', rather good-looking and has certainly very taking ways. He has been out here since October 1914.[40]

10 June 1916
Relieved William Roberts,[41] 'Wilkie', a 2nd Birmingham City [battalion] man who learnt his German at Stuttgart and says that for a time he was in the German Army. This afternoon we brought our furniture over, fixing up the table and mattresses.

11 June 1916
Every spare moment filled improving our new home. Excitement and fun combined by exploring the cellars of neighbouring ruined houses. Discovered some crockery and mirrors, also a picture which owing to its design we call 'Chatting'. Went into village and had a bottle of wine.

---

40 He had been a pre-war Territorial.

41 1488 Private William Roberts, 'B' Company, 15/Warwicks.

12 June 1916

Owing to [a relief] there was some difficulty over breakfast rations which were very small. Taffy and I built a latrine, quite classy with proper wooden seat. The weather is wet and cold. We have got the well in proper working order, though there is no bucket and having to use a light biscuit tin is unsatisfactory. The [infantry] have opened a good canteen, so we bought some pineapples, biscuits and chocolate. Two officers came down and told us that Mr Bryden,[42] our OC up to now, had left us and that a Mr Redgrave[43] would be our new boss. Brought one of the mirrors out of a cellar, also a chair we found. Jock started yarning, some stories quite good, but towards the end he began pulling our legs with some very juicy lies.

13 June 1916

Worked at the IT until noon … Were visited by the two officers who asked if we were quite comfortable. They seem to be very decent sorts. Said two more men would be coming shortly to relieve Wilkie and myself.

14 June 1916

Started work at 7 am and then fetched breakfast with Taffy, afterwards working on and off until dinner. This is a delightfully free and easy life. We are practically our own masters and most of the time is taken up in improving our new home. I was disappointed that no letters had come; it seems strange being a week without any news and our isolated Robinson Crusoe existence increases one's 'alone on an island' feeling … At tea we began pulling down each other's country, Taffy and Wilkie getting quite excited over Lloyd George and the Insurance Act.

16 June 1916

Wilkie called me at 4 am and at once started work … During quiet intervals, wrote letters … Kept on until after breakfast, when Wilkie relieved me. Had a thorough chat hunt and put on some Harrison's pomade. It pricked like pins and needles.

---

42 Second Lieutenant Sydney Brydon RE. A research physicist commissioned in November 1915, by 1917 he was responsible for all listening sets in First and Third Armies: War Office to Brydon, 18 November 1915; 'Statement by an officer concerning his own [medical] case', 18 April 1921; Protection Certificate, 30 September 1921, WO339/46392, TNA.

43 Second Lieutenant Harry Redgrave RE. Twenty-two-year-old electrical engineer and pre-war Territorial, commissioned in December 1915: WO374/42009, TNA.

17 June 1916

Up at 7.30 am, had wash and shave, made out reports during breakfast and directly after left for Arras ... Saw Corporal [Frederick] Francke[44] and had bath and change of clothing ... Found letters had been sent to the 5th Divisional Intelligence Corps ... Put blue and white Signals band on tunic sleeve for first time ... Jock and I fetched two REs who are to help us with the laying down of our wires.

18 June 1916

I am reading *The Ne'er Do Well* by Rex Beach.[45] Good book. Corporal Francke, the Intelligence man lent it to me. Went to church ... During service, swallows kept flying in and out of hole by window and I noticed they had a nest in a corner. A dog also casually strolled in during the service and sniffed around, then was led out.

19 June 1916

Wilkie told me more of his life, how, after his turn in the German Army, during which he was stationed in Zanzibar, he took up navigation and following some trips from Antwerp to Hamburg, spent some time on the Rhine, sailing between Cologne and the sea. He was on this when War broke out but managed to escape to Antwerp and get over here before the Germans reached it.

20 June 1916

Wilkie woke me up to take his place at the IT whilst he fetched rations ... Jack and George came back from Arras with glowing accounts of how they had been treated. Had some bother about rations with these new men but thanks to a man ... of the [Durham Light Infantry], we settled things. All the same it was not until midnight that I reached 'home' with our rations and having to go on duty straight away, it was 4 am before I got to bed.

21 June 1916

After tea, being off duty, sat on the porch, part of which has been converted into a seat and read the bundle of papers which has come. Then went with Jock and Jack into Achicourt village where a very young, officious MP stopped us. Jock told him off beautifully and after that he felt too cowered to stop us. Brought that heavy old cupboard out of the ruined house and carried it along to our abode-of-love.

---

44 99190 Corporal Frederick Francke, Intelligence Police.

45 Rex Beach, *The Ne'er-do-well* (1911).

22 June 1916

Cleaned up the billet after breakfast, breaking bottle of pickles whilst doing so. The sandbag curtain shutting off passage caught fire whilst I was fetching breakfast but Jack managed to put the flames out … The two REs have just left, so now we shall have more room. Had supper of Army ration, plus pineapple and cream and a cup of cocoa.

23 June 1916

Had a row with George … When morning came, he found his bed too comfy, neither would he fetch breakfast, so we avoided each other until tea which he offered to fetch after a tremendous thunderstorm with mud lying about thickly everywhere. This morning I gave him a piece of my mind, but on offering to fetch tea, met him halfway and at night peace was restored. Went to Achicourt to fetch accumulators … The tremendous weight of the box of staples decided us to dump them until tomorrow.

24 June 1916

Great activity around us – guns and trench mortars firing all day and over on our right a continual rumble is audible. Rumour says our troops have broken the German line at Albert and advanced five miles with our cavalry starting the ball rolling, infantry following up. Casualties about 6,000 'tis said.[46]

25 June 1916

Day started with a hot trench mortar bombardment on our lines. They are 160 pounders and when they explode, make an ear-splitting roar, shaking the earth for hundreds of yards around. Jack and George came into abode quite nervous after narrow squeaks.

26 June 1916

The bombardment that has been going on our right for some time, still continues, giving the whole earth a slightly trembly feeling. Jock turned up and after a pleasant chat, he fixed up some pictures, greatly improving our 'living room' … Rumours of further successes at Albert.

46 The Somme offensive's artillery barrage commenced that day, but the infantry did not attack until 1 July.

27 June 1916

Went on shift during morning; the work results obtained will probably make Captain [Grassett[47]] sit up in his chair ... Bombardment has knocked our wires about.

28 June 1916

During afternoon the bombardment on the ridge recommenced, a very fine sight. We all agreed that certain folks at home would pay £5 to see it. At times the ridge was one cloud of smoke and the roar of guns incessant. For certain reasons we were obliged to stop work and Wilkie and I had some interesting talk on our various experiences, also of Germany and the Germans. My boots are worn through at the toes and, with the mud outside, my socks are nearly always wet, so I take them off and slip sandbags over my socks and hobble about on them.

29 June 1916

We were awakened at 3 am by violent shelling. I lit a candle and we lay in bed listening to it. Some shells fell rather close. It then died out and just as we were asleep at 5 am, the same things happened again, but less violently ... The damage done was quite considerable. The room next to the Orderly Room was smashed in whilst fellows were sleeping, one having his legs blown off. Wilkie and I fetched [battery] cells and were pumped by officer and RFA man on our work. Got no change ... Have been here three weeks today and are feeling strain of almost continuous day and night work and much shelling. Rest would be very welcome but no signs of it yet.

30 June 1916

Went into Arras and drew new boots, had a bath and a change of clothes ... Had dinner with Intelligence men, one of whom said "leave and letters stopped". Had hair cut and later was paid, thus having quite a successful day.

1 July 1916

Wilkie woke me up with "They're shelling the road". At the same moment a loud crash sounded just outside. Later we found a shell had hit our wall, just where wall and pavement meet. Found nose cap and I am keeping it as souvenir. Line has become quite lively here. Whilst stripping wood

47 Probably Captain Arthur Grassett RE, GSO3 VI Corps.

off a roof conveniently blown down by a shell, a sniper's bullet passed between us, hitting wall behind, then a machine-gun began peppering away but nobody was hurt so we had some apple pudding made over a fire.

3 July 1916

Just before tea, Mr Brydon bounced downstairs bringing some much needed stationery. He told us of the successful fighting round the Somme and generally cheered us up. Stayed for tea and made himself quite at home. During evening, after he had left, footled around, did no work and then lit fire, indulging in some general chit-chat.

4 July 1916

Owing to the usual trouble (*1968 comment*: interference from our own signallers) work very slack ... Things still seem to be going well with us down Albert way.

5 July 1916

Work here still slack. I am reading a book of Jack London's called *The Iron Heel*,[48] a powerful novel bearing on the Socialistic Movement of the future. A general feeling of 'fed-upness' exists; we want a change or a rest badly.

6 July 1916

Dad's cigars are a daily treat and one feels at peace with oneself and the world in general when smoking one, lolling in our armchair. It is difficult to imagine a war is going on as just now the line is very quiet.

7 July 1916

Rain began pouring in torrents and soon our floor was about an eighth of an inch deep in water. We tried to sponge the water up with sandbags, also the passage and top of stairs where the water threatened to pour down. Vigorous sandbag sweeping prevented this, but we had to stop the entrance up. Started our oil lamp up though the light could hardly be called dazzling. In fact it just about lights enough for us to see from one side of the room to the other.

---

48 Jack London, *The Iron Heel* (1908).

8 July 1916

Bosches started sending over some heavy stuff that fell just behind out place. Had one hit on our abode, it would have been all up with us as I sat here, I was 'all of a sweat'. Later we saw one of our aeroplanes brought down, a ball of flame. Ghastly sight.

9 July 1916

Went into Arras … fetched letters from 43rd Infantry Brigade HQ and had bath … Read Jellicoe's despatch of Jutland battle and a heated argument between Wilkie and Jack ensued.

10 July 1916

Whilst others were inspecting the lines … I gave this place a regular clean up, clearing rotten rations away and burying them … When Jock had fixed up instrument, found something else had gone wrong and whilst he was tinkering away with it, Captain [Grassett] paid us a surprise visit, saying we probably would be leaving here.

11 July 1916

Trouble [with lines] discovered at last. [We] went to Achicourt, where I drank a bottle of stout. Then waited outside Brigade dump for rations from 10.30 am to 12 noon without anything turning up.

12 July 1916

A new battalion have come in and they wear shorts like the Gallipoli men.[49] Seem rather decent sorts and their cook has behaved very handsomely towards us … Wilkie came back [from Arras] with the upsetting news that we were leaving this Abode-of-Love. After the time spent on the place improving it, we feel rather sorry.

13 July 1916

Mr Brydon turned up and confirmed Wilkie's statement about moving … Both sides are [bombarding] … Out of bravado we went out again and brought in some wood collected earlier in the day and whilst the din outside continued, fried bacon and Welsh rarebit to distract thoughts, also yarned a bit.

49 5/King's Shropshire Light Infantry replaced 5/Oxfordshire and Buckinghamshire Light Infantry within 42nd Infantry Brigade (14th Division) area: VI Corps, 'Dispositions of Troops', 13 July 1916, WO95/769, TNA.

14 July 1916

Hardly … seemed to have fallen asleep when the booming of guns woke us up again at 3 am. After an hour it stopped and we slept until 8 am … Mr Brydon and a Corporal turned up. They would not give password until just as I was going to shout to Jack to bring up rifle, then Brydon gave it. At 11.15 pm heard noise of somebody breathing heavily outside. Fixed bayonet and began poking round unable to find anything. As soon as we reached the spot where the breathing seemed to come, it came from a different place. Eventually, after we all had been searching, discovered that the noise came from rats sleeping and snoring.

17 July 1916

Went down to Achicourt for cells, but none had turned up … Got wire from Mr Redgrave telling us to fetch them from 43rd Brigade HQ … Collected the cells and with a lot of growling and cursing, returned to billet. Had chicken and asparagus for supper from Auntie Truda's parcel and then went to bed whilst Jack and Wilkie had heated argument over merits or otherwise of Intelligence men.

18 July 1916

A Captain Redgrave called and informed us that he may possibly become our new boss. He had a long chat with us and offered us some 'baccy. We all took to him and hope he will really be put in charge.

19 July 1916

Had a very successful morning at work which was lucky as Captain [Grassett] turned up. Otherwise the visit was a disappointment; no relief, no interpreters, no cycles, no nothing. We feel we are being played with after promises of all kinds and both Wilkie and I are sick of this game. Glorious weather prevails outside and it makes one wild to be cooped in here when a little management would secure us a few days' rest … New men are guarding the barricade outside who say that in the case of bombardment, they propose to shelter in here – which we have orders not to allow. There won't be any difficulty over this but tonight I have a feeling that before many days something is going to happen.

20 July 1916

During night a working party pinched our washing basin, two towels, a pair of socks and soap and brush. As soon as I discovered the theft, I reported the loss to two officers and at length one of them recovered the basin for us but the other things are gone. We have been here six weeks today and the monotony has brought us to a state when the smallest provocation produces a row. The place is shelled daily, continued changing of troops prevents us from getting rations properly and the last three days we have only had bread. All this is unsettling and now comes news of our moving and Taffy, who has come from the new place, says the dug-out is awful and that this is a palace in comparison.

21 July 1916

After tea, the trouble I thought was brewing, came to a head and we had a right royal row. Quite cheered me up. Took cell to usual place, sent wire to Mr Redgrave, crossing allotment gardens, then had a bottle of beer at Blanche's café and returned. Found atmosphere cleared after row. George came from stores bringing a terrier for rat catching.

22 July 1916

Mr Brydon turned up … Told us we were moving tomorrow to quite a decent dug-out … George's dog has disappeared, to his sorrow and our delight.

23 July 1916

Had wire from Mr Brydon to get all equipment etc. to Guard Room. As our goods and chattels stood there, all stacked up, looked like as if somebody had hastily turned us out of a house. We left the Abode-of-Love at night, had last glass of beer at Blanche's, then loaded everything into a motor van … Arrived at Wailly late at night, tyre bursting just as we stopped. Carried furniture etc. to new quarters, had supper and then turned in.

24 July 1916

This is quite a nice place, three dug-outs knocked into one, reminding me of cabins leading out on to a deck or kind of corridor, as outside is a passage and steps at both ends lead to the trench above.

25 July 1916

Felt in rotten humour, but Mr Redgrave called and to my great delight heard that two interpreters are to be expected from XVII Corps. This has cheered me up immensely and I am feeling quite bucked up … [We] went to Wailly village. The owner of the café where we were drinking, a woman … entreated me to look at her house [near our dug-out] to see if it had been knocked about. Although now living only ¼ of an hour away from her old home, it is nearly two years since the Germans swept down and turned her out. Luckily the dwelling part is still intact although the outbuildings are very knocked about.

26 July 1916

Wilkie being ill, with chill on liver, I think, had to stick to IT set without relief. Just before dinner, Mr Redgrave turned up and said two interpreters would come tomorrow. Very cheering this, and that tomorrow Wilkie, the day after tomorrow I, would come out for a fortnight's rest … News that we had captured Pozières.[50] Kept on duty until tea, after which went into Rivière village and told woman about her house. She was delighted and in gratitude gave me a bottle of beer for nothing … Jock isn't feeling over-well but was sporting enough to take over IT set until 11 pm, when we closed down, having to sleep through sheer exhaustion.

27 July 1916

Jock has got some fever, caught first when he was stationed in New Guinea and both he and Wilkie are down, leaving Taffy and myself to run the show. Mr Redgrave came with letters but to my disappointment, no interpreters. Jock is groaning in next cabin and one can hear his moans quite clearly. Took Mr Redgrave to the CO of the Dorsets[51] where he arranged about rations for us.

28 July 1916

Thanks to new ration arrangement, got hot breakfast … Suddenly Mr Redgrave appears with two new interpreters. We had to pack up at once and in a lorry had a glorious ¾ hour run to Noyelle-Vion where we are to rest. The motor run was fine, the day being perfect. By degrees the trench zone was left behind, the villages began to look less damaged, more civilians were about and the country looked really pretty … Quartered in a hut with Royal Engineers. We were warned about an 8.15 am Parade which surprised us a bit on the wrong side.

29 July 1916

Was told to deliver cells to our station with Wilkie … Came back … Had tea, then a bath and spent evening writing home and reading *Nash's* magazine and eating chocolate.

---

50 Pozières had been attacked by the ANZACs on 23 July.

51 Lieutenant-Colonel C.C. Hannay, 5/Dorsetshire Regiment (34th Infantry Brigade, 11th Division): VI Corps, 'Dispositions of Troops', 28 July 1916, WO95/769, TNA.

30 July 1916

Went on 8.15 am Parade without wash or shave. Lucky we weren't inspected too closely. Cleaned [motorcycle] up and in a fit of energy, wrote Philip. Slept until tea and then went with Wilkie … to Avesnes-le-Comte. Had stout at 'Hotel le Pol', exchanging pretty speeches with barmaid, then came back and had supper of poached eggs on toast.

31 July 1916

Took Mr Redgrave to Wailly, saw boys, returning to Warlus, taking road in view of German trenches, there dropped Mr Redgrave and proceeded … to Arras. Had dinner with the Intelligence bods, got a pair of riding breeches from QM Stores and collecting letters, started on journey back … and motor bike ran a treat … Arrived back here covered in dust.

1 August 1916

Was called out at 3.30 am to take cells to station. Like reporters, I suppose we Intelligence men are liable for work at all times, anywhere. With dawn just breaking, had delightful run to Wailly … returning with a *Daily Mirror*, arriving in time for breakfast. Got new tunic and pantaloons and chatted with Madame and daughters at café at bottom of road … After tea, Wilkie and I tramped to Avesnes-le-Comte and went to cinema – the first one we had been to since leaving Blighty.

2 August 1916

Went to Avesnes-le-Comte to have a look at local market. Expected to see a lot of peasant costumes and colour but was disappointed. Had a long chat with some Minister in Church Army who told me some interesting things about guns at Liège and deeds during the Mons retreat. He was in Arras a week before the war broke out. Later sat … and listened to concert in chateau grounds, afterwards having drinks at special café where a rather pretty and decent girl lives. Quite different from the usual café type.

3 August 1916

Wilkie and I were called out on Parade and told we should be transferred to the REs. Later had this confirmed and got orders to take papers down for men at station to sign … Had dinner with boys, then returned … Went and saw Susanne and was joined by rather decent Red Cross fellow. Outside in garden, carried on quite a jolly flirtation which we all enjoyed.

4 August 1916

Last night read in *Daily Mail* that Philip had been wounded,[52] so wrote to him and his mother. Wrote letters and read *Nash's* magazine until dinner, then slept a bit, had shave, followed by some *vin blanc et citron* at Susanne's, returning to billet for tea. Afterwards went … and saw German prisoners in farm close by. Dirty lot, all types, big and small, some fine fellows, others rotten physique. Met Susanne there and we walked back through fields, later sitting in her garden, drinking *vin blanc et citron*. It is very peaceful there, very quiet and I enjoy these evenings. She improves on acquaintance and although at first gives the impression of being fast, one soon discovers that she can look after herself. She reminds me of 'The Girl Phillipa' in Robert Chambers's story in *Nash's* magazine.[53]

7 August 1916

Went in Red Cross van … to Avesnes-le-Comte where bought towel, shaving brush and got wristlet. Back here, cleaned razor and rifle. Wrote letters and after tea read a rag called *Blighty* … The German [prisoners] were busy writing letters. Tomorrow they get new underclothing. Judging by the numbers looking for lice, they want it. Back at billet, heard that prisoners' camp is out-of-bounds.

8 August 1916

Went on Parade unshaven, but was not copped … After dinner went and said goodbye to Susanne … [and left for the IT station].

9 August 1916

At dinner we had so much steak and mashed potatoes we had to give some to a fatigue party, resting close by before finishing their job. They were glad. On till tea, then Jack and I went to Rivière … We had three glasses of *vin rouge* and grenadine, very sweet stuff, too sweet for me. I had to leave café as I was going to be sick but nothing turned up. Jack was quite lively although he acted a lot as if he had had too much.

10 August 1916

Went to new cookhouse to fetch breakfast but they had no rations for us. However, the cooks put us right. I found our rations at HQs and made arrangements for them to be taken to [the] cookhouse.

---

52 Titterton had been seriously wounded in the right arm at Longueval on 22 July 1916: WO339/60265, TNA.

53 Robert Chambers, *The Girl Phillipa* (1916); serialised from March to September 1916.

11 August 1916

Went to Arras, walking along forbidden road as short cut in full view of Bosch lines. Had a lovely view of their lines … George and I had some lemonade and tea at the YMCA, newly introduced in Arras and listened to gramophone. Intelligence men were very nice to us. Came back after tea … Went on duty at once, the while eating College Creams from Dad and having pineapple chunks for supper. Line went 'dis[connected]' at 10.30 pm and so had a good night's sleep.

12 August 1916

At night, Wilkie gave me a good lecture on my untidiness because I happened to have my stove, mess tin, knife, tongue and ham tin and other objects in the 'office' in readiness for meal when I come on at 3 am tomorrow. Had a nice game of repartee, which we both enjoyed.

14 August 1916

Heard that train bringing up rations had been shelled and hit, consequently got no rations until late in the morning and had to rely on cooks for our breakfast. A *Graphic* and *Sphere*, both old, however, worked wonders and we got a fine serving. Mr Redgrave came at 12 noon and hardly had he left when Captain [Grassett] turned up. Being just dinner time, unfortunately things were a bit untidy. He looked round, said nothing, but his silence was most eloquent … A trench mortar has broken our lines and Jack and Taffy have gone out to mend the break. They returned so late I was getting anxious. Went to bed but could not sleep. A rat, running down Wilkie's back, woke him up with a start.

15 August 1916

Felt very fit during my 3 am to 9 am spell. Thought a lot about Dad's business and what would happen if and when I got home … Wilkie suggested our back Infantry money being paid up before we start getting RE pay … Line went 'dis' after tea so while Jack and Taffy went round line, Wilkie and I discussed politics … Watts and Vine[54] (two new interpreters) who came to relieve us, turned up … The usual boxcar ride back followed, but it was dark when we reached Noyelle-Vion.

54 1264 Gunner Arthur Vine RFA. Twenty-seven-year-old jeweller and pre-war Territorial from Birmingham who was educated partly in Stuttgart: WO374/70663.

16 August 1916

Went to Warlus … During the short stay there, Wilkie and I discovered a very decent Church Army hut with a dream of a gramophone. Could hardly tear myself away from it.

21 August 1916

Major Paxton[55] gave me a talking to because my [motorcycle] was dirty. Could have given him a straight answer but thought it best to mention subject to Mr Redgrave first, which I did when I met him at Warlus. He told me that Paxton up to 11 am is more like a fiend incarnate than a human being. Mr Redgrave is letting me use his tent wherein I am reading, writing and quite enjoying myself. He expected to be back by dinner but didn't turn up, so had dinner myself in kitchen and then went on enjoying myself in his tent … Ran back to Noyelle-Vion, got into 'bed' and read *The Infamous John Friend*.[56]

22 August 1916

Went to Avesnes-le-Comte to the pictures and leaving early, dropped in at Susanne's whom I found in a flirtable mood. At 8.30 pm left in boxcar with the Quarter-Master Sergeant and others who seemed to be duly impressed with the mystery of the trenches as we approached the station, especially when a few bullets whizzed over.

23 August 1916

During our stay at Noyelle-Vion [the IT station had] moved to a new dug-out, a real beauty. They scrounged round and succeeded in getting quite a good assortment of chairs and tables and have made the place most comfortable, with mattresses to lie on. This dug-out is similar to a log cabin with log roof and wooden beam at sides, the earth walls firmly kept up by wire netting. Mr Redgrave turned up with an acetylene lamp; not a tremendous success as yet but with a bit of coaxing, it keeps alight. Went to Rivière and village was shelled a bit whilst in café but nothing much.

24 August 1916

We had too much given us for dinner, so gave some to a couple of infantrymen outside. When I asked them whether they wanted some of the stew, never have I seen a more expressive "Rather".

---

55 Major Alexander Paxton RE, commander VI Corps Signal Company. Thirty-four-year-old regular officer.

56 Martha Garnett, *The Infamous John Friend* (1914).

25 August 1916
Was on IT from 4 am to 9 am, but then had a quick wash etc., and cleared off to Arras ... Was stopped by Military Police Corporal when passing railway out of Arras and had name taken etc. because was without pass and was told I would be 'crimed'. Took matters very coolly and considered the whole affair gas and bluff.

26 August 1916
Mr Redgrave came in. Looked worried and run down. Gave us passes to go into Arras and told him how I was 'copped'. He said he would see Major Paxton and put things right. Jack, Taffy and George came back from their round in not over good spirits, but [we] went into Rivière and drinking beer, Banyuls and *vin blanc et citron*, soon got very lively and the after-effects made it difficult for me to keep awake when I had to sit at the instrument.

27 August 1916
Had very jolly evening deciding not to swear after 11 pm. Penalty one franc per word for first punishment. Before midnight Jack owed umpteen francs.

28 August 1916
[Fetched dinner] It is a job, ½ hour through narrow trenches, ruined houses and a road. When wet, as the trenches are now, it is no joke. Line went 'dis' just before tea and was on way to Rivière when met Mr Redgrave with cells. Long talk over lines followed and the poor man looked very unhappy. After he had left ... Jack came in in a fine rage, his language being most picturesque. Decided to go 'dis' for the night and so settled down to a good night's sleep.

29 August 1916
Whilst Jack and Taffy were out on line discovering break, Wilkie and I cleared up, washed and took things easy. It is when the line is 'dis' that we score and although always most sympathetic to Jack and Taffy, yet we cannot help chuckling up our sleeves. Their slack time is when the IT set is working well.

30 August 1916
Jack isn't feeling well. He was out most of yesterday in the rain, his breeches are wet and I am afraid the damp may be affecting him. He

has no pants or means of drying his breeches. However he bucked up after tea, just before which Mr Redgrave and a Captain came down and proposed several new things. After they had left and we had had tea, we had another game of whist which was interrupted by the arrival of the relief.

31 August 1916

Went in Red Cross van to Avesnes-le-Comte and spent quite a nice morning in the town, writing home, buying books and talking to German prisoners, though was warned off on approach of an officer.

1 September 1916

To our unspeakable disgust, were told off to work in a chalk quarry. Wilkie and I are furious, as also others with us. We are supposed to be resting yet are put to picking, shovelling, loading and unloading lumps of chalk. We are most emphatically going to complain to Mr Redgrave and I have already written a note to him saying that I want to see him when he comes. Today is the limit. We put in passes to go to Avesnes-le-Comte and the Sergeant-Major refused to initial them. Went … to a café, the main attraction being a girl called Hortense. We imbibed freely and as a result felt better.

2 September 1916

Again on chalk picking but took things easy and in a more philosophical manner though at times a wild feeling would surge up and I longed to dash off and have it out with Captain Grassett. Wilkie and I managed to get our passes and went to Avesnes-le-Comte but found the cinema closed. With things as they are, it is not worthwhile coming here for a rest.

3 September 1916

Blasted inspection and had to get up at 6.30 am to get things clean. All this is almost worse than being in the trenches at our set. Later hoped a Church Parade would improve my spiritual state of mind, but at the time of writing I cannot detect much difference.

4 September 1916

Instead of working in the chalk pit, had to shovel and stamp down gravel and stones to make foundations for some stables … After dinner … [we] had usual drink at Hortense's then I bought some chocolate, returned to billet and went to sleep. Wilkie is still in a dangerous mood and is best left alone. At 6.30 pm suddenly got orders to proceed to Wailly in the boxcar with two linesmen. En route, stopped at Warlus and saw Mr Redgrave who said he would try and arrange for Wilkie and me to rest at Warlus.

5 September 1916

This time we had to load [General Service] wagons with stores from the side of the road, but the Sergeant-Major, being in a good mood, let us off early … Met two Mounted Transport men and we had a bottle of champagne in a café in Avesnes-le-Comte and altogether had a lively time, a girl named Maria showing flirtatious inclinations and before I left, we had a kiss. Pity I have not run across her before as possibly may not see Avesnes again.

6 September 1916

Found ourselves working beside German prisoners, so after little talking with the guard and they did the work for us. We also arranged to have our wagons loaded at the station, so this morning Wilkie and I looked on whilst the Germans filled up and eventually resulted in our getting the praise for three more wagon loads being loaded than if we two only had loaded. Afforded me great pleasure tricking the Sergeant-Major and 'Piggy' [Paxton] … [Back to the] Log Cabin, had a good feed and decided to do no work that night. If 'Piggy' can't be square with us, neither shall we be with him. So making a big noise, singing and drinking, we passed the evening away.

8 September 1916

At night we had a shock. A trolley line has been laid just outside this place up the road and the Bosches spotting it, began shelling it, some falling quite close. After a long spell of comparative safety, I understand what Robinson Crusoe felt like when he first saw the footprints.

9 September 1916

Mr Redgrave surprised us whilst I was having breakfast and took George away to attend a Court Martial of a man over [a] report. Before dinner a General of Artillery appeared and began to ask awkward questions. He expected more than he got. Back from the Court Martial, where the man was let off with a caution, George and I went to Rivière, though a brisk bombardment (for here) at first made us hesitate. However, we decided to go and had a chat at the various cafés and almost got our names taken by the Military Police.

10 September 1916

Wilkie had had another book (shorthand) sent to him and a lot of time is spent studying it. Knowledge of shorthand is very useful in this specialised work.

11 September 1916

At 6 pm [we] went to Rivière and started with a bottle of champagne and later followed with a couple of bottles of wine and eventually wound up with beer. We all got lively, Jack most talkative, Taffy sentimental, I both. Taffy wanted me to translate all sorts of harmless but impossible things to the various females in the *estaminets.*

12 September 1916

I am writing this on the midnight to 4 am spell. Except for a bit of a headache, the natural result of last night's revelry, feel OK. Was just up to fetch dinner, with Wilkie in bed and the others up the line when 'Piggy' [Paxton] and Captain Rathbone[57] turned up. Had they come but two minutes later, with Wilkie in bed and me gone, we should indeed have been in the cart … As it was, Wilkie feigned sleep and left me to face the music. Then Taffy strolled in and nearly gave his show away by saying "he had only just come in from Rest", whereas he, George and Jack are supposed to be 'in' always, the 'Rest' they get being a private arrangement made by Captain Redgrave but fortunately neither 'Piggy' or Captain Rathbone twigged. After some questions, they cleared off and we were left in peace.

13 September 1916

Wilkie and I came to words over reports. Honestly I thought I was in the right, but thinking the matter over before falling asleep after dinner, it dawned on me that he was right, so naturally I apologised … Wilkie and I were hard at it until 45 minutes after Watts and Vine had come in to relieve us. We then got aboard the boxcar … and were then dropped at Warlus. Mr Redgrave, quite merry after a glass or two in his tent, gave us waterproof sheets and lying on the ground in a tent, Wilkie and I had our first night under canvas since we landed in Boulogne.

14 September 1916

Plenty of rumours – Vimy Ridge, Somme, Ypres etc. Spent evening boozing in the local *estaminets* and then walked to Bernaville and looked

57 Captain William Rathbone RE. Thirty-six-year-old Liverpool financier: WO339/27556, TNA.

in at the Church Army hut … Mr Redgrave turned us out after we had gone to bed and in strong moonlight we had to run down to IT set with cells, much to the disgust of men there who had reckoned on a quiet night.

18 September 1916

Mr Redgrave and I patched up [the broken] sidecar springs with wire but after falling in a shell hole last night, it was in a very rickety condition and I did not start off very confidently. Managed to reach our station despite pelting rain and appalling roads … Sidecar tilting at a very nasty angle but somehow kept on to Gouy-en-Artois. There miscalculated depth of water at bottom of hill … and with water over axles, after a protesting gurgle, the machine stopped. Had to push her back, through water, knee deep to Gouy. Having Mr Redgrave's officer's waterproof togs on and steel helmet, impersonated an officer and by this means got a lift in a Red Cross van to Barly where managed to wire Mr Redgrave. Stopped a motor lorry train on return journey and still impersonating an officer, 'requested' a lift back to Gouy. Arrived there, soon found a house where obtained some fried eggs, coffee and bread and butter … The boxcar turned up. Between us, the driver and I took the sidecar off the machine, which, after a bit of tinkering, began to run, so we returned to Warlus. There put on dried socks and proceeded to Arras … [We] swallowed two bottles of champagne in 15 minutes in café of Jack's girl, to whom we were introduced … Met boxcar, returned to Warlus, made wireless report translations and went to bed.

20 September 1916

Whilst reclining on bed, old Redgrave came along with a woeful face saying station wanted cells. 'Phoned to Corps for boxcar but was told it had been sent to Paris. Eventually arranged for cells to be taken in the Divisional Staff car … En route were often taken for officers and [we] were kept busy returning salutes to our huge amusement. One sentry actually presented arms.

21 September 1916

Read *The White Army* by Max Pemberton[58] until Wilkie relieved me at 4 am … Busy during afternoon washing handkerchiefs and socks, also giving Jack a hand at building up some sandbags outside the entrance. Went on to IT after tea, during slack period wrote part of letter home and

58 Max Pemberton, *The Great White Army* (1915).

continued reading … but somehow felt a bit fed-up. It took over an hour to make out reports although Wilkie gave me a helping hand.

22 September 1916
Cells ran out and Taffy, Wilkie and I went to chateau to wait for new ones which we were informed would come up "after 10 pm", however they didn't. During our wait, line lively, several machine-gun bullets pinging round.

25 September 1916
Reynolds, of the Intelligence, turned up and had dinner with us after settling some case in Rivière; we talked and chatted for a long time. He was once a Secret Service man round here and went about in civvies, investigating suspicious cases, including that of Luce, one of the girls at a café in Rivière where we often have a drink. After tea, batteries went 'phut' … Got oil for stove and the warmth induced us to yarn again. Lately these yarns have been superseded by cards.

26 September 1916
Usual rumble audible from the Somme, but at 12.30 suddenly became very violent, reports seeming to go off as fast as machine-guns. This went on until 2 pm when the range apparently lifted and the firing sounded less fierce.[59] George and I went to Claire's and to celebrate Dad's birthday, had a bottle of champagne apiece, indulging in quite a jolly bit of fun with Clare and Luce.

27 September 1916
Heard that Combles had fallen and Wilkie, who brought up breakfast, came with news that Thiepval had also been taken by our men … New lot of [infantry have] come in, up from Somme. They fought at Delville Wood.[60] Very nice young cook.

28 September 1916
Had a good dinner and Francke, Bob Hutt[61] and we four from the IT had our photos taken. … At 7 pm we went into the town and I bought some eggs at Mlle Mathiny who is supposed to have had a lively past. At 9 pm we commenced our 'do', I starting off with the *Pink Lady* and

59 The British had launched a major attack on the Thiepval Ridge.
60 41st Infantry Brigade (14th Division).
61 99520 Sergeant Robert Hutt, Intelligence Police.

soon things were going merrily, Taffy being in great form at the piano. Bernard played the cornet, Francke danced a clog dance, the gramophone had its turn, Wilkie sang a German *Studentlied*, Reynolds began the *Marseillaise* and then broke down and 'Bobagin' the cook did his best during it all. We drank wine and smoked Dad's cigars. At 11.30 pm we adjourned to supper and Bobagin in typical broad Irish described to us his opinion of the Army, keeping us in fits of laughter. We then went to bed where Taffy was sick and later slept fully dressed.

29 September 1916

Left after breakfast and walked to Warlus where Mr Redgrave showed us our new billet, in a cottage. After dinner, got a handcart and wheeled our belongings to this place.

30 September 1916

This used to be an officers' billet and apart from two canvas beds, our room has a stove, a table and four chairs. We bought some pens and ink last night, so for the first time for a long time we are able to write with ink.

3 October 1916

Later went to Bernaville where bought the usual eggs, had beer at usual café and came back. Played a bit with the kiddies here, had a cup of coffee and went to bed early. On the whole, these days are most uninteresting and quiet, the wet weather preventing us from going out, besides which my boots are very leaky and I have to dry my socks every night beside the stove.

4 October 1916

Played again with the kiddies here. I rather enjoy this, as after a spell of rough and ready life, always in men's company, to come back and play 'hide and seek' etc., listening to the chatter of lively little girls, is a change and it appeals to me very much.

5 October 1916

Boxcar came and took us to IT station. Heard that a big howitzer had dropped a shell two yards from roof of dug-out. Marvellous escape. Both Taffy and Watts were thrown across the dug-out by concussion. Trench outside blocked up and greatly knocked about.

6 October 1916

During my 4 to 8 am spell, things being quiet, had a look at the shell hole outside, tremendous hole. It happened last Tuesday [3 October]. Began reading *A Knight on Wheels*[62] lent me by Mr Redgrave … Went to Luce's and had a couple of bottles of champagne, improving our acquaintance with the damsels there, with Claire in particular. After a row with Wilkie, upset because we had been away such a long time, had another game of cards [which] put Wilkie in a good humour again.

7 October 1916

Worked till 1 pm, then had dinner and took washing down to Luce's, had a chat with her and back here, cleaned rifle and slept until tea after which we all turned to and wrote out reports as it has been a very busy day … Mr Redgrave did not turn up so we had a good night's sleep as the batteries went 'dis' at midnight.

8 October 1916

Heard that [our] transfers [to the Royal Engineers] had come through at 2/2. Very disgusted. In the middle of a game of cards, terrific row started outside, a bombing raid on and for the first time the emplacements round here were manned.[63] This broke up our game at speed and we got ready to move but later, as things quietened down, we resumed our game. No doubt things are hotter here now than they have ever been before.

10 October 1916

The Sergeant of the Platoon in the road is luckily a good sort and is helping us a lot with food, otherwise we should be stranded … Line was noisy. [We] had a booze in Rivière during which carried on the usual flirtation with Clare. Quite harmless but we both enjoy it. Back at station, started a game of cards, then quite unexpectedly Mr Redgrave appeared. The way cards etc. disappeared as he came down the steps into the dug-out was like a conjuror's trick.

---

62 Ian Hay, *A Knight on Wheels* (1914).

63 At 2000 the Germans fired upon the front lines with rifles, machine-guns, artillery and trench mortars. The firing then subsided, but a raid was launched at 0400 on a neighbouring brigade: 41st Infantry Brigade (14th Division) war diary, WO95/1894, TNA.

11 October 1916

Helped Jack rip up wood from attic roof of house close by. During course of this operation twice my leg broke through the rotten wood and once I nearly followed it.

12 October 1916

Was hard at work on duty until tea, after which began to pack up as probably we shall move out to rest tonight. How the time flies. Wilkie is in a silent mood again, won't speak a word to anybody unless necessary. Funny sort of fellow he is. We waited in vain for the relief, so after some cussing we had to carry on. Naturally I was disappointed but decided to philosophise and so turned in and went to sleep.

13 October 1916

George and Wilkie tried their hands at cooking the meat on the stove we brought in yesterday and I must admit that the result was quite a success … The boxcar driver called for us and brought us back to Warlus for rest.

15 October 1916

Reached Warlus … Mme Rosa, whom I asked for some bread, gave us a whole dinner instead, ending up with beer and coffee. This woman is quite a character, but very kind hearted. Lay down after this dinner but then got up to give a helping hand at carrying coal. Quite amusing. This done, we sat down to a cup of coffee and chatted. Very homely and nice all this. Bought some *sucre* for the kiddies.

16 October 1916

Slacked about most of the day … [We] spent the usual evening at Bernaville and on way back listened to band playing outside mess. Leaned against the open dining room window and sniffed the glorious roast beef smell.

17 October 1916

Went with Mr Redgrave on my rickety No. 22 [motorcycle combination] to Corps. Just managed to reached Noyelle-Vion before a general collapse. Had dinner … at Corporals' Mess and then went on to Avesnes-le-Comte having shave at Maria's by woman barber there. Eventually came back … in boxcar and helped load up some of the broken parts of Mr Redgrave's charging engine. After tea [we] went into Arras … [for a] booze [with the

Intelligence Police] in honour of 'Blitz' Mason's birthday.[64] Had roaring time and all turned in very merry.

18 October 1916

Felt bit thick headed but the walk to Warlus took some of the cobwebs away. Arrived too late for dinner but just in time to buy some tinned things. I asked Mme Rosa for bread and instead she hauled us in and gave us a nice warm meal, some beer and coffee, keeping up a lively conversation in her deep voice, accompanied by the usual expansive smile. We had a lie-down during afternoon, but chats prevented me from sleeping, although I felt very tired.

19 October 1916

New boxcar turned up and when Mr Redgrave asked if I would like a ride to [Saint Pol-sur-Turnoise], was not slow in saying "Yes, sir!" … Having two hours [there] to ourselves, looked about for where to have a meal. Suitable spot found in the Café de la Place and had a good feed, also good beer. Walked about town, novelty seeing women wearing hats, not dressed like farming folk. Also strange seeing trains and smoke coming from factory chimneys … Took some corks bought in Saint-Pol to *estaminet* and was given two glasses of Muscat in return and had a long chat with Mr Redgrave. Thinks he is going to Blighty next week. Lucky man.

20 October 1916

Wilkie came in and told me that Mlle Ivonne was in Warlus. Later, on way to dinner, called in at café and had a long chat with her. Her mother treated me to a glass of beer and a cup of coffee. Ivonne is supposed to have created some heart-burnings in Arras. She certainly seemed very self-possessed and cocksure of herself.

21 October 1916

Packed up and ran down to 'Log Cabin'.

22 October 1916

Helped cook dinner and afterwards went with Jack up the line … Mr Redgrave and a Mr Doust[65] appeared with a commutator which they

64 Another member of the Intelligence Police said he was known as 'Berlitz', presumably due to his language skills and was 'a dapper little chap one of the best, good German scholar': D. Manning memoir (1919), 80/1/1, IWM.

65 Second Lieutenant Joseph Doust RE. Twenty-nine-year-old electrical engineer and pre-war Territorial, commissioned in January 1915: WO374/20456, TNA.

fixed up. Instrument being new, we are kept very busy and have little time to ourselves.

23 October 1916

Whilst preparing dinner, the Brigadier[66] appeared, asking why he had not had our reports. He tried to get into our dug-out, but not having a proper pass, would not let him in … Wilkie obtained some rather interesting looking news, so Jack and I went to chateau, giving the news to the Brigadier himself. Then with a candle to light the way, the night being coal black, we passed through the chateau grounds to Rivière, had a drink at Claire's, gave her the group photo, was thanked in a very practical and pleasing manner and together, [we] stumbled through the dark to the 'Log Cabin'.

24 October 1916

Met George coming in. Usual talk; Bapaume rumour, leave rumour etc. Wilkie and I came to words over the real meaning of the German word *Abteilung*. When he failed to convince me, behaved in a rather childish manner, not doing his share of the chores. When in this mood, best to take no notice of him, but it's annoying all the same.

25 October 1916

Wilkie raised Jack's monkey by not getting up and giving a hand at breakfast … Line more lively and afterwards George was obliged to go out into trenches to see what was causing disturbance … Later found out we hadn't been handed over to new battalion coming in. As soon as I had my reports ready, trudged through wet to see the Adjutant and soon fixed things up with him, then left reports at Brigade HQ and went to Claire's where a kind of smoking concert was going on. Wilkie and I are on bare necessity speaking terms now – best thing.

27 October 1916

Directly after brekker [we] scrounged round for wood, finding some by the fallen down barns adjoining the house … Cut up and began cooking our dinner; steak, chips, onions and beans. There was so much, none of us could finish our share. I am now reading *The Harvester*[67] and am enjoying it tremendously although it does take some getting into. [We] went into Rivière and saw Leontine, then spent most of the evening at Claire's, listening to gramophone records.

66 Probably Brigadier-General Percy Skinner, commander 41st Infantry Brigade (14th Division).

67 Gene Stratton-Porter, *The Harvester* (1911).

28 October 1916

Wilkie and I still at loggerheads and I was just contemplating the prospect of spending a week with him at Warlus when the relief came in. To my great joy, Vine and Watts had had a row together and so we soon arranged for Wilkie to go out … and I am to stay with Vine. Felt like dancing out of sheer happiness at prospect of getting away from Wilkie.

30 October 1916

George … has completely changed from the sullen, lazy and difficult to get on with fellow he used to be at the 'Abode-of-Love'. Whilst he is as he is now, one could not have a better companion. With Vine being a good help, things are working very smoothly at the station.

31 October 1916

Part of the parapet outside fell in and [we] saw Sergeant in the huts for the trench to be cleared … I made a scrounging raid to the Company HQ above and got a table, some canvas and wire … Jack and Taffy came in after tea, furious that Mr Doust would not let them have boxcar from Warlus to come down; "Now if it had been old Redgrave". Took a long time for Jack to calm down … I had just settled down for a couple of hours' sleep before the midnight to 4 am watch when the Bosches suddenly sent over some big stuff, several shells falling close by, breaking our wire and making me jump into my clothes in double quick time. However, after ¼ hour stopped as suddenly as it started and I was able to go to bed again.

1 November 1916

Very tired when Jack woke me and for the first hour or so on the IT was all I could do to keep awake … Mr Doust came down during morning and whilst here, all the others … went out on the line … I had [an] exciting time as Fritz was firing from Mercatel way, the shells dropping all around this place. Between the pauses, I calculated with the help of two maps whereabouts they were fired from and when things quietened down, cut bacon, peeled potatoes and onions for dinner. Dinner over, went with my information to Brigade HQ, spending about 20 minutes with Brigadier. (*1968 comment*: I [had] heard the German Forward Artillery Observation Officer quoting the range to his battery in the rear. In and between the bursts, I rushed out of the dug-out … to ascertain the site where the shell explosion took place, plotted this on a map and with the help of a ruler and compass … [pinpointed] the actual position of the battery firing.)

2 November 1916
Have got a bit of a cold, the first of the season, so as soon as the breakfast things were cleared away and the place cleaned up, I went to bed to sleep, but woke feeling queer and with a headache.

3 November 1916
Busy morning, spending afternoon writing out reports and then was on duty until 9 pm. With things as they are, we have no time to ourselves during the day, as time off-duty is taken up cooking or making out reports or scrounging round for something or washing. All my letters I have to write during my night watches, when things are quiet.

5 November 1916
Found that Mlle Ivonne was staying with her aunt at café at the corner, so we … spend a lot of time chatting to her … Went to Bernaville at night where I attended a rather crowded Church Service, later buying eggs and indulging in another chat with Ivonne.

6 November 1916
[To rest] … I am going for a drink at Ivonne's. She is curious about our visit to Bernaville. Think she is a bit of a sly, intriguing minx, but all the same, very jolly to talk to. Half way through tea … the boxcar driver, burst in saying he could take our things … to Dainville. A bottle of beer and three bottles of champagne enabled us to get very fluent with two damsels there, Colette and Denise by name, both very 'Frenchy' and inclined to be *gaies*, especially after they had drunk some of our champagne. In fact, we had the doubtful honour of having at one time Madame and the two girls at our table, making a lively party. We were lucky in getting a lift in a limber wagon back to Warlus. I wonder how we should have got back otherwise as we were not exactly in a fit state to walk back that distance.

7 November 1916
Both Arthur and I feel very 'dry' after last night's events, so as soon as the time came, we went to Ivonne's for another drink. With a great deal of secrecy, she asked me to call that afternoon to fetch two letters to take into Arras and was not to show them to anybody. Smelt a rat so promised to do so. Called for them on the way back from Bernaville after a bath … Ivonne once more impressed on me the secrecy of these letters, one of which was for Francke, the other for her mother. Gave Francke the letters

and he said he would deal with the matter … Looks as if some queer game is on. Went and saw Seraphine at night. Looked rather nice.

8 November 1916

We spent the usual midday café hours before and after dinner chatting to Ivonne followed by a talk with Mme Rosa. These days at rest are very nice in their way but one does run through some cash – and some drink. However, as long as one does not overdo it, why worry?

10 November 1916

Spent time at Ivonne's … Seated around the stove, we passed the time with the usual silly talk, though excellent practice for my French, especially as Ivonne is very good in correcting me.

13 November 1916

[Back at the station] … The boys went out to get wood and in the course of 'working' in a house, they brought the top storey floor down … We started a game of cards … but in the midst of it, firing of all description, making quite a noise, started outside. Conferred together what to do but eventually decided to go on with game.

14 November 1916

Arthur showed me the way to make stew. It was slow work and took nearly two hours and when it was done … didn't feel inclined to eat any … Went to Claire's after tea and indulged in much light-hearted talk which did me good.

15 November 1916

Sent off a wireless message to Mr Redgrave … During morning, answering message came saying I was to walk to Warlus. Walking along crest of hill, had good view of German shelling one of our gun emplacements some 300 yards away, not far from where road crosses railway at station. Between the cemetery and ruins of station some 15 shells must have dropped. Was very glad when I had got out of sight the other side of railway, the last two shells falling uncomfortably close … Then spent afternoon at Bernaville, at first watching football match, then saw the ceremonial 'Retreat' of pipers of a Scotch Pioneer Battalion marching up and down the main street, the Battalion lining each side of the road, the villagers seemingly taking a huge interest in the bagpipes.

16 November 1916

Bitterly cold and it took 20 minutes to start motorbike. At Avesnes-le-Comte dentist kept us waiting 1½ hours. English nurses at hospital, yet when one asked me "Has the postman come yet, Corporal?" was so taken aback at hearing a woman speak English, for a moment I was unable to answer. The dentist, a Dr Parkes, told me to come [back on 21 November] ... Ran into Arras ... Found card for me from Ivonne at Intelligence.

18 November 1916

[Back at the station] ... Usual morning of cleaning up and starting on dinner as soon as ready. Line very active and George is not very amiably disposed ... Collected money for Primus stove and then returned to Warlus.

19 November 1916

Went to Saint-Pol. Bought Primus stove ... Went to the Dainville place to collect a set to take back. Outside the building, a Sergeant of Artillery and a Police Corporal had a row, the former knocking the latter out. Bleeding and muddy, saw him being carried away on a stretcher.

20 November 1916

Had tea and a chat, during which Arthur told me of his *affaires de coeur* in Germany, we had two bottles of beer at Mme Luce's and two more at the Wanquetin café where the girls were quite lively.

21 November 1916

Left for Habarcq to have teeth seen to ... Kept waiting two hours before dinner and 1½ hours after, then dentist, a new one, said "Dr Parkes has your teeth in hand, I think it best for you to continue to be treated by him". After the long period of waiting, this cool statement made me feel really ratty, but all I could do was swallow my feelings and say nothing. Went into Arras, consoled my feelings by seeing Ivonne.

22 November 1916

I ran into Avesnes-le-Comte and bought pots and pans for our use in the 'Log Cabin' ... Tested the Primus making some cocoa. Boiled water in less than 5 minutes ... [We] strolled over to Bernaville for a bath, but were told 'Nothing doing'. Tried to get tea at an *epicerie*. No go. At length a Norfolk Regiment cook made us some. We went to a ripping concert party patronised by the Major-General who nearly broke his eye-glass laughing.

23 November 1916

Met Breakey[68] and Griffiths, two No. 24 IT instrument station men and went to Café Blondel where the best beer in Warlus is supposed to be served. Breakey was taken prisoner by the Germans in the Cameroons and was a prisoner for 18 months, not once getting news from home during that period.[69] He returned to England when the British released him and joined the Royal Garrison Artillery, later transferring to the REs and our job. Said he was not badly treated by the Germans but was given little to eat. The other man, Griffiths, was as good as thrown out of Cardiff College through wine, women and song, then made a clean breast of it all to his father who 'squared' him and when War broke out, he was a most respectable bank clerk. We three went to the Bernaville pictures and thoroughly enjoyed seeing some old films again. The band was very good [and] we had a jolly good supper of salmon and chips.

24 November 1916

To Noyelle-Vion. Once there … the Quarter-Master, had a lively ½ hour and we left him with our arms full of shirts, vests, pants, new boots, puttees, new tunics etc. Old Blackstaffe[70] is a good fellow, too kind hearted to refuse anything, very different from the average Quarter-Master Sergeant.

25 November 1916

A miserable ride into Avesnes-le-Comte; headwind, mud and rain. Waiting to see dentist, chatted with an RFC man who had once been with Lieutenant [Albert] Ball,[71] the winner of the MC, DSO etc. Told us a lot about him – most daring airman in the world. Doesn't care a hang about anybody or anything. Flies in his pyjamas with just overcoat and wraps over … Down to 'Log Cabin'. Indulged in usual chat, had game of cards, then turned in.

---

68 206935 Corporal Walter Breakey RE.

69 The British began operations against the German colony in September 1914 and the Allied campaign continued until February 1916: Hew Strachan, *The First World War*, Vol. 1: *To Arms* (Oxford: Oxford University Press, 2001), 522–39.

70 560479 Sergeant Harold Blackstaffe RE.

71 Promoted to Captain in mid-September, by the end of the Somme he was the RFC's top-scoring pilot with thirty-one confirmed victories: David Gunby, 'Ball, Albert (1896–1917)", in *Oxford Dictionary of National Biography*, www.oxforddnb.com.

26 November 1916

We had a great shock today. The boys were just going into the village when news came that we were to prepare to leave Tuesday or Wednesday [28/29 November] … This is a staggering blow to us as we thought we were settled here for the winter with everything working like clockwork. Now the future is undecided and heaven knows what will happen. We are to go to GHQ for some course of instruction.

27 November 1916

Into Arras … [and] had a last look around the town. I've spent some hard but also some very pleasant days and nights there and shall always look back to the town with affection. The Intelligence men were very sorry at the news of our departing. Said goodbye to Ivonne, giving her her birthday present.

28 November 1916

Went to Claire's. We had four bottles of beer and Taffy was quite fluent on way back. The afternoon and evening we spent in a state of expectancy, wondering whether the boxcar would come to take us away. The first shock of having to leave has worn off and now we are to move, we feel the sooner the better. At the same time, all real interest in the working of the station has ceased and we do our spells just as a matter of routine and duty. Luckily the new man, Eoll,[72] is very keen and enthusiastic and he makes up for [our] present slackness. Eoll spent 12 years in Germany and his English is now like a foreigner who speaks with just a trace of an accent, carefully choosing his words.

29 November 1916

Sergeant Shepherd came down saying we would be leaving tonight. Messed about and did nothing all day. At length, round 8 pm, just after the last game of cards in the 'Log Cabin', the new lot came up … At Warlus, our billet was out-of-bounds because of mange so we decided to sleep in boxcar … We kept up our spirits, playing whist until 1 in the morning. Then we somehow unpacked our blankets and like sardines, lay down on the boxcar floor.

30 November 1916

Felt rather stiff when climbing out of boxcar and in the cramped space we had, there was plenty of confusion and swearing when packing up. We had

72 198109 Corporal Joseph Eoll Queen's Regiment.

a last chat with Captain Redgrave who said he would do his best to get us back. He also thought there was a good chance of our keeping together.

Vince was sent to General Headquarters (Second Echelon) at Hesdin.

1 December 1916

Arrived at GHQ. Rather awed with everything. As per usual, we made ourselves scarce and spent most of our time in cafés drinking coffee and rum. The weather is freezingly cold and on the whole we are not charmed with the place. Further enquiries show that the chances of our staying together are not so rosy … Some time spent in blacking shoes and polishing buttons, accompanied by much cursing.

2 December 1916

Up at 6.30 am. Bitterly cold. CO Inspection at 7.30 am and was dished for a dirty rifle … Then had some drill by a Warwicks officer, a martinet on discipline … We are all already fed up with the place, 'all dressed up and nowhere to go', except to the local cafés and the drinks are not up to much.

4 December 1916

We went for a short march after breakfast and then practised buzzing [messages]. This place is full of schemes but so far the best one is Jock's who used to be with us … and is now a Sergeant. His scheme was a march during the afternoon, the tit-bit being a straight walk to a café outside the village which he knew and there passing away ½ hour drinking coffee and rum, talking over old times. My feet still tender [from new boots] so when Jack, Wilkie and I had a feed of cutlets and chips in an *estaminet*, I took my slippers along with me and put them on, greatly relieving the pressure.

6 December 1916

The morning's work was a farce. Before the mid-morning break we did nothing. After that, something was dictated to us over the 'phone. Each man ought to have kept his copy to himself, instead of which, each began comparing with the other, thus eventually every copy being well nigh correct.

7 December 1916

A little wangle of mine turned out successful today. Although there is nothing radically wrong with my teeth, when I heard that the dentist was in Hesdin, I thought it worthwhile going sick. This I did, escaped the 6.30 am Parade and had a run … into the town. I soon got attended to, a tooth was stopped and then I had a jolly walk round, left my watch at a watchmakers, was given a shave and then ran across the others. Being market day, the place was fairly full and presented quite a picture. We left, after dodging the Sergeant-Major, for drinks; a man keeping guard outside the café in case he should surprise us. Have just finished preparing for the old pastime of being on guard tonight.

Had first watch and the Sergeant-Major pulled me up for walking with rifle slung over shoulder, infantry trench fashion and for having a hand in my pocket.

8 December 1916

We were given German dictation by an Alsatian deserter and in the midst of it, Mr Griffin,[73] the Intelligence Officer quietly walked in and catching sight of Arthur looking at Mason's sheet, calmly said "No cribbing there, Vine". Rather humorously indignant collapse of Arthur. We all met at the 'Black Dog' and had a good supper of chips, eggs, and steak, drinking healthy proportions of beer. We nickname the pubs here ourselves, the 'Boulangerie' being opposite the 'Blue Laundry', another the 'Round Stone Steps' because of their leading up into the premises. Then there is the 'Black Dog' because the owner owns a huge black dog.

9 December 1916

The German dictation was easy, so a fellow I have chummed up with called Stolzle[74] and I went to a café to write letters and of course we had coffee and rum but actually also wrote a couple of letters. Generally the case is that some acquaintance turns up and the letter writing is forgotten in the chat that ensues. We then strolled from one café to another talking to all the Mademoiselles worth talking to; which shows how slack we are with nothing really worthwhile to fill up the time.

11 December 1916

[Bill] Auckenthaler, an Englishman, as he calls himself, but who speaks French better than English, is very eloquent in his denunciation of the unfair behaviour towards us interpreters. He and 'Jacques', the French-

73 Second Lieutenant Sydney Griffin East Yorkshire Regiment. Intelligence Corps from September 1914 and at 'Wireless GHQ' in January 1917: LO430, Griffin to War Office, 12 January 1917, WO339/87701, TNA.

74 197899 Corporal Gustav Stolzle RE.

Canadian, always talk French together and together with the German spoken, our hut is like a miniature international conference room … Went to an out of the way place to play billiards. The table was not a beauty but this was counteracted by quite a good-looking girl who served us with beer.

12 December 1916

Spent the whole [morning] buzzing. I can just about do 12 words to a minute. There was some row over our having to get dictation in by 3 pm, in consequence only half the translation was done … At [a] café I went to, I met an ANZAC who came out with the first Australian Expeditionary Force, went through Gallipoli and now somehow, is here, lying low, doing nothing at all.[75]

13 December 1916

This life is just like being at school again. We are supposed to attend a 6.30 am Parade, but if one fellow does not turn up to answer his name at Roll-Call, his pal, with a change of voice, does so. Meals we have in a large dining hall 'as soon as morning or afternoon classes are over'. We have a certain [German] dictation and the moment it is over, in quite a frank, brazen fashion, one man compares his work with that of another, cribbing without a second thought. By 3.30 pm it gets too dark for real work, yet we must not be dismissed until 4.30 pm. The time is killed by throwing paper balls at each other and other tomfoolery. I expect there with be one big right royal row one of these days.

14 December 1916

A bit of a stir has been caused by the arrival of some 50 new men from Blighty, the funny thing being that they think a tremendous lot of themselves and swing the lead in grand style. We don't take much notice of them though the Sergeant-Major is greatly down on them on Parade, making them hop and skip about to the huge delight of everybody else. They are called 'the conscripts' and as such the wind is being slowly but surely put up them.

15 December 1916

Things seem to be coming to a climax here. We had a lecture by a Staff Officer, OC of the [Intelligence Corps] of the BEF. A timetable of our

75 For Australian deserters in the BEF's rear areas, see Peter Stanley, *Bad Characters: Sex, Crime, Mutiny and Murder in the Australian Imperial Force* (Millers Point, NSW: Pier 9, 2010), 185–92.

work has been issued and buzzing is much in evidence. Those incapable of more than 10 words have to stay in from 6 to 7 pm … Just when my financial resources had run down to 10 centimes, Dad's welcome Xmas money came and so … to a supper where Jack was much upset by a fellow flirting or, as [he] called it, 'hauling her about' with a girl behind the bar.

16 December 1916

The boys here had a football match … near [Montreuil], so I went over with them on a lorry. On the way we passed the residence of 'Duggy' [Haig], an ugly red building plumped down in the middle of a plain.[76]

17 December 1916

Bad throat and cold, so reported sick and saw doctor at the RFC dressing station. Got medicine and was given 'light duty' … Feeling as miserable, without being actually ill, as possible … [so] sat in front of log fire … dosing myself with liquors.

18 December 1916

We had our first official day today, lectures during the morning and the amount of items to be learnt rather frightened us. Mr Griffin impressed on us the importance of discipline and our great lack of it, "a very ragged crowd" – a thing, we are told, he has said to every company of men down here for a Course. Caused us great amusement. Auckenthaler gave me surprising news that I, Wilkie, ['the Major'] White[77] and he were going up the line to a station just after Xmas.

19 December 1916

We four to be sent up the line have been taken in hand by a Corporal Gauge[78] who explained things to us during the morning. A lot of electrical theories which, had I not had a lot of practical experience up the line, would have floored me. We sat in a hut in 'Tin Town', round a stove and listened while he talked.

20 December 1916

My previous signalling course at Codford St Mary had stood me in good stead and I am aiming for 15 words and superior pay. To my delight,

---

76 Presumably Chateau de Beaurepaire.

77 Vince later described White as 'the oldest member of our Set. He was a good interpreter and considering his age and settled habits, adjusted himself to our mode of life very well': photograph annotation, Vince Shirley typescript diary, Vol. 3, 9, MIM.

78 106028 Corporal Joseph Gauge RE.

Mr Griffin informed us we should leave on 30 December for VI Corps, which means our being under Captain Redgrave again.

21 December 1916

Mr Griffin had us into his office and we had a special private lecture, just we four who are going up the line … We have a rotten stove in our hut, it smokes everybody out and, living up to Army traditions, to make matters worse, some dear fellow has pinched a length of the pipe. So to equalise matters, we pinched a length from another hut when nobody was looking.

22 December 1916

As Auckenthaler is to be one of the new station crowd, he and I always have dinner together at 'The Circular Steps'. He reads the *Petit Parisien*, I the Continental *Daily Mail* and we exchange titbits of news. We have steak and chips and usually have to double back to camp as we find the café clock invariably slow. We are getting through a lot of tests and have to work hard. Was working until 8.30 pm deciphering a code message.

24 December 1916

We worked practically all day but after duty were given passes and a lorry took us to Hesdin. Out of curiosity, [we] went … to the Red Lamp district but went no further, soon came out.

25 December 1916

Had Communion at Hesdin, also attended service, the Artists Rifles being there in great forces, a feature of the service being a solo sung by one of their men for the anthem … At the camp a fine dinner of turkey and vegetables had been prepared for us, the mess room really beautifully decorated. The usual toasts were drunk and everybody was very lively and jolly. Later [we] went to a neighbouring village, visited every café and got very genial with everybody. I have no recollection of returning to camp but know we were singing all the time … Under the circumstances, a very happy Xmas day.

26 December 1916

Usual morning schemes, though very tactfully Reveille and first Parade were fixed for an hour later. Mr Class[79] gave us a good lecture and another

79 Probably Lieutenant Herbert Class Royal Warwickshire Regiment. Forty-six-year-old music professor of German extraction; seconded to wireless work in January 1917: WO374/14123, TNA.

followed after dinner by Mr Griffin. He showed us some interesting original German [listening set] reports.

28 December 1916

These days we are having our real tests for pay. I cannot touch on the main thing, it being secret. (*1968 comment*: The item … was a new valve, in appearance like an ordinary electric light bulb, which not only possessed far greater volume than any previously used amplifier, but also enabled the interpreter to pick up German conversation from far greater distances. Another secret factor was being able to switch from one wavelength to another, thus allowing the operator to cut out irrelevant local talk in favour of far more important matters being discussed perhaps further afield.)

But on others, I can. We were supposed to do 15 words a minute of English and German in Morse. ['Winston'] Churchill,[80] who will be one of the men to come up with us, buzzed the messages, but nearer to 10 words to 15, so that Auckenthaler, who cannot do 10, simply put down the dots and dashes and then later turned them into letters and thus words.

29 December 1916

Another test this morning, with jamming, but think I did alright. These days, so full of concentrated work, are making us 'loony'. We are almost expected to cram our heads in a fortnight what others will take 8 weeks to absorb.

30 December 1916

[Examination] on the IT instrument, each man having to put the whole thing together and answer certain questions. I managed to pass … Worked until after tea, then hearing that a party was going to Hesdin, got in with them without a pass … Had a lively time, singing all the way back. We stopped at an *estaminet* en route for a drop … and the Corporal in charge nearly had a fight. Was very glad to get to bed.

31 December 1916

Felt very fit and dodged a march. Went to Church Parade in morning and played football during afternoon. Being last day of year, a good excuse to

---

80 Vince later described Churchill as 'no longer young … as tough as leather … as hard as nails and could out walk any of us when trudging round the trenches. He was the type of man who could turn his hands to anything and proved invaluable in our rough and ready kind of life': photograph annotation, Vince Shirley typescript diary, Vol. 3, 6, MIM.

go to 'Black Dog' and spent a very merry evening. However, I left early and returned to camp. Later, when the boys came back, they were nearly all hopelessly drunk. Can't blame them. They will mostly be up the line again in a few weeks' time.

1 January 1917

The New Year started well by [hearing of] a paper on which it was stated that I had been proposed as capable of being in charge of the new set. Then shortly after I heard that Auchenthaler and I had passed our tests for superior pay … We are all heartily tired of this place and longing to go. We had a kit inspection and I am afraid we shall have to swap our old infantry kit for that of the Royal Engineers. The disadvantage is that with RE equipment one cannot carry anything like as much as when wearing infantry tunics and trousers. There are number of interpreters here from various stations, all of whom have been up the line and they have banded together and meet in the parlour of the 'Black Dog', calling this meeting the OTC or 'Old Timers' Club'. A kitty or pool is made and drinks ordered accordingly. The chairman sees that drinks are kept going with plenty of singing and thus we can spend a very pleasant evening.

2 January 1917

During the afternoon I was called into Mr Griffin's office and there told that I would be in charge of the new set. This bucked me up fine. Drew my new Corporal's stripes and Carmen of the 'Black Dog' sewed them on.[81]

4 January 1917

At Warlus … had a long talk with Captain Redgrave, heard exactly what we had to do and the last stage of the journey then commenced. He came with us and at the end of the boxcar part of the journey, showed us our cellar. As soon as he had left we had supper, mostly of things sent us from home. A strafe then started and with the barking and booming of guns all around, I fell asleep on the cellar floor.

Vince was now in command of No. 26 IT Station at Arras.

81 These were presumably RE lance corporal's stripes for his new uniform.

Lance Corporal Vince Schürhoff with Sappers Bill Auckenthaler (left) and Cecil Stallworthy (right), 1917.

5 January 1917

Once more back among the ruins, trenches all around, mud everywhere, the familiar sight of mud-covered men, all now wearing tin helmets … I went out on the line in the trenches. After recent rains, some were in a fearful condition and we soon looked absolutely charming. Taffy began to give way but Cecil [Stallworthy][82] and I pulled him along and at length, after going through one disused trench after another, following our IT line, we hit a good trench and our progress became more rapid. Our artillery then started bombarding the German front line and the shells were falling so close to the end of one of our saps, that a man who was on guard there, came back without orders and when ordered to return to head of sap, he refused, though eventually obeyed when the Sergeant threatened to take drastic action. The poor boy was almost crying with fear … He wasn't wrong. We finished working in the sap and began mending the breaks in our wire, slowly nearing the [support trenches]. Whilst engaged on this, trench mortars began popping over, bursting all round us. How we missed being hit, I don't know. The climax came shortly after. I was helping Cecil mend a break when 5 duds fell behind us – at least so they seemed. We joked about the rotten stuff the Jerries were turning out, but suddenly a whiff of a peculiar smell came over. Cecil said "Gas" and in a twinkling we had our gas masks on … Luckily no more gas shells were sent over and we were able to take our gas helmets or masks off. All the same, we decided to push on for the cellar without wasting time and got there safely, covered with mud. Bill had a good dinner waiting for us. He is proving to be invaluable as a cook.

6 January 1917

I'm writing this down whilst the whole thing is on and whilst the impressions are on me. A raid is anticipated,[83] we are bombarding the German lines like hell and for three hours there has been a continuous succession of ear-splitting bangs and crashes of guns all round, the droning of heavies from our rear, the barks of 60-pounders close at hand and all this noise is increased by the exploding of shells from the Bosches. First the shriek of the shell, then the crash followed by the rumbling of falling masonry or merely the continued reports of our own guns. The noise is deafening and I frankly admit that my hand is trembling as

82 151829 Sapper Cecil Stallworthy. Thirty-one-year-old Post Office sorting clerk and telegraphist from Exeter. Having previously registered under the 'Derby scheme', he was called up in February 1916 into the Royal Engineers (Signal Service).

83 26th Infantry Brigade (9th Division) conducted a raid with two infantry companies: 'Report on raid carried out by 8/Black Watch and 10/Argylls, 6 January 1917', WO95/1762, TNA.

I write … Only Bill and I are together in a cellar, lit up by an acetylene lamp that pops up and down with every crash. The presence of danger and this awful noise has loosened our tongues and we have had a talk on things fellows don't talk about as a rule, at least under ordinary conditions we two would not have done so. The nearness of a Higher Power under conditions as at present, whether those at home – in his case his fiancée – are affected by mind or thought waves and have a kind of instinctive feeling that we are thinking of them more than ever. As Bill said "If they were to hear this, they would go dotty".

A shell has just fallen into a house very close by. As we only moved in such a short time ago, I found there was no pick or shovel. To be here without would be foolish, so I ran the risk and ran to an RE dump up the road. But I saw two Scotties walking along not far ahead and their calmness and apparent unconcern affected me, so I stopped running and walked, got a pick and shovel and returned to the cellar. We occupied our minds as much as possible, tidying up the place, fixing up a shelf, making a dixie out of a petrol tin, cleaning the acetylene lamp. Throughout we kept up a cheerful run of small talk, stopping at intervals when we thought the whine of a shell seemed to come extra near or the crash of an explosion seemed almost on top of us. At last there was absolutely nothing more to do and we began our unusual talk as mentioned above … Whilst writing this page and a half, there have been either explosions or shells fired at the rate of one to every two handwritten letters. No idea how much longer this will last. I feel as if I want to run outside and shout myself hoarse, at the same time dash about like a mad being. Yet it is simply a case of waiting. Our cellar looks quite theatrical. Grey stones with an arched roof and a flight of steps at the further end from where I am writing. The light shines on our faces but otherwise the place is in the shade – cold, damp and grey.

Another appalling crash. Bill is now writing too. We write a few sentences, then comes a crash and we relieved our feelings for a moment by talking a bit, then settle down to write until the next crash. During a lull in the firing, I went up and drew some water and we quickly gathered some wood and then lit a fire for tea in the cellar. Very smoky and Cecil has borrowed my tear shell goggles. The din had increased outside and is louder than ever; without doubt the raid is on now. The firing went on until 4.30 pm then died out and the evening has been as peaceful as the day was loud and noisy, with hardly a single shot being fired now.

8 January 1917

There is still a general feeling of dissatisfaction with this cellar. We keep looking round, at times hit on one that seems good at first sight, then some great defect is found and we have to look elsewhere. This afternoon, though, Bill went into the cellar next door … and it so pleased us that we sounded the Captain in charge of the billets in this road … [He] gave us permission to move in … when the battalions in the line are expected to be relieved. The knowledge that at last we have a definite place to go is very satisfactory.

10 January 1917

At 3 pm we moved into our new quarters … Before settling down, the cellar had to be cleared of numerous cobwebs, the floor thoroughly swept and so forth. Then each one of us selected a place to sleep in, dumped our belongings down there drawn from the general heap, and had tea … Went into Arras at night … [and] spoke to Francke about beds and arranged for a Continental *Daily Mail* and a *Petit Parisien* to be kept for us. On arrival back, heard that definite results had been obtained from our IT set.

11 January 1917

We have got a stove – brought here on a perambulator found on a rubbish heap – and some tubing next door came in useful as a chimney. Also a cupboard found in a neighbouring ruin is just the thing for our crockery. Tables abound and these together with the chairs are giving the place a slightly more homely appearance … For the first time got potato rations, one each, a great event.

12 January 1917

Bill very wild about our brick fire, so decided to scrounge another stove. After dinner, [we] found one in a ruined house, brought it over here and started a fire. Being very damp, it took a lot of starting, but once going, we soon got water boiling for tea, and how nice and warm the stove was … Went to Mme Pruvost's and had a very nice supper, putting us on good terms with ourselves. Back in cellar, found the stove going nicely and had a nice quiet sit round it with a pipe of 'Chairman's' tobacco.

13 January 1917

During my night watch found the stove a great nuisance, it would keep going out. So during the day we went to the RE dump and collared another stove. We fixed it on the old perambulator and wheeled it to our cellar ... Cecil and I took [an IT] message to Battalion HQ, a message which the Adjutant did not seem to relish. The boys went out at night as owing to batteries the station was 'dis'. Winston [Churchill] repaired the armchair and I had a very pleasant evening sitting in this armchair, smoking, dreaming about leave, home etc. The new stove brought out from the dump was a great success, burning quickly and giving out a good heat.

15 January 1917

First thing, old Winston trotted across to the [RE] dump and he and Davy spent the morning making beds. Cecil and I went to No. 21 Station and sent a wire to Mr Redgrave from the wireless there ... All afternoon and evening we worked on the beds, old Winston being called 'OC Beds'. By 8 pm we had three fine double-deckers ... I am beginning to find out that in Bill as cook and Winston as a Jack-of-all-trades, I have two very useful men.

16 January 1917

At night [we] went back to the Intelligence Police office and then we all went out to have a drink at Magniez's café ... Later, we had one of our old time 'do's' with Taffy at the piano and each man singing and generally enjoying himself, drinking beer or red and white wine.

17 January 1917

After only three hours' sleep, felt decidedly like 'the bottom of a birdcage' during my night shift ... Just now, during these last days, there exists a general feeling of bitterness towards Redgrave for not having looked after us more. We are expected to keep things going and yet get no assistance. I have sent messages galore, wired by wireless but nothing is done. Just above us is a bomb store. I want to ask him to have the bombs removed. A chance shell in them would blow us up miles high. Also I want to hear something definite about my leave ... White, the third interpreter, came and will be a very welcome addition to the staff.

18 January 1917

Stallworthy was in Arras last night talking to the Intelligence Police and [was told] about underground galleries. These, in connection with our work, would be invaluable. The possibilities were discussed over breakfast and agreed upon. Having no one to turn to, we acted on our own responsibility. All morning we explored these galleries and found them even more favourable for our purpose than we expected. Whilst the boys were reeling wire after dinner, I tracked down the OC of the galleries and got a written permit in duplicate allowing us to work in them.

19 January 1917

The instrument being 'dis' we all were able to turn out except Bill who remained behind to cook. All morning we worked hard and had incredible luck. First, Mr Redgrave appeared at last and put things right, explaining his long absence. Told me he was staying with us and that I could expect my leave shortly. Was very enthusiastic about our new scheme and went along one of the galleries … Captain Rathbone from GHQ appeared. Luckily the machine was 'dis' so he could not indulge in his favourite pastime of testing by galvanometer. Had the machine been working, he would have found every earth gone. He also, was very keen on the gallery and I had to show him all round our lines. Trenches rather knocked about by trench mortars, hence our wires were not as neat as they could have been. Still, he was very nice and did not ask any awkward questions … All the boys are in a good humour now, very different to what they were a few days ago. They take this work and life, the 'carrying on' of it, much more to heart than the unknowing outsider would imagine.

20 January 1917

Shivering and cold to bone, got up … to make breakfast. Directly after started reeling wire and then went up to front line to continue laying more. Trench mortars were fairly active at this time. 'Whizzbangs' also flashed over us from time to time and some shells could be heard sailing over in the direction of our cellar … Proceeded again to the front line. The trench mortar activity had increased and we had three very narrow shaves, one in particular we saw coming straight at us, but very luckily it fell short. All the same, crouching low in the trench as we were, we were smothered with dirt and earth. [Davis] burst into almost hysterical laughter after the shower of earth had subsided – reflex action from the strain. I must say, I was not sorry when wire and staples gave out and we had good reason to return. After dinner, saw Adjutant of the 6th Buffs[84] who used to be in our sector at No. 22 to arrange for us to be rationed from his Battalion. Like this, we get 8 men's rations from him and 8 men's from Brigade, altogether 16 and we are only 7 men here at the moment.

84 Captain J.C. Page, 6/East Kent Regiment (37th Infantry Brigade, 12th Division): WO95/1860, TNA.

21 January 1917

We worked hard all morning and finished the wiring by dinner. At 2 pm we switched on and had instantaneous success, all in turns taking down as hard as we could until after tea when atmospherics slowed matters down. All of us delighted. Had two messages for Battalion HQ.

22 January 1917

Mr Redgrave himself came round dinner time with a Mr Marsh,[85] his substitute.

25 January 1917

The thought of going on leave never leaves my mind and reminds me of the way I counted the days for going home when I was at school at Hildesheim ... Winston and I created a bit of excitement trying to remove a writing cabinet from a room upstairs. We got up by an iron ladder, through a window, the actual staircase having previously disappeared. Very gingerly we managed to get this cabinet to the floor overlooking the cellar entrance. The wall had been blown away so all we had to do was to lower the cabinet. This we did with a piece of wire ... but for some unknown reason, it toppled over, crashed down the stone steps and lay there, a crumpled heap of wood. We extricated the central part, left intact and collected the rest for firewood. All this gave us a lot of amusement. The centre part, shelves and pigeon holes serve admirably for literature, stationery and oddments and generally improves the appearance of the cellar.

26 January 1917

A very exciting morning from an official point of view. Altogether, we had to notify the Battalion twice during the day and as a result of the morning's information, I believe we gave Fritz a hot time during the afternoon.

27 January 1917

The Kaiser's birthday was announced by a shell exploding outside in the road, too close to be pleasant. At the time I was standing at the top of the cellar, cleaning my nails, but very quickly skipped down with a shower of masonry behind me ... After tea, had the greatest disappointment I have had for years. Sergeant Shepherd came down and told me that

85 Lieutenant E.V. Marsh, attached Army Signal Service.

my leave had been cancelled for the time being. During evening tried to be cheerful but what touched me was the quiet way the boys left me an extra tot of rum allowance and I must say the warmth did buck me up considerably.

28 January 1917

Mr Redgrave [visited] with an Intelligence officer and this man and I went over some pages of reports relating to information we had obtained … At night went to service at the YMCA and enjoyed singing. Never realised what beautiful words there are to some of the hymns. Afterwards met Francke and Reynolds and we went to Mme Magniez's café where we had a very pleasant chat. The former told me our leave was only postponed for a few days owing to congestion of traffic at railheads. Let's hope he is right.

30 January 1917

Again aroused by mortars falling not far away and, as usual, they stopped for breakfast. Don't know why, but felt very nervy. We had a 'council of war' on the state of our lines, parts of which have been levelled and knocked about horribly. As a result, we did some more wiring and … at last, we connected up and found the line OK. It is just like a story the way we carry on; things go splendidly for a couple of days, then something happens and a 'council of war' follows. The suggestion agreed upon is then carried out until something else happens, say the batteries run out. More cursing, urgent wireless messages for more batteries and then we go on again. Or the wire gives out. Then we pinch wire right and left and then manage to keep on again. There are many more difficulties I may not mention, but it gives a feeling of adventure and romance to the whole, the way we keep things going.

1 February 1917

Was on duty when at 11.15 am Sergeant Shepherd tumbled down the cellar steps and after recovering, told me to pack up … for going on leave. For a few minutes behaved like a kid of five years old.

Vince took leave in England.

15 February 1917

After 3½ days' travelling, which completely made me realise I was back in the army again, I reached 'The Cellar' and saw the old familiar faces.

16 February 1917

Back into the old life again. A bit strange but I am not feeling as down as I expected. These comfortable quarters atone for a great deal ... In place of Taffy we have a new man called Kiff whom everybody speaks well and no doubt will be an improvement on Taffy, whose nerves were beginning to tumble to pieces. Troubles have not been backwards in coming forward. The whole Station is furious with Mr Marsh because he has made arrangements to dump our batteries at a spot about a mile away and we have to fetch them. These batteries are heavy things and it took Davy and myself ¾ hour to fetch one. Unfortunately there is a nasty feeling of suppressed anger, 'fedupness' and "if you don't play the game with me, I won't with you" towards Marsh and that rather puts me between two fires. We had a long discussion on the subject and decided to give this battery carrying a week's trial. By that time I hope tempers will have simmered down, perhaps other arrangements.

17 February 1917

Winston discovered reason why results had not been very satisfactory. [We] brought up two more batteries. It's not such a terrible job in daylight ... The feeling in the air is still there, though since better results have been obtained, not so pronounced as last night. The IT is a kind of temper barometer. If OK, all spirits rise, if not OK then down they go and everybody is irritable and it takes a lot of tact and patience to keep things going peacefully. A bit of excitement ... [We] had gone to the dump to fetch more wood for another bed. Whilst there, a shell exploded which sounded not far from 'The Cellar'. When we got in sight thereof and saw smoke pouring out of the windows, I thought that "Summat's happened to Bill". Doubling along the last 50 yards I dashed downstairs and found Bill calmly writing, smoking a cigar, having just lit a fire, quite unconscious of the stir he had created upstairs ... The chimney had caught fire, hence the volume of smoke, officers came along, throwing their weight about and I had my name taken. Gradually the excitement dies down and then since nothing has been heard. Still it was lucky that the slight mist outside prevented the Jerries from observing the smoke.

18 February 1917

Went to the YMCA for the usual service and found that Gipsy Smith,[86] the well-known Evangelist, was going to speak. I must say, he could

86 For Smith's work in France, see Snape (ed.), *Back Parts of War*, 78–9.

speak, the best speaker I have ever heard. I could not decide which I liked most, listening to his speaking or listening to what he was speaking about. Certainly the man had all the tricks of oratory at his finger ends and knew how to get a firm grip of his audience … At Magniez's café, Cecil and I discussed the idea of taking a cave for when 'the Push' starts, already taking down rations etc. A chat with Bob Hutt of the Intelligence Police confirmed our intention. We held one of our war councils in 'The Cellar' on our return.

19 February 1917

We spent the morning looking for a suitable cave and eventually found one. Awfully weird wandering round these caves and on two occasions we actually lost ourselves but soon found our way back. Saw Mr Barrance,[87] the New Zealand Tunnelling Officer, regarding permission to move in, but were told we should have to apply to the 'Cave Major'. Another unpleasant interview with Mr Marsh. After the loud talking about having to fetch batteries, when I asked for volunteers, to my surprise practically every man volunteered. Was rather touched by this.

20 February 1917

Just before dinner, [Marsh] turned up with Captain Rathbone and Lieutenant Coke.[88] Luck was again with me. The place was quite clean and tidy, though part of line 'dis'. Cecil had gone out with White to repair it and the fact that both an operator and an interpreter were out seemed to impress Rathbone favourably though the fact that they were both out was pure luck. I was also able to settle the battery question with Marsh alright and now peace once more reigns.

21 February 1917

We understood from Marsh that batteries were awaiting us at the Battalion HQ but when we got there, there was nothing. So we went to the 'Van John's', a pierrot troupe and said a damn to Marsh and the boxcar. Jolly fine show, well staged in a large high theatre in Arras, more suited to orchestra concerts than to pierrot troupes and it was difficult to realise oneself but 3 kilometres from the firing line as except for one hole through the wall, the place was absolutely untouched.

87 Lieutenant K.M. Barrance New Zealand Engineers.

88 Second Lieutenant Edward Coke RE. Thirty-eight-year-old actor: WO339/73960, TNA.

22 February 1917

Fairly successful morning but the chief thing of today was that Cecil and I went and routed out all the RFA signallers and gave them a quiet but very "suggestive of what will happen to you if you don't listen to us" talk. (*1968 comment*: This was because, despite repeated warnings, their signallers would persist in irresponsible talk over their 'phone lines.)

23 February 1917

Bill in an energetic mood, so we gave the place a good spring cleaning. Meanwhile, Davis refused to get out of his bed until 10.30 am and so gave him a piece of my mind. After dinner ... Went into Arras and had a bath at the College followed by a dashing tea at the Tearoom. Getting there early, we had tea in the august presence of officers and seeing some having to stand, awaiting their turn, whilst we placidly kept on eating was as sweet as an extra cake to us.

24 February 1917

The artillery activity is still bothering us during Bill's turn on duty, his exclamations, gesticulations and general behaviour resembled a pantomime. Although he was seriousness personified, he made us all nearly choke with laughter. I had to write ... about the 'phone activity on our lines but have little hope of improvement. The general aspect of our cellar has been improved by some red lamp shades. I am afraid that officers coming to visit us will find this place so comfortable they will want to stay longer than would be pleasant for us. As it is, what with admiring our furniture and pictures and postcards, they stay a good time and the longer they stay, the greater the chance of their popping us some awkward questions.

25 February 1917

We are going through some peculiar phases of life just now. The ever-present thought of 'The Push' starting soon is beginning to haunt us. At times we never give it a thought and as the IT is going well, the general spirit barometer is excellent. Meal time is when we are most cheerful and White, the 'Major', the oldest member of the party, a man of about 45, gives vent to some very dry remarks ... On the other hand, at times the talk veers round to the other extreme; extreme pessimism. Boyce, of No. 21 Station came over to see us today. He is a nice chap but three months in the trenches have worn his nerves to shreds ... [On way back from Arras] we were nearly hit by machine-gun bullets along road. They hit the trees all round, making bark fly about and bringing out sparks when they hit a brick wall.

26 February 1917

The excitement started [while we] were preparing breakfast. Suddenly the guns, as if from under our feet, started firing and in a few seconds we had to shout at the top of our voices to be heard. Through the window of the door upstairs, we had a view of our shells bursting. It wasn't long before the Bosches started and we could see his trench mortars exploding the other side of the barrier, sending up huge columns of smoke and flames. We had just taken the breakfast downstairs when shells began to fall in the road and back of our house. A party of Gordons passed me as I was bringing some wood down and asked if I knew of a cellar close by. I showed them one but after 20 minutes they were shelled out, so although against orders, I brought them in here. One cannot refuse men shelter when shells are 'crumping' all round and the poor devils are aimlessly wandering round, trying to find their units. Several shells fell quite close, the concussion of one ripping some baize off our door … We had dinner of bully as it was not safe to cook upstairs. Afterwards, though, things began to quieten down and Mr Marsh came up, informing us that Mr Redgrave had come back … I spent the evening writing home … and then lay in bed reading *Pip* by Ian Hay.[89] The Bosches had spasms of hate, sending over salvoes of trench mortars in the midst of one of which our trench mortar crews dashed down the cellar steps and broke in here for shelter before we had time to stop them or ask who they were. They all seemed too breathless or scared to speak for some time. However, they soon calmed down, satisfied me of their identity and left when things quietened down.

27 February 1917

We witnessed a very sad sight. Eight German aeroplanes seemed to appear from nowhere and like hawks flashed across at two of our machines cruising over Arras. Our planes had no earthly chance against these fast German machines, the like of which we have never seen before. One Bosche darted ahead of the others, dipped down over one of our machines, a big biplane, there was a faint rat-tat, our plane swerved, seemed to right itself, suddenly glowed red, next moment burst into flames and fell, a ball of flame, to earth. Our other machine was forced

89 Ian Hay, *'Pip': A Romance of Youth* (1907).

to land, but as far as we could see, it landed in safety. Then the Germans turned round and in two minutes had disappeared. The whole affair lasted less than 5 minutes.[90]

28 February 1917

Ran out of paper, so strolled over to Boyce's [station] to get some. Usual depression there, so didn't stay long … A quiet and rather boresome evening. Not for long though … 'Crrump, crrump, crrump' came shells exploding quite close. We thought the Bosches had seen the beam of light from our lamp shining out of the ventilation shaft. We 'dimmed the wick' and sat tight and eventually lived to fight another day. However, when [our Wireless visitors] were leaving, we saw the cause; it was the flashing of their electric torch across the road that the Germans must have seen. A few sweet words from our lips put their wind up, also promptly extinguishing the light.

2 March 1917

Saw the 'Light Blues', a very cheap pierrot troupe, cheap in two senses, it not being much good and entrance being free of charge. One or two turns were painful.

3 March 1917

A lot of changing about of troops, result we get rather messed about with rations. Thus this morning we got no tea, sugar or meat from the Battalion. Our stock in hand came in most useful … Feeling in a pugnacious mood, I wrote a very clear, frank and in places thinly veiled sarcastic note to various quarters and although I may get into a row about this, I don't care a damn. We have got over our 'nervy' feelings and as a result everybody is extra cheerful. Rumours are very current that the Bosches will retire round here as they have done in the Somme [area] and we are keeping a sharp look-out in order to be the first to find out when they do. This would be a big feather in our cap. This underground life is beginning to show in our faces. Both Bill and I are getting quite a yellow complexion and all say I am getting a bald patch on my head.

---

90 That afternoon a BE2e of 12 Squadron RFC conducting artillery observation was shot down, probably by Second Lieutenant W. Voss of Jagdstaffel 2, killing Captain J.H. McArthur and Private J. Whiteford: Trevor Henshaw, *The Sky Their Battlefield* (London: Grub Street, 1995), 139.

4 March 1917

Saw the Sergeant-Major about our rations. As a result, we got extra tea and sugar and pork and beans, after putting on the usual professional beggar's wail and semi-starved facial expression.

5 March 1917

Went to fetch our rations. The Sergeant-Major gruffly informed us he knew nothing about us and was just going to clear off when I said "We'll go over and see the Adjutant straight now". This got his wind up and as a result he went so far as to arrange rations for us himself which we have to fetch tonight. In consequence, we have no actual meat except Macconachie and [we] are experimenting with a rice pudding. Four of us had a beautifully quiet evening together round the stove, chatting and reading.

6 March 1917

[Marsh] came with Newton 'The Skipper' … [a] Sergeant … He used to be in charge of the Wireless Station by No. 22 IT. Has the Long Service Medal for the Navy and for service on the Royal Yacht. He's one of the nicest fellows I have met out here. Although over 50, in himself he's more like 25. Altered the shifts to 4½ hours each. Felt restless and nervy all afternoon and could not settle down to anything … [To Arras and on return to] 'The Lounge' we found everybody's eyes running and in a couple of seconds, ours were too. The Germans had sent over a tear gas shell which exploded just outside our cellar in the road. In a moment the place was filled with the stuff but vigorous blanket shaking blew the fumes away. Still, our eyes were running continuously for an hour after the explosion.

7 March 1917

At 5.45 pm Cecil woke me up with the news that a gigantic rat was in the cellar. I said "Oh?" and turned over as I had still another 10 minutes before going on the IT. Suddenly I heard a scratching and rustling immediately beside my head and opening my eyes, saw the rat within two inches of my nose. My start woke up the others. Bill got out his revolver and whilst we took cover, he fired. When we looked for the rat, which had jumped to the floor, it had gone, but further investigation showed it calmly nibbling some cheese. Bill's second shot knocked over a box behind which it had disappeared and the third finished it off. 'The Lounge' still has a peculiar mustardy smell from the tear gas shell and I think the fumes affected us all, as we all were somewhat groggy and I felt it only needed the spark to set tempers going … Bill and I brought the stove down. Cooking outside in the yard was getting too dangerous after the recent livening up. This rather upset White, who objected to the smoke and in the midst of our rather snappy argument, an officer from the Brigade Staff came down. This put an end to the talk. He listened to what I had to say and luckily in less than 15 seconds he had proof of the points I had stressed in my note. He was very nice and promised to see the Brigadier about our move to the cave. All afternoon we laid wires to our prospective cave and after tea.

8 March 1917

Marsh came down with batteries and I'm afraid we rather pitched into him regarding removal to the cave. He had been very slack with us and so I felt justified in speaking out my mind. Cecil and Bill afterwards remarked how he squirmed and wriggled and shifted from one foot to the other.

9 March 1917

[Told that] the General was coming to see us, so … the next hour saw very active preparations in the way of cleaning up and in making ourselves look 'posh'. Everything was ready at 11.30 am and Bill lit his cigar. The *Berliner Tageblatt* and *Leipziger Neuerste Nachrichten* lay apparently haphazardly on the table and I was glancing casually at *La Vie Parisienne.* Thus we waited, picture of understudied comfort and ease, Bill and his cigar, one example, 'The Lounge' in itself the other; of 'learning' as shown by the German and French newspapers 'lying about'. The same thought seemed to strike us all, "We'll show the Brigadier that there are others beside himself who live well and know a good thing or two". Weakness of human vanity, I suppose. So we waited, even postponing dinner until he should come. At 1 pm I said "Damn the Brigadier, let's have dinner". So, being late, we had just plain bully and cheese. Naturally he appeared in the midst of our very frugal meal. Nothing resulted from this visit. On duty until 6 pm after which … a lot of excitement was caused by one of the reports we sent in being repeated.

10 March 1917

There is a lively lot opposite us and life is no dream. Shells fall around and all we can do is grin and bear it and hope for the best. Winston and Kiff went out just before tea; I never noticed them go out although there was a lull in the bombardment. Suddenly I heard Winston shout "Oh

God" and next fraction of a second there was a tremendous crash outside and both men came stumbling down the steps in a cloud of dust etc. It was a narrow squeak for both of them. I find chewing a match a great nerve soother.

11 March 1917

Awakened at 3 am by a very insistent bombardment all around. It's beastly being awakened during the night, one never knows whether it's a raid or a strafe and at night, in this hollow cellar, the noise sounds much louder … We cooked some dinner with fear and trembling. Our kitchen stove is downstairs and we fixed a pipe leading up to outside the cellar entrance and our great fear when cooking is that the Bosche may see the smoke and fire on us. The activity continued until 3 pm when four of us went to our cave to level the ground. But we found the thaw had cracked large lumps of chalk and it only needed a knock of the spade to bring these lumps down. This made us look out for another cave. We ran across the 'Cave Major' to whom I put our difficulty. He was not exactly overwhelmingly encouraging and on our return to 'The Lounge' we felt worse than ever … Went to see Lieutenant Quinn, the Brigade Staff Officer who had been rather decent to us. He behaved like a brick, suggested other caves we might have.

12 March 1917

Mr Quinn came round. [We] went round the caves he had in mind for us, but they were too advanced and so we had to cry off … Returned to 'The Lounge', once more at a loss about where to find safer quarters than this place. It looks as if the cave question is knocked on the head. The prevalent idea now is to have a passage made from our cellar to the tunnel close by. We should not feel so much like rats in a hole then, having two exits. Whilst we were discussing this … [in came] the news that our wires had to be moved from one side of the tunnel to the other – some undertaking. On top of this came orders concerning our earths. Result, all cleared out during afternoon bar Bill and myself. He was in one of his nervy moods and his talk was hardly cheering.

13 March 1917

About 9 pm went to bed with some rum, cake and chocolate. Felt very comfy. Had fallen asleep when at 11.30 pm was awakened by Wilkie and found everybody rather excited over information received. As a result, we packed up. This information was to the effect that we were to be heavily shelled between 2 and 4 am. Our cellar not being proof against heavy shells, we retired to 'The Well' (*1968 comment*: A dry well with a ladder down by means of which we can enter the cave system.) ... After warning Lieutenant Barrance we tried to settle down to sleep, but none came my way.

14 March 1917

It became rather cold and damp and the rough chalk floor was not very soft to lie on. Still, we fixed things up and awaited the eventful hour. It came, it passed, 3 am came and passed, also 4 am. I got fed up with things then. Our cosy cellar seemed especially cosy, so ... went over at 5 am and made breakfast. With a piece of D5 wire, we pulled things up the well and all feeling a bit raw-edged ... A 4.2 [shell] fell into a house opposite ours. The concussion knocked a glass off our cupboard. The shell must have just skimmed our roof.

15 March 1917

At 5.30 am a tremendous bang and the noise of falling bottles, tiles, bricks etc. woke me up. It was not necessary to leave the cellar to know that a shell had hit the outhouse adjoining ours. We were speechless with the shock till somehow I managed to gasp out that we should now have some firewood for breakfast. A rotten bit of humour but it relieved the tension ... For two hours, 5.9 and 4.2 shells, 'whizzbangs', shrapnel and heaven knows what else fell around, then ceased. When the Orderly came round for reports, he told us the Germans had made a raid on our left, in the region of the road and had penetrated to our Second Line, which would have brought them close to us.[91] Ignorance is bliss. Later, four of us went to fetch rations ... All the way we were chased by 'whizzbangs' and shrapnel and one 5.9 exploded just in the road where we should have been had we not stopped to take cover ... Things are quieter now but we are all screwed up to a pitch of nervous strain, expecting any moment the 'c-crumph' of a shell. It is not a pleasant feeling. At every unusually loud intake of breath or rustle of anything, we suddenly stop and listen, thinking it is the whine of a shell approaching. White's snoring is a source of great annoyance to us in that respect.

---

91 The raid killed eight, wounded thirty-two, and six were taken prisoner: 8/East Yorkshire Regiment (8th Infantry Brigade, 3rd Division) war diary, 15 March 1917, WO95/1424/2; 7/Suffolk Regiment (35th Infantry Brigade, 12th Division) war diary, 15 March 1917, WO95/1852, TNA.

16 March 1917

Just now, following the German raid, there is a spy mania on. The Adjutant of the local battalion himself told me a spy had been caught in the tunnel dressed as an RE officer, also another man is supposed to have been caught. It is quiet today and that nervy cloud is falling off and we are regaining our usual spirits. Mr Redgrave and Marsh turned up after dinner and spent over two hours [discussing] future plans for work, our respective jobs when 'The Push' starts. Cecil and Winston showed Redgrave their 'earth' idea, and had their names taken to be recommended.

17 March 1917

A Continental edition of the *Daily Mail* had just been brought in. In it the British communiqué says 'A German raid was attempted early yesterday morning NE of Arras but failed to reach our trenches'. A big lie. The Germans evidently not the only people who make out lying official reports. During the day the usual shelling but it is such an everyday occurrence, we are getting quite used to it, in fact, a quiet day is something abnormal. Experience has shown us to be just out of reach of trench mortars, 'whizzbangs' are not strong enough to hurt us and what gave us some big frights in the shape of loud bangs we found was shrapnel so there only remains real heavy stuff falling directly on us that could do us any harm.

19 March 1917

More good news, suggesting a general retirement along the line,[92] also with the news that Péronne had been taken.

20 March 1917

Except Wilkie, who was making breakfast, White, who was on duty on the IT set and Cecil, who happened to be up, we were all asleep at 9.30 am when Marsh appeared on the scene, quietly, like a spirit. He is always quiet when entering, as if trying to catch us by surprise. I hopped out of bed, slipped on my trousers and looking as pleased as possible at seeing him, very charmingly asked whether he would have some breakfast with us. He was just going to make some remark about our staying in bed rather late and my invitation somewhat took the wind out of his sails. He then thanked me and said he was expecting Mr Redgrave. Mr Redgrave

92 The German withdrawal opposite Third Army had started on 17 March: Cyril Falls, *Military Operations, France and Belgium, 1917*, Vol. 1 (London: HMSO, 1940), 149–51.

in fact did turn up shortly after and told us his plans. So Winston and I buckled on our shield and armour and the lot of us sallied forth. We were soon splashing through mud half-knee deep. Our destination was the old German lines we had just taken over. At length we got into the newly-dug communication trench, connecting our old front line with the Bosche's. Mud appalling. The trench was in parts only waist high and we had to keep low ... In the German lines, the mud was, if anything, worse. Their front line was wider than ours, but in parts nothing but a series of shell holes ... Continuing, we ran into an English working party. Told us there was a post of ours 30 yards on and that it was also about 30 yards from the nearest Germans. A most uncanny silence reigned everywhere. We got the information required and returned by another communication trench, shallower than the first one. Back in the cellar we talked things over and discussed future plans ... The boys, except Bill and Wilkie, had gone over to the German lines to work in accordance with plans and came back about 5 pm, literally caked in mud from head to foot, but successful despite numerous close shaves. They saw a Northumberland Fusilier man carry a wounded man across the exposed communication trench, in full view of the German lines – another example of an unheard and unrecorded deed of bravery.

22 March 1917

An interview with Mr Barrance resulted in there being no chance of a passage being dug to the tunnel as yet as some big things are expected [on 1/2 April]. I hope to heaven we shall come through alright. Between us we have tried in every imaginable way during the last six weeks to obtain a safe place to fall back on, caves, passage from cellar to tunnel, strengthening of this cellar, special dug-out etc. Had we only had Redgrave, I have no doubt some steps would have been taken, but Marsh is hopelessly helpless. Although in charge of us, he does not want to do anything and when it comes to a bit of tricky work, like procuring this cave and getting a working party to dig a passage through to tunnel, he just backs out. Should this place be shelled down and the lot of us, or any of us be killed or wounded, the blame will be on that man's shoulders.

Kiff and I went to a performance of 'The Thistles',[93] a pierrot troupe ... They were magnificent, one being a girl [impersonator] who might have walked out of *La Vie Parisienne*, her make-up was so good.[94] Every action

93 9th Division's concert party.

94 For the different psychological levels at which the female impersonators had resonance with their audiences, see Laugesen, 'More than a Luxury', 235.

was an exact imitation of a girl and her singing of *The Broken Doll* just fine … Another member was a Padre who won the Military Cross in the Somme,[95] another ex-professional music hall man who the evening before had been on a fatigue party in the newly-taken German lines. As I saw him, in evening dress, top hat, swagger cane, white gloves etc., I could not help thinking what he must have looked like the previous evening.

24 March 1917

The water supply has broken down and now there is an everlasting crowd round our well. How long it will last out, I don't know. Also what makes me nervous is the frequent appearance of hostile aircraft above and should this crowd be spotted, we should rather quickly hear things buzzing around rather too close to be pleasant.

25 March 1917

Taffy has come back to the line but as a result of some diplomacy, he is at No. 24 Station and not with us. Davis is back again and Cecil is at rest … Once, during my absence, [Taffy] and Bill had a real rumpus. They never agreed, neither did Taffy get on well with the others. The boys thoughtfully said nothing to me about this row, although I knew something was in the air. Taffy's teeth gave an excuse for him to leave us for them to be seen to … This row … must have reached a lively state as all say it took three men to keep him from springing at Bill. Taffy must have completely lost his head. On my return from leave, found Kiff, a man from No. 24 had come *pro tem* instead of Taffy. Kiff is an A1 fellow, a fine worker and very popular with us. I foresaw more difficulties should Taffy return here … so I tackled Marsh … Taffy … came down here to collect some things but left in a fuming rage. In a way I was sorry for him as No. 24 is not an ideal place.

26 March 1917

Newton, [the] ex-Navy man who was with us when we went over to the old German lines, is missing. Nobody has the slightest idea where he is. He was last seen on [23 March] at 11 am and since then, not a trace. Absolute mystery … Into Arras … found the cinema and concert hall closed, also the Church Army Rest hut, found a canteen but they had sold out of tobacco, and so drifted to Mme Pruvost … and we had a

95 'The popular Padre Brown was best known from his connection with "The Thistles" concert troupe': John Ewing, *The History of the Ninth (Scottish) Division, 1914–1919* (London: John Murray, 1921), 393.

nice supper. On way back, we had just passed the railway station, two long distance 'whizzbangs' came over. We didn't even hear the report. One second we were calmly strolling along, the next, or a fraction of the next, we heard a shrill whine that had passed us and given vent to two loud crashes before we had had time to realize that we had heard them. We bolted into vague darkness and somehow got down the cellar steps of a ruined house. Eventually we dared to come out and returned by the tunnel. I am afraid our language was not pleasing to the ear.

28 March 1917

A wire informed us that two more operators are coming tomorrow night and Winston is out all day with other men on special work in connection with 'The Push'. Feverish activity is apparent everywhere and personally I think the next fortnight will see a great change in our lives. Also I think we interpreters will be separated from the operators and we shall be switched on to Intelligence 'B' work proper.[96] Just now, I'm not taking much interest in our work, only hanging on to keep in touch with the Bosch. Altogether, a general feeling of expectancy prevails … Mr Marsh told me that Newton had turned up and the case against him will be that of absenting himself for several days, as good as deserting and also of misappropriation of money not belonging to himself. He had 800 francs to buy stuff from the Officers' Canteen at Avesnes-le-Comte but bought 32 bottles of champagne and some rum and had big bust-up instead. The day after, he disappeared. Personally, I think it's a case of temporary insanity.

29 March 1917

Outside, artillery on both sides going at it hammer and tongs. We expected Marsh up with batteries but a wire came saying we were to fetch them. Needless to say there was a general hymn of hats, suggestions of frightfulness, of "what I should tell him if I were to meet him after the War". This went on starting shortly before tea, during tea and for some time after tea. When I calculated the outpourings of hate had reached their climax, I asked for volunteers to fetch them – and every man volunteered. So we cut cards.

---

96 Within the British army at this time I(b) dealt with espionage and counter-espionage. Vince was not to be employed on such work. Presumably at this time he associated general intelligence duties with the Intelligence Police because he had not had much contact with other intelligence personnel.

30 March 1917

Just as I was hopelessly bored stiff, a Brigadier-General Potter[97] came down and inspected IT. He was tremendously interested, especially as I happened to have a very complicated report … [To the] IP's office where … we had a real lively evening, wine and cigars galore, songs and stories.

31 March 1917

I lay down for a nap but hardly had I fallen asleep when I was awakened by shouts of "Corporal", to find that Brigadier-General in the cellar. He came with a Brigade Major, but after a short time they left. So I again turned in and for the second time, just when in dreamland, another shout of "Corporal" woke me up, to find Redgrave with a string of officers. We had a friendly chat and Reddy proposed that we interpreters should be brought back for a rest. Otherwise life resumes its normal course. The artillery of both sides go at it hammer and tongs, from after breakfast to dusk … Going into Arras now is always risky. We go via the caves and then the sewers, the latter reminding me of the Underground passages in London leading to the railway platforms. The electric lighting installed adds to the appearance. In Arras, we go about our work, buy stores, fetch rations and letters and then come back as fast as possible. We live like moles.

2 April 1917

General feeling of resentment and dissatisfaction against Marsh, particularly about batteries and candles. An agreement was made by which on Mondays we should fetch the cells from a Battalion Signals Office and on Thursdays, the boxcar with Marsh would come to give us our stores. Now, first the paraffin runs out and we have to rely on candles, bought out of our own pockets, but does Marsh try and get us a supply of candles? Not he. Doesn't move a hand. Then recently wireless messages keep coming up on Wednesdays saying "Boxcar disabled, bring cells to YI" (a certain spot in Arras). This means carrying 4 batteries, each between 40 and 50 pounds, through the caves, to this spot, about a mile further away than the Signals Office. This is enough to get one's monkey up, but what made matters worse was that when once the boxcar was supposed to be disabled, it was seen in Arras. In other words, what Marsh had wired was a lie.

97 Brigadier-General Herbert Potter DSO, commander 9th Infantry Brigade (3rd Division).

3 April 1917
Everybody still within an ace of semi-mutiny still, but White, Wilkie and I went to 'YI' with remaining cells. We waited in vain for Marsh and new cells. Nothing turned up so quite decided to let Marsh and the running of the Station go to hell. On return, found Redgrave had called, saying that Bill and I would be going out tomorrow to Corps … I shall be sorry to part with Winston. He has been a fine help, teaching me a lot of things. In a few days he will be an acquaintance of the past. Funny how certain characters in this life drift into one's circle, influence you one way or the other and then, as if their mission fulfilled, vanish again.

4 April 1917
At 1.30 am I was awakened by a voice calling "Corporal, Mr Marsh is here". I know that my predominant thought was to give free vent to my feelings. He had funked coming up during the evening and now … when there was nothing to fear, was expecting us to move out at once. He first remarked that he was surprised we weren't ready. This gave me my opening and whilst I was slipping on my togs, I asked him how he could expect us to be ready with a vague wire without time or date as he had sent us. I then went on to the battery mix-up, informing him of our needless journeys through the tunnel … his contradictory instructions, asking why he never came up himself, the light or candle question … In short … I let rip. Marsh did make some excuses, saying something about having to obey superior orders. Well, the end was I didn't answer his excuses. I said goodbye … and casting one last look round, followed the others, stumbled through the dark to the boxcar and by the Verey lights shooting up, saw silhouetted against the sky for the last time perhaps, the ruined, hollow, gutted and battered ruins of Saint Sauveur.

This brought a certain period of my kaleidoscopic life to an end … But I shall always look back to the cellar as a portion of my life, equally mixed with excitement, comfort, danger and homeliness, an atmosphere of independence and a feeling of Bohemianism never felt before. The song sung by the 'Van John's', *Oh for a Night in Bohemia* will at once, no matter where heard, bring me back to that dimly lit cellar, slightly mushy smell and the feeling of comradeship with real fine fellows, equally fine in sharing danger as well as pleasure.

Bill and I slept at Warlus … During the afternoon, left in the boxcar for Corps HQ, passing en route mile after mile of transports and lorries. I noticed also that what had once been bare fields by the Arras – Saint-Pol road, were huge camps and growing ones too. … [Then] went into

Avesnes-le-Comte, made purchases, looked about, bought some Vaseline for Marsh who overtook us and very much thawed when he had to ask us to speak to the lady in the chemist's shop, he not knowing French.

5 April 1917

An Orderly informed us that Major Thompson[98] wished to see us … one of the reasons, we … were brought back here, was to have certain instructions given us … The interview resulted in us being informed that we should be used as interpreters and prisoner interrogators at the Dainville Prisoner-of-War Cage.

6 April 1917

Adjourned to Café Bordeaux for lunch. Bill was very pleased with 40 francs pay, so was I and he was quite excited over my new tunic and general outfit; he actually made me feel a little excited too and I had to let him take in a bit of the hip to improve the fit … Had another look at the Pictures, one being Harry Lauder on the Blackpool Golf Links.[99]

7 April 1917

Bill and I spend all day strolling about in the lanes and walks round here … Nobody would imagine a war is on though when the wind drops for a moment, the continual rumble of guns is audible … [We] were shown some captured German papers and letters. The latter were rather interesting as we were able to get some idea of what to do in future. The newspapers seemed to delight in printing columns of hate against England and in showing up to what a state we had been reduced.

8 April 1917

This village, Noyelle-Vion, is remarkably quiet, hidden away from all the bustle and traffic always existing closer to the line. Only a few batmen, signallers and clerks live here and officers … We got the word and moved off … and proceeded to the Corps Prison Cage, being held up times without number owing to congestion of traffic. The journey took three hours altogether although normally it takes half an hour.

We got out at the railway embankment at Dainville and found, as usual nobody expecting us, nobody knew about us and nobody cared. But somehow we found a tent and met a [Despatch Rider] … whom I had met at Corps. He put us wise to several things, including some hayricks, from

98 Major F.V. Thompson DSO RE, GSO2 (Intelligence) VI Corps.

99 [Unknown director] *Bunkered at Blackpool* (1917).

which we obtained straw to lay on the ground of our tent. Then 'midst the usual cursing and growling, we settled down to sleep. Just done so, when Benoly's[100] crowd turned up. More confusion and excitement. After endless snapping and back-biting, they got down too, Benoly and Bill, who do not love each other, indulging in a series of sarcastic veiled insults.

First and Third Armies launched an offensive across the Arras front.

9 April 1917

Got first instructions on what to do and hardly had time to look round when first batch of prisoners turned up. They were an undersized, unkempt, unshaven, filthy, rowdy, muddy, nondescript crowd of ape-like human beings. The pictures seen of crowds of German faces, drawn by Bairnsfather,[101] give a very good idea of their appearance. Our precise job is to marshal them up, take down certain particulars, search them, do some questioning and altogether make ourselves generally useful. Also, I have to do a certain amount of clerical work. Mr Bury,[102] our OC, is a very nervous, restless man who never can let you work alone, but must keep poking his nose in, giving an order one moment and a different one the next. The other officers are all very decent. All day batches of prisoners came up and we had no time for meals, just chewing biscuits when possible although we got a drop of tea at 5 pm. We kept on, entering the details on special forms provided until dark and then continued by the aid of lamps, when the whole things became a farce. At length, by 11.30 pm the last batch moved into the main pen and we were able to return to our tents.

10 April 1917

Very cold and windy with frequent snow and sleet showers. Must be awful for the prisoners. There are 1,500 odd in the cages.[103] The cage is a large area bordered by barbed wire; it is sub-divided into three others, the first into which the prisoners enter, the second in which they are examined and

100 197194 Corporal Herbert Benoly RE.

101 The famous cartoonist: Mark Bryant, 'Bairnsfather, (Charles) Bruce (1887–1959)'', in *Oxford Dictionary of National Biography*, www.oxforddnb.com.

102 Lieutenant Edward Bury Suffolk Regiment. Transferred to the Intelligence Corps, January 1917. In 1918 he was removed from his duties for 'peculiar' behaviour and later left the army on mental health grounds: IG261, Third Army Intelligence to Assistant Commandant, Intelligence Corps, 10 January 1918; Fourth Army Intelligence to Assistant Commandant, Intelligence Corps, 21 April 1918; 9/12/1634 MS4t, War Office to GHQ, 21 June 1918, WO374/11291, TNA.

103 On 9 April the corps took 1,802 prisoners, with another 379 the following day: VI Corps, 'Notes for General Staff on Operations: Arras Battle', [July 1917], WO95/771, TNA.

the third, main, one into which they enter when examined and searched. The examination and writing down of details is a tedious and monotonous job and as the conditions are far from pleasant, at times it becomes downright nasty. Imagine a sixty-mile an hour wind driving across the ground, a blinding downpour of sleet and snow and myself, with the thin sheets we have to write on, being blown right and left, endeavouring to jot down, whilst standing, the rank, regiment, name and date of birth etc., of a gorilla-faced Teuton, stamping his feet and shaking and trembling with cold. Still, when we once got used to it, somehow the whole affair struck us as vastly humorous – if only Mr Bury would not be so fussy.

11 April 1917

Mr Bury came to our tent at 6.10 am and asked why we were so late but cleared off before I answered. We ran through 50 before breakfast and the lot were evacuated. Altogether, close on 2,000 prisoners have passed through here … The prisoners taken are nearly all a most sullen, evil-faced, stupid looking lot of men and it is only here and there that one drops on an intelligent looking fellow. These few are kept in separate pens and later are interviewed by Intelligence Officers though we also do some quiet questioning under the guise of enquiring how they fared. Just now, the old lot have cleared out and we are waiting for another 400. These never turned up so whilst the others had a bit of an evening free, Bury kept me in the office, making me daft by saying "I want to know how many of each regiment have been through here" and when I had almost finished (in spite of many interruptions, calling this man, finding that, with Bury dancing up and down the room, popping a continual stream of questions), he would suddenly change his mind and say "Oh, Corporal, instead of the number of men of each regiment, I think it would be best if you were to register them in divisions" and so on, continually contradicting, changing his instructions. He is very unpopular with us, especially since he referred to us as "those interpreter persons" and treating us as muck. There will be rumpus before long.

Before turning in, the RAMC Corporal told us about the wounded. How some of these wounded prisoners managed to walk from the trenches to here is a mystery. Many have shrapnel etc. in their legs, one had still two small pieces in his head and several have body wounds and practically collapsed on arrival. Red Cross vans were 'phoned for and the worst cases taken away. One thing I must admit, they are all very plucky as the conditions are rotten and these wounded lie huddled together, 30 in a tent. The unwounded simply tramp up and down all night … It was pitiful seeing the eagerness with which 6 of them clung to some large biscuit tins to sit on and to the way they hauled them about everywhere. Uncomfortable as we are in this tent, hearing the ceaseless tramping going on during the night in the cage outside makes me feel glad that we are in our own boots and not theirs.

12 April 1917

The rumpus came to head today. I complained about the rations first thing in the morning … All prisoners were sent away before 8 am. The usual excitement and messing about ensured and tempers became short. My complaint did not improve matters, but the usual "Will attend to this" was promised. Then a 'Court of Enquiry' was held and Bury blamed us for sending some 'special' men into the main cage. We denied this and enquiries showed that it was the fault of one of the Intelligence Officers. This made Bury more ratty still. Being altogether in the office, Bill spoke to him about our tent. Bury, desperate, told us that if we wanted a better place, we could find it ourselves. This was precisely what we wanted. So Bill and I went to Dainville and found an A1 place where the woman promised to cook our meals. Bury was obviously both surprised and a bit relieved and at any rate, it showed him we weren't fools.

After tea he held a 'lecture' on the formation of the German army from some of his notes, but it sounded so similar to ours, I remarked to him about it. He then discovered he had made a mistake but tried to blur it over. This opened out the others and in a short time we had Bury cornered, unable to answer our questions which we settled amongst ourselves. To some of our questions, his answer was "I'll ask Mr Woodhouse",[104] who was feigning sleep but we think thoroughly enjoying the 'lecture'. To others, "Well, that has changed during the war and is being reconstructed". At the end, we think Mr Bury felt very sorry he tried to lecture us – it was almost the other way round.

13 April 1917

Fine breakfast, once more round a table, decently, and not like pigs in a sty. At the Cage, no news of more prisoners, so we are all lying in the tent (as we may not leave the camp). We chat, discuss Bury, write letters and kill time as best we can … It seems strange that we should be so peaceful here while not 5 miles away there is continual fighting. The wind is blowing away from the line and we do not hear a sound.

---

104 Second Lieutenant E. de C. Woodhouse.

14 April 1917

Still nothing doing so we lay on the railway embankment and basked in the sun.[105] I went to Arras in the afternoon about pay and letters. The town is fuller than ever, every available square inch used, lorries and men everywhere. Saw Marsh about pay, who was very affable and chatted quite nicely. The whole lot have moved up from Warlus … Coming back to the camp after the roar of traffic was a great contrast, but to everybody's excitement, a batch of 9 appeared. They were Bavarians and looked a better lot than the first crowd. We went through the usual examination and I found a paper showing infantry signals to aeroplanes and vice-versa. One man was also more intelligent than the others though we could get nothing out of him. So Bury told Bill and me to come back at night and see whether with some whisky and soda, we could succeed. 9 pm saw us round a fire in the office, whisky and soda and biscuits on a table, everything very cosy. Bill fetched the man in, saying the officers were out, that we were on duty, had a fire, there was nothing doing, so would he like a chat? Yes, no objection – so in he came. We chatted about all sorts of things, Zeppelins, the use of Zeppelins in the Jutland Battle and by gradual stages, led on to the topic we wanted to know about. We pumped him hard and the whisky and water added to the enjoyment. The man, under the impression that all was just a friendly chat, became more open and frank and told us one or two interesting things. I must say, he was a nice fellow, had a refined face and as Bill remarked later, during the whole proceedings he maintained a very quiet, calm, possessed and dignified manner. One or two of our questions, he answered by a frank "I may not tell you" and "My honour prevents me from informing you" and when we left him, it was with a certain feeling of admiration and respect for the man.

15 April 1917

Towards evening a small batch of prisoners came in but there was nothing remarkable about them. They had been kept at Arras prison for fatigues and there being nothing more for them to do, they had been sent on here. Lederer,[106] another No. 24 Station IT interpreter, somewhat livened matters up by holding a pheasant supper which, together with other oddments bought, made us all sleep badly.

105 Between 9 and 11 April the corps took 2,294 prisoners, but from 12 to 30 April only 509: VI Corps, 'Notes for General Staff on Operations: Arras Battle', [July 1917], WO95/771, TNA.

106 206948 Sapper Richard Lederer. Before transferring to the Royal Engineers, he had served with 1/London Regiment.

16 April 1917

Nothing doing in the office, no prisoners came in and thus, to say the least, our job was a soft one. During the day, a train passed en route for Arras, filled with civilians and gaudily dressed officials, so evidently the line is through and civilians are returning. No doubt there will be a regular train service soon. News had come through that tomorrow we leave here for the prison at Arras.

17 April 1917

The news of our move was confirmed first thing and the arrangements were a masterpiece of muddle and incompetence on the part of Bury … An ASC man gave me a lift on his cart and in a blinding snowstorm we reached Arras. At the prison met Breakey & Co., had our new quarters shown me and we all started scrounging beds, paliasses, chairs etc. Towards evening the others came in, in a fine frame of mind, cursing Bury blue. In spite of his saying that all kit should be carried by limber wagon, he went back on his word and consequently the boys were again thrown on their own. Thank heaven that man has little or nothing to do with us in future … Slept the night in the local Intelligence 'Office', a cellar, in order to answer the 'phone, which happened to be broken, but red tape laid down that a man must be continually there, day and night, so telephone in order or not, being my turn, I had to be there.

18 April 1917

This continual biscuit and bully have made me constipated and my humour is not sweet. In fact I'm feeling decidedly pugnacious. This prison is a large stone building with whitewashed walls and the cells are on either side of the many corridors. Our sleeping quarters are in three of such cells and the doors still have a little peephole and slide hole … As regards work, there is next to none. It consists of detailing four men per day for duty in the office, one at night and otherwise expecting the arrival of more prisoners that never come. During the day we installed a stove in the front room and Bill had a big row with Lederer who, without doing a bit towards fixing it up, butted in and expected to enjoy all the privileges. Both men had certain points in their favour so I only tried to calm them down, but at the time of writing there is a stated of armed truce between our lot, the old No. 26 Station and No. 24 … Towards evening we had a stroll down from the Rue Saint Aubert to the Rue Gambetta, the road appeared like a seething mass of khaki. To get things at night is impossible unless you wait for ages in a queue and outside most shops there is a queue four deep.

British troops delivering German prisoners to Arras Prison, April 1917: IWM Q3573.

19 April 1917

Last year I remember that on my birthday I had to help dig a grave and especially recollect wondering where I should be 'this day in 1917'. Certainly Dame Fortune has been good to me last year as my most sanguine hopes never dreamt of the cushy and yet interesting future in store for me. Our chief [Captain Bowle-Evans][107] took us in hand today … [He] seems a jovial man, whose chief aim is to combine business with pleasure. The artistic arrangement and fitting up of his 'office' in Bill and my hands, to him is more important than the actual office work itself. We have scrounged some old tapestries and curtains and these we are putting up in an oriental fashion behind his 'desk', a good-sized table covered by some green cloth from heaven knows where, which I found in a cellar. He is a stickler for 'effect' and as if to excuse this fad, says "Nothing like a well-looking room to impose and impress those Bosche devils, eh what, by Gad?" Then he puts on his monocle, looks round and says "Beastly hole, this, what? But just wait until I've finished." He

107 Captain Wakefield Bowle-Evans Rifle Brigade. Thirty-eight-year-old former Honorary Attaché at the British Embassy, Tokyo: *Foreign Office List*, 1913; WO339/8753, TNA.

spends a long time deciding on the best position for something to be hung and when he seems to have definitely made up his mind, suddenly raps out "Damn it, pull the thing down, I don't like it after all". Although a typical 'knut', still, he's all there, is not afraid of speaking his mind, had plenty of damn and altogether has a peculiar mixture of both male and female characteristics which continually follow one another in 1001 ways, mannerisms, gestures, ways of talking, slight affectation, the *tout ensemble* making the man very attractive.

20 April 1917

Had breakfast in bed. For the first time since leaving Corps had some bread and rations other than iron rations. There is no doubt we are leading a very easy life. All this morning I tramped round town. I called in at a Monsieur François who showed me his shop – a nice state. It seems some men broke in … and stole all they could, even goods quite useless to themselves. They were Scottish troops and four were caught but managed to drop their stolen articles en route to the Town Major's, so when they got there, the evidence against them was slight and they got off with only a light sentence.

21 April 1917

Bill and I were on duty during the morning and put up the tapestries, making the office look more like a harem than an office. Captain Bowle-Evans was delighted and [we] went on a scrounging expedition to a forbidden portion of the prison, the pre-war Governor's quarters. We found another rug and hat and coat pegs. Bowle-Evans himself thoroughly enjoyed the scrounge, slinking about, as much afraid of being caught as we. Strolled over to the Wireless people, saw that Bill and my papers for skilled pay had come through and was not satisfied until I had seen the Lance Corporal fill in the increased rate of pay.

Saw Francke beautifully take the wind of out of the sails of two MPs. We were at Magniez's at 8.30 pm, half an hour after closing time. Francke was talking to Mme Magniez when, after a glass of beer, one of the MPs in his most officious manner howled out "Now then, Sergeant, time's up. Out you get." Francke never answered until, after a couple of louder 'howlings', the MP came right up to him and after repeating his statement, with all due pomp took out his notebook and asked "Who are you?" Francke calmly took out his cigarette case, coolly selected a cigarette, very quietly and slowly lit it, exhaled and just as nonchalantly answered "You ask me who I am – well I am Sergeant Francke, in charge of the Intelligence Police". Like two pricked gasbags, the MPs slunk out of the *estaminet*.

23 April 1917

Already during the night things became interesting and the drumfire at 4.45 am was terrific. We were up early and witnessed a continual stream of walking wounded passing our place … During the morning, the first batch of prisoners came along, about 6 of them, some wounded, the same weary, dirty, unshaven gorilla type of men we had at Dainville. As the day wore on, more and more came in until the impression I had towards night was that of a never-ending mass of round filthy faces, fatigue caps and gibbering voices, visions of wounded, bandages and red blotches, continual running about to see this and to see that, collecting the register sheets.

24 April 1917

We interpreters do not confine our work to interpreting alone. One of the main things we do is carefully discover 'specialists' of some kind, such as liquid fire operators, gas operators, trench mortar men, telephone experts and Listening Set men. Having found one, he is 'pumped' and all results given to Bowle-Evans who 'phones them to Corps. Very few have turned up and those that have are naturally extra wary and suspicious. Of course, each man requires a special treatment, some talk by almost being shouted at, others by gentle persuasive methods and others do not talk at all, averring that their 'feeling of honour' does not permit them. Again at times very simple facts provide the 'open sesame'. One man was quite communicative when he heard that I knew Hannover, where he had been. Another wounded man was the same because I got him some water quickly and had his wound dressed.

25 April 1917

The more I see of Bowle-Evans, the more do I like him. He is essentially a man who understands men, sees very deep and is quite capable of holding his own against anybody, but to the casual observer, to the average prisoner brought into the office for cross-examination, he must appear a bit of a harmless fool, yet his method of questioning is very tricky. The poor prisoner, scared at the idea of being in the presence of a highly placed officer and awed by the impressive office, is usually bowled over by Bowle-Evans's first question, "Well, my boy, where do you come from? From —" (referring to which part or sector behind the

German line) and according to the regiment, which Bowle-Evans knows, he asks from where in Germany the man hails. This is so different to what the prisoner expects that he soon rattles off his family history, as Bowle-Evans has a very sympathetic and taking way. Very gradually he works round to the actual state of affairs and it is rare that a man leaves without giving away some information. Round tea time, two prisoners came in from 121st Württembergers. One had been in a listening sap, sharing with another two-hour shifts, the length of time they had been in the trenches when our men came over without artillery preparation, his pal, in front, was killed and the body blocked the trench preventing the man behind from getting away.

28 April 1917

We got a small batch of prisoners ... Württembergers and on the whole are a fairly intelligent lot. Chatting on things in general an *Unteroffizier* was very down on our blockade. He said that we might rave about their killing women and children but that we were doing the same by the slow process of starvation and that whereas possibly they may have killed some in the heat of the moment, our was a systemic cold-blooded murder. I pointed out the Siege of Paris, to which he replied that the inhabitants had time to escape, and when I said that the blockade was only a means, if not the only means of quickly ending the war, he said "Then how little you know us Germans". Another prisoner was a boy, looking 16, though he was 19. He belonged to a machine-gun Company and was posted 500 yards ahead of their frontline, so when our barrage opened up, he got cut off and with the remainder of the team, were taken prisoners. He had only been a fortnight at the front. Sad stories one hears galore ... Felt rather queer all day and was glad when the examining and cross-questioning was over, enabling me to have a walk around.

29 April 1917

Still felt funny until I realized that it was bad constipation, so visited the RAMC Corporal who gave me a pill. An Alsatian was brought in and he absolutely hated the Germans and gave us as much information as possible ... I went to the YMCA service, but halfway through the pill worked and I bolted out. Much relieved and feeling better than for days past, returned to the Prison and had a long talk with Benoly on whether certain circumstances of sexual intercourse were immoral or not.

1 May 1917

Just as I casually strolled into the office, Bowle-Evans hung up the 'phone receiver and in a very excited voice said "Corporal, an airplane, German, has been brought down at Saint Catherine's (an Arras suburb) this morning. Cycle over at once and get all particulars and be quick about it." In the way fresh information has to reach the Intelligence HQ, our work is very similar to newspaper work – first man with the news gets the feather in the cap. So, with Wilkie, we lost no time and pushing along through the stream of lorries and general Army traffic, clouds of dust and usual hubbub, we ran into the APM. He informed us that the prisoners were with him, also the documents and the machine was further along. A big crowd surrounded the aeroplane. Shoving our way through, we gained the inner circle and for a few seconds just gazed at the machine. I then approached an officer, who gave me some information. It seems it was brought down at 9.30 am by the first shot of a Canadian Anti-Aircraft Battery. The pilot, after temporarily gaining control, tried a nose dive, but although skillfully handled, the undamaged landing was more by luck than management … One of the officers caught jumped on the machine's tail in an endeavour to smash it, but some of our fellows close by pulled him away. There was some doubt on the type of machine, most being in favour of an 'Improved Albatross Two-Seater Biplane', 250 horsepower, 6 cyclinders. Wilkie and I took down all bits of information possible. Except for a hole in the side showing where a piece of shrapnel had penetrated, jamming the engine and the slightly damaged tail, the whole machine was intact. This kind of 'work' is just to my taste, my one regret being that I could not make out a real exciting account of things in my report … [Then] Bowle-Evans turned up [and] I chanced to hear two officers talking of [a] camera thrown out [of the aircraft and that] it had been bagged by an officer in charge of an ammunition dump close by … We ran the officer to earth and collared the camera.

Towards evening, another bit of interesting work came my way. A 'phone message came through that a certain Division wanted a man to translate a captured document. I was sent … and found a plan of the Scarpe river showing over 20 machine-gun emplacements with details concerning them. I knew at once that this would be of tremendous interest to Bowle-Evans … I copied [it] word-by-word off the original on to the copy I had obtained and showed it to Bowle-Evans who seemed delighted. We worked at the thing, making out an intelligence report until 11.30 pm when it was sent to Corps by special despatch rider. As a result of this, the exact situation of these machine-guns will now be searched and photographed by aeroplanes, developed and handed over to the artillery who in turn will register on them and knocking them to hell, clearing the way for our infantry to pass over.

2 May 1917

Rumours about a 'do' tomorrow have been confirmed officially and as I write, the guns are going at it hammer and tongs. Benoly has had orders to pack up and be ready to move off to the Advanced Corps Cage and tomorrow night ought to see a new lot of men in ... [Here] in the office, whitewashed walls, barred window, maps all round, footsteps re-echoing in the building and outside the continuous 'c-crumph' of guns, with occasional louder ones as shells from the Bosches fall in the town, whilst somewhere, marching up and down the streets, the faint swirl of bagpipes is audible.

3 May 1917

The third 'Push' took place early this morning and as before the colossal gun fire kept on all night without a moment's pause.[108] Prisoners came in during the day and were not a pretty lot to look at. We had our usual work to do, but the sun was so hot, it made all and everybody, Bowle-Evans included, a bit slack and towards night he became, as he himself admitted, 'addled'. All the same, he is splendid man and very popular with us. He has decided personal magnetism and it is treat to see how polished and free his every movement and behaviour is when with officers, and also with us.

4 May 1917

Chatting with Bowle-Evans, he told me he was with Captain Bairnsfather during that period written about in *Bullets and Billets in Ploegstreet*[109] ... During the day he told us he was in Serbia during the war ... He also managed to obtain quite good information out of a Pole who came from Osowa, a place that Bowle-Evans knew well and which was the means of making this Pole quite chatty. The Poles are a very unsettled element in the German Army and this man frankly told us that the Poles he knew were dissatisfied and unruly in the extreme. He said that all Poles are

---

108 'At 3.45 am an attack was launched on the whole of the corps front, as part of a general offensive by the Fifth, Third and First Armies'. On that day and the next the corps took 158 prisoners: VI Corps, 'General Staff Summary', 3 May 1917, WO95/770; 'Notes for General Staff on Operations: Arras Battle', [July 1917], WO95/771, TNA.

109 Bruce Bairnsfather, *Bullets and Billets* (1917).

brought to fight on the Western Front, the Alsatians on the Eastern. Another tricky dodge to keep unruly spirits quiet.

Cycling down to see about letters, met Francke who remarked on a large column of smoke coming from somewhere. I cycled to the scene or as near as I dared – and heard an ammunition dump had been set on fire. As I stood watching the smoke, the noise of odd shells exploding was audible. Just as I had mounted to move off, an earsplitting, deafening roar, which nearly threw me off the cycle, together with a rocking like an earthquake, made everyone run for shelter – and I made off too and did not stop pedaling for all I was worth till I reached the other side of the town, where the Prison is. Half the ammunition dump had blown up. I was slowing up, when a shout was heard and everybody bolted … A second voice shouted out more distinctly "Gas". So, noticing that I was cycling with the wind, what there was of it, I again tore on, reached the Prison and then, comparatively safely, donned my gas mask. But the gas – a lot of the shells in the dump were gas shells – blew past without affecting us, though the Bosches, noticing the column of smoke … started shelling us galore as we lay in bed, gas masks close at hand, it was to hear one series of explosions, big and small, with an occasional extra loud one, rattling windows, making the ground rock and sending up a huge belt of flame that lit up the whole town, showing that another pile had gone up all together. It was both awesome to watch and awesome to listen to.

5 May 1917

Bowle-Evans had us in the office and gave us a very nice little lecture on how to do better, during the course of which he mentioned that thanks to the documents about machine-guns collared on 1 May, we had been able to take out all those guns. This was very encouraging.

7 May 1917

We heard the Warwicks were in this district,[110] so Wilkie and I cycled over to Saint-Sauveur, but after jumping over innumerable trenches, hauling our cycles along, we had no luck and were forced to return. All that district, once so well known, though only by trenches … is now a gigantic transport park with miles and miles of tents, horses, wagons and transport odds and ends.

110 16/Warwicks had arrived at Roclincourt on 4 May: WO95/1574/1, TNA.

9 May 1917

Borrowed [a] cycle and made a determined search for Linder and eventually ran him to earth right in the midst of nowhere. Found he was suffering from a boil on his leg and had been sick for several days. We talked about everything imaginable … It was a great treat seeing the fellow again and luckily I found him little changed.

10 May 1917

I saw Linder again during the afternoon and heard that Captain Martin,[111] one of the most popular officers of the old battalion, had been killed. I left Linder early as he had to go on Guard and cycled back through the heat and the accompanying dust and bustle of traffic. In great contrast was the calm peacefulness of the Divisional Band's evening concert. [We] lay on some brushwood and enjoyed every item. I kept closing my eyes, trying to imagine myself on some seaside pier, but the shock when opening them was not pleasant. Dead and stunted trees all round, shell holes, bare ground where once was a park and a little wood, all surrounding the bandstand, across which a tree had fallen, hit by a shell. The tree lay slanting across the top of the bandstand, not quite broken off at the roots and thus it still managed to show green leaves and thrive in general.

12 May 1917

Lederer, one of the old No. 24 Station men, began making himself obnoxious, stating that working for Mr Partridge, the Camp Commandant, he considered himself absolved from office work and night duty, to which I would not agree. We had a good set-to, he calling me picturesque things, I calling him a pig-headed, obstinate Jew. This having no effect, I used my authority and ordered him to sleep the night in the office as it was his turn and when even then he hesitated, I had him up before Bowle-Evans who soon told him his position. I now await his revenge or next move.

Just recently several rumours have been flying around about Bowle-Evans moving away and to cap all, Cecil Stallworthy, the old No. 26 Station operator, who has been up the line almost continuously, told [us] that ITs were being fixed up and that there was a good chance of our being used. This was rather a tickler, so we conflabbed with Bowle-Evans on our return to the Prison. We asked point-blank, "Are Signals the people who can shift us, or the Intelligence?" and he said straight "The

111 Captain M.J. Martin, died 9 May 1917.

Signals are the Powers that be". I then asked "Are we to understand that any day, considering what we have heard concerning ITs, we can expect to be sent up the line to a station, leaving this work and you behind?" and he answered "Yes, you are really only lent". So we went to bed, once more with visions of shells dropping all round, trench life etc., as just now, where these new stations are, trenches are mere shell holes joined together – no dug-outs, shelters, trench boards etc.

13 May 1917

Bill and I decided to see Mr Redgrave, but saw Mr Marsh instead. He cheered us up greatly, stating that we should only be wanted if these stations proved themselves successful and the chances were one in a million. So far, the lines had been blown up as fast as they had been laid down and the prospect was far from promising. In the meantime, Bowle-Evans has made a report to the effect that just now we are more useful in our present work than on IT work, that we work together well through mutual understanding and has asked for us, or some of us, to remain with him as assistants.

14 May 1917

We moved from our old rooms to different quarters in the Prison … This move is a great improvement as our old rooms, once-time prison cells, each had a sink hole, used by prisoners as lavatories and what not and an unhealthy, smelly, close atmosphere always used to hang over the place. Our lot, No. 26, now live in one room, No. 24 in an adjoining room. They are large rooms, have a window and in every respect are healthier and brighter. Whilst carrying our belongings across, we saw the lunatic, or shamming lunatic, having his lunacy driven out of him.[112] The general belief is that the man is acting and morning and afternoon he has to double, with knees up, all over the building, up and downstairs, everywhere.

17 May 1917

In spite of supper, slept well, only awakened by sudden shouting of the lunatic during the night. Rather ghastly. All facts concerning this 'lunatic' are being kept very secret. Had breakfast in bed. What a life this is. Were it not for the three months in the cellar, I should be ashamed of myself – but I'm not! The mystery surrounding Bowle-Evans somewhat cleared

112 For a summary of the army's approach to mental health, see Harrison, *The Medical War*, 110–19.

up by the news that he was attached to the British Diplomatic Legation at Madrid where he was when the war broke out and I knew from previous conversations that he had been in Russia, India, China and Japan, not to mention Egypt, Germany and France … Met Linder outside the entrance and we saw a splendid show, of which an exquisite rendering of the *Valse Triste* by an ex-conductor of Drury Lane Band with the pianoforte accompaniment was a feature, also a skit on the Revue *Of Course*. The whole was grand, beating both the 'Van John's' and 'The Thistles'. To get a seat, one had to book two days in advance.

19 May 1917

Still nothing doing here though it is said that we now are to do the examining of documents which means the work of another department on our shoulders but as we have so little to do now, it will be a change. We are told to expect prisoners tonight or tomorrow morning. With so little doing, I am reading some French books to kill time and improve my French.

20 May 1917

Our guns opened out at 9 pm last night and kept at it until this morning. I 'phoned through to the Advanced Cage where Mr Simpson informed me that no prisoners had turned up and that the whole affair seemed rather unsuccessful … Heard that the first Red Cross train had run into Arras and that nurses had been seen 'doing' the town. Would have liked to have had a view of them myself! Just outside the Prison here, a crowd from a Canadian Pioneer Battalion put down a narrow gauge railway. I noticed that half the men were Asiatic – prominent cheek bones, half yellow complexion, slit eyes and thick black hair.[113] The men working the line, shoving trolleys laden with stores, are from Barbados, a typical black lot, always smiling, singing with eyes and teeth flashin'.[114]

21 May 1917

To kill time, Bowle-Evans gave us a lecture in the shape of a chat, 'the first in a series', on the Bosch Army. [We] went to an afternoon performance of the 'Bow Bells' where Bill met another acquaintance of his, who informed us that he was the girl of the troupe succeeding the

113 For the recruitment of Asian Canadians, see Timothy Winegard, *Indigenous Peoples of the British Dominions and the First World War* (Cambridge: Cambridge University Press, 2012), 147, 152.

114 For Western Front labour units from the West Indies, see John Starling and Ivor Lee, *No Labour, No Battle: Military Labour during the First World War* (Stroud: Spellmount, 2009), 243–4, 247–8.

'Bow Bells',[115] namely the 'Barno's'. This fellow struck me as a bit soft, an amusing boaster and a most humorous liar. Amongst other things, he is supposed to have had given him 765 francs – during Xmas week, to have dined with generals, staff officers and what not and his experiences and relations with the fair sex can hardly be put down on paper.

22 May 1917

Bowle-Evans is having fits of artistic temperament, changing table cloths about, cutting rugs up and generally creating an atmosphere of nervous restlessness ... Things very quiet on our front. The Prison only has British prisoners, men misbehaving in the town, drunk etc. They have to do fatigues, are handcuffed to posts for two hours and do pack drill.[116] The lunatic, an athletic looking fellow with a beard, long hair and a large red sash like the Spaniards, still keeps up his game and is made to double up and down and round this building, followed by a Police Corporal shouting "Knees up there", "Go on you bastard" etc. – not a pretty sight.

23 May 1917

One German prisoner, an *Unteroffizier*, brought in. He was acting as a guide to the 119th Regiment, got lost in the ground mist, told his men to wait until he had found his way and trying to do so, walked into our lines ... Before the man was brought in to the office, Bowle-Evans said "Give me my staff cap, it looks more imposing". This done, the door opens, the prisoner walks in, clicks his heels, throws up his head and stands to 'Attention' until told to 'Stand easy'.

24 May 1917

On way to fetch dinner at Prison, ran into Bowle-Evans who gave me the staggering news that he had been ordered to Corps, that we should after all be separated and that our work here had come to an end. I need not emphasise how upset we all are. Nothing else was talked of all afternoon. Truly this is a life full of uncertainties. For a long time the hideous thought of returning to Signals haunted us, but just before falling asleep, an idea came into my head.

---

115 56th Division's concert party.

116 For the army's field punishments, see Clive Emsley, *Soldier, Sailor, Beggarman, Thief: Crime and the British Armed Services since 1914* (Oxford: Oxford University Press, 2013), 64–5.

26 May 1917

A bit bilious and not over fit. General Haldane[117] and Lord Loch[118] turned up this morning, but position concerning our movements unchanged … Later on, had great attack of 'fed-upness', no doubt due to our uncertain future. The office is half empty of things. Bowle-Evans clears off tomorrow and tomorrow I tackle Marsh to see whether we can remain here.

27 May 1917

Toddled round to Marsh and 'put things' to him. Result, Marsh thawed visibly and was 'graciously agreeable' to our remaining billeted at the Prison, though he did mention the feared threat about our attending the 8 am Parade. Heaven forbid. I quickly switched the conversation round to Bill's leave … Captain Bowle-Evans eventually left this afternoon. He had us in his office, said a few appropriate words of farewell, shook hands and dismissed us, locked the office up and off he went. I have an idea we shall meet again; I most sincerely hope we shall work together. But if not, I shall always think of him as a tall, broad-shouldered but rather stooping, well-bred, refined and polished type of gentleman, extremely tactful, slightly nervy yet not nervous, very clean in every way, with a weakness of setting straight any object out of line – a book not in line with others beneath it, a picture slightly slanting on a wall, a man's cap not straight on his head. I felt genuinely sorry to see him go.

28 May 1917

Captain Partridge, the Camp or Prison Commandant, had me in his office this morning. He asked me what the plans were. I tried to look clever and answered we were awaiting news from Corps. However, the man is a good sort and laughed and said "I know your game but I won't be a spoilsport. Join the men in physical drill in the morning and do a bit of gardening." He showed me a patch – once the exercise ground of special prisoners – and this patch we have to cultivate. Benoly and I started 'cultivating' it and an hour's work showed us that certain muscles needed 'cultivating' too … To Mme Candas at Achicourt … She put me on the track of a seed seller at Achicourt, but found the man was out so had to return empty handed.

---

117 Lieutenant-General Alymer Haldane CB DSO, GOC VI Corps.

118 Brigadier-General Lord Loch CMG MVO DSO, BGGS VI Corps.

29 May 1917

The No. 24 Station men indulged in their usual grumbling about the physical training, all the more because it was fixed first for 9.15 am, then 10 am, then 11 am ... Met Bill who is now fearfully excited about his leave being granted. It starts from midnight tonight. Saw Linder at Neuville-Saint-Vaast but he had to go on Guard at 5.30 pm which suited me very well as it left me time to again look up the elusive seed merchant, but he still eludeth me.

30 May 1917

During morning we had physical jerks in the garden behind the Prison, usual exercises, followed by games. Some Major of Police came round, kicking up a stink about the place being dirty and of course Partridge vented his wrath on me and I cursed the others and we had to clear things up.

31 May 1917

Unexpectedly five prisoners turned up. Their arrival almost upset the Prison, so much excitement. At once started cross-examining them and in the meantime our old friend Captain Bowle-Evans arrived on the scene. It was delightful having something real to do. These prisoners were intelligent enough but had little real news to impart and the Captain left before tea with all that he wanted ... Another prisoner [arrived], this time a deserter. He was a fearfully slow, ponderous kind of man, in fact I'm surprised he thought of deserting. He came over to us at 3 pm in broad daylight. I spent nearly 15 minutes trying to get out of him where he came over. The man was willing to talk but too dense to describe anything ... Later on in the evening [Bowle-Evans] came himself. The deserter, a Pole, was brought before him and Bowle-Evans gave him a short cross-examination. The Pole, obviously bored, perhaps a little off his head, sat, picking his nails and scratching his hair whilst Bowle-Evans addressed him. Instead of shouting at the man, Bowle-Evans thought the whole affair rather humorous.

2 June 1917

Ronnie Myers[119] turned up and he and I spent the morning together. I didn't know he had a commission ... It was quite nice seeing him. It shows how immersed one gets in this life and its doings as we hardly

119 Lieutenant Ronald Myers Intelligence Corps. Despatch rider in France, August 1914; commissioned April 1915: WO339/28679, TNA.

talked about anything else but the war, only just slightly touching home topics ... Ronnie is another 'I' man who thinks the war will end this year in a kind of stalemate.

3 June 1917

Linder was in a quiet mood; there is no doubt the fellow has become more quiet and silent though I wish I could get him alone for a chat, there are always so many dodging around. I had a light supper in order to fall asleep early, which I did, but an enormous crash shook me at 11.15 pm and hearing the hum of an aeroplane, knew a bomb had been dropped close by. Lying in bed, listening to the diminuendo and crescendo of the machine humming, expecting the next explosion, was a novel experience. More bombs were dropped, shells also came over, but I fell asleep as soon as things died down a bit.

4 June 1917

At Mme Pruvost's met a French interpreter who for six years, from 1906 to 1911, was Professor of French at Birmingham University at Bournbrook.[120] Was a very nice man to talk to. We had a splendid meal; soup, mutton, peas, carrots, cheese and fruit, with white wine, beer, red wine, champagne, coffee and rum. Soon after I got back to the Prison, Bowle-Evans turned up and brought some documents for us to examine. He also settled some little differences with Partridge and encouraged me by arranging lectures to take place here ... As I thought, soon after 10 pm the hum of aeroplanes became audible, first faintly, then louder, until we knew that they were over the town. A couple of distant crashes showed that two bombs had fallen and a minute or so after, five terrific crashes close by shook the building. Later on I heard 30 horses had been killed but no men.

5 June 1917

Captain Bowle-Evans came down and gave us a lecture. We are keeping well in touch with him. He brought us down a pile of German newspapers to wade through in search of interesting news. Looking through one after dinner (*Die Frankfurter Zeitung*, 27 May), it mentioned the admission made by a German doctor of the [corpse factory] ... This admission was

120 Probably Paul Demey, lecturer in French at the University of Birmingham from 1902 to 1920. During the war he served in the French army as an interpreter attached to the BEF; information supplied by Cadbury Research Library, May and October 2013.

first made in this Prison by a German doctor – a prisoner.[121] The point is "Are dead human bodies used or only dead animals?" Everybody seems to jump to the conclusion that the chemicals are drawn from the bodies of dead human beings, though I fail to find anywhere any proof – though of animals there are proofs enough.

6 June 1917

Spent all morning trying to discover bits of interesting information from the Bosche newspapers. One reads a few things outsiders do not hear about: Siberia rising up and trying to make herself independent, also Finland. These papers naturally contain a lot of lies, but also a lot of truth. I notice that the Allied official reports are always published, more often than we publish the German. The leading articles all try to prove that our 'Pushes' have been unsuccessful and have been knocked on the head.

8 June 1917

Communiqué states that Messines and Wyschaete have been taken with 5,000 prisoners.[122] Let's hope this continues … Bowle-Evans, speaking over a private wire, informed me that five prisoners were expected … The Bosches came towards dusk and we each questioned a man. Later Bowle-Evans himself came down and we cross-examined a man through and through, though at this time of night the whole affair is a bit of a farce – the prisoners tired out, we too rather inclined to yawn and altogether one is not at one's best.

9 June 1917

Busy all morning with the prisoners. They are a placid, docile group, very pleased at being out of everything and very chatty. They belong to one of the regiments (the 163rd) of which we nearly captured a whole battalion in April and these men are drafts and tell me they have heard from their pals (in London). They all hope to go to England.

I still continue my midday meal at Mme Pruvost's and have a very good insight into a typical French family's meal customs. There is Monsieur Martel, the 'patron', also called 'Papa Martel' who has stuck here since the beginning. Before the war he was a gymnastic instructor. Then there is Monsieur Masquelin, a French Sergeant who has to do with the

121 Third Army intelligence summary, 29 April 1917, WO157/151, TNA. For a discussion of this infamous propaganda story, see; Beach, *Haig's Intelligence*, 54–5.

122 On 7 June Second Army captured the Messines Ridge south of Ypres.

local railway and Monsieur Crainket, who always wears a white tie and a fancy waistcoat and a frock coat, also engaged on the railway. And lastly, Monsieur Carpentier, belonging to the Prefecture whose business is to visit those places where repairs are deemed possible. We start the meal with potage, vegetable soup, and then Mme Pruvost fills our glasses with beer, at the same time serving us with meat and vegetables. The party all tuck their serviettes in at the neck and make a big noise whilst slopping the soup down but otherwise are extremely polite … The talk is usually about the War, the dropping of bombs and local gossip. After the meat and several glasses of beer, the latter are emptied and we also have a glass of wine with the cheese and fruit. Peculiar but nice custom this. Then after an exchange of cigarettes, folding up of napkins, we shake hands, bow slightly, wish each other *au revoir* and *bon chance* and depart. If guests are present, the drinks vary. I have had white wine, beer, red wine, more white wine, champagne and coffee and rum, all for lunch and all for the ridiculous price of 2½ francs.

10 June 1917

Got a surprise today. Mr Partridge is going on leave. The infantry are leaving here and he had no Quarter-Master, so he has made me Quarter-Master. I did not relish the appointment, but the man being in a hole, he appealed to my 'helping him' in his difficulty. I could not very well refuse, so most of the day I spent messing about with indent books, ration strengths and 'if 41 men eat 13 loaves, how much tea and sugar do they consume?'

11 June 1917

In pouring rain, Benoly and I went to fetch the rations from the fishmarket. On return to Prison, had an arduous job chopping the meat into various pieces; 12 for rations for Advanced Cage, 5 for the infantry and 7 for us. Still, I managed it, feeling a cross between a butcher and a grocer … The APM came to see me. His interview with me was remarkable to say the least. He informed me the Hun prisoners were being removed with escort, also that the British Police Guard were leaving and that we interpreters would be the sole inmates and that I would be nominally 'OC Prison'. I have imagined myself being a lot of things, but never 'Governor' of a prison without prisoners in.

12 June 1917

Bill and I had lunch at Mme Pruvost's and on arrival back, found Benoly busy with a Hun prisoner. Captain Bowle-Evans arrived and took him in hand. Benoly has had a row with Lederer who is and has been the *bête noir* of our crowd. Lederer refused to give a hand at helping and when Benoly asserted his authority, Lederer told him to go to hell. Of course, Benoly could do only one thing, report Lederer, which he did. The Captain took short measures and ordered Lederer back to Signals – in other words, gave him the sack. We are well rid of him and I am jolly glad that he has gone.

14 June 1917

I soon found out that … today was going to be eventful. The first hint was the arrival of rations for 500 men. Then came a batch of 10 cyclists as guards. Then followed a visit of the Provost Marshal, a Major Graham, and lastly, of Captain Bowle-Evans himself. Result, I had the arranging to do of the cooking and rationing of prisoners, of their disposal in cells, of their being searched, registered and cross-examined and 101 further details, too minute to put down but which had to be attended to and which took up time.

At length the Huns turned up, an ungodly mass of men, dirty, unshaven, partly with steel helmets, though mostly with fatigue caps perched on their round heads.[123] Things went off well, considering. I had to march them round to be searched, detail the Guard to accompany them (after a bit of 'Order arms, fix … bayonets'), detail the boys for taking down on the Register Forms and then, when that was done, see the Huns had tea, bully and biscuits. But I was never still for a moment and the last thing I saw in my mind's eye before falling asleep was a crowd of ape-like faces, fatigue caps, jabbering voices, a lot of English and German talking, a continual horrid smell of 'sweat' and the whole jumbled into one, resembled a jigsaw puzzle before being put together.

15 June 1917

It seems our attack came as a complete surprise. There was no artillery preparation, our men just hopped over and gained their objectives in 7 minutes. All today I have been cross-examining or comparing the Register Forms with the actual number come in; was a man short. The Captain was naturally rather upset … The men [were] paraded and that the missing man [was] found, so once more peace reigneth.

123 On 15 June the corps took 178 prisoners: VI Corps, 'Notes for General Staff on Operations: Arras Battle', [July 1917], WO95/771, TNA.

17 June 1917

News that 26 of the prisoners were to leave. This they did ... Just round tea-time, instructions came for 88 men to be evacuated. I put the *Vize-Feldwebel* (Sergeant-Major) in charge, explaining what I wanted to him and he saw to the rest – very simple way. Amongst these last prisoners were some very decent men. One particularly, a man called Wachsmann, who had been in New York for some years, also a lot in Pernambuco [Brazil]. He was a refined fellow and it struck me how, whereas a soiled appearance, unshaven face etc. makes a common looking man appear more of a brute – in a way, it makes a refined face and dignified bearing appear still more refined and dignified – though only if looked at from a certain point of view. [We] accompanied the Huns to the station and I could not help saying "Good luck to you, Waschsmann". One becomes rather hard and callous with the general crowd, but when one, obviously above the average, comes along, then one's sympathy gains the upper hand.

18 June 1917

We got through the cross-examination ... but just as we finished, some men of the 76th Regiment came in and more questioning ensued. Then the documents have to be dealt with. They are in Tucker's hands and I must say he is very good at the job. When these papers first come in, a huge pile like a big mail in business, they rather frighten one. First each letter, notebook, slip and postcard is read through. Any containing items of economical or military interest are scored with blue pencil and put on one side, the remainder are torn up. Those put aside are then again divided into 'papers giving addresses' and 'names of town of sender' and 'papers of exclusive military or economic interest'. The former are then entered on special forms and through reference either confirm previous reports of the position of a regiment, or determine a new position taken up. The latter contain more actual information such as machine-gun defensive methods, artillery observations, diaries, all of which come under this heading. But this work entails a great deal of care and time. I was up until midnight on this job.

19 June 1917

In batches of one and two, Huns come in, all pleased to be away from the fighting. Some are quite decent fellows and fraternise with the Guard here in a really laughable manner. One fellow, called Hentze, spoke a bit of English and knew Hildesheim well. He with two others help the cooks and they are the best of pals. Many may object to this, but on the other hand, when these prisoners can write, they will give the lie to the many statements flying round in Germany of how badly we treat their prisoners.

20 June 1917

The documents have been finished and most of the cross-examinations. Just after luncheon, a batch of 39 left, leaving only 4 behind, and now, for the first time since [14 June], I feel I can lean back in my chair and take things a little bit easy. But still, irritating trifles arise. Although I counted this batch four times over, yet one beggar managed to slip in unnoticed and, of course, one too many was found the other side and he was returned with the escort together with polite hints for 'the NCO responsible' to take further lessons in counting.

21 June 1917

Bar the Alsatian [Brandenbourg], all prisoners now cleared out. This Alsatian is quite a good fellow and hates the Huns like poison. He says he is ashamed of being in the German uniform. He is to be taken over by the French authorities and is very keen on getting away and to start on some work or other.

22 June 1917

Captain Bowle-Evans informed No. 24 that they would have to go to Wireless. This came as the climax to many talks and discussions, both to the fact that we should never return to Wireless and also that we should … His management has been an adroit mixture of keeping us here together up to the present, presumably for our benefit (and no doubt it was) and in reality for serving his own ends. But to do the man justice, he had treated us better than any other officer I have known and personally I consider myself very lucky in not being one of the staff of No. 24 Set.

23 June 1917

Got another Hun in. He was a tough customer. Refused all information and acted the silly goat until pulled up. Falling into one or two traps we put during the course of questioning woke him up a bit too. But little or nothing was to be got out of him. Eventually I had an idea. I went to into the kitchen … and told Brandenbourg … to act as decoy, play the *Vaterlands-liebe* [love of country] game, and chatting with the man, get out of him all he could. This plan worked well and after dinner, when Wilkie carried on, we had already the regimental resting village and the news that a relief was taking place [on 25 June]. Cycled over to Corps with my report, which I gave personally to Mr Sykes and he advised me, considering the type of man we had to deal with, to leave him alone for a time.

25 June 1917

Many rumours fly around of recommencement of IT sets up the line, of moving up, of numerous promotions, Benoly and my names being mentioned. There is no doubt that great changes at Wireless are in the air. Nearly all men already promoted are leaving altogether for the Divisional HQs … But we interpreters remain at Corps and as far as I can make out, Redgrave will only have the two IT sets and two Wireless stations to run … No. 24 are already up the line and I suppose we of No. 26 will follow too.

26 June 1917

Went up with the ration cart to Advanced Corps Cage where at present Bill hangs out … I found Bill in a tent on a crest overlooking the valley with a good view of the Bosches shelling one of our batteries. He and I sat down, opened a bottle of whisky and sat chatting and smoking.

27 June 1917

A further chat with … Brandenbourg, yielded interesting points about the Wotan Line. It seems the Bosches are making dug-outs 150 metres in front of the front line to crawl into and shelter in when the front line is being heavily shelled. I had not finished making out my report on this when a French interpreter came and, taking particulars of Brandenbourg, told him he can expect to leave here any day now … Mr Partridge [the Commandant] has returned from leave.

28 June 1917

Two more prisoners came in and got average amount of information out of them. They had to deliver a message to the HQ of the Battalion in the line, but lost their way. In front of our line, they heard a sentry calmly say "Come on, come on", thought it was a German "Komm, komm" and suddenly found they were among the British.

29 June 1917

Went up to Advanced Cage to relieve Bill [for the day]. Just now I am once more in the wilds, with guns booming all round. Surrounding me is desolation with tracks and roads and old trenches cutting through the grass. Here and there are artillery and transport parks, dug-outs and patches of brown waste land. During the lulls between the guns firing, nothing is heard beyond the hum of aeroplanes flying and the singing of larks. An ideal spot for philosophising and thinking of things in general. There is just enough on to make the surroundings interesting – as far as it goes – but not dangerous enough to cause any anxiety or nervousness.

1 July 1917

The surprise of the day came as I 'phoned as usual through to the Intelligence. A thin voice curtly told me to be prepared to move tomorrow morning at 10 am. I recognised the voice as that of Captain Evans,[124] the chief of intelligence, not Captain Bowle-Evans' voice. Damned nuisance, this short notice, so many things still to be done … Made out an inventory of stores, packed up Bill's things here in his box and I am now going to have a last read in bed.

2 July 1917

We were all bustle, packing up, settling this, settling that and just as we were ready to move to the bottom of the road to meet the lorry … The move was typical of the Army. The arrangements were that we should be at the bottom of the road at 10 am to meet a certain lorry which would take us to Duisans. Actually, the lorry never turned up and we waited patiently, at first in good spirits, later on more and more bored … at 3.15 pm I sent Wilkie to 'phone up and just as he returned, the lorry came. At Duisans, the Camp Commandant's clerk gave us our billets but at each one we had some difficulty, so after tea in the Church Army hut we tackled the Camp Commandant personally who told us to take 'No. 25'. But the good lady at No. 25 was not disposed to take us even into her room. I suppose she thought us just common or garden Tommies trying to get a good billet on our own. Thus we fell back on the French Mission whence an interpreter came round and settled everything so well with Madame of No. 25 that she actually agreed to cook for us … We had to pass through the chateau grounds and I particularly noticed the flowers, the atmosphere of luxury, the walks, the beautiful flower beds and trees, all at their best. Further on, three officers and a French girl were playing tennis. My, it *did* make me long and crave for a game. I found myself clenching my fists and yearning for one free afternoon to meet with

124 Captain Arthur Evans RMLI, GSO2 (Intelligence) VI Corps since 26 May 1917: *Navy List*, January 1919.

those officers on an equal footing and play, with a yearning really quite abnormal. One gets these spasms when something forcibly reminds one of the dear old home days.

4 July 1917

Felt hopelessly fed up and bored after tea and went out to read close by the Hospital Camp. Several nurses were strolling around but hospital rules and etiquette prevented them from so much as looking in my direction as they passed. Still in a very funny mood, returned to billet, then went out again to a field and sat on a log, trying to make out what was the matter with me. Eventually saw some men having a game of football so went and joined them and had quite an enjoyable bit of exercise which completely chases away my morbid humour. Back in the billet, had a cold tub and much refreshed and with my humour quite restored, went to bed.

5 July 1917

Saw Benoly who has come down here as Corporal in charge of escort to some British prisoners, including Denton, Redgrave's batman, who was found drunk and disorderly … Have been trying all day to catch the Captain who seems to spend the greater part of his time on a motorcycle. I have some letters for him to censor.

6 July 1917

We leave tomorrow for the 'desert'. Have heard nobody give the place a good name yet.

7 July 1917

Up early, everybody packing, getting in each other's way, tripping over odd pieces of kit, but gradually the disorder became less, things disappeared like magic, I settled up accounts with Madame and we left for the lorry starting point … We were one of a column of several lorries and the dust thrown up soon covered everything, making us look like bakers.

Passed through Arras and at Beaurains, which used to be in German hands, saw several parties of men and repatriated civilians digging for treasure, i.e. money and valuables they had buried in the ground before the Germans took the village. The country we then passed through was one vast panorama of desolation. Ruined villages, razed to the ground, in many cases already so overgrown that one had to look twice before noticing that once a house had stood there. Transport lines, huts, temporary shelters, somewhat relieved the monotony, but on the whole the picture can be best described as a series of rolling brown plains, with occasional green patches, with here and there some shapeless wall, overgrown with creepers, showing the site of a once-time village, a few miserable trees, the whole dotted with tents and horse lines and carts.

We reached our destination, Bihucourt, [north-west] of Bapaume, about midday and after the usual bit of looking around for a billet, fixed up in the Intelligence Clerks' Hut and we also mess with them … We are in the grounds of a once-time chateau but of the chateau itself there only remains a sad pile of bricks, stone and masonry. The garden must have been pretty, though our huts, built in every nook and corner, disfigure it most horribly. Of the village, only one house is standing, all else in ruins, with roads cleared through. The nearest civilians are 10 miles away.

8 July 1917

Walked over to the next village, Achiet-le-Grand and found it quite interesting. A number of Indo-Chinese troops are stationed there and wear khaki, not like the usual French troops.[125] It was strange to hear them jabbering away in their lingo. Besides a YMCA there is a Church Army hut, an Expeditionary Force canteen and [45th] Casualty Clearing Station.

9 July 1917

Signs of wanton German destruction are everywhere. All these villages are in ruins and it does not take long to see who did the damage; very few shell holes are visible, yet every house, without exception is uninhabitable. The destruction is such that one cannot picture what the village appeared like in one's minds' eye as one looks round – just one monotonous sequence of bricks, stones, plaster, general debris, wood, rafters and weeds and grass and flowers growing over the pile, meets one's eyes.

10 July 1917

Redgrave … informed us that Wireless was moving today to Béhagnies, a village close by and that he would call in here, Corps HQ, for paying us. He also gave us the welcome news that almost each week, on Wednesdays, the boxcar would be going to Amiens and that we were to arrange

125 The French army recruited four combat and fifteen labour battalions for service on the Western Front, mostly from Annam and Tonkin: Kimloan Hill, 'Sacrifices, Sex, Race: Vietnamese Experiences in the First World War', in Santanu Das (ed.), *Race, Empire and First World War Writing* (Cambridge: Cambridge University Press, 2011), 53–6.

amongst ourselves, who was to go … The YMCA men, two ministers, were very decent, gave us some cake and had a chat with us.

11 July 1917

Had tea at a Church Army Hut. The town is full of Australians and I enjoyed watching them as much as anything. There are some fine types of men among them with sharp, clear-cut features.

12 July 1917

We are beginning to find this place not so bad after all. Wilkie and I had a rare treat this afternoon. We found [a] swimming bath … and the sun being warm, we had a simply gorgeous swim. It is months since I so enjoyed myself. These baths were originally built by the French as a reservoir, presumably destroyed by the Germans and now restored by us … After tea, we again went to the pictures but on return found that a German prisoner had turned up. The 'Major' was 'doing' him; later Captain Bowle-Evans took him in hand.

13 July 1917

Actually did a bit of work, dealing with documents and translating a leaflet of Bosche Gas Precautions. I suggested to Bowle-Evans that when the [Intelligence] Bs leave, we take over their hut and introduce an office system. However, the usual 'bear it in mind' answer only was forthcoming. Well, I can only show willingness to work and if work is slack or even nothing forthcoming, I am not letting the chance slip by to enjoy myself, so after dinner, [we] had another glorious swim.

14 July 1917

A number of the Indo-Chinese 'patronise' the reservoir. They are small muscular fellows, very much like Japs. Excellent swimmers and their diving very clever …

I am beginning to know the fellows here a bit more. They are a quiet lot. The mealtime politeness is almost painful, "After you with the butter, please" or "Please help yourself first" – like a bally girls' school, very different to our "Chuck the possy over" or "Hurry up with the bread" or "Are you going to keep me waiting all night for the butter?" etc. Still, it's good to be amongst more refined men again. They are all draughtsmen, surveyors, chemists, engineers and so on attached to Corps Staff, the same as we are now, on Intelligence.

15 July 1917

Bill went over to Béhagnies [to see] Captain Redgrave … It seems [he] began to fight for us interpreters to have higher pay. He got to fairly high quarters when all his endeavours went 'pop'. The reason was, unfortunately just at that time we were all very much under suspicion, in fact being watched, because an interpreter at a neighbouring Corps Hun prison cage was caught in the act of helping a cousin of his, a German prisoner, to escape. Let alone asking for our pay to be increased, poor Redgrave had to guarantee each one of us, give our whole history individually and, according to Bill, when Redgrave told the powers that be that he mixed with us, when alone, as equals and treated us as superior to others owing to our superior education, they were supposed to have held up their hands in horror, like a pack of old Mrs Grundys.[126] We thought this a rare bit of humour.

17 July 1917

I paid a visit to the Stores and drew a new tunic and cap, so feel fairly 'posh' … This lazy life is making me feel unsettled and for the first time I have thought of offering to go up the line; only the idea that the other lads may be incriminated and that Bowle-Evans is away on leave prevent me from doing so at once.

18 July 1917

Drove in the boxcar to Amiens. The drive to Albert was along the main road, cutting through the scene of the Somme fighting of the summer of 1916. Le Sars, Courcelette and Pozières were just masses of almost completely overgrown bricks, stones, wood and general debris. This almost tropical-like overgrowth hid very ugly sights. All woods were just tree stumps, quite black and charred, not a touch of green and all around, the ground was churned up, revealing remains of blown-in or crushed dug-outs, stakes sticking out, haphazard remnants of barbed wire, the only ordered thing being the beautiful macadamised road cutting through it all. The shattered remnants of 8 or 9 tanks were visible, some quite close to the road and at one spot a German train had either been bombed or severely hit by shellfire – the trucks and engine lying upturned beside the road. Passing through Albert, saw the famous church and hanging Madonna figure. The other side of the town, the scene changed completely – everything as peaceful as could be, beautiful

126 Fictional character renowned for her conventional social views.

woods, cultivated ground, civilians, as great a contrast as could be, if compared to the Albert–Bapaume side. At Amiens, as before, my greatest pleasure was watching people, the trains (just as bed seems to be one of the items of 'home', so trains denote a complete return to civilisation), the shops etc. … Today, though showery, everybody was dressed in summer things and the effect, especially of the damsels, was quite pleasing to one's eye … Unfortunately our stay in Amiens was short and by about 6 pm we were once again back in the wilds, far away from anywhere.

19 July 1917

Down here at Corps HQ necessity had at last compelled me to shave every day. I often wondered how long I should manage to keep on the 'shave every odd day' system. Still nothing doing in the shape of work and a lot of my time is spent reading. All manner of books come one's way and I've read some by Elinor Glyn and Victoria Cross[127] that are commonly known as 'hot'. There is no doubt of their being immoral, dealing openly with sexual questions, but looking at the themes and the general working out of the plots, without letting oneself be influenced by the suggestiveness or lower meaning, from each one book some good can be drawn.

20 July 1917

During the day we had some documents and newspapers to wade through. The articles of the latter about the reconstruction of the German mercantile fleet, of the 'Dutch Potato Question' and our treatment of neutrals, were interesting … A chat with Bill … [and] broached the question to him of my offering to return to Wireless, being fed-up with present conditions. We hummed and haa'd and eventually agreed that Bill … [would ask] if we were being kept here for a certain reason, the real object of which was still to come, or only for 'in case something unforeseen should crop up'.

21 July 1917

News came through that Redgrave's IT set had had good results and that we could expect to be called on any time now to Wireless. Although I prefer the work here, especially when something is on and we are busy, nevertheless I prefer Wireless when things are so quiet here.

---

127 Pseudonym of Annie Sophie Cory.

22 July 1917

Captain Sykes … told me to get "the time, circumstances and method of escape of a German prisoner recaptured". I found him in the 49th Casualty Clearing Station with a wound through his abdomen. But he was quite cheerful and after a little tactful clapping on the back, he told me the story: [On 16 July], he and another decided to escape, the night being dark, with rain falling. They had noticed the barbed wire had been cut some 10 metres to the left of the latrines. At 11 pm they left the hut, ostensibly to visit the latrines. The sentries were having a chat together some 30 metres to the right of the latrines. So they took this chance and wriggled through and disappeared unnoticed. Travelling by night and hiding by day, living on a tin of bully and four biscuits, by [19 July] they got as far as our Third Line. A sentry of ours, however, saw them passing through a chalk pit. It was a moonlit night and although 15 metres away, they were visible. He gave the alarm and when the two Germans were close enough, they were fired at. One was killed, the other wounded and then he was brought down to this hospital where he told me his story.

24 July 1917

During the morning Sir Douglas Haig turned up.[128] Passed him close to and had a good look at him. Looks a bit different to pictures. Although oldish, had very keen features. I wonder whether as a result of this visit something is going to happen here? … This idle state bores one to extinction. Never believed that laziness could so get on one's nerves.

25 July 1917

Bad news about Russia, things seem to be in a hopeless mess.[129] I'm sorry for Kerensky,[130] but admire him fighting against all these odds.

26 July 1917

[To Doullens where] we had a sit-down and drink in a proper café, with marble tables outside on the pavement, with creepers and trees in pots, all complete *à la real Continentale* … During the afternoon we wandered about, I had my photo taken, bought things for the boys and then we returned with the stuff. Judging by the roads and the jolting, the eggs

---

128 Haig arrived at Bihucourt at 1130 to meet with the Third Army commander and three corps commanders: Haig typescript diary, 24 July 1917, WO256/20, TNA.

129 Russia's new provisional government had launched an offensive on 1 July, but on 19 July the Germans responded with a successful counter-offensive.

130 Alexander Kerensky, Russian Prime Minister and War Minister.

must have suffered. I just gave them to the Mess on arrival and cleared off before any complaints could be made.

28 July 1917

Bill had a good post in so treated us all round to beer, biscuits, toffee etc. He thoroughly enjoys treating us when he can. We went for our usual bathe and lay as bare as when born in the grass, drying in the sun … We had also received an invitation to play tennis! The court was in the field the other side of the wood behind here. The net is some wire-netting tightly drawn and the ground is not too bad, though still requires a lot of grass tufts removing and I expect the next mornings we shall spend pulling them up and trying to roll the surface. Bill and I had quite a good game, very warm, but most enjoyable.

29 July 1917

Walked over to Achiet and listened to a band, though the antics of a very officious, fat, ginger and perspiring Sergeant-Major acting as conductor amused me almost more than listening to the band, which played rather gingerly itself.

30 July 1917

Bill and I had a spell of digging or shovelling away tufts of grass off the so-called tennis court but a sharp spell of rain put an end to the work. We then went to the EF Canteen at Achiet and had tea. I bought some very nice nougat tablets which, failing chocolate, take the place of my usual 'snack in bed' tit-bit before falling asleep. Thence we strolled to the pictures and saw a magnificent show. One film, called *The Mysteries of New York*[131] being especially good. Not much of a mystery, really.

31 July 1917

We had our usual morning lecture and were told that the offensive up north had started, so far with the two first objectives taken.[132] The Captain gave us certain work to do, dealing with some selected villages behind the German lines opposite us. It is surprising how from various sources we get to know the construction of each house, the wells, underground passages, sunken roads etc. Bill and I marked out the tennis court and had a set against two fellows whom we beat 6–5. Very enjoyable playing though the court is not exactly *à la* Wimbledon.

---

131 Possibly William Parke, *The Mystery of the Double Cross* (series) (March 1917).

132 The infantry attack of the Third Ypres offensive commenced on 31 July.

1 August 1917

News came that Wilkie and 'The Major' had to report to Redgrave prior to going up the line. This came as a shock and seems to be the thin end of the wedge before [Bill and I] go up … Personally, I should not mind.

2 August 1917

Caught the 7.45 am train to Amiens … [which] is quite a nice town but soaked with loose women and temptations are not lacking … Now, I am subject to the weaknesses of the flesh as any other fellow, especially so after months of more or less life away from female attractions. With plenty of cash and time to spare, the desire to pick up an attractive looking loose girl was great. However innocent looking they may seem a certain look, nod of the head, motion of the arm, soon show what they are after the moment you slightly stare at them. Most of the morning I was debating with myself whether to risk the game or not. I frankly admit that it was more than fear of the results than any other reason that decided me not to, but temptations never ceased all day. First was outside a shop listening to a gramophone. Two quite smart girls, with a most ingratiating smile, enquired whether I was fond of music and then went on to ask whether I would accompany them. Later, just as I was getting on a tram, some very magnetic smiles made me decide to keep off. Heaven knows how much I wanted to follow them. At luncheon, a girl was sitting at the next table. For a time I thought she was different, just a girl clerk. Then I started chatting with some French soldiers opposite and somehow, whenever I happened to glance at her, my look was answered by a faint smile. As I rose to leave, she rose too and started talking, but I politely left her and went to a café for a coffee and rum and soon after two others came in with their trade written on both faces and clothes. Again those inviting looks and beckonings. The rum got into my head and I began to think "Damn the consequences" but something, some sleeping second personality or willpower made me get on a tram and standing on the rear platform, the wind cooled me a bit. Then went to a cinema where my restlessness also the terrible piano playing made me go out half way through the show. Some idea prompted me to visit the lowest quarters of the town. I strolled up but the atmosphere was so disgusting I quite decided that the game was not worth the candle.

3 August 1917

Lederer and Tucker have now come here instead of Wilkie and White. The former is very fond of showing off his German and I had to choke him off at tea … Altogether, although on the surface we scrape along somehow, beneath there is not much love lost and half our talk is in the shape of veiled sarcastic remarks, slights and insults, one trying to outdo the other. Bill hates him and he and Lederer have had one or two open rows. Towards evening I met Mr Redgrave and he gave me the interesting news that with the expansion of Corps, another IT set was to be put out and that if results were obtained, he would have to call on … Bill and myself.

5 August 1917
The bubble of excitement caused … [by] Redgrave's news about our being wanted, has died down and now tennis is the main attraction. In boiling weather spent an hour rolling the court, but then, although by no means perfect, we could not resist the temptation and so Bill and I went at it hammer and tongs till tea and after tea, until dusk. The War doesn't concern us in the least down here.

6 August 1917
We played a set [of tennis] which I won 6–1. In his endeavours to beat me in the second set, when at two games all, [Bill] broke his racquet which put an end to things.

7 August 1917
Had a chat with Redgrave … Perhaps next week he will take me up to a likely spot where out IT set could be laid out and what with talking of this and talking of old times, we chatted quite a long time together.

8 August 1917
A bathe with Lederer who on the strength of his going on leave on Friday, bought me a cigar. A very talkative fellow who ends every sentence with "Now don't you think so too?" It gets on one's nerves.

11 August 1917
Had a glorious run to Amiens. Marsh came and was as charming as a man could be … The driver and I had lunch together and later met Marsh outside 'Charley's Bar', an American bar. The visit there seems to have put him in an excellent humour. He and I went shopping together and when he was not paying compliments to the girls in the shop, he was paying them to me for the excellent way I had helped him. Shopping in Amiens is a combination of flirting and business, the two go hand in hand. One does not see the black-dressed girls as in our shops. The average

girl is something pleasant to cast one's eyes on and she herself knows it, and how to dress too. Marsh's game was to put the flirting before the business and in his broken French he got on famously. I understood that he wished us to be, so to speak, on an equal footing, i.e. shopping to be quite informal, but I had enough tact to keep in the background until, floored himself, he should call me. This keeping in the background enabled me also to carry on several tête-à-têtes with damsels whilst he was busy elsewhere. Furthermore, he wishing to take things only to be bought in high-class shops, shops which we rankers would not be served in, gave me the entrée and the female attractions were all the greater. To say that he and I enjoyed ourselves in the 6 to 8 shops we went into would be to put it mildly; it was screaming.

12 August 1917

A run to Étrun. Hurried shave and wash and Bill and I found ourselves with Captain Bowle-Evans in a 15/20 horsepower Sunbeam staff car … [There] we found we had to examine some prisoners taken and particularly we had to obtain some information of the front opposite here, where some of the men came from. I was not very fortunate up to dinner, which the local prisoner-of-war cook made us but afterwards struck oil. I strolled into the NCO's cage and chatting with them, asked one casually where he came from. He said "Lothringen" [Lorraine]. When I further questioned him as to whether he had been around Bullecourt way, he denied it and looked round at the others so furtively and curiously that I grew suspicious. Later, I had him out alone and what I half guessed at I found correct. Being from Lorraine, he was at heart pro-French, but of course being questioned by me in front of the others, he very exaggeratedly denied knowledge of anything. When I had him alone to myself, he was like wax, out came his grievances like a torrent and in no time I got to know all I wanted. Back at Corps I drew up my report which Bowle-Evans told me would appear in the Intelligence Summary … It appeared alright, of course greatly cut down until hardly recognisable, but nevertheless, the main points appeared and I was quite bucked.

13 August 1917

[To Amiens] with Tucker … [who] cannot be called highly amusing or sociable, in fact he rarely opens his mouth unless addressed first. We spent the morning looking at shops, indulging in tram rides and watching people, but on the whole I felt fearfully bored. After dinner I had a brainwave. Tucker is a tremendous bookworm, so I escorted him to the

Town Library and seeing him happily engaged with his books, I left him, arranging when and where to meet him for tea. Once on my own, without his following me like a poodle, I felt happier and shortly after ran into Shepherd who was the RAMC man at Dainville and Arras Prison with us. Through him I became acquainted with a *demoiselle* called Lulu and she and I spent a delightful hour together until it became time for me to meet Tucker. Then we had tea, once more strolled about and had supper with some French soldiers from our front in Belgium. We chatted together, discussed our respective armies, the war in general and the future, all of which made time fly and we had to leave hurriedly to catch the return train.

15 August 1917

This last day before returning to the trench region spent quietly writing letters (one to my new friend 'Lulu') … I had a final dip in the reservoir followed by the usual tea at the EF Canteen. Towards evening, packed things up and then Bill and I had a final walk in the fields by the tennis court. I think he felt sorry at our parting after being together over six months without a day's break, excepting his leave. I know I shall miss his invigorating personality.

Vince went to No. 24 IT Station, 2,000 yards east of Croiselles Church.

16 August 1917

Proceeded [by boxcar] to Croiselles. It could go no further so we walked to the IT Station … Our dug-out,[133] 30 foot deep, is just outside our support line and the view from above overlooks a valley on the other side of which lie the remains of Croiselles … Of course, all around us is one vast area of shell-holed waste ground in which thistles and buttercups and daisies grow at random. The dug-out really consists of three sections or cabins, the centre of which is ours. On one side in an RAMC dressing station, on the other the Medical Officer's room. A corridor connects all three and at night, with the lights of each shining into this corridor, I am reminded of the interior of a small liner where lights from cabins shining into the passage outside produce the same effect. Once more on an IT instrument though results are bad owing to a defective loop, but it is a case of hoping in the future.

---

133 Map reference U.19.b.5.4: 102nd Brigade war diary, 21 March 1918, WO95/2461, TNA.

17 August 1917

Benoly relieved me at 2 am and the next thing I heard was the sizzling of fried bacon. We have an oil stove, the best procurable in this wilderness and it takes 3 to 4 hours to boil our tea water, thus the man on duty … puts the water on 4 am and by 8 am it begins to boil. During the morning I went with the boys round the loop. In places the trenches were quite dry, in others the mud went half up to the knees.

18 August 1917

The boxcar turned up with rations and letters. This happens every odd day and is like the arrival of a vessel at a lonely island as of course here we are completely cut off from everywhere. Redgrave and Marsh also came, the former kicking up a bit of a stink over the loop though I succeeded in calming him. But I foresee hard work ahead.

19 August 1917

We were out laying wire by 6 am … Luckily the enemy trench mortars were quiet, but the Battalion HQ,[134] consisting of dug-outs and shelters built into the far side of an old railway embankment, got shelled heavily but the only casualty was caused by a 'dud' which smashed through the cookhouse and killed the cat. Placed as we are on the ascent of an incline towards the trenches, we can observe the shelling beautifully.

20 August 1917

A furious strafe started and the firing on our trenches was so great that I did not think it worthwhile turning out to fix the loop until working parties had cleared and built up the trenches a bit … [We] went to fetch rations. The boxcar comes up to Croiselles where we meet it. We take down from here the four empty tins of water and exhausted batteries and return with four full petrol tins with water, new batteries, rations and stores and mail. Today it was swelteringly hot and when I got back, my shirt was wet through … Benoly and I had a chat on his intention of applying for a commission. I advised him not to. He is very unsettled in his mind. When things go well with him and when he is on good terms with everybody, he doesn't want to apply; the moment things go wrong, then he wants to. Owing to his peculiar character, few can get on with him and he himself frankly admits the knowledge that he is known as a troublemaker. But since I've been here, we have got on well together.

134 9/King's Own Yorkshire Light Infantry (64th Infantry Brigade, 21st Division): VI Corps, 'Dispositions of Infantry', 19 August 1917, WO95/771, TNA.

22 August 1917

The boxcar came up this morning, relieving Benoly ... Two new men, Hicken[135] and Corker,[136] linesmen, came up and I soon had them out on the loop, continuing the work begun yesterday. Found them very willing workers ... As usual spent the evening till dusk sitting on the wire drums and coils of wire outside the dug-out, smoking and chatting. Then when dusk comes we return to our 'room', put a blanket on the IT box as table and have an hour's whist, to which the RAMC men often come in and crowd round. The game over ... we lay down our waterproof sheets and blankets and after a last look round upstairs, turn in. The 'last look round upstairs' is sometimes very pretty, as this evening. Both far up north as also further south, the sky was lit up by continuous flashes, here and there one saw the red flame of bursting shrapnel or of a trench mortar and everywhere, all along the line, never stopping, Verey lights shoot up in a thin streak, suddenly break out, illuminating the whole surroundings, then, gradually falling, eventually disappearing amongst the number of others that have shot up meanwhile.

25 August 1917

Breakfast at 6.30 am and then Haines'[137] lot went out to try and finish the loop. It is supposed to be in working order by 12 noon today but some shells falling ... may have broken the wire in places. I am now going to clean the acetylene lamp and then cut the meat for dinner. The working with wires in the trenches, hammering staples, cutting staples, continuous fingering of wires, the many items of manual labour in the dug-out have covered my hands with blisters ... After the long spell behind the line, I was getting my hands quite decent looking again, but a week up here soon fills the nails and cracks in the skin with grit.

26 August 1917

The boys went up to Croiselles to fetch rations and our one battery being exhausted, had to close down until the fresh one arrives. As I sat outside waiting, taking in some fresh air, Redgrave turned up. He and I had one of our confidential chats on things in general which we generally indulge in when alone. He is a charming fellow. He opened his heart to me, so to speak and complained of the many difficulties he has to contend with,

---

135 127119 Sapper Charles Hicken; nineteen-year-old mechanic from Birmingham.

136 127635 Sapper William Corker; twenty-two-year-old former wireless school student from Durham. He had arrived in France four months earlier.

137 108243 Sapper Cyril Haines; twenty-one-year-old student from Hull.

especially about the fed-upness of his men, even blaming Mr Marsh, his second-in-command. As regards the Station, I told him that the instrument, the headpieces and the commutator were faulty and he is sending someone up tomorrow to repair them.

27 August 1917

Was on the 2 am to 8 am watch. I always take things easy as until 6 am nothing much ever happens. Tucker gave me a tin of *café au lait* which I turned into a very rich and delicious cup of coffee, at the same time eating some bread and butter and gooseberry jam. This jam has come very welcome after a long run of marmalade. Then lit a pipe of 'Waverly', which is the only tobacco I can get and read *Ann Veronica*[138] until 4 am. Thereupon got our writing materials and wrote letters. However, I had to break off and pay attention to work but around 7 am started stove which, by the way I have found can boil water in ¾ hour if attended to properly.

28 August 1917

Slept for once a full night on a stretcher out in the passage. It was not so bad, only water gathers there and forms a stagnant pool of mud which collects as soon as it is cleared away. Wilkie relieved Tucker. The former was quite pleased at being up here again and spoke disgustedly of his treatment down at Wireless when at rest. All sorts of fatigues and the last days was as cook's mate … As usual, he was full of rumours and stories: Corps are moving, Wireless are also moving, White might get a cushy job somewhere at GHQ, there is a general weeding out of clerks at Corps HQs. [Davis] on his return to Wireless from here was detailed off to cook and refused and in short, the people there seem to be in a state of semi-mutiny.

29 August 1917

The rainy weather continues and outside is a sea of mud, whilst everyone coming in brings a few lumps stuck on the boots, so this place requires a lot of sweeping up. Owing to the intermittence on the instrument, Haines and I had a look at the inside,[139] cleaning the terminals and valve prongs, tightening screws, but no difference. Afterwards we examined the high-tension battery, without tracing a defect. This intermittence is horribly irritating. When I first came up, the instrument was OK and the line 'dis', now the line is OK and the instrument faulty. Breakey, Haines and I did a

138 H.G. Wells, *Ann Veronica: A Modern Love Story* (1909).

139 In violation of regulations; see this volume's appendix, section 9.7.

useful piece of work by pulling up the boards in the passage over the mud pool, clearing the mud and water away, then digging a sump hole. I also lay the logs of wood left on the bank outside our dug-out on the ground to form a kind of path over the mud to the spot where we wash.

30 August 1917

Whist games have come to be the feature of the evening. With the instrument unsatisfactory, one is liable to get rather irritable but this game restores the balance. The table consists of a sandbag on two paraffin tins, we squat round on the floor or blanket rolls or upturned petrol tins and a couple of candles stuck on cigarette tins lids or anything illustrates the scene.

1 September 1917

Ration day, so strolled into Croiselles to meet boxcar … Eventually a limber came up with a new instrument which Benoly, who had ridden up, helped to carry to dug-out. On the way he started his tale of woe and quarrels with all and everybody … The new instrument fitted on, we at last obtained results. In a high pitch of excitement went round to Battalion HQ to strafe the signals staff.[140] The IT once more in order cheered us up a lot and as usual, altogether raised the general spirits. A slightly strained feeling was beginning to pervade the station. Hicken gets on one's nerves. He is still a kid with lively spirits, plenty of youthful impudence and cheek and a ceaselessly wagging tongue. Periodically he is told off, then, after a few minutes bobs up again until the next telling off. But he is a good lad at heart and I do not forget how well he worked the first few days up here.

2 September 1917

First symptoms of a sore throat which became worse later on. Neuralgia added to the fun. I think this underground life with the damp and lack of fresh air is beginning to tell a bit. The moment I go outside and face the driving wind which had been on for days, the pain leaves and it always comes on when I lie down.

3 September 1917

Heard that Intelligence were pleased with the work of the Station which is some consolation for the work we have had to do … Wilkie and I strolled

140 1/Royal Munster Fusiliers (47th Infantry Brigade, 16th Division): VI Corps, 'Dispositions of Infantry', 1 September 1917, WO95/771, TNA.

into Croiselles and brought up a tin of paraffin. When we got back the sun began setting. After several days of cold and wet weather it is more than a treat to sit and watch the sun and let one be influenced by the peculiar mixture of silence and noise that reigns … The quiet is broken by peculiar noises, the loudest being two big 6-inch howitzers in Croiselles banging away every minute whilst, as if to meet them half-way, one of the Bosch shells comes whining over and, with the whine still in one's ears, the column of dark brown earth and smoke can be seen shooting up, the sharp 'cc-rash' of the explosion being heard the moment the whine ceases. Then, perhaps a moment's silence until the ear catches the hum of an aeroplane above. Far over towards Monchy-le-Preux an anti-aircraft gun is popping away, distinguished through its characteristic 'whew-whew' and then one hears the 'cr-crumph', 'cr-crumph', 'cr-crumph' of shells bursting around the plane, the sky meanwhile being dotted with many little black and white puffs of smoke … From below in the dug-out I hear a snatch of song, probably Hicken's *I Hear You Calling Me* – he has got it on the brain these days. A cart is rattling along the road in the valley and from here and there, columns of blue smoke slowly rise up, showing the evening camp fires.

4 September 1917

A new station is being opened at Bullecourt with Benoly in charge. I am to remain in charge of this Station … Redgrave asked whether I wanted to come out for a rest, but when I heard that resting would mean helping the Wireless to move … shifting stuff, building shelters etc., I decided to remain up here.

6 September 1917

The doctor has left here, leaving his partition in the dug-out free so the man who has every third night not on duty sleeps there. Thus I slept gloriously there last night but was awakened by another spasm of Boche hate. This morning shelling seems to be his fad now.

7 September 1917

I found that the rations had come up in a very bad state, the sugar wet through, through contact with water and it settled on the meat, making a nice mess of everything. On the spot I tore out a leaf of my notebook, writing a complaint to Redgrave and I hope we shall be better treated in future. Benoly was to blame and being present, he looked rather black. This has happened before, including leaky water tins and I did not feel like standing any more nonsense. The IT set is not as it ought to be and altogether, just today, I am not over-amiable.

8 September 1917

A sleep after my 2 am to 8 am spell did me some good and after dinner a walk to Croiselles to fetch water did me still more good. Instead of the well, a pump has been rigged up and this is a great improvement. During my 4 pm to 8 pm spell came to the conclusion that the Bosches had been relieved and, advising Battalion HQ, found my conclusion was justified and so went to bed feeling much lighter-hearted than for some days past.

9 September 1917

At 8 am a big roar outside made me rush upstairs and I saw a huge cloud drifting towards the Bosche lines. Gas! The IT set is going well again and have been very busy this morning. This gas does not seem to have been all plain sailing. 700 cylinders were discharged in the shape of missiles from our Support Line. They were to have fallen between our front line and the Germans, but some fell short, thus gassing our own men. There is a man groaning and gasping in the RAMC partition now as I write – it is ghastly. Later: The poor fellow died; good thing. More men have turned up, feeling the effects, also an officer, but none seem to be really bad. During the morning we heard (over the IT) that the Bosches had been badly hit and Breakey and I informed the local Battalion Adjutant. At the same time we 'ear-rolled' some tins of Macconachie of which we are in want, the rations having been very low recently. Have mostly existed on bully and biscuits. (*1968 comment*: 'Ear-rolling' denotes the acquiring of something by cajolery.)

11 September 1917

Rations … came along during the afternoon and rotten rations they were, no meat or Macconachie, milk or butter. Practically just plain bread and bully. Redgrave and Marsh came up and made matters worse by informing us that in future we are to draw our rations from a spot in [Écoust-Saint-Mein], a village close to Bullecourt. There we dump them on a truck and have to push this truck for over an hour across the open, exposed to machine-gun fire and ordinary shell fire, every other night. It is sickening. One works like the devil and as a result, instead of having the work simplified, it is only made worse. Even Breakey, who has been splendid, gave way to strong language.

12 September 1917

It's remarkable how only one month changes one. When I came up here, I felt full of dash and go, above all, in excellent spirits; nothing put me out. This morning, in contrast, because Haines lay in bed late, it was all I could do to control myself, instead of pulling the blanket off him and chucking him out bodily. And there was no real reason why he should have got up. Just the fact that he was in bed whilst the others were up annoyed me. When I spoke to him 'gently and firmly' instead, he got up and why I was in such a temper I can only put down to the confinement of this place and a general feeling of 'fed-upness'. The ration fetching affair from Écoust was discussed – actually it consisted of cussing Redgrave and Marsh, "anything is good enough for the men up the line", "their own convenience is all they trouble about", "what's the good of slaving and trying to get IT results if you are only treated like muck". Naturally I had to defend Redgrave and Marsh, but it was not a very spirited defence. One grain of consolation was that the Munster Adjutant was very decent in indenting for rations for us and they turned out to be really excellent.

13 September 1917

We had our usual early morning dose of shelling. The lines were broken and it was 11 am before Haines & Co. could go out. During their absence, decided on working things on a more business-like basis: two men detailed each day for certain jobs, thus washing up, sweeping up, fetching water, fetching rations and so on. As these men have to be detailed for their turns to be outside their regular duty hours, the arrangement is rather complicated. Haines, of course, objected, but was squashed by the majority. One of these days I shall have a row with this young gentleman.

14 September 1917

The new arrangement of detailing men worked well and ought to be a great improvement. Haines and I had a row this morning. The line was broken by the usual morning strafe. He ought to have turned out at once, but obviously dallied to annoy me. Result was, quite calmly I gave him my opinion of him and he seemed somewhat surprised! He has certainly been more civil and willing during the day … We had our nearest shave this morning, one shell bursting outside our dug-out. Anybody sitting at the entrance or outside would have been 'napooed'. Half a dozen yards shorter and it would have landed on top, smashing the entrance possibly.

Fetched rations from Écoust … by means of a trolley truck which starts from a place called 'Porter's Dump', about 150 yards away from our dug-out, to 'Guinness Dump', the terminus of the motor railway coming up from the rear … The trolley made a low, grating noise which in the silence of the night, seemed deafening. The journey was stopped once through the lines being broken (we had to unload, lift truck on to unbroken portion of rails and load up again) and then two or three times through stones derailing the truck and once to bolt for an adjacent trench when some shrapnel came over. We reached 'Guinness Dump' safely, exchanging old stores for new, groping about in the dark, stumbling over logs, timber, some loose rails … and peering through the darkness to see one's way. The train came in, drawn by a big motor engine, working parties jumped out – silent shadows disappearing into the night. A red light was all that showed, though an occasional Verey light would light up the scene. Everything was done at great speed, no time lost. The train staff no doubt were in a hurry to get out of harm's way. Haines and I loaded up and started the return journey … Were glad to reach 'Porter's Dump' after an hour. In the dark we nearly missed the way to our dug-out but a Verey light just showed us the brown earth patches against the dark green grass round the entrances.

16 September 1917

Hicken and I were walking up the incline towards the dug-out after fetching rations from Battalion HQ when, to my surprise, I saw Bill's unmistakable brown boots and eventually I recognised the fellow himself. During our absence, he and Benoly had come up to relieve Breakey, Haines and myself. So we almost turned the place upside down, packing up, Bill giving graphic accounts of the last month's doings in his old excitable, gesticulating style, the total conclusion he had come to was that everybody seemed to have gone mad.

We left Croiselles in a boxcar and pulled up at Boyelles. Found a decent Armstrong hut and spent some time making myself comfortable, rigging up shelves and the like. A visit to a canteen provided some excellent stout and it was a pleasure to be able to splash some money about … We ran into Achiet where I changed my £1 note and back here, had a long talk with Redgrave, discussing the working and results of the Station, also pointing out the dangers of the present ration fetching system. Later, I translated the German and Austrian evening Wireless Press.

17 September 1917

Had a glorious full night in bed … Saw my first Yankee soldier.[141] This feeling of rest is glorious and I am appreciating it all the more after the hard month up at Croiselles. I just lazed away all day, visited the YMCA and canteen, had a kick at goal with some fellows playing about with a football and ended up with a nice read in bed.

19 September 1917

Redgrave, the driver and I ran into Amiens … It was an ideal day for motoring, dry and warm, yet not dusty or stuffy. On the way picked some apples off trees lining the road, Mr Redgrave climbing the trees and enjoying himself as much as we. At Amiens as usual did the necessary shopping and then wandered round to kill time, indulging eventually in a tram drive. Unfortunately it was 'no tea' day and so the cafés were closed. The YMCA came in handy.

21 September 1917

To Claire's and we had a very jolly ½ hour together. I was really pleased to see the girl, when at No. 22 Station, we visited her *estaminet* regularly and we became quite friendly.

22 September 1917

A conversation with Redgrave about Breakey and his leave resulted in my being detailed to go up to Edwards' Station tonight … Reached [it] after a lengthy walk … and found my companions to be Lederer, Davis, a fellow I only know slightly called Bob Watson, but who seems to be a very decent sort and Sergeant Edwards who is in charge.

23 September 1917

This is not a bad dug-out, though rather bare. Some beds have been erected, one above the other … The place is wooden-walled and roofed, some 25 feet deep and a draught prevents the air from becoming oppressive like it sometimes used to be at Croiselles. The cooking is done over an improvised brazier cut out of a petrol tin and the tea can and frying pan likewise. We are in the trenches proper and from outside can look over Riencourt, in German hands … Bullecourt is to the left, quite close, but invisible from here. Hundreds of dead, British and Colonial,

141 The first combat elements of the American Expeditionary Force had arrived in France on 26 June: David Trask, *The AEF and Coalition Warmaking, 1917–1918* (Lawrence: University Press of Kansas, 1993), 13.

are buried round here in the trenches and in working in the trenches one constantly digs up against the remains of some poor beggar.

24 September 1917

Things are very slow here and no results obtainable. Sergeant Edwards, an old soldier, usually called 'Daddy' or 'Uncle' is handicapped by having Davis, that intolerable, pig-headed lazybones whom we got to cordially dislike at 'The Cellar' and also at Croiselles. He is just as lazy and obstinate here and casts quite a gloom over the station. If it were not for Bob Watson, an excellent fellow, old 'Daddy' would be in a hole. Then there is the other bête noir, Lederer, a Jew, called 'Dirty Dick', who also is detested by all, tries to get out of everything, swinging the lead where he can and is as thick-skinned as a rhinocerous. The one thing that pleased me was that yesterday, at nap, he lost 6 francs. That riled him. He got a special leave on the plea that after 10 months it was imperative to see his wife with whom he had only been 24 hours since their marriage.[142] Now he is going out for two days in order to observe some Jewish fast day of atonement.[143] We are all sure that it is only a means to get out of the line for a bit and he was told more than once that for him to atone for his sins, he would have to fast to death and continue his fast in hell. He went out at night and as nobody came up to take his place, 'Daddy' closed the Station for the night.

25 September 1917

I walked over to Croiselles to see the boys at my own station … Found everybody seething with indignation against Benoly. He and Wilkie seem to have had some priceless rows. The ration fetching is still a sore point. To do away with the truck pushing game from Écoust to the station, Redgrave arranged for three infantrymen and a Lewis gun cart to be used along the road and this experiment was tried yesterday, but it made such a noise, the Bosche heard and shelled them. They escaped alright, but Bill and Wilkie put the wind up Benoly to such an extent that today he walked to Boyelles to see Redgrave … Otherwise, little doing, the chief subject being complaints against Benoly's impossibility as NCO-in-charge. As Bill said "We do all the suggesting and he meekly tries to carry them out".

142 The marriage of a Richard Lederer is recorded at Hammersmith in June 1916.

143 Yom Kippur, 26 September 1917.

28 September 1917

We have had no fresh meat since I have been up here and continuous tinned stuff makes the skin terribly irritable.

29 September 1917

Was sitting outside dug-out, having a breather, when a message came saying I was to go out, i.e., be relieved. Not sorry as life and work has been very dull at this Station, though I knew I was only here temporarily. It was whilst I was waiting at Écoust for my train to turn up that I had a narrow squeak – a machine-gun bullet hit the heel of my boot. When I picked the bullet up, it was too hot to hold. Luckily it was a spent bullet, but then again, how nearly a Blighty touch! At Boyelles … found my old bed occupied and the one I had to resort to as good as collapsed when I lay down, so was obliged to turn out, find a sandbag and with some nails I luckily had in my pocket, hammered the ripped open sandbag over the collapsed portion. It was close on midnight before I was able to lie down safely and for some reason or other, could not sleep.

30 September 1917

Redgrave told me that I had to go up to No. 24 Station at Croiselles, so had a bath, a change of washing and after dinner went in the boxcar to Saint-Léger with Haines and Ormerod, the latter a new man, this being his first experience of line. At Saint-Léger, met Benoly, Hicken and Corker with handcart and transferred luggage. After a hot pull, reached the dug-out safely and heard the reason I was wired for was because Benoly had had troubles and rows without end and this coming to Redgrave's ears he had decided for Benoly and I to swap Stations. Incidentally, Redgrave told me this morning that he had recommended me "for something" and "if my name did not appear on the next papers it would not be his fault".

1 October 1917

The sump-hole in the passage had turned out to be a small well and after every meal, we lift up a small board and find a plentiful supply of water, just right for washing up the crocks. Most convenient! The stove question and lack of paraffin are the only drawbacks and as I have to cook breakfast tomorrow morning, I made quite a nice brazier out of a petrol tin and using a trench board from outside, chopped up the wood required.

2 October 1917

Was very mystified by finding the code key list missing and was still more mystified in finding same in the rubbish bag. Although I trust everybody here, I am keeping an eye open as this is inexplicable … Paraffin came up with the rations but now the wick has disappeared into the inside of the stove. Spent nearly two hours fishing it out and when at last I had patched it up, it was a pretty sight with paraffin, soot, grease and oil all over me.

3 October 1917

We've fixed up quite a jolly kitchen upstairs at the dug-out entrance. The brazier stands on two old petrol tins which let a good draught through. The sides have been banked up with sandbags and corrugated iron sheets, with shelves etc. for cooking utensils. Bill, who cooks, sits on a box and is quite happy.

4 October 1917

[To] the Saint-Léger crossroads … Found the infantry carrying party and as the boxcar did not turn up, we adjourned to the YMCA where cocoa is served up free. The moment we got in, the men left behind came running along saying the boxcar had turned up. Hamilton and Hicken were on board … From other sources I heard that next week we can expect some 'doings' here, in the shape of strafings. The moment I got back had to go on duty and then make tea. This latter was quite a job. The warm weather has changed to a gale and the wind howls round the cookhouse. The only way to start the fire was by pouring paraffin on the wood and paper. During the process, to guard or screen the fire, fixed up a curtain and had hardly done so when rain came on cats and dogs, so bolted out to get in what wood I could. A piece of log, whilst being chopped up, hit the sugar and sent it flying whilst I slipped and knocked over the tea. But somehow got water to boil and mix the tea.

7 October 1917

I called Wilkie to relieve me at 2 am and went to bed. After a sound sleep was awakened by what I thought to be Wilkie getting up. Next was an unusual dashing about preparing breakfast at speed. When I asked him what time it was, he didn't know, the Station watch had stopped; shortly after he heard it was 8 am. When I cross-questioned him, he stated that he got up early alright but that the watch had stopped at 4.30 am, then again later. Personally, I believe he got up but fell asleep again and then was late in starting breakfast. Anyhow, spoke a few words to him and then thought it best to say no more.

8 October 1917

Breakey came up and relieved Wilkie who had been up here seven weeks and deserves a rest. Breakey has come back from leave and brought up a bottle of whisky. We opened it and soon became most amiable and genial. I am glad Breakey is here; he is a very steady and reliable man and excellent to get on with whilst Wilkie is without doubt a peculiar customer who has to be humoured and who tries one's temper sorely at times.

10 October 1917

Was called out by an RAMC Captain who told me he wanted the room Bill and I sleep in clean and ready by 1 pm tomorrow. He also added that two stunts were ready to take place shortly, probably tomorrow. The Battalion Orderly did not come to fetch our despatches so had to stroll down to Battalion HQ[144] myself to fix up arrangements which was soon done. At same time saw the Adjutant and informed him that if he wanted anyone to interrogate or cross-examine German prisoners taken in any of the stunts, there were three interpreters in our Station at his disposal.

11 October 1917

Both Bill and I felt touchy and had words on two occasions, but having words with him is a tonic, one can reason with him and he admits himself in the wrong if he is. This cramped life is very conducive to periods of snappiness and one has to keep a tight hold over one's self, especially after a couple of nights of but little sleep … The doctor turned up, a most cheerful customer and at length settled down with the RAMC men, leaving the other room to ourselves. At 8 pm the stunt started, gas cylinders I believe, followed by artillery. There was a lot of noise until after 11 pm but I did not let it interfere with my night's sleep.

12 October 1917

Haines refused to get up when Bill called him. I gave him a warning "and five minutes" and then, as he still refused to get out, I felt I had good cause and decided to report him for refusing to obey orders and asking for him to be replaced. Have just written report to Lieutenant Lane who

144 1/Royal Munster Fusiliers (47th Infantry Brigade, 16th Division): VI Corps, 'Dispositions of Infantry', 10 October 1917, WO95/772, TNA.

is in charge of Wireless during Redgrave's absence on leave and I devoutly trust Hicken will come up instead.

13 October 1917

Breakey and I went round the loop, noticing a big improvement in the front line. After the gas stunt of [11 October], things have quietened down and the expected Bosch retaliation has not come about. In fact, there are many rumours that the Hun was on the point of retiring here. He has certainly ceased talking just opposite us though machine-gun and rifle activity show that he is not far away. Otherwise, life goes on in the same old way, the one amusing thing being my relations with Haines. His own silly conduct forced me to report him after several little differences and not over-good feeling between us. Now, after having been reported for having disobeyed orders, far from sulking or wangling, he is as decent as can be, excessively cheerful and is more open and willing to help than ever, as if he quite relished the idea of having been reported. Still, I'm afraid he's mistaken if he imagines this new behaviour will make me change my mind. I did it once, but not again!

14 October 1917

Went to Boyelles for a bath … [and] had my proper first impression of Mr Lane, Redgrave's now second-in-command. Made a good impression and we ought to get on well together. At one time he was a plain Sapper, cook's mate at GHQ, now Second Lieutenant. Spoke to him about Haines and as a result, he will go to Écoust Station and Hicken will come here again, the successful result of a little diplomatic treatment. Wilkie is having a good time and otherwise my chief delight was to splash about in a bath and once more have clean underwear.

16 October 1917

I had just called Breakey [at 0200] when was told that I was wanted at Company HQ as interpreter in case prisoners should be brought in [from a raid].[145] I had to be quick in order to avoid the German answering barrage

145 An 'unpretentious' infantry raid with ninety men was conducted, assisted by the Royal Engineers who feigned a gas attack with compressed air cylinders causing the German defenders to don their respirators. It achieved its primary purpose of reconnaissance and was commended by both army and corps commanders: 7/Leinster Regiment (47th Infantry Brigade, 16th Division) war diary, 15–16 October 1917, 'Enterprise by 7th Battalion Leinster Regt', 16 October 1917, 47th Infantry Brigade to 16th Division, 18 October 1917, 16th Division to VI Corps, 19 October 1917, VI Corps to 16th Division, 26 October 1917, WO95/1970/4, TNA. Frederick Whitton, *The History of the Prince of Wales's Leinster Regiment (Royal Canadians)*, Vol. 2 (Aldershot: Gale & Polden, 1926), 433–4.

to ours. The guide and I slipped along in the dark, stumbling into and over shell holes as we crossed 'Porter's Dump' and then slithering over the trench boards in the trenches. It was very dark and quite silent. An exciting little touch took place as I arrived at the Company HQ. Outside, by the aid of a flash lamp, two officers were counting out seconds: 20, 10, 5, 4, 3, 2, and 1. Then up went three rockets, "Off you go my lads and the best of luck to you", another second and the silence was shattered by the roar of our guns, opening out dead to a second. It was just perfect.

Down in the dug-out, the Colonel[146] and Adjutant[147] were very decent, offering me cigarettes and drinks. Had some very fine Curaçao. At length a Hun was brought in, a very simple *gemütlicher Unteroffizier.* He seemed to be in a dream and evidently did not realise his sudden change of fortune. I asked him the usual tactical questions and then translated questions put me by the officers present. Later on the men returned, the raid was a success and all and everybody in fine spirits. A young Captain[148] gave an account of the affair: the timing of the barrage and of their moving in perfect order. Our shooting was also most accurate. Also, he and a Lance Corporal got through the wire into the German front line without any resistance. The raid was a complete surprise. Flashing his lamp, he turned it full on a head peering round the curtain of a dug-out entrance. He called "Kamerad?" and the Hun very promptly answered "Kamerad" and was at once taken prisoner. Working along the trench, a *Mebus*, or concrete dug-out was found to be occupied and an exchange of bomb-throwing took place. But the *Mebus* was found to be too strongly held. The entrance to a tunnel was discovered, examined and then had a couple of Mills bombs thrown in. Time was then up and the raiding party returned. In all 140 men went out and only 4 or 5 got slight wounds, including two officers.[149]

A second prisoner was said to be at Battalion HQ to which we proceeded but found he had already been moved to Brigade. The other man, however, was still detained and I could not help thinking what a picture the whole made. The Officers' Mess, lit up with candles, the remains of dinner still on the table. On one side of the table stood the German prisoner, behind him the two wounded Irish officers,[150] one with a bandaged head, the other with an arm in a sling and sitting or standing

146 Lieutenant-Colonel G.A.M. Buckley DSO.

147 Captain E.L.L. Acton.

148 Captain R.A. Dench MC.

149 The casualties were officially recorded as one killed and seven wounded: 47th Infantry Brigade war diary, 16 October 1917, WO95/1969, TNA.

150 Lieutenant C.H. Magahy and Second Lieutenant J. Ryan.

around, their faces lit up, all more or less muddy, the other officers who had come back from this raid. And nobody seemed more pleased and childlike in his delight than the Colonel himself. The Irish spirits of all were very evident and not much thought was given to suppressing them. There was indeed joy in the camp!

An uneventful day otherwise, just a return to the usual cut and dried routine though, after weeks of silence, in the midst of pontoon, Breakey suddenly heard "Allo, wer is da?" (Hello, who is there?). It was an agreeable surprise.

18 October 1917

A morning reminiscent of the IT at its best – busy from the moment I sat down to when Breakey relieved me at noon … I cooked dinner and got on famously, in fact was quite bucked with my fried chips.

19 October 1917

Had to walk to Saint-Léger, it being my turn to meet the ration boxcar. It turned up alright but not the infantry carriers. No doubt the outgoing lot failed to 'handover' to the incoming … I had to leave the rations in charge of the policeman at the crossroads and eventually they were called for by Wilkie & Co. this afternoon, who sallied forth from here with the handcart 'midst much growling and cursing and arriving back likewise.

21 October 1917

Wilkie and Hicken went down for rations and returned late owing to the boxcar having broken down. The infantry ration party turned up and were rather suggestive in their language en route of what they thought of us … The Irish RAMC men next door sang some hymns. One of the men has a very nice voice and it was good to listen to … Mice are becoming a nuisance, scuttling all over the place, dropping little lumps of earth on the table, on one's head, down one's neck. One had eaten right into a sandbag with rice in and when I went to investigate, jumped out of the hole it had made and disappeared like a flash.

23 October 1917

Had a bath at Boyelles, settled various minor affairs and returned to the Listening Post. Was on duty to 8 pm and felt very tired. It then struck me that I had only had three hours sleep last night, had been up since 2 am and during the day had walked nearly 15 miles in very heavy weather. One incident heckled me on my return. Breakey told Sergeant Edwards when they met at the crossroads that I had gone into Boyelles to which Edwards replied I should be arrested for leaving my Station without permission. Sergeant Edwards' leg will have a serious pull in return for this.

24 October 1917

Breakey, ruffled at having to move [to the other station] threatened yesterday to 'swing the lead', making himself obnoxious. I gently pointed out that it would be doing the dirty on us at our Station, to which he replied that it was only by doing the dirty that one got anything one wanted in the Army, witness Lederer, 'Dirty Dick'. This morning, being his turn to sweep up, I wondered whether he would stick to his word but his common sense prevailed and he gave the place a good sweep out. Still, I know he will lead poor old Benoly a merry dance at the other Station.

25 October 1917

Bill came up from rest to relieve Breakey … Hicken accompanied [Breakey] and returned for tea. Said the other Station, No. 26 at Écoust, was in a filthy state, smelt horribly and everything seemed to be in a most untidy, slipshod state, so much so he was glad to leave it. There was no denying the lad's genuine delight at being back with us again.

28 October 1917

I pride myself on making some excellent steaks and fried potatoes for dinner and which received all due appreciation from all. Hickin and I went wood hunting in the ruined sugar factory. I didn't like climbing over the ruins at all, one never knew when a hidden box of tricks might go 'pop' and was careful to see that Hickin only touched the wood we were after. Wilkie came back with the rather staggering news that Goritzia had been recaptured by the Austrians and 80,000 Italians taken prisoner.[151] This is too great a pill to swallow until further news comes along.

29 October 1917

Saw that Wilkie had [only] partly swept up without having had time to finish the job, being due to relieve Bill at noon. Well, I told Wilkie off and then Bill barged into him with his well-meant but blustering and overbearing manner. Result, he and Wilkie went for each other without actually coming to blows. I adopted my usual policy and let them have

151 The Austro-German offensive, later known as the Battle of Caparetto, had been launched on 24 October.

it out and when they had exhausted themselves, I chimed in in my best persuasive manner and poured oil on the ruffled and troubled waters. I then suggested *vingt et un* and managed to win 5 francs after being 10 francs down at one time … I have just noticed that except for Bill, we are all Birmingham men here now, as Wilkie and Hicken come from Small Heath and Davis from Aston.

2 November 1917

The much looked forward to parcel from Dad [came], with the new fountain pen … and with the news that I have been promoted full Corporal in the Royal Engineers.

3 November 1917

Bill went to Boyelles, the rest camp, on private business and came back with the news that according to the German Wireless, 300,000 Italians and 180 guns had been captured. It seems incredible. 'Dirty Dick' [Lederer] is still sick and won't relieve me tomorrow … With my promotion I find I get 26 shillings and 10 pence … A heated row on the Italian fiasco was kept going until 9.30 pm. I then retired to bed, having to be on duty at 2 am. At 10 pm Bill magnanimously suggested that the argument should cease, enabling me to sleep, but at 10.30 pm asked Davis in a loud voice whether he would like some more toasted cheese, as he could not eat all his. This woke me up. I was just dozing off again when suppressed laughter and giggles from Bill woke me up once more. He was highly amused that the men next door had taken up the Italian argument we had been discussing. I here broke in and announced that I wished to sleep, but at 12.30 am, Bill (whose full night in bed it was) started to tell [Davis] off for making such a noise. Of course, [Davis] replied and in a moment the two were shouting at each other hell for leather. It was then I felt inclined to kick up a row, but instead kept control and spoke a few home-truths instead. At any rate, the row ceased.

4 November 1917

Corker came up from rest and Hicken left us. I am sorry as in spite of his shortcomings, he is a very useful man on a Station. On the other hand, I could see that he was getting on Bill's nerves and I am sure there would have been a rumpus before long. Had a bath in Bill's tin in the cabin next door. First heated water over stove, then laid two sandbags on floor, placed water on shelf of cabin and then had a sponge and wash down. Very nice, except that I could not indulge in splashing about.

5 November 1917

I was unlucky at *vingt et un*, losing 9½ francs but expect to win it back again. The theme of the discussion this evening was on the British Consular Service and drifted round to the attitude British manufacturers will take towards German post-war competition. This is getting quite a debating society, let alone a gambling den.

7 November 1917

I slept soundly till dinner, afterwards having another tin bath. Bill was grooming himself at the same time in his pyjamas and as I was smoking a clay pipe, standing in a tin bath as bare as when I came into the world, we must have looked a comical picture. As Wilkie said "If our people could see us like that, only a few hundred yards from the Bosche front line, they would have fainted".

8 November 1917

When Bill came back with the rations from Saint-Léger, it was with the surprising news that I was being relieved … Down at Boyelles, spent an evening unpacking and fixing up my things, also to sewing on my two stripes; beastly fag, more bother this sewing than the stripes are worth. Began reading *Sonia* by Stephen McKenna,[152] a much talked-of and well-criticised book.

9 November 1917

The advantages of being a full Corporal are beginning to show themselves. I am entitled to being in the NCOs' Mess and thus had a very nice breakfast of porridge, bacon and dipped bread, and bread, butter and jam. Had a trip to Amiens, but Sergeants Edwards and Shepherd boozing with friends in Albert delayed us and we arrived at Amiens too late for a good restaurant meal. Result, we had some omelettes, ham and beer in an *estaminet* in one of the dark side streets. The rest of the time spent shopping, one whirlwind of a rush from one shop to another, though I arranged to take everything to Suzanne's at the fruit shop, my particular friend and this allowed us to have a little tête à tête. She was in a very nice mood and we parted in a most friendly fashion.

---

152 Stephen McKenna, *Sonia: Between Two Worlds* (1917).

10 November 1917

Took the boxcar to Saint-Léger crossroads with rations etc. and had a drink in the Hants canteen. Sergeant Edwards is a glutton for his drop of beer, typical 'old soldier' touch. However, as he pays, I don't mind.

11 November 1917

Today was a bit out of the ordinary. I had a pass to Arras and was lucky in getting a lift in a staff car nearly all the way … I made my peace with Jeanne Magniez – simply could not think of her Christian name and eventually got it by asking how she spelt it. Then proceeded to Mme Pruvost and was very nicely received, having a top-hole lunch at a party nearly a dozen strong. The meal was three courses, with beer, wine, cider and coffee. After the usual *au revoirs* and *bon chance*, went to the cinema but cleared out at 4 pm and went over to Magniez's for tea. Madame was very effusive and invited me to luncheon next Thursday [15 November], to celebrate the return of her daughter, Ivonne, from Boulogne. In the days gone past Ivonne and I had been good friends. When I had accepted, Madame further informed me that four more girlfriends of Ivonne's were coming to lunch, so I shall be in clover, surrounded by six young French girls. In fact, I almost feel nervous! Jeanne came in during tea with one of the friends and she was a very decent sort with quite her share of good looks. In fact, living up to the customs of the country, when Jeanne 'offered' her cheeks for a kiss, I could not but respond and repeat the performance with her pretty friend, quite harmless, but most pleasant nonetheless … To Corps HQ and at length was lucky in running White to earth in Claire's *estaminet*. We discussed various things, the new pay, our future and the future operations on our front … Claire and I had one of our semi-flirtatious chats and parted in the most affectionate manner – a great day with the girls!

12 November 1917

Had my box respirator examined, spending three minutes in a chamber filled with tear shell fumes … To the pictures featuring Charlie Chaplin's *Carmen*.[153] A good film spoilt by a bad light.

13 November 1917

I met [Reynolds] and White at Claire's where we passed a very nice hour and being the last time I might see her, kissed her goodbye. Got a lift

153 Charles Chaplin, *A Burlesque on Carmen* (December 1915).

as far as Boisleux-au-Mont where I witnessed, quite close to, four tanks proceeding southwards.

14 November 1917

Went the round of the stations with rations – very cold in the lorry. Hicken is a good companion, so over-bubbling in spirits and vitality. He is 20 today. At times his bobbishness is rather irritating but at other quite entertaining.

16 November 1917

Aroused out of my slumbers by being told to go on a limber to the Corps Soda Water Factory. It was a most cold and monotonous journey, very slow and boring. Having a box of empty bottles prevented us from trotting, hence our speed was snail-like.

17 November 1917

During the morning had to cut up and sort out rations, always a distasteful job to me and as the rations (composed of meat, bacon, potatoes, onions, bread, butter or margarine, cheese, jam, tea and sugar) had to be divided in lots for 20, 12, 9, 6, 5 and 3 respectively, it took some reckoning. Feeling very greasy, had a bath in the afternoon. Later, Mr Redgrave told me that … the day before 'the Push', together with Bill and Wilkie, we would report at Corps for further prisoner interrogating.

18 November 1917

Things are in a very transitory stage. One gets orders and counter-orders, directions and instructions which are changed the next moment. First I was told to sort out the rations, then not to. Then to go up with the boxcar with rations and stores, then not to. At length I did and met Bill at the Saint-Léger crossroads. He was very fed-up with Wilkie who it seems is in one of his erratic moods. Luckily Davis, of all men, is playing the game. The Corps operator at the Station has fallen sick and is in hospital. Life too hard for him, I expect … Touring round, one can almost feel the atmosphere the proximity of a gigantic something; continuous traffic, general activity, more frequent inspections of iron rations and gas helmets and a look of expectancy on everybody's face.

19 November 1917

After a long period saw Captain Bowle-Evans again. I honestly think he was glad to see me again; he shook hands with me at once … Definite news has come through that for 'the Push', Bill, Wilkie and I go to Corps ... That means that we shall work again with Bowle-Evans interrogating Huns ... Left for Brétencourt, frankly glad to leave the Wireless *pro tem.*

20 November 1917

'The Push' started this morning and the distant firing woke me up. News was slow in coming through ... We had a look at a tank, for some reason left behind and I managed to get right inside. Very confined and when in action the noise must be deafening.

After dinner, the first batch of Hun prisoners turned up.[154] We only get specialists here, the bulk remaining at [the Cage in] Boisleux. They were a miserable lot, half-starved. It was 3 pm when they were brought in and they had had nothing to eat since yesterday morning. Bowle-Evans was away and as these men were specialists, I did not want to question them before he had seen them, so saw that they had something to eat given them, also arranged for some sandbags for them to sit on instead of bare wet earth. They are under canvas so are not really badly off. Examined documents until 9 pm and then closed down for the day. 'The Push' seems to be going fairly well, only one of our Corps doing badly.

21 November 1917

Carried on with interrogation. This is not easy as suitable accommodation is scarce. It is essential to have the man away, separated from his comrades, so we have had to discover quiet spots amongst neighbouring ruins, or perhaps a mess hut, an old Nissen hut and therein conduct our questioning ... The day's questioning work over, we started searching the documents, sorting rubbish from readable material, but at 6.30 pm we visited our friend Claire and there ... had a fine meal of omelettes, chips, wine, coffee and cheese. Quite bucked us up.

22 November 1917

Very depressing day and did not feel like hard work. Captain Bowle-Evans was in a touchy mood too. The majority of the Germans were sent off, only a few extra specials remaining. There are one or two sick, one feverish with a temperature of over 100 degrees. He was sent off too. During the document examination, Bill was lucky in finding an Iron

154 'In order to assist in the main attack of the Third Army against the German defensive system west of Cambrai, the VI Corps was ordered to carry out certain operations whereby the enemy's attention might be drawn north of the area where it was proposed to pierce his lines, and ground of importance might be gained.' The corps took 775 prisoners in this operation: VI Corps, 'Operations of the Corps, 20–26 November 1917', 5 December 1917, WO95/772, TNA.

Cross. The next best I could do was finding two ribbons. The rumour and news atmosphere is very lively as of course being at Corps HQ we get news very quickly. Whenever we meet in the Mess, i.e. the clerks etc., the first question is "What's the latest?" also when the men come into the hut at night. On the whole, rumours are scarce, official news for a change being the actual news heard.

23 November 1917

The greater part of the day spent on documents. The Intelligence Office is too small for this and we have to work in the Mess room and clear everything away before a meal. Bill and I went to Claire's and had another good meal. Claire had improved in looks and is more attractive looking than before. I think Bill is a little taken with her ... Everybody very pleased as Bourlon Wood and village have been taken, the wood being a splendid point of observation, high up, overlooking miles, something like Barr Beacon, near Sutton Coldfield.

24 to 26 November 1917

These days have been exactly alike, so I am giving a general summary of our work. It has largely consisted of reading through documents which are mainly made up of purely military data and general correspondence. The former are naturally of official value, the latter of general interest. The chief impression one gains is the great longing for peace by everybody. *Wenn nur der Schwindel ein Ende hätte*[155] is the commonest expression and shows how all regard this war as a gigantic farce, or hoax or 'swindle' for the benefit of a select few called *Die Capitalisten*. One reads many sad letters, but also – and this is remarkable – a great many religious letters. It is striking what faith a large number have in the Lord and his being able to bring the War to a favourable end. There is no doubt about the sincerity of most of the writers and one feels sorry at having to tear up a lot of these letters. It is but a test of Martin Luther's doctrine of absolute faith in the Lord being put into practice and after an account from home of the privations that are at present being borne, three out of four letters end with words to the effect "but we must have faith in *der liebe Gott* who will bring everything to a happy ending". It compels one's admiration. Many letters begin with "God guard and watch over you". The great hope and longing is for peace. Even the German successes over

155 'If only the [*Schwindel*] had an end.' *Schwindel* – giddiness, vertigo; extravagant project; charlatanism; swindling; fraud, cheat, humbug: Karl Breul, *A New German and English Dictionary* (London: Cassel, 1909), 530.

the Italians only make the populace hope for an earlier peace, no wild jubilation, just a renewal of hopes for peace. I am convinced that given a vote, the German people would welcome peace at any price, even to the giving of Alsace-Lorraine to France.

27 November 1917

Today was a breather. There were a few documents to read through before dinner but they were of no real interest. Afterwards sat in the Church Army Hut and wrote letters. The accumulation of letters from only slightly known but well-meaning people almost becomes a nuisance and after a time weigh on one's mind.

28 November 1917

Documents still trickle in. Bill is in one of his childish, excitable moods and feels offended because Bowle-Evans is rather suspicious of our taking German postcards as souvenirs.

29 November 1917

After 'standing to' all morning for something that didn't turn up, we went for a walk after dinner. Some documents I looked at were interesting. They were German instructions to men to listen for our light trolley railway, the times of arrival and departure and to report these times in order for the artillery to open fire. As these reports were captured from the Battalion exactly opposite our station at Croiselles and very probably the noise heard was that of the wheels of the trolley we pushed to Écoust and back for rations every other night during the middle and end of September, we might have had a warm reception one night had we not asked Mr Redgrave to introduce another way of having the stuff brought up.

30 November 1917

Had usual meal at Claire's though being pay day, was on a larger scale than usual, including wine and champagne.

1 December 1917

Life is easy now, next to no work. We just report at 10 am to Captain Bowle-Evans, look over whatever reports or documents may have come in and otherwise amuse ourselves as best we can. Claire's was a bit of a rough house tonight, that cousin of hers, Georges, on leave, being with other French fellows in a very lively mood, and Claire herself could not keep up her first attitude of seriousness and so soon became quite larky.

2 December 1917

Attended Church Parade on my lonesome. A company of a labour battalion marched up. All the staff generals (who also attend service) stood on the right and the poor lieutenant in charge of the company, gave 'Eyes left' instead of 'Eyes right'. Fortunately for him, the men of their own accord gave 'Eyes right', so all ended well. After dinner we witnessed a boxing tournament at which several Yankees boxed and were quite sporting. A feature of the tournament was a kicking contest between men of the Indo-Chinese Labour Company in this area. Marvellous balance. Small men, long hair, with native beads as necklace and bracelets, quite picturesque.

3 December 1917

Walked to Boyelles … [and] found Redgrave in a bad humour but learnt that leave was starting again shortly and that he hoped to get 'at least' 12 away this month, in which case I would go as there are 9 before me. Discomforting news being that of a return to the line shortly, in fact, any day. This did rather upset me, being so sudden.

5 December 1917

Packed up and arranged for boxcar to meet us at the Signals Office for 6.30 pm. I feel this parting from civilisation and rest more than on any previous return to the line. Somehow, without being windy, I dread the idea of returning to the rough old life. The stay down here has been so pleasant, the Intelligence and other men have been so decent that without doubt I have been spoilt. In due course [we] were picked up by the boxcar and reached Boyelles and, packed like sardines, kipped down anywhere.

7 December 1917

Went to see 'The Chequers'[156] at night, jolly good show. Had an omelette at the one and only civilian house in this region at Boisleux … The concert party was excellent, there was a full house and the cars waiting for officers when we came out gave quite the 'taxi' or 'ride home in the car' touch familiar in the pre-war days after a theatre night. Several men called out "Taxi here". Found everybody half drunk in the hut, celebrating the reopening of leave … Haines … rather oiled, asked for past rows and differences to be forgotten. We had had several. The most interesting thing to me was the news that I go up the line tomorrow.

156 34th Division's concert party.

8 December 1917

Packed up and with several others cleared off in the boxcar. In due course Lederer … and I arrived at the old No. 24 IT Station [run by Sergeant Edwards]. Found everything in a very dirty state, few rations, and my room occupied by officers and in fact, the whole very depressing … They have been laying new wires in lieu of the old ones which were destroyed during the last attack and have had no time to bother about the upkeep of the dug-out. As soon as their work is completed, this place will be thoroughly swept and cleaned out and I shall run it on the same principle as before.

11 December 1917

Had breakfast of biscuits borrowed from next door and bully beef, and feeling miserable, tried to look cheerful. Redgrave came up again and brought the news that Jerusalem had fallen.

12 December 1917

Dick relieved me at 6 am and I was just dozing off when the guns opened out hell for leather. It sounded as if the much discussed and expected attack on this front was coming off. I went upstairs and, risking the shell splinters, had a quick glance round. Over the trenches, fountains of earth were shooting up, just visible in the early morning mist, nasty red flashes kept cutting through the gloom and without ceasing, one heard crashes, bangs, roars, whistles, whines and shrieks of shells, fizz-thud of shell splinters hitting the ground. Then from Croiselles and the ridge, behind us, hundreds of bright red orange flashes, some big, some small, some almost dazzling and others bringing into sharp relief the outline of the ridge, all combined to make up a scene one could never tire of watching. A splinter entering a sandbag behind me brought me to my senses and I dived below again. The noise went on for about an hour and then gradually died down. I heard that on our right the Germans made an attempt but that only three men had reached our lines.

13 December 1917

Gas alarm at 1 am in the morning, so for half an hour we lay on our stretchers waiting, but not a whiff. Next morning several complained of feeling queer … 'Dirty Dick' [Lederer] reported sick and to our astonishment was booked for a Casualty Clearing Station. His departure from here was typical of the man's denomination, a Jew. He forgot his puttees and umpteen other things but, besides his own tobacco (good stuff), he almost upset the dug-out for common ration tobacco and cigarettes to give away should anyone ask him for 'baccy or a fag when away.

14 December 1917

A very normal day during which nothing much happened. I cut up meat for dinner and peeled potatoes, also made tea and then sat with the others listening to the RAMC Corporal from 'next door' who often comes into our place for a yarn. He is an 'old soldier' and when he and 'Daddy' get going, there is plenty to listen to. Both have an old soldier style of story-telling, with plenty of swearwords intermingled with "Says I to 'im" and "Says 'e to me" with the same gesture and screwed up facial expressions.

16 December 1917

Today we had the first snows. Instead of the view of dirty brown-green rolling plains, all was white, though, the fall being slight, the bare ground was visible and has a more miserable aspect than if completely covered in white. Cecil and I went to fetch rations and were met by Sergeant Shepherd who, as usual, was like a wet blanket. As Cecil remarked, meeting that man casts a gloom over one for the rest of the day.

18 December 1917

Heard my leave was not due on the 24th. Bit by bit it gets postponed … Redgrave is ill and in hospital at Boulogne. Life just now consists of hanging on to the day I go on leave. I don't take a genuine interest in anything just now. Feeling stale. I go on duty, come off, give a hand with 'household' work, make my usual cups of cocoa, read and sleep during spare times and generally feel rather fed-up.

19 December 1917

Introduced the timetable system by which every fellow knows what he has to do on that day. Each man read it through and agreed to it, so there should not be any trouble. 'Daddy' left us today – to put out a new Station 'tis said. This leaves me in charge, a position rather more responsible in these months than ever before … As I come on duty at midnight, turned in early after reading Mr Asquith's speech in Birmingham.[157] Considered it sounded like President Wilson's, only in other words.[158]

157 Asquith spoke on 11 December in the context of Lord Lansdowne's 29 November letter to the *Daily Telegraph* 'calling for a reconsideration of Britain's stated war aims': John Turner, *British Politics and the Great War: Coalition and Conflict, 1915–1918* (New Haven. CT: Yale University Press, 1992), 248–51.

158 The US President had made his 'State of the Union' address on 4 December.

21 December 1917

Several parcels have greatly added to the enjoyment of our meals and in between, I suck toffee and other things continually. Things running quite quietly and smoothly here. The RAMC men have a gramophone and to lie on my stretcher and listen to it was one of the greatest treats I have had for a long time … The sensation of the evening was the news that Tucker and Meredith have been awarded the Military Medal. It seems that during the German attack on [12 to 14 December] at Bullecourt, they stuck it out in the dug-out until the Brigadier gave orders for them to retire … So the fellows packed up and cleared off at midnight and safely reached Écoust. Tucker told me the whole thing was a farce and would not even shake hands with us as he considered the award was not deserved. Had there been heavy shelling on at the time, perhaps, but just then things were quiet. In fact, after they had brought the instrument to safety, they returned for their blankets. Tucker gave as his opinion that they had gained the award through obeying an order to run away when it wasn't necessary.

23 December 1917

We had the usual men in to tea and the Signals Corporal and a friend came for supper. It is quite the thing to stroll in calmly and take a cup of tea or cocoa for granted. Cecil was active at the instrument and as I lay 'in bed', was called out several times to translate.

Vince took leave in England.

12 January 1918

I came back from leave today and feel somewhat like a snowball in hell. It seems strange that a fortnight could so change one's views of a place. I certainly never liked this camp [at Boyelles], but now I consider it awful, with the draughty dirty huts, the cold wind howling and whistling and such an atmosphere of bleakness and desolation all round. It strikes me all the more forcibly after the crowds and life and bustle of Birmingham and London. More than ever one feels absolutely in an out of the way corner of the earth. Meanwhile, no news of my going up the line, so I am intending to take things easy here and make the best of things. Once the natural feeling of depression after return from leave is over, I shall be quite OK again.

13 January 1918

I walked to Boisleux to see the dentist but found he had gone, so after a cup of tea and slice of cake at the Expeditionary Forces Canteen, I attended a service in the YMCA. Out of the six hymns sung, there was only one I knew. The address was poor, so returned to camp, still feeling rather depressed and not as cheered by the YMCA service as I had hoped.

14 January 1918

Again visited the dentist, this time more luck. Pain due to abscess in tooth. The stopping was pierced and the pain thereby relieved. On way back met boxcar en route for Corps HQ so had a ride there. We had to give a hand with lifting a piano from the Church Army Hut to a cart … and after doing so, gave the fellows a performance of *The Pink Lady*. My endeavours did not seem to be appreciated and a fussy policeman came up and told me to stop the row. I spent the evening with Cecil [Stallworthy] in his hut up on the hill overlooking this camp. We discussed Marie Corelli's book *The Sorrows of Satan*[159] and Satan in particular, later having supper of tinned plums, condensed milk, cocoa and biscuits. In this Wireless hut reports are both received and sent off. A few days ago, during the German-Russian armistice, Cecil took a message wherein Berlin and Petrograd exchanged compliments and whilst I was there, a British station sent out a wireless warning vessels of the whereabouts of submarines in the Mediterranean.

15 January 1918

Fetched rations from Boisleux, anything but a pleasant job. Boisleux station is where the rations are given out and at the time of distribution is it is the centre of great activity. Lorries, limbers, GS wagons, carts, boxcars, all are jumbled together, but the rationing is done quite quickly in spite of the long queues waiting. All the stuff is shoved into sandbags or any other available bags and put into the boxcar and when ready, we slowly wade through the crowd, cross the railway after which the traffic is less and our progress more rapid. Later on, we had to take rations to the Directing Station, a kind of local telephone exchange and then to my station near Croiselles … [On my return] I had to change my things, being wet through, but now I am on my bed, with the rain rattling against the corrugated iron roof and the wind blowing as if to blow down the hut.

---

159 Marie Corelli, *The Sorrows of Satan* (1895).

17 January 1918

Redgrave told me he wanted me to buy things at Amiens for the Mess … Got [there] in time for a good luncheon in the hotel overlooking the station and afterwards did the shopping, indulging in the usual flirtation with my friend, Suzanne, which resulted in her giving me a bag of apples and tangerines. These visits to Amiens are always similar in one respect, a visit to Suzanne at the 'Jardins Espagnols', to a *demoiselle* in a stationer's shop whom I give whatever foreign stamps come my way and from whom I get a packet of envelopes in exchange and lastly to a 'Miss Lulu' at the American Bar who treats me to some weird concoction which makes me feel on good terms with myself and the world in general.

19 January 1918

After dinner, had to take rations up to Croiselles on a limber wagon. The horses were restless, all the more as one or two guns were firing close by. At length the driver lost control and I hopped out, landing on my feet for once in a way in some marvellous fashion. The horses dashed up the road and one of them eventually caught its foot and crashed down. Between us, the driver and I got it free, when, before where we knew where we were, the brutes dashed off again but luckily made for a pile of debris, once a wall, and this stopped them, though one of the horses again became caught and tripped up. Hicken and Haines meanwhile appeared on the scene and helped us to unharness the animals as everything had become hopelessly entangled. In spite of much jumping and shying, we somehow harnessed the beasts and only just prevented them from making off again by hanging on to their heads like grim death, and it was indeed a relief when we left Croiselles and the startling bangs of guns nearby, which caused the mischief.

20 January 1918

Walked to Béhagnies, intending to see pictures but found the Irish Guards were holding a concert. The place was packed and the music grand, really excellent. The pieces were very mixed, like a Llandudno 'popular' night. Thus selection from Gilbert & Sullivan operas, *William Tell*, *Chu Chin Chow* and *Bubbly*. Also a potpourri of various pieces by famous composers … Towards the end, the electric light flickered and went out but the band managed to play on in darkness, a flashlight from one of the audience just shining on to the conductor until candles hastily lit and handed round relieved the situation.

21 January 1918

To Croiselles … [and] once again I am in a dug-out with Sergeant Edwards in charge … Lost toss with Walter for Bill's stretcher, so have to sleep on floor … Before Bill left, I gave him a taste of Dad's parting gift – Curaçao – went down midst much lip-smacking. I had some shortly before turning in; it's like a health tonic.

22 January 1918

Cooking is now performed downstairs. Both the Beatrice stoves are in working order and a very excellent frying pan arrangement had been made out of a biscuit tin, made by Bill. Dinner over, I washed up and thereafter had a most necessary wash and shave myself. All our washing water we get from the well-filled shell holes around. Very convenient. After tea lay down on 'bed' and read *The Vultures* by HS Merriman.[160]

23 January 1918

The rations were brought up and Wilkie cooked meat and spuds, the process taking close on four hours. The dug-out was filled with the most unholy stink of coke fumes from a brazier next door and our own cooking … All of us had headaches, while frequent visits outside to inhale fresh air made no difference to how we felt. By 8 pm we were ravenous and I think hunger was upsetting us as much as anything for as soon as we had eaten the meat and potatoes, we began to feel better.

24 January 1918

Walked to Saint-Léger in order to breathe in some fresh air, to enquire about baths and to buy odds and ends … Had some tea at the YMCA, installed in the stables attached to a sugar refinery. Whilst there, Croiselles was being shelled, but old Jerry very politely ceased when we started to return. I bought some sardines for tea and after spreading them on bread and butter placed them on a slab of wood (acting as a plate), putting it on the floor, a very usual thing. But this time, unnoticed in the semi-darkness, the cat we have for killing mice, silently approached, attracted by the smell of sardines and thus, just as I was putting the bread into my mouth, I noticed that all signs of the sardines had vanished, eaten up by the cat. The day's work over, I pulled out the stretcher and squatted down, reading *The Laughing Cavalier*[161] and enjoyed a really peaceful evening.

---

160 Henry Seton Merriman, *The Vultures* (1902).

161 Probably Emmuska Orczy, *The Laughing Cavalier* (1914).

26 January 1918

Every sixth day one's turn comes round to take the reports over to Battalion HQ when coming off duty at 6 am.[162] It was my turn this morning … Everybody was 'standing to', except the runners in the Orderly Room, who were sleeping on the steps, the floor, anywhere in the dug-out. Struck me in what comparative comfort we live now and how much worse off we were during the 1915/16 winter with the Warwicks than even these fellows … After tea [we] had one of our old time games of pontoon in which I won 2½ francs, not much, but it's better than nothing. Poor old 'Dad', after losing last night, he swore he wouldn't play again. I wonder how long he will stick to his word!

27 January 1918

Walked into Saint-Léger for a bath. We found the baths in the usual patched up barn, but quite passable and clean. The only thing lacking was the water which dripped out of a douche drop by drop at a most amazingly slow rate. Still, we managed to get rid of some dirt and, with a clean change of washing … felt better.

30 January 1918

Walter and I went for our walk to Saint-Léger; the exercise always does us good and at the same time we buy things from the YMCA. Walter is rather prejudiced against the YMCA for selling at a profit – if they do – but that does not prevent him from buying off them. Found the usual crowd waiting in a queue. They make quite an interesting picture. The General Service man, unfit for trench duty, getting on in years or physically unfit, usually with a uniform that hangs on him, a soft hat covered by a cap rain protector. Or one sees the transport driver with his short 'British Warm' overcoat and collar turned up, top boots and spurs. A sprinkling of signallers with blue and white arm bands or artillery 'blokes', usually big hefty men. Then, of course, the infantrymen out of the trenches, covered with mud, wearing equipment with the ever-present rifle, a fag in mouth or stuck behind the ear and, naturally, wearing a tin helmet. Some of them sit around a fire in the 'reading room', others lie on the floor, others sit at a table, if available, their heads buried in their arms, fast asleep, or trying to snatch some sleep. We buy what we want, have a cup of tea – the cup being an empty cigarette or condensed milk tin – and then we return the way we came, in time to get back for a proper tea in

162 19/Royal Welch Fusiliers (119th Infantry Brigade, 59th Division): VI Corps, 'Dispositions of Infantry', 26 January 1918, WO95/773, TNA.

the dug-out. Tea over, out come the cards and the usual evening pontoon starts and so the time passes until one or other interpreter takes over for the first half of the night's shift at the IT instrument.

2 February 1918

I am reading quite an interesting book taken off a German prisoner relating to the adventures, life and diary of the U-boat commander who shelled Madeira and Funchal.[163] Rather a novelty reading a German book and seeing us spoken of in about the same fashion we speak of the Germans.

3 February 1918

Had a great treat today. Walter Breakey and I strolled over to Saint-Léger and at the baths found our old friend Corporal Noble in charge … A hint of something to be had induced him to give us a bath worthy of the name. As a result, we had the officers' bath to ourselves, water at first so hot we couldn't stand it (or, as a matter of fact, sit in it) and lastly, Noble gave us a complete change of new underwear.

4 February 1918

Corker lost 30 francs at pontoon but he was very sporting about it. He is quite a remarkable character, short and fat, a very deep gruff laugh and a long intake of breath sounding like a hiccough, are his chief characteristics, but a round chubby face, a fat little body and a continual smile is the picture that remains in the mind's eye. We call him 'Jelly Belly'.[164]

6 February 1918

We toddled into Croiselles, each with 60-pound exhausted accumulator on his back which at the best of times is awkward to carry but with the sticky mud now prevalent is, if anything, more awkward. We waited at Croiselles for the boxcar, but in vain and so walked on to the Directing Station, a couple of miles further away … arriving back at the dug-out fairly whacked by 4 pm. We were in none too good a humour then and having to turn to at once and cut meat and cook dinner for six did not improve mine. Everything seemed to go wrong. Stoves would not burn, candle would not stick up but kept falling over, meat was tough

163 Max Valentiner, *Dreihunderttausend Tonnen versenken! Meine U-Boot-Fahrten von Max Valentiner* (Berlin and Vienna: Ullstein, 1917). On 3 December 1916 U-38 had shelled Funchal.

164 When he joined the army in September 1916 his height and weight were recorded as 5' 3" and 116 lbs.

and sinewy and Walter and I had words over the tea but they passed by without further ill feeling. A fitting climax to the whole day was that I lost 20 francs at [pontoon].

7 February 1918

Good or refined language had never been a strong point with us and it seems the doctor, who in his partition of the dug-out can hear all we say, said a few words to 'Dad' on the subject. So when we were all assembled at dinner, he announced in a very grandiose tone, "Gentlemen, there have been complaints about the language. In future there must be no swearing". At that precise moment the acetylene lamp popped out and as he turned round to attend to it, 'Dad' exclaimed "Who the bloody hell has damn well been fucking about with this bloody lamp?" Considering the virtuous way he had opened the sentence, the ending rather belied his words and made him look decidedly sheepish.

9 February 1918

Rotten bacon for breakfast, resulting in everybody having indigestion. I made a quite passing stew of bully beef, potatoes, onions and pea soup powder.

12 February 1918

Dug-out almost upside down through packing up. Marvellous how things accumulate and how invaluable sandbags are for keeping them in … Came out and waited for the boxcar at Croiselles and on nothing turning up, continued on to Saint-Léger, meeting it halfway. Back in camp at Boyelles, as usual felt a bit out of it with all the strange faces, even more so through having taken a bed in Staff Sergeants Floyd and Gosney's hut.

13 February 1918

This could be a most comfortable hut were it not so cold. Without a fire, it is rather bleak. Another thing, the company is not quite to my liking, nothing personal against any individual, only I don't feel so much at ease with them as in the men's hut, to which I shall try to return at the first opportunity. Also, this seems to be the camp's wet canteen as Bass's beer is sold to everybody and several fellows 'drop in' for a 'chat' and end by 'dropping out', singing. Needless to say, any quiet evening reads are 'napoo'.

14 February 1918

I have to fetch rations from Boisleux every morning. This consists of a ride in a boxcar to Boisleux, a railhead, post office, canteen and general meeting centre. As one approaches, all roads have lorries, limbers, general service wagons on, all making one way, towards the gigantic ration dump. We take our turn in the queue, eventually get served, dropping raw meat, bacon, loaves of bread and so on into sandbags, carry them on our backs to the waiting boxcar, flounder through the mud to the 'office', presenting the indent for the next day, call at the post office for the 'Wireless' mail, cash any postal orders, buy any wanted, then proceed to the Canteen, buy what we want from there and so at length slide in and out of traffic to the boxcar and eventually reach camp, where … the officers' chef … takes the rations, whilst I distribute the mail and canteen purchases … Tomorrow I am Corporal in charge of the 'Sanitary Squad', yet another post I have never filled.

15 February 1918

The worst part of [the] job was having to get out of bed rather early. But otherwise the job was easy and simply consisted of supervising the work done in connection with the sanitary arrangements of the camp.

17 February 1918

Bill and I obtained a day's pass to go to Brétencourt … Lunch at Claire's was very nice, pork chops, chips, wine, cheese, coffee etc … We attended a 'sacred' concert in the Church Army Hut, rather weak through the performers' lack of practice, nervousness and squeaking instruments. Soon after, Bill and I started back but the poor fellow suddenly had such an attack of neuralgia, we called in at a Casualty Clearing Station where he had given him a kind of drug and the pain lessened until we reached camp, where he went to bed and even a bombing raid failed to get him out of it.

18 February 1918

Saw the searchlights trying to pick up bombing raiders. In camp, everybody was outside following the direction of the humming, counting the dull booms as the bombs dropped, all talking when the humming was not our way, with dead silence when overheard, only the occasional voice saying "They're right over us now".

20 February 1918

Owing to the recent [air] raids, there is a dug-out-building epidemic and this spread to our hut. This afternoon we had the boards up and Gosney and I dug a few feet down. One can continually see men emerging from huts, carrying loads of brown earth and depositing same in odd corners. When it comes to one's own safety, it is marvellous how energetic one can become.

21 February 1918

The rumours about a new station are true and tomorrow 'Dad' comes down for a conference with Lieutenant Lane. Things are otherwise quiet but I think it is the quiet before the storm. One hears many stories about what Jerry is doing, what he is going to do and what we are going to do – and meanwhile there is nothing doing.

23 February 1918

Cecil and I had a walk after tea during which, on my pressing him, heard certain things that 'Dad' Edwards is supposed to have said concerning me and which will very much put me on my guard against him.

24 February 1918

Bill and I paid Arras a visit today … To Magniez's café. Met Jeanne there and Jeanne's friend also called Jeanne, a very strikingly handsome girl, if not pretty. She and I had a long chat together and in the end felt I should like to know more of her, but 'wot 'opes'. Mme Magniez, in tears, told me the café was being put out of bounds for a month owing to her having sold ½ dozen eggs to an officer's batman after hours. The batman himself came in later and I managed to get the officer's name, his Mess and address for Madame and she and Jeanne, who speaks a little English, at once went round to interview him. When I called at the café at night, Madame told me in high glee that the sentence had been reduced to one week only. Bill and I met at Mme Pruvost's and had a splendid luncheon, washed down with two kinds of wine, beer, cider, champagne, coffee and rum. Needless to say I felt on good terms with myself and the world in general. Discovered a 'reading room' in a certain club, reserved for officers but which NCOs can use if no officers are present … We went to a large cinema, the chief film being *The Girl who was Nothing*[165] … Journey back to camp rather slow, half walking, half on a GS wagon filled with empty bottles.

165 Maurice Elvey, *The Woman who was Nothing* (June 1917).

27 February 1918

Left for Croiselles in the boxcar en route for the new Station. We then proceeded on foot, each man carrying something. Judging by the absolute quiet and lack of life, we might have been surveyors in some unexplored land. We tramped across country, through sunken roads, bordered with the remains of dug-outs, in single file along tracks winding in and out of shell holes and obsolete trenches. The features of this walk were the enormous belts of barbed wire and the new trenches for defence zigzagging across. At length we entered the trenches proper and passing some old German ferro-concrete fortresses, eventually reached a certain shaft of the Hindenburg Tunnel in which we found Sergeant Edwards' party. They have beds built in the passage and a recess in the side as the office … We did not stay long.

28 February 1918

Bill and I went up the line … The dug-out, as usual on relief days, seemed to be upside down with things, equipment etc. lying about everywhere … Bill and Tucker almost had a row. Bill wanted the bacon outside because of the probability of it smelling. Tucker said the bacon was eaten up before it turned bad. Bill replied that at the faintest smell "out the bacon would go *and* no mistake!" to which Tucker answered that if it were thrown out a minute before it started smelling Bill's hair oil would be the first thing to follow, as that was always smelling … Then we settled down in our respective quarters and spent the evening fixing up shelves and improving other knick-knacks. Had supper of duck, cocoa and rum, the duck being one of Bill's delicacies.

1 March 1918

Hicken and Haines came in from the line with the news that all shafts leading into the Hindenburg Tunnel had been closed and as this would rather interfere with their work, I decided to go out and investigate … We took this tunnel and the front line above last November, our present front line being the old German front line. The tunnel runs along under the old German front line for miles … Inside the tunnel, except for a few German valises and occasional tin shrapnel helmet, there was nothing worth noting. In places where the wooden walls had been taken away, the chalk had already fallen in. We went along the front line, practically a path between gigantic shell holes and churned up earth on both sides and with nothing visible but mounds of brown earth or mud, the general effect was most weird … From one of our trenches there was such an excellent view of Jerry's lines that I considered discretion was the better part of valour and made off before old Jerry should have an excellent view of us … Quiet evening during which Bill amused himself by making some soup.

3 March 1918

In spite of the persistent rumours of a great offensive by the Boche, things are very quiet round here and we carry on our happy-go-lucky existence down here in the depths of the dug-out that in saner moments surprises me somewhat. It's difficult to realise that the day may come when a terrific bombardment will prevent us from leaving this dug-out and that the moment the firing ceases, Germans may be at the dug-out entrance and we ourselves prisoners. Just every now and then we discuss our chances of dashing through the barrage outside but obviously a definite conclusion is never reached … Bill and I had a discussion over Alsace-Lorraine and in the end both of us decided we had better go to school again and swot up our history.

4 March 1918

Owing to unsuitable meat, made a stew of chunks of meat, onions, bully, pea soup, mustard, pepper and Devonshire sauce. Tucker handed round some cake for tea which was a great treat and as margarine came up with the rations today (we have been without for several days) we all had an extra good tea.

5 March 1918

Besides the one cat we have had for some time, two more have appeared on the scene from somewhere and during my midnight to 6 am spell there was a pretty concert between them which ended in my chasing the lot into the officers' portion of the dug-out, whence they were chased out altogether. Things are still very quiet, the days passing by in monotonous regularity without any outstanding incident. I often wonder how long it will be before the storm bursts.

7 March 1918

Yesterday … Lance Corporal Gosney[166] came up with a Wireless set. This afternoon, Mr Redgrave came up himself concerning it. He told me the much talked of German offensive was expected to come off next Sunday

166 77672 Lance Corporal Charles Gosney RE.

[10 March][167] and the object of this station was to transmit to certain HQs any and all information of interest and importance, at all costs, anyhow. Until it is smashed, we have a Fullerphone wire to Brigade,[168] then the Wireless set must be used and besides that, a Power Buzzer to local stations. We are to stick here in this station to the last, then at the last moment smash the valves into atoms, burn all the papers and join the infantry should they fall back past this spot and so get back to Boyelles as best we can. Delightful outlook. The one thing is, similar warnings have been so often spread with nothing happening that even this one, calculated as it would be to put the wind up one, leaves me rather dubious. Still, I shall do all the necessary and after tea we started putting up the aerial for the Wireless set but could not finish the work before dark. The evening was spent discussing our chances of survival, excitedly by Bill, sarcastically by Tucker.

8 March 1918

I could get no answer from the line to Brigade. I rely on this wire to Brigade for all outside messages from Redgrave and also to send any messages from here. Until I got no answer to my repeated calling, I little realised what importance I laid on this thin little length of wire running across country, down odd trenches, through ruins of houses and under seas of mud. In the end, investigation showed that the batteries were very run down so we changed them and with immediate better results.

9 March 1918

I arranged with the 'Marconi House' amplifier fellows about our calling them up on the Power Buzzer, settling calls and address codes … then walked to Saint-Léger for a rather pressing bath and change of washing. It was a beautiful day and quite warm. Back in the dug-out, heard that Redgrave had been up with 'last minute instructions'. Everybody seems to have the wind up about Jerry attacking tomorrow. Although I find it hard to believe, one is still haunted with the thought that he might, and, as I mentally went over the last instructions given, remembered that we had plenty of paraffin to pour over instrument and papers to burn in case we should have no time to escape, remembered that Hicken had

167 For expectations regarding the timing of the German offensive, see Beach, *Haig's Intelligence*, 279–81.

168 102nd Infantry Brigade (34th Division): VI Corps, 'Dispositions of Infantry', 7 March 1918, WO95/773, TNA.

promised me his sleeping bag to slip the instrument in should there be a chance of our getting through, remembered that we had a pick and shovel in case entrances to the dug-out should be blown in. Well, as I recalled and classified each one of these factors, I felt something like a criminal disposing of his last goods and chattels before giving himself up to justice. As a final treat, I had some sardines on toast and after that said "Let 'em all come" and fell asleep.

10 March 1918

After all, another false alarm. Morning came and went and everything remained quiet … Beautiful day, like real Spring, heaps of larks singing. I lay on top, just outside the dug-out entrance and basked in the sun as soon as I had finished work. Having screwed up one's nerves for this morning's feared attack by the Germans it is almost disappointing that nothing has happened.

11 March 1918

Without doubt the Hun's artillery was more active today and everybody expects something to happen shortly. The morning of the 13th is the date forecast now. Haines and Hicken came back from the line with the news that the tunnel is being blown up by us in parts, the front line filled with barbed wire and the infantry withdrawn to our old front line. When the Germans come a barrage will form behind them, force them to our front line, into the barbed wire and there finish them off.

12 March 1918

Another final list of instructions from Reddy. One would imagine us being besieged and cut off from the outside world, what with several days' 'emergency rations', 'emergency water tins' and the wording of the instructions quite smacks of the melodramatic, ending with the words "To be destroyed and burnt when read". Once again I turned in with that feeling of "I've done all I can, so let 'em all come".

14 March 1918

We have quite resumed our normal mode of living after the state of expectancy of the last few days and all agree to a feeling of disappointment.

15 March 1918

Walked over to Boyelles. First had a long chat with Reddy over the working of the Station, the keeping up of the lines. We discussed various items and came to the conclusion that for the time being the Boche offensive would not break out.

16 March 1918

I accompanied the lads into Croiselles to fetch rations. In the sunshine now prevailing, the place looks doubly desolated and depressing. It is not so razed to the ground as some of the Somme villages and the walls stand often as much as 3 foot high with the remainder of the house within the square formed by the few feet of wall, just a hopelessly jumbled pile of debris. Some houses were mined and instead, the centre of the house is a large cavity with the superstructure lying all around the stumps of wall. But nevertheless, it is all so mixed up, no definite outlines of buildings can be traced. I think the most complete object still standing is a little overgrown summer-arbour in what I supposed was once a garden. Nobody seems to have had the heart to pull it down and use the wood for firewood. We heard the startling-to-us news that 'Dirty Dick' [Lederer] had turned up again. The cunning beggar, he's the next for leave.

19 March 1918

Went to Saint-Léger for a bath. The water was warm but we got a rotten change of washing. The dry weather spell has broken and today it rained on and off continually. Once more everything is soaked in mud and we were both fairly tired on our return.

20 March 1918

Bill and Hicken went out to rest, Wilkie and Corker coming in instead.

The Germans launched their offensive against Fifth and Third Armies. The Croiselles sector was at the northern end of their initial attack.

21 March 1918

I shall never in my life forget today. It first started by my hearing Wilkie (who was on duty) exclaiming "Well, I'll be damned, what smell is this?" I quite woke up then (it was about 4.30 am) and also smelt obvious tear gas. We had to wear our goggles for a time and investigation showed that a tear gas shell had exploded just outside our dug-out. Round 5 am,[169] up to which time everything had seemed normal, a terrific hullabaloo started. The icy truth dawned on me that these were not our guns but those of

169 The bombardment commenced at 0445: 102nd Brigade war diary, 21 March 1918, WO95/2461, TNA.

Jerry firing. At 5.15 am I called up on the Brigade line and obtained no answer – line smashed. At once I called up the Advanced Battalion [HQ] – same result.[170] I was thus cut off completely from receiving orders on how to act from Redgrave or anybody. Our intercepting lines went west one after the other and it was only by marvellous commutator combinations that we got any German messages. Twice during the morning I bolted across the field to the Advanced Battalion [HQ] for them to be delivered. The Signalling Corporal was in despair, every one of his lines was smashed and he could only rely on rumours. Ghastly sights were already to be seen in our trenches.

By 11 am we knew that the Germans were attacking Bullecourt on our right; against our sector so far nothing had been done. Haines ran out a couple of earths, a very plucky thing, 50 yards each side of the dug-out and we sent a Power Buzzer message to 'Marconi House'. All the time, without a second's interval, shells were coming over at a hideously terrifying rate, luckily mostly past our dug-out but playing hell with the railway embankment, the ravine, the 10 trees of Saint-Léger we so often saw silhouetted against the sunset, the valley of Croiselles, Croiselles itself and the Saint-Léger valley, sending up huge columns of dense black smoke, fountain shape clouds of earth, smoke and debris. One never heard a single whine, one only heard the monotonous, continuous uneven keyed roar of explosions. One only had to look at a spot for a couple of seconds before it would suddenly rise up as if forced up by some subterranean power; the whine of the shell would be lost 'midst the whines and swishes and reports and explosions of 1001 others. It *was* a sight. At 2 pm, peeping out from the dug-out entrance towards Écoust, we saw 3 long lines of dots crossing in extended order from the other side of the Ten Tree ridge to the railway embankment. Thank heaven, I thought, our reserves are coming up. But never shall I forget when, nearly an hour later, fierce machine-gun fire and rifle fire made me realise that those three lines of advancing dots were Germans and that more were following.[171]

170 22/Northumberland Fusiliers (102nd Infantry Brigade, 34th Division).

171 VI Corps was attacked by German infantry at 0930. In their southern sector 59th Division came under the heavier pressure and by 1530 had been forced back upon their rear defences. At this point 'large bodies of the enemy were reported to be moving north-west towards Croiselles'. 34th Division had also been attacked in the morning but, in the case of 102nd Infantry Brigade, had only lost their frontline positions. By 1300 the brigade became aware of the danger to its southern flank and began the process of withdrawing from east of Croiselles to avoid being cut off. In the late afternoon, under heavy fire, the German attack stalled and did not capture the village that day: VI Corps, 'Narrative of Operations, 21 March to 4 April', [April 1918], WO95/773; 102nd Brigade war diary, 21 March 1918, WO95/2461, TNA.

I at once gave orders to pack only the most necessary kit. I disconnected the instrument and definitely told the others we were going to try and run the gauntlet. As I wrapped the instrument in a blanket, destroyed all papers and just shoved my towel and shaving kit into my haversack, I remember half trying to pray, half thinking of the next thing to do and all at the same time saying to myself "Now keep cool, it's up to you".

Outside the dug-out, poor Corker's nerve nearly went and I honestly thought we should have to leave him. It was only by my telling him sharply that I could not run the risk of sacrificing four men for him that he at length moved out. For about 200 yards one felt like shrieking with laughter or crying.

Haines was fine, a typical Englishman, as cool as a cucumber. He and I stuck together. I could not help thinking how odd that he was the one man I once was never able to get on with. Wilkie, Tucker and Corker strayed more to the right. As long as they kept in sight, I did not mind. We were right in the open and to our left the murderous ploughing still continued. We had our close shaves, too, but I need not dwell on them; it only struck me how close a shell can burst without hitting a person.

We reached the outskirts of Croiselles and tried to get into a trench and a nightmare of a search after the gap in the barbed wire ensued before we found it. Alternately relieving the other, we carried the instrument to a crossroads where we came across the other three. For a moment, at a loss of our position, it was decided to cut through to the Croiselles–Saint-Léger road. We climbed up the bank on the sunken road to a field and were most promptly fired upon by machine-gun bullets. We wriggled on our bellies to the crossroads and decided not to go that way. So we blindly took a track leading west towards Boyelles and in spite of the attentions of a German plane flying very low (machine-gunning us from above), also of a nasty big gun firing, the shells exploding far too close to be pleasant (marvellously enough the three nearest were duds) we at length reached a spot I considered safe and out of danger and there we rested for the first time.

The boys were simply fine, I felt proud of them. Then we carried on and when I saw the aerial of Wireless Station at Boyelles, I gave a hoarse kind of cheer – we were as dry-throated as leather, although soaked in perspiration. Then we got into sight of camp itself and everybody turned out to welcome us. Bill's unfeigned delight at seeing me again was the sweetest thing, though Redgrave's words gave me a great amount of pleasure. We had quite been given up as lost, two wires with orders for us to return never reached us and Redgrave and Sergeant Shepherd could get no further than Saint-Léger when trying to reach us during the morning, owing to the intense shelling.

We must have looked an interesting picture, hot, dusty, dishevelled, dirty, just rifle, bandoliers and box respirators slung over our shoulders and our haversacks containing our few necessary belongings. I've lost my overcoat, valise, blankets, waterproof sheet, change of underwear and umpteen other things. But I shall get replacements in time.

(*1968 comment*: The first or earliest reaction I remember was listening to the German drumfire bombardment just after 5 am and realising with a horrid sense of reality and consciousness that 'this was it' – the much talked-of and feared prelude to the German offensive. It must be remembered that we were in a dug-out some 30 feet below ground and although providing shelter against shellfire, nevertheless gave one at the same time a nasty feeling of the risk of being trapped underground, either through the entrances being blown in or because the concentration of the shelling outside was too great to risk making a dash for safety. The dug-out exits gave on to a field which provided no cover whatsoever and the nearest trench was many yards away.

This first reaction was soon followed by a second, one which haunted me all morning and part of the afternoon – that of making our escape whilst the Germans concentrated on shelling our back areas leaving the vicinity of our dug-out comparatively alone. Despite the many difficulties in keeping our wires 'open' or 'live', as described in the diary, we managed to obtain the odd German message, both spoken in plain German and in Morse, the Germans surprisingly sending out the latter in plain, not in code as was customary. My orders were to 'stay to the last' and then to use my discretion. Thus, as long as we were able to receive spoken or Morse German messages, I felt it was my duty to stay on. I may add that the second of the two messages I took to the Advanced Battalion HQ mentioned in my diary was to the effect that the Germans occupying the sector opposite ours were advised to be ready to advance when the appropriate codeword signal had been transmitted. The other message was just a brief summary of the advances made in various sectors. What I also remember were the innuendoes, querying glances etc. cast my way suggesting that 'now' was the time to leave whilst the going was good. In the event, we stuck it until about 3 pm when I was convinced the Germans were advancing in a kind of pincer movement which, if completed, would have cut off our route of escape.[172]

172 'At 3.30pm RE operators of Listening Apparatus … left (after destroying apparatus) having received no messages since 11am.' The area was finally abandoned by the infantry two hours later: 102nd Brigade war diary, 21 March 1918, WO95/2461, TNA.

As we emerged from the dug-out, to our relief we found that the Germans were concentrating their fire mainly on the back areas where our artillery batteries were sited. In the diary I mention 'a nasty big gun' firing. I won't say that it was this gun, but I have a clear mental picture of watching the team of one of our batteries working full out, loading and unloading after firing and then, a sudden fountain of smoke intermingled with earth, a red/orange flash, a deafening crash and when the smoke drifted away, just nothing – a direct hit wiping out gun and team.

Nor shall I forget poor little Corker, a lad of about 19,[173] and his refusal to leave the safety of the dug-out. It is a terrible thing to see a young fellow with whom one has worked and played for months, in abject terror, crying and trembling like a frightened child. After I had told him, even ordered him to follow us, Wilkie and Tucker had to drag him for the first dozen yards, by which time he realised that things were not quite as bad as he feared. Corker was a fat, cheerful little fellow and I shall never forget how unconsciously his fat 'behind' kept poking up as we 'wriggled on our bellies' to that crossroads. I remember shouting to him "Keep your bloody behind down" and at the same time laughing hysterically at the funny picture he made.

I have been awakened in my dreams at the evil picture of that German airman, with his goggles and helmet, peering down at us over the side of the cockpit of his machine as the plane flashed past us, rooftop height only … On his second run, the pilot started machine-gunning us. The natural reaction was to fall flat but some lesson learnt somewhere sprang from the sub-conscious to the very conscious that lying flat would offer a far better target than standing up, so I shouted to the boys to keep standing, no easy task whilst listening to the stream of bullets whining past and watching them make a pattern in the ground. We were not hit and as the plane flew on, knowing it might return, I ordered the boys to make for whatever cover they could or lie flat, absolutely quiet, as if hit, but nothing further happened. The whole incident only took a few seconds.

Approaching Boyelles, Captain Redgrave's and his Wireless HQ, we had to cross over a railway embankment. Our figures must have been silhouetted against the sky as hardly had we come down the other side of the embankment when, so it seemed, the whole camp staff turned out to welcome us. I have rarely been so touched in my life. All day I had been tensed up and for the first time, knowing that I was safe at last, I was afraid I would break down and make a fool of myself. Bill, in his

173 Corker was twenty-two; see 22 August 1917 entry.

delight to see me, nearly did so. It was Captain Redgrave who saved me. He just asked me to come to his tent; I remember he ordered his batman to bring two large bottles of beer and there I told him the whole story and this I suppose acted as a safety valve. I was to tell that story, modified according to circumstances, many times that evening to the other 'boys' of the Wireless camp.)

22 March 1918

Living over the past 24 hours prevented me from sleeping much, tired as I was. Sad to relate, the Hun is having a marvellous run of success and during the morning the Wireless Camp got moving orders. Bill, Wilkie and I had orders to go to Boisleux Prison Cage. About a dozen prisoners there. Everywhere signs of a retirement and, needless to say, spirits were not good. The Expeditionary Force Canteen at Boisleux was set afire and the cloud and smoke and flames must have been visible for miles around. Then, during the afternoon, sudden orders to pack up and proceed to Brétencourt, Corps HQ. The German prisoners' undisguised pleasure at the obvious reason for this move was very galling. An officer, in particular, was very pleased, so rather to that gentleman's disgust, he was put to ride in one of the lorries on top of the pile of stores, tents and camp paraphernalia. … Rumours of a most fantastic description fly round. Corps HQ are moving tonight. We are to hang on at the Prisoner-of-War Cage.

23 March 1918

We are under a Captain Barrow,[174] a very decent sort, though a Lieutenant Bradgate[175] also interrogates. He is a very disagreeable type. Few prisoners come in and there is not much to do except arrange shifts in Prisoners' Cage and office hours during day.

24 March 1918

Things are not going well with our Army. The Germans are said to have taken Péronne and Bapaume and are still advancing. Everybody hears and says different rumours until one hardly knows what to believe and of course these stories lengthen with the telling. This morning I heard that the Germans had shelled Paris with a gun firing a distance of 70 odd miles.[176] By night it had grown to 100 miles! … Towards evening I was

174 Captain P.L. Barrow.

175 Lieutenant Lionel Bradgate. Joined VI Corps headquarters January 1918: WO339/972, TNA.

176 The actual range was around eighty miles: Zabecki, *German 1918 Offensives*, 80.

told [tomorrow] I had to go to the 43rd Casualty Clearing Station [at Bac-du-Sud].

25 March 1918

Packed up again and cleared off. What a game this is. Reached the 43rd CCS … Wounded were coming in fast, ghastly sights and they required attention before anything else … Spent all day giving a helping hand at any odd job, carrying wounded, stretchers, taking messages, anything, though I also had to interrogate some Boches, wounded. And so the day passed quickly. But some of the sights are hideous and the way the wounds are borne without a groan is marvellous. I shall often think of that long reception hut, filled with either silent, motionless covered up forms on blankets, or the walking cases, with their torn, dirty and tattered uniforms, with white bandages showing up strongly, often with a dull red blotch.

26 March 1918

I have meals in the Sergeants' Mess and fare very well. The RAMC Sergeants aren't bad either. During the morning I heard that no more wounded are being admitted and that the hospital was moving. On the strength of this I did not see the sense of my staying so [tried to find the wireless headquarters] … An American gave me a lift on his lorry and I heard the Ostende yarn which we were supposed to have taken, but I think it is only another 'Russians passing through England' story to buck our men up … After tea I packed up and drew some very useful things from the stores (including a waterproof sheet cape) and then walked to Gouy. Here found everybody rather disgruntled as it seems moving orders came late last night and it was 1 am before Gouy was reached, and of course every body had to sleep out in the open. These cold nights, this is no joke. Then Bill had a lot of his kit pinched and naturally the poor fellow is very upset. Towards evening we hit upon a first-class billet, most conveniently close to the Cage, a large room in a cottage, a dear old woman and an excellent log fire round which we sat and chatted until late.

27 March 1918

Things very slack as regards work and I'm not bothering about the prisoners. My chief object is to make the best of life. We have one of the Huns in here to act as a general valet. He blacks our boots, polishes our buttons, washes up, draws water from the well, chops wood, lights the fire, warms water for washing and altogether is quite a useful and genial young man … [We procured] 3 bottles of Johnnie Walker [whisky] and thus, after fried eggs and bacon and coffee, we stayed up until after midnight, chatting and singing. This life is 'very much so'. As one of us said "If this is the life when retiring, then I'm going to retire for life".

28 March 1918

Early this morning, Captain Barrow came with a string of new orders which will scatter us all over the place … Bill's wedding present, 4 pipes in a case from Dunhill turned up and he seemed pleased with it – at least a little consolation for the loss of his other pipes. After dinner got a lift on a lorry to Avesnes-le-Comte and there managed to get into a train leaving for Frévent, where 43rd Casualty Clearing Station had moved to. But on arrival there and discovering whereabouts, found everything in a very backward state, with the prospect of having to sleep in the open or on wet grass … under a tent.[177] So went in search of a billet. Luck was with me. The proprietress of a restaurant where I had a couple of eggs and coffee recommended a certain house, and there, after a little talking, the old couple took me in.

29 March 1918

The old woman was very decent and gave me some hot water for washing and shaving and after the night's rest, I felt fine. Went out to find breakfast somewhere and got some tea and cold ham in a rest camp near the station. Then strolled round to get my bearings, found there are some restaurants about, so won't starve, though as soon as the Sergeants' Mess is opened in the hospital, I shall live and mess there.

30 March 1918

Nosed round for a bath and struck oil again. Had a fine warm shower-bath also a change of underwear. The last bath I had was … only 10 days ago, but it seems ages now after all that has happened. Whilst going up to the Hotel de la Gare for lunch, heard a lot of cheering and then, slowly turning round the corner at the top of the road, a magnificent car appeared with the Royal Standard on the radiator. The car passed quite close on my side of the road and I saw His Majesty splendidly – the first

177 Configured as a 700-bed hospital, it had just arrived from Bac-du-Sud and was not ready to receive casualties until 1 April: 43rd CCS war diary, 26 March to 4 April 1918, WO95/416, TNA.

time I have ever seen him. Suppose he is out to give the troops some bucking up.[178]

1 April 1918

These long sleeps are doing me a world of good. I sleep as long as I like, dress leisurely and then have breakfast at a little restaurant close by. Thereafter I walk over the uneven, cobbled pavement to the hospital to see what is doing and I am then free for the day … Was told that from tonight they would be taking cases at the hospital so … trudged through the streets with valise and the inevitable mailbag filled with blankets on my back to the hospital where I soon got fixed up.

2 April 1918

Unfortunately there is no 'sleeping out' like at the old billet. One has to get up at about 6.45 am, willy-nilly. During the morning made myself a basin out of a petrol tin and a 'dressing table' out of an old box, then did a little work in the office. Things are slow otherwise, no Boches coming in and I do a little work in the office just to justify my *raison d'être*. Saw a Hun, a great big hulking fellow, being returned to his prison after escaping, by a little fat *Gendarme*, bubbling over with importance. They made quite a humorous picture walking through the street.

3 April 1918

An Australian band played during the afternoon. During one of the intervals got talking to a Corporal who turned out to be a professional dancer and singer … He told me of an *estaminet* where, last night a suspicious looking fellow, without badge, otherwise dressed as an English soldier, asked for "Zee boddle beer" but in such a peculiar way, the old woman became quite nervous. I went round during the evening and she repeated the story. Stayed as long as I could, but the fellow didn't turn up. Had he done so, would have had a little game of 'intelligence' on my own.

4 April 1918

During the day about a dozen wounded Huns were admitted. After the recent period of inactivity, this almost came as a shock. However, it was a welcome shock and I went through the usual game of the classification

178 At Frévent the king made an impromptu inspection of 6/Gordon Highlanders (152nd Infantry Brigade, 51st Division) and 1/NZ Entrenching Battalion: Photographs Q301, Q306–307, Q312–313, Q315, Q11465, 29 March 1918, IWM; 6/Gordons war diary, 29 March 1918, WO95/2868/1, TNA. For the perceived positive effect of royal visits, see Englander, 'Discipline and Morale', 131.

forms, searching, then having a chat. The commencement of work again, without being too great, is just what is wanted to prevent this life from getting a wee bit too boring.

5 April 1918

Odd Huns trickled in and kept me pleasantly busy. The documents are quite fruitful also the men are quite willing to talk.

6 April 1918

There are three other hospitals besides this one taking in Germans, so took the 2 pm train to Avesnes to obtain authority from Corps HQ to see wounded prisoners of these other hospitals ... Saw Major Evans and got authority to act as I thought best ... At Frévent, went at once to the other hospitals and saw wounded Boches, having quite interesting chats with them. Also had a nice chat with one of the nurses (bow-wow!).

8 April 1918

I've arranged with ... the cook, to have breakfast about 8 am. So when I hear the other Sergeants in our tent called at 6 am for the 6.30 am

Wounded British troops at 43rd Casualty Clearing Station, Frévent, 7 April 1918: IWM Q331.

Parade, I can afford to smile and turn over whilst the poor beggars have to get up. Being a kind of freelance, I can do as I like. We sleep on stretchers in a marquee kind of tent.

10 April 1918

Heard that the spy referred to on [3 April] was caught in the Hotel d'Amiens, a place only for officers. He never revisited that *estaminet* after the first visit. Tremendous distant rumble of guns and during day heard that we had advanced 10 kilometres in the Albert district. Let's see what the communiqué says.

11 April 1918

The rumours heard yesterday of an advance of ours at Albert have turned out to be a reverse of ours round Armentières.[179]

12 April 1918

Went on my first fishing stunt but in spite of the expert advice of a very genial Frenchman, didn't even see a fish, so ate the bread and cheese bait I had brought along and returned empty-handed.

13 April 1918

Went to a performance of 'The Stars', a pierrot party. Collectively, not much, but individually good. The Divisional Band was great. Afterwards had my new tunic from the tailor's and felt very 'posh' – turned up collar, waist taken in etc. Now that I look like having a time behind the line, a good fitting tunic is worthwhile; one can afford to take a certain amount of pride in one's appearance.

14 April 1918

On the Regimental Sergeant-Major's invitation, went to [Ligny-sur-Canche] and spent the evening in an *estaminet*, to a great extent translating the bantering flirtatious remarks of the RSM to Madame who seemed to derive great pleasure therefrom and whose equally complimentary answers I translated for the RSM's benefit.

15 April 1918

A first class performance of 'The Stars' new programme, not a weak turn and again the band excelled itself. Bill thought it was the best

---

179 On 9 April the Germans had launched their second offensive on the Lys front overrunning Armentières.

performance he had ever seen in the Army. Certainly one would never see a show like this one for ½ franc in Blighty.

16 April 1918

[To] Noyelle-Vion … Said goodbye to Captain Redgrave who is leaving the Section for a Blighty position.[180] I think we both felt the parting; we've worked together since June 1916 and always have got on well. I gave him our home address and he repeated he hoped and believed his recommendation for our having the Military Medal would bear fruit and then, with a final shake-hands, we parted. I shall always think of 'Reddy' as one of the most decent and 'understanding our position' officers I've had to work under, an officer who always played the game with us – in spite of contrary statements by others who professed to know better – and through the confidence he had in me, made it a pleasure for me to do my utmost for him.

17 April 1918

The time passes, one day much as another. Every morning at 7.30 am I ask one of the Sergeants sleeping in our tent "Well, I suppose it's time to get up now" to which he answers "Oh no, heaps of time". But by 8 am I have breakfast, then have a quiet smoke and read and follow by sitting on my bed and clean my buttons, tunic and overcoat. Next, empty out dirty water and draw clean water from tank and, taking my time, wash and shave. By 10 am I am ready and if not too cold, squat down in the Sergeants' Mess 'next door' and write a letter. About noon I proceed to the Expeditionary Force Canteen where the *Daily Mail* is sold and have a glass of coffee in a nice little *estaminet* close by. During this time I just look in at the hospital and after the usual "No, no Jerries in today", we have a little chit-chat and then I go on my way until dinner time comes, after which I spend the afternoon reading or walking – just today I had another try at fishing – until the evening comes and results in a visit to the cinema or the concert party. Such is an idea of my day's 'work'. But for how long will it last?

20 April 1918

A lot of French soldiers have been appearing in this district. Frévent is now full of them … Went to a café on the road to Ligny where a family, refugees from Lens, have settled. Quite nice, girls quite cheery but with the place full of *Poilus*, hadn't a look in with the *demoiselles*.

180 He was posted to the signals depot at Fenny Stratford, Buckinghamshire: Redgrave to Schürhoff, 12 May 1918, Vince Shirley typescript diary, Vol. 5, 49, MIM.

21 April 1918

I do wish some Huns would come in and so enable me to justify my existence. I've long given up the 'very busy with documents' touch, an excuse that usually carries on over several days. I frankly admit to those who make polite remarks on how I am being overworked, that at present I am making the best of an easy time, as any day may bring a change. Meanwhile, to ease my conscience, I do a lot of talking with friendly damsels here and there in order to improve my French – in reality it is to enjoy a bit of female company.

22 April 1918

Last night, again in order to improve my French, I went to an *estaminet* where one, Lucianne by name, reigns supreme. I went for the first time and was smitten. Her French seemed to be quite pure but what impressed me were her eyes, a soft mixture of brown and violet. When she and I chatted together, they fascinated me, so expressive and but yet so soft. At one time, however, they changed. A couple of drunken Canadians went at each other and had a rough and tumble fight. Didn't those eyes suddenly flash! The difference was startling. The two men were chucked out and when we resumed our talk, those eyes were just as soft and attractive as if nothing had happened. I must say, it is a long time since I met anyone with eyes like Lucianne's.

23 April 1918

It seems that in the brawl last night, 5 bottles of Champagne were stolen, glasses broken, also a windowpane. I went to the *estaminet* after dinner and Lucianne, or Lucy as she prefers to be called, asked me to go with her to the Canadian Camp where she intended lodging a formal claim. Of course I couldn't refuse, but except for keeping us waiting for ¾ hour and then not being able to see anybody in authority, nothing happened so we returned without being molested.

24 April 1918

Each day is so like another, so uneventful, that of absolute facts there are few to write about. During three days of enforced idleness I must admit to spending a lot of time at Lucy's place. Whether for business or for her safety, Madame asked me to come as often as possible, as she is in mortal fear of the Canadians. Tonight a fellow, half-drunk, came in and started a regular blood and thunder speech of the stain cast on the Canadian name by the claim lodged by this *estaminet*. He talked a lot about justice, about the culprits being others, but not Canadians and ended up by calling on the other Canadians present to ask for an apology from Madame. But his appeal was met by silence and stony stares all round, simply because the few Canadians drinking belonged to a different crowd. Result, this fellow looked like a pricked gas bag and all he did was to pick up his glass half full of white wine and throw it on the stone floor, thus endeavouring to make a most dramatical and theatrical exit, but which only called forth roars of laughter and jeers. Incidents like these are certainly amusing and do make café hours a little interesting, the one drawback though is that the women get so scared.

25 April 1918

At Lucy's last night, a woman of about 30 called Mme Jeanne was working. She had burnt her wrist badly so I said I would bring some cream. Today, after dinner, went round to Lucy's again who showed me where this Mme Jeanne lived. I was just on the point of walking there when Lucy called me and said "Prenez garde, Madame aime à s'amuser avec vous autres".[181] I felt grateful for this warning, so just put the bandage and cream on Mme Jeanne's wrist and left her without time for her to "s'amuser avec moi". After tea … went to the cinema and saw an excellent film called *Daddy*,[182] by the United Film Company, about the best company going, I should think and English, too.

27 April 1918

Still nothing doing although there is considerable movement of troops round here. Fighting up north is fierce round the Kemmel and the Lys areas and the Huns made another attempt down south to break through to Amiens. But except for the number and mixture of troops of all countries, the flashes of guns in the sky at night and the distant rumble, here one would think no such thing as a war existed.

28 April 1918

Orders that all tents have to be surrounded by earth from the inside of the tents, as protection against bomb splinters. So practically all today we spent digging, until blisters appeared and the muscles of both back and arms seemed to creak. At the end of the day, we all felt we had earned our pay!

---

181 'Beware, Madame likes to have fun with you people.'

182 Thomas Bentley, *Daddy* (July 1917).

29 April 1918

Toddled along to Lucy's; we are quite good friends and my French is making excellent progress, especially in the art of paying compliments, polite repartee and flirtatious chit-chat.

30 April 1918

For the first time for weeks a wounded German was admitted into a local hospital, No. 6 Stationary. Made me quite excited. He was captured during a raid made by the Canadians near Neuville-Vitasse and was hit in the arm by shrapnel. Quite a decent talkative fellow.

2 May 1918

To break the monotony I had a bath at the bath house near the laundry and got a new change of washing, but felt fearfully bored all day, even the evening at Lucy's failed to rouse me. I went to Mme Jeanne's for a cup of coffee after leaving Lucy. For a certain reason Mme Jeanne and Lucy are not on good terms. Most unfortunately Lucy saw me at Mme Jeanne's and Lucy's expression and behaviour towards me was distinctly that of "napoo, c'est fini". When I next go, I shall have to put things right with her as she is the one girl I enjoy talking and chatting with.

4 May 1918

The monotony of life was broken today …. Was told to return to Corps HQ [at Noyelle-Vion] as Military Medals were being awarded … During the afternoon we practised the ceremonial drill for the actual affair tomorrow. A feature of the drill was the way in which the 'medal recipients' had to practice marching 'smartly and briskly' up to 3 paces before the supposed Corps Commander, then halt, salute, then take one pace forward for the ribbon to be pinned on, then one pace back, salute, about turn and march back. Of course, the Sergeant-Major had something to say against each one of us. One had as much idea of 'smart and brisk' marching as a man after an evening's boozing over *vin blanc*. Another man's salute looked more like scratching his ear, another man's 'Halt' was "more like an exhibition of the figure 8 in the air by the left leg" and so on. Still, at length he seemed satisfied.

5 May 1918

Miserable, rainy weather delayed things and the Parade did not take place until after 11 am.[183] There was a mess-up with an order, 'Order arms'

183 The VI Corps Signal Company war diary records that the 'corps commander inspected [and] presented decorations', but gives the date as 6 May: WO95/793, TNA.

from the 'Present' and ended in the happy medium of 'Slope arms'. All the men on the Station, Wilkie, Haines, Tucker and Corker have been awarded … A most glowing and exaggerated account of our exploit was read out in stentorian tones to the 200 men on Parade – almost made me blush, I really had to smile. Old 'Reddy' stuck it on thick if what was read out was what he reported. The Corps Commander, General Haldane, then pinned the Military Medal on our breasts, said "I congratulate you" and shook hands. I felt like saying "Have a drink, old thing?" but said "Thank you, sir" instead.

6 May 1918

I seemed to spend the greater part of the day shaking hands with fellows in response to 'congrats' on the MM and at the 'Café at the Corner' Madame gave me a pancake, a glass of Banyuls … and a tot of rum … After tea went to Lucy's who seemingly had forgotten the [recent] incident … Monsieur is back on leave and Lucy has to be on her best behaviour, much to her disgust. Met Grimes, of the 'office', and he insisted on our 'celebrating the occasion' again, so after leaving Lucy's, went to two more *estaminets* and by the time we got back, we were rather oiled.

9 May 1918

Today, Ascension Day, was a big feast day for the inhabitants. Wherever one went everybody was dressed up and there seemed to be a continuous stream to and from the Church. The two local factories were closed and as most of the girls in the town work there on ordinary days, today one saw them walking up and down the streets mostly looking very self-conscious in their 'Sunday best' and giggling 24 to the dozen in answer to Tommy's "Bonjour, Mademoiselle". Here and there one saw them, or a couple of them, 'parleying' with one or more of our men, the conversation punctuated by outbursts of laughter, but on the whole our men are very popular with the *demoiselles*. Spent the evening with a party of the local hospital orderlies, having some supper with them at the Hotel de la Gare.

11 May 1918

Noticed that Chinese coolies were working on the railway.[184] They are a mixed crowd, dressed anyhow, old felt hats, odd tunics, some had slacks, some puttees and the majority had long hair down to the neck. Smelt

---

184 For the Chinese on the Western Front, see Xu Guoqi, *Strangers on the Western Front: Chinese Workers in the Great War* (Cambridge, MA: Harvard University Press, 2011); Gregory James, *The Chinese Labour Corps (1916–1918)* (Hong Kong: Bayview, 2013).

horribly of garlic. All the time they work they keep up a very high keyed rumbling, disconnected sing-song, like one hears little children singing. Went … to the last show of 'The Stars' who are moving off, had supper in and enjoyed quite a good evening, ending up with whisky in the mess.

12 May 1918

Felt a bit thick after the whisky last night, the amount drunk being somewhat more than usual; we all felt disgruntled. Felt clearer on the whole during the afternoon after a nap and at length went over and had a row with Lucy to break the monotony so they won't see me there for some time again.

13 May 1918

I am beginning to know the way into Frévent by now, considering I have walked it, backwards and forwards a couple of hundred times. On leaving the hospital by the main Hesdin road, the turning on the right leads to the Canadian Engineer Camp which nestles under the great, huge trestles, pillars and beams of the bridge which they are building. Just about opposite this road the first cottages begin and incidentally, the first *estaminet* at which a woman refugee, since departed, sewed the stripes on my overcoat. Outside a house a few yards further down is a notice "Washing is done hière" … Just about opposite, on a little bank, is a faded and very weather-beaten crucifix, surrounded by a group of trees, just now beginning to look green. Adjoining is a brick depot and a dump at which a sentry always is supposed to be on duty, but most times when I pass, he is chatting with a Madame who lives where the cottages start on the further side of the crucifix and only hurriedly springs to attention when a motor car with officers is seen coming along. On the other side of the road is a house where two strikingly pale girls, sitting at the window and door in one, are always sewing. They never have the window open and they never seem to move from their positions, but are always sewing. Houses and cottages by now line both sides of the road and one has entered the little town properly. On the left, sandwiched inconspicuously with the other houses is the place where I buy eggs, chocolate, boot blacking etc. and on the right lies the entrance to the Canadian Hospital. An uninteresting portion of the road follows until a lorry square opens on the left. At 12 noon all men and women leave the cloth works and pass through the square for their homes and the lorry drivers and the girls indulge in such banter and chaff, that it's worth strolling down to listen. "Bonjour, mademoiselle, you promenade avec moi ce soir?" – "Oh, brigand, you no bon, me beaucoup travail in estaminet ce soir" – "Tress beans, moi vous au revoir estaminet ce soir" – "Alright". (The girls have learnt 'alright' like little boys all over the world.) And so one could go on giving examples enough to finish this diary. The resource, imagination and quickness of divining what 'he' or 'she' wishes to say is at times really marvellous.

17 May 1918

Much excitement in the hospital owing to the arrival of a most unpopular Matron to relieve one exceptionally popular one.[185] If this newcomer were to hear the things said about her, I am afraid she would blush. Walking down to meet Nuttal, two little French kiddies started chattering with me. Feeling their little hands grabbing mine, I just felt as I hadn't for years and gave them the wherewithal to go to the cinema, much to their delight … Looked in at a café in which the girl always works at the telephone in the station. Have given up going to Lucy's after our row.

18 May 1918

Awakened by Sergeant Glover saying that No. 19 Hospital had 'umpteen' wounded in, also Bosches. Much excited, got up, dressed and went to the 19th, but found only our men there. Most of our men had been hurt through bombs being dropped over rest billets. One expects danger in the trenches, but when out resting, to have to expect the same thing goes very much against the grain.

19 May 1918

Have had a large number of letters recently congratulating me on my getting the Military Medal … The hospital staff are being photographed so, as interpreter, had to make arrangements with the photographer, a fat, round little man, excitable and always perspiring.

20 May 1918

More gushing letters – I'm beginning to feel a bit of a humbug. Can see some busy mornings ahead answering them. Went round and called for the photographer who naturally was far from ready, couldn't find this, had lost that and so on. But at length reached the hospital, decided on a

---

185 Nora Dalrymple had replaced Mary Laing as sister-in-charge. She was a forty-five-year-old New Zealander, married to an RAMC colonel, who had previously served with the unit in 1916 and 1917. At the end of that period she had been judged a 'strict disciplinarian' with a 'strong character': 43rd CCS war diary, 16–17 May 1918, WO95/416; 'Confidential Report', 12 November 1917, WO399/1998, TNA.

convenient spot and in due course [all] were photographed – the present unit and those remaining of the original unit looking very puffed and self-conscious.

21 May 1918

Went into Frévent and had some eggs at Julianne's, during which we had a chat over the respective customs of England and France on the subject of 'paying attention' or courting. Most entertaining.

22 May 1918

I called for the photo proofs and then installed myself in style in the canteen with my pipe and a bottle of beer and proceeded to 'take orders' from the men and in an hour booked about 460 francs worth.

23 May 1918

Was awaiting my turn at the dentist's when an orderly came in saying I was wanted in the dressing tent. There found a woman with a very thin baby and Major Manser,[186] one of the doctors. Had to explain the directions and instructions to the girl and in turn translate her questions to the Major. Altogether, I'm being of more use as an Interpreter for French than German – an unexpected way of justifying my existence. Later on, during the day, looked in at the girl's house and had a nice glass of coffee … Went to see 'The Crumps',[187] a new Concert Party, not as good as the previous one, but having all the same one or two quite original turns. We then met other members of the Sergeants' Mess and imbibed beer, cognac, Banyuls, a kind of gin, and later, in our own mess, finished up with a bottle of whisky.

24 May 1918

Escaped the one hour's gas helmet wearing stunt … by taking a novel and hiding in a wood down by the river.[188]

25 May 1918

The Hun has been sailing round this place at night, but without dropping any bombs. Instead he had dropped poisoned sweets; a child picked one up – said it was like a chocolate sweet – ate it and died soon after.

---

186 Major F.B. Manser RAMC.

187 41st Division's concert party.

188 For the period 22 to 26 May, Commandant Third Army Troops had decreed that respirators should be worn for an hour each day by all personnel: 43rd CCS war diary, 22 May 1918, WO95/416, TNA.

26 May 1918

Morning spent letter writing. The applying for a commission question has arisen again, so to please folks at home have agreed to put in another application, this time for Intelligence, not Signals – at least not until as a last resort ... [Also] thought of transferring to 'Intelligence B', though some 'IB' men I met ... and what they said about 'IB' rather gave me fruit for thought.

[A] concert, by a French band, was quite the Frévent society afternoon event. It was held in a park and the small ground was crowded with soldiers of all kinds, from Yanks to Algerians. The female element was also there *en force* and so dressed up and disguised, so distinguished looking, that one had to look twice before recognising Lulu from such and such an *estaminet* in some back street, or Jeanne who sells newspapers on weekdays, or Florence, the female barber. The music was quite a secondary matter, the showing off of dresses, stupendously gorgeous hats and fantastic shoes was what mattered most. Afterwards attended service at the YMCA (The Birmingham Hut), had Communion and ... during [the evening] witnessed a fight between a policeman and a Canadian, both showing the signs of strife. Usual cause, girl in *estaminet*, first joking, then insulted, row, fellow drunk, others tried to pacify him, ended by chucking him out of *estaminet*, he shouts and kicks up a hell in street, police arrive, another row, crowd gather round, until some fellows give policeman a hand and the culprit is marched, carried or kicked and pushed to the Guard Room.

28 May 1918

Frévent had a very nasty shock today. For the first time in its calm, quiet and happy existence, it was shelled by a heavy gun. The first shell ... killed 5 and wounded 7, all civilians, bar one soldier on leave, knocking the houses nearby into ruins. I went into the town and the people I talked to and the groups of women standing at street corners or entrances to houses, showed and made one feel the anxiety, doubt and uncertainty, wondering "is this the beginning of regular shelling?" and "should we clear off?" Many had their doubts settled by more shells falling during the afternoon, only a few though. [In the evening] ended up at Ligny, a neighbouring village. Several women and children were in the *estaminet*, all refugees from Frévent. The women mostly talked amongst themselves and I gathered they had only come out for the night and would return, if the shelling quietened down, next day. But there was a little girl, about ten, who looked so miserable, sad and strange, that out of sympathy for her, [we] gave the mother a couple of francs "pour vos petits"[189] and then bolted.

29 May 1918

During these last days I have been 'interpreting' the case of a girl or 25 about with a thin, semi-starved, miserable baby. Its condition was brought about by an internal abscess and after certain correspondence etc. with the Mayor of Frévent, this hospital had agreed to operate and get the abscess out, to the mother's huge relief. This was performed today and now one of the wards had the novelty of a crying baby.

30 May 1918

I witnessed the funeral of the 5 victims of [the] shell. It appeared wedged in between a long column of artillery and transport proceeding through the town, a most incongruous picture – the dejected and sad figures, all in black of the coffins' mourners and the dusty brown of khaki following straight behind. Just during the dinner hour, two shells fell by the factory (or cloth works) and this, coming in the centre of the town, put the wind up the populace proper and from 1 pm to 2 pm one steady stream of old men, old women, women, girls, boys and little children passed along the road beside the hospital for Ligny and Boulers. Calmly watching them and yet powerless to help, every now and again catching sight of a familiar face, it made one downright wretched. Somehow it seems so wrong that a harmless, peaceful little place like Frévent should suffer, and above all, that all these poor people should, after nearly four years of war, also learn what it is to gather up one's most precious valuables, hurriedly pack them into a bag and clear off, never knowing whether they will return or not, or if they do, to find their home a gutted out mass of ruins … I gave a hand pushing the wheelbarrow of an old man of about 80 and lame, who was leaving with his daughter. She had gone on ahead to try and obtain a place for them to sleep in somewhere. I had to leave the old man at Ligny and returned with many of our fellows who had given others a hand.

31 May 1918

I bought the photographs taken of the hospital [staff]. The photographer and his wife have been chased out of three places and now that they are leaving here too, this is the fourth move. He admits that through the Germans shelling Frévent and the business in photographing our men

189 'For your little ones.'

being lost, he has lost 4,000 francs. Similar incidents, tragic family affairs, can be heard on all sides.

1 June 1918

I go every day to Mme Degonne for a cup of coffee. She is the mother of the baby in the hospital and as I act as interpreter we have become quite friendly.

2 June 1918

Mr Sykes, Corps Intelligence Officer turned up with a 'lame pigeon', i.e. a kind of Secret Service man, a Pole. This man's job was to pass off as wounded and lie beside a really wounded German in the 19th CCS. So, under Major Sampson's[190] supervision, he had a bandage put round his head, iodine painted, he donned pyjamas and as a casualty was admitted into the ward. My job, pre-arranged with the Pole, was to call in the morning, ask the usual questions, chat a bit, always as if he were a real German. But on my asking "Nun, wie fühlen Sie sich?" (How do you feel?), he would answer "Och, ganz gut", by which I should know that he had obtained the information he wanted and could be evacuated. However, if he replied "Nicht besonders gut" (Not very well) it meant that he wished to stay on. So this morning, after advising Major Sampson, I blew in, proceeded as arranged and got "Ganz gut" (Quite well) as the answer. I 'phoned this through to Sykes and got the rather staggering news that Frévent not being in our VI Corps area, I was to be relieved today. I need not state how this has upset me. I made a quick tour round, saying goodbye to the various civilian friends remaining and at noon, Mr Sykes arrived and conveyed this 'lame pigeon' and me to Candas, the [Third] Army Prisoner-of-War Cage. The motor car run was glorious, but Candas, as I later discovered, is a most miserable, depressing place.

3 June 1918

There are about 50 Huns in the Cage and they keep me pleasantly busy ... Mr Hogg, now a Lieutenant, who used to be with Francke's 'IB' crowd, turned up and wanted to know several things about equipment, boots, make of shirts etc.[191] Seems as if this is his branch of Intelligence. Promised to do my best for him, so when, just after tea, 17 more came in, had a good look, but there was nothing new about them. Spent the

---

190 Major P. Sampson RAMC.

191 Hogg was presumably collecting information for GHQ Intelligence's 'War Trade' sub-section: Beach, *Haig's Intelligence*, 113.

evening with [Charlie Horne] the Corporal Quarter-Master, who seems to be one of the best men here. Was told one or two things regarding the men in this camp, from which it would appear that half of them are prison birds and whilst I was being told this, a loud thick semi-drunk sounding voice was shouting outside to a fellow in another hut "Come on, you bloody —, I'll show yer who's the better man, pull your coat off ye — coward" etc. and a few moments later a fellow came into our hut, sobbing like a child, because he had given the Sergeant-Major a thrashing and only realised too late what the consequences would be.

4 June 1918

Mr Hogg kept me busy with the Huns. An airman NCO was one of the men he interviewed. The airman was asked to give up his 'flying' trousers, but refused. Hogg then got into a rage and wrote a note for Squires, the Prison OC, who happened to be out, asking for official permission to obtain the trousers. When Squires returned, after Hogg had gone, he and I tackled the man again, who again refused, even when ordered to surrender them. Two sentries with fixed bayonets then came into the compound and this put the Hun's wind up and as he was marched away prior to giving up the trousers, he asked me whether he was going to be shot! I reassured him that he was not. The whole crowd were evacuated tonight.

5 June 1918

Obtained a pass for Noyelle-Vion … I got a lorry lift to Doullens, a motorcycle lift halfway to Frévent and then got to Frévent on a lorry. Had dinner at the hospital and saw several old friends again … People were still windy owing to shells having fallen in the town, one close to the railway station. The Hotel de la Gare is closed and the town seemed more deserted than ever. Caught train to Avesnes and walked to Noyelle-Vion, got Mr Schönland[192] to sign my 'Shirley' papers … and got to Avesnes just in time to catch a return train. At Frévent … then got lift on a lorry which broke down outside Frévent, but hopped on to another one passing and reached Doullens. From there had to walk it to Candas where I arrived about 10.30 pm, covered in dust.

192 Lieutenant Basil Schönland RE. Twenty-two-year-old physicist who subsequently became the chief scientific advisor to 21st Army Group during the Second World War and later Director of the Atomic Energy Research Establishment: T.E. Allibone,'Schonland, Sir Basil Ferdinand Jamieson (1896–1972)', in *Oxford Dictionary of National Biography*, www.oxforddnb.com.

6 June 1918

This Prisoner-of-War Cage is about 10 minutes walk from Candas and lies alongside the main road to Doullens. Adjoining us are 6 hangars, once used by the [RAF], now used as stores, whilst across the road lies the station, or railhead to give it its military designation. All day and night we can hear the puffing and whistling of engines and clattering of shunting trucks. At night, with the railhead and the hangars so close, one feels none too safe owing to the Hun bombing planes. As soon as they are signalled, a big bell starts clanging in the station and shortly after the 'poof-poof' of the [anti-aircraft guns] opening out. However, we have been very lucky here, not one bomb has fallen.

7 June 1918

Mr Hogg has a nasty habit of appearing just before dinner which not only prevents me from having a refresher in Candas, but also keeps me from dinner an hour or so longer … Had a walk to Gézaincourt, where Dick Lederer is attached to the CCS there, as interpreter. We indulged in our usual sarcastically polite repartee, patronised a few *estaminets*, had some eggs and coffee and during the course of our talk heard of the possibility of an IT set being put out again.

8 June 1918

I have a Pole into this hut every morning who sweeps up, blacks my boots and polishes my buttons and generally makes himself useful.

10 June 1918

This is a very monotonous existence. Charlie Horne is the only passable fellow and he and I always go out together. The other men are most typical old soldiers, though luckily the ones sleeping in this hut, all officers' batmen, are quiet enough. In his hut, as assistant, Charlie has a character, 'Ernie' who has seen 15 years service in the Army. He prides himself that no man in the Army carries his years, 40, as well as he does, though my opinion is he looks older. He is at his funniest when 'oiled' and can then keep us in fits of laughter for hours.

11 June 1918

A few days after I arrived here, a very decent fellow, Jimmy Wolridge, attached here for rations, was recalled to HQ. His job seemed to be that of going out at nights on his Triumph motorcycle on the lookout for spies, possibly dropped from Hun planes. Obviously he said little about his work. Well, he told me about a certain *demoiselle* who was not adverse to being friends with an English Tommy, quite a decent girl in every respect and would I like to be introduced? I answered "Yes", so with Charlie, we walked to Bernaville, some 8 kilometres away, but although she was quite nice, didn't see anything remarkable about her and in fact doubt whether I shall walk (there and back) ... nearly 10 miles, just to see her. As arranged, met Jim there who evidently was quite *persona grata* with the sister.

13 June 1918

Had a 4-page letter from Captain Redgrave which gave me great pleasure[193] ... By paying the cooks a 'consideration' I get my meals brought in here, also have extras but have to be on the lookout as these cooks are old Army men and very sharp to take advantage of one. They are willing to do anything to earn the tip but that 'anything' is as little as they possibly can do.

16 June 1918

Commission Form paper ... came by post – one step in the right direction. The Sergeant of the Guard had the wind put up him by a German *Unteroffizier* – one of the few decent [*Unteroffiziere*] we have had. It seems there has been a lot of illegitimate 'souvenir hunting' by the guard. As a result, Captain Squires, OC Cage, put a notice up which I had to translate into German, stating that any prisoner proving that an article of value had been stolen or forcibly taken off him, had the right to lodge a complaint with him, the OC Cage. This German NCO thereupon told me that the Sergeant of the Guard had taken his gold wedding ring and that if the Sergeant did not return it, he was entitled to lodge a formal complaint. This I repeated to the Sergeant who considered discretion to be the better part of valour and thereupon handed the ring over 'without a murmur'.

17 June 1918

With the prisoners all evacuated I had to polish my own buttons.

18 June 1918

This evening I got another insight of Charlie's 'Sky Pilot' position in camp. As already mentioned, the men here are all a most unruly, rough, drunken and low set of fellows, Sergeants included. Charlie is the only

---

193 Redgrave said that he had previously recommended Vince twice for the MM: Redgrave to Schürhoff, 12 May 1918, Vince Shirley typescript diary, Vol. 5, 49, MIM.

exception. Through sheer superiority of character, brains and breeding he has more influence with the whole crowd than any other man. Every evening the senior Sergeant and another man come in drunk, or at least the worse for drink. They came to Charlie to get some clothing – Charlie is Acting Quarter-Master, though only a Corporal. Charlie refused them clothing, they became offensive, the Sergeant in particular. In cases like this, tact is of no use. Charlie quietly said "Sergeant, you don't know what you're talking about. I don't stand words that you've said to me from anyone, let alone you. If you want to fight me, say so, if not, here's a candle, go to bed." As the Sergeant hesitated, Charlie just as quietly said "I give you 30 seconds, if you are not out of here by then, I shall throw you out and you know that what I say I mean". And out the Sergeant and the other man went. They dared not refuse as in spite of their drunken state, they knew that if there was one man who would get them out of trouble or some scrape, it would be that same man – Charlie Horne.

20 June 1918

By a tragic coincidence, Charlie and I are almost broke. We ransacked our pockets and managed to find 3 shillings and 8 pence for which the YMCA gave us 5 francs. Then we met 'Ernie' who asked for 5 francs to be lent him until he could change two 10 shilling postal orders tomorrow, it being too late at the time. Besides the 5 francs from the YMCA, I had about 4 francs on me, so Charlie lent Ernie the 5 francs asked for, intending to borrow 10 francs when the two postal orders had been changed. This man 'Ernie', being Charlie's storeman, is the only man we could borrow money from, all the others being twisters, more or less. If they were to lend us some francs one day, they would later on always be pestering us for a loan.

22 June 1918

There has been an epidemic of a kind of influenza[194] and this morning Charlie was down with it. Half the camp is laid up. Consequently I went out for the first time here alone and toddled to the pictures, 'featuring' Douglas Fairbanks in *El Americano.*[195] Still short of funds so cannot go much to cafés and the whole time go about with a "mustn't spend or you won't have anything at all left" feeling.

194 For the influenza epidemic in the summer of 1918, see Anne Rasmussen, 'The Spanish Flu', in Jay Winter (ed.), *The Cambridge History of the First World War*, Vol. 3 (Cambridge: Cambridge University Press, 2014), 336–45.

195 John Emerson, *El Americano* (December 1916).

23 June 1918

A great many Yanks have been marching through; infantry. They struck me as being of good physique but with rotten march discipline and with a decidedly 'new to the game' appearance about them. However, the stuff was there alright.[196]

24 June 1918

This district seems to be invaded by Americans; one sees them in every street. One has to admire their physique, also their well-fitting tunics which greatly add to their appearance. Also, on the whole, they strike me as being mostly of a good standing, like the 1st Birmingham City Battalion at its formation. I went over to Gézaincourt to see Dick and his favourite café was full of Americans. They had just been paid, the first time for three months, so one could hardly blame them for having a bit of a bust-up. But I also noticed that although intoxicated, the respectful way they treated the girls, somewhat different to sights witnessed amongst our own men, though one can say that familiarity breeds contempt in their case.

25 June 1918

At last we were paid and the period of financial embarrassment was relieved.

26 June 1918

The evenings are really at times more entertaining than the day. 'Jack', Captain Squire's batman, quite a good sort when sober, usually comes in drunk and entertains us for an hour or so with his views of the war, work, women and wine, ending up by working himself into a frenzied fury because everybody agrees with him and doesn't want to fight him. He pulls off his shirt, strikes boxing attitudes, shows his muscles as further enticement for a fight and when nobody offers himself to be knocked out, he suddenly comes over sentimental and speaks to himself, calling himself a "bloody fool" and other unprintable names, ending up the evening's show by a general and oft-repeated "God bless you, my lads, bless you, bless you". Hardly has he fallen asleep when the clanging of the railway station bell shows the Hun bombing planes are on their way over. Soon the quiet outside is broken by the banging of anti-aircraft guns, the crashing of bombs, the whirring of machines and looking up, on all sides

196 For the AEF units attached to the BEF, see Mitchell Yockelson, *Borrowed Soldiers: Americans under British Command, 1918* (Norman: University of Oklahoma Press, 2008).

one sees searchlights, starlights, flares and flashes of explosions. Then the noise gradually dies away and peace eventually once more reigns.

28 June 1918

A dozen Huns were brought in last night, taken by the Canadians at Neuville-Vitasse. On the whole a very poor set of men, a large number being quite young boys. The *Unteroffizier* hadn't a good word for one of them … At night the Hun bombing planes were very active … I lay on my bed and looked out of the window at the many searchlights. One machine was picked up by them and looked like a silvery bird being supported in mid-air by the long beams of light. For several minutes it travelled thus, in the centre of six or more searchlight beams with every anti-aircraft gun and machine-gun in the neighbourhood firing at it, but by a miracle it escaped.

1 July 1918

We had an interesting case in the Cage, a German, taken at Messines, who escaped from his Prisoner-of-War Cage at Étaples [on 28 June] and who was caught yesterday. He was working at a repair shop close to a dump of old clothes. When nobody was looking, he took an [RAF] tunic and cap – he was working in khaki breeches and puttees already – and hid them in the repair shop. Then, last Friday after the dinner hour, he saw his chance, slipped on the tunic and cap and calmly walked past the sentry. Reading through his correspondence, I read that he vowed to himself to escape as often as he could.

2 July 1918

Went out with Tommy Kay, a 'fly' gentleman of many tricks, including 'Crown & Anchor'. But he was amusing company and one could be sure that something would happen whenever going out with him. This time it was an arrangement of selling 10 kilos of sugar to certain people at 1½ francs the kilo, a clear 15 francs profit for Master Tommy.

4 July 1918

Had a letter from Bill from which I heard that Cecil Stallworthy had died.[197] It was a great shock to me. He was one of my greatest pals during the beginning of last year and he again showed his qualities last December when I was up in the old dug-out with him. His advice on anything was

197 He had been admitted to hospital on 26 June and died the following morning. Cause of death was given as nephritis; an inflammation of the kidneys.

worth listening to; one could discuss music for hours with him and he was very well-read, even writing essays and short stories himself. I always considered that he was thrown away as a post office clerk.

5 July 1918

To Gézaincourt where I looked up 'Dirty Dick'. The recent bombing has evidently frightened this gentleman as he told me most naively at having obtained a civvy billet at the cottage of an old couple, where he slept in the same room as they. If he intended going to bed early, he informed them and after he had got in, he whistled and then they came into the room, undressed and got into bed. If, however, he expected to come in later, they retired first and he followed after they had tucked themselves in. I thought the arrangement very simple and at the same time screamingly funny.

6 July 1918

We've got some German bombing squadron officers in. They were brought down [on 2 July]. I had a long talk with them and must frankly confess, it is very difficult to convince oneself and to imagine these men deliberately bombing hospitals. They emphatically denied that instructions were ever, at any time, given for hospitals to be bombed and could only account for this having occurred through accident or having mistaken the hutments or tents for billets. The Red Cross marks cannot be seen during the clearest moonlight when higher than 500 metres and bomb dropping is calculated by landmarks visible at night as shown on special maps.

11 July 1918

Got some Jerries in today – a couple of flying men, NCOs, night bombers. An anti-aircraft gun brought them down. On landing they blew their machine up and had to wait two hours before anybody came to take them away. One was a cheeky, impudent fellow, a regular boasting Hun, the kind one snubs with diabolical delight.

12 July 1918

[Went] to see 'Dirty Dick' who still works like fury to make his position at Gézaincourt a cert, interrogating every prisoner down to the smallest detail, all for fear that he should be sent up the line again.

13 July 1918
All day was busy with the Jerries, with Mr Hogg and the Jerry documents, by which I identified a regiment of foot artillery near Albert and a regiment north of Arras. Was not able to leave until 7 pm, an unheard of late time for me.

14 July 1918
The Jerry who I had in to polish my buttons gave me the interesting news that last month he saw a battalion of Austrians at Cologne. Why and what for and for how long etc. he could not state. He spoke very disparagingly about them.

15 July 1918
Another batch of Germans in, including a Polish Sergeant whose sentiments I quickly divined by asking him whether in his opinion the newly formed 'Independent Kingdom of Poland' would settle the differences between Poland and Germany and gradually bring about a more peaceful atmosphere. His answer ["never, never, never"] was a most emphatic indication of which way his feelings lay.

16 July 1918
Had a long talk with the Polish Sergeant. Struck me as being like a safety valve suddenly opened after years of throttling down. We discussed the Polish Question at length, the Ukraine, the disappointment in Germany over the crops (he stated that Germany had actually had to send seeds to the Ukraine for future harvests), the situation in Austria – not rosy but neither quite as bad as one would have expected – the fighting on the West Front, the gradual feeling of disillusion creeping into the German ranks and many other points, almost enough to fill this book. Lieutenant Hogg questioned him after dinner and was with him for two hours, which time I lay on my bed and took things easy. Hogg was very pleased with the information gathered and said he was the best man he had had for months, though considered that the man's relief at being able to air his grievances freely against the Germans apparently made his tongue run away with itself at times.

17 July 1918
Amongst many other things, I have to give each Jerry a postcard by which his people or whoever he wants to write to, can see that he is safely in our hands. By an oversight one such postcard was not sent off with the

others [on 15 July]. As I looked at it, a pang of sentiment came over me and – I don't know why – I vividly pictured a scene of the man's family, wondering at the man's silence, the questions they would have asked each other, their hopes and fears, the uncertainty and it struck me what a great relief the arrival of such a – to me uninteresting – piece of paper this postcard must be to the family.

18 July 1918

Had the busiest day today since I've been here. All morning was occupied with odds and ends connected with the Huns – medical inspection, detailing fatigues, explaining points, nosing out information. Then just after dinner, 25 more came in and they kept me busy until teatime. In the prisoners' enclosure a special hut is reserved for me. New prisoners are shoved into another hut and brought to my hut one by one. Each man I have to enter on a certain form, then quickly get to know certain details, such as if the man had been employed on special work, in fact anything that might interest Mr Hogg. I also have to look quickly through the man's papers and personal belongings and then, when finished with, the same process is repeated with the next man. Had a jolly evening at Adrienne's and her people being out, she was delightfully flirtatious. Ended up with the usual supper but then met Sergeant Bayliss who was drunk. Wanted to go to the café at corner after closing time but headed him off and in order to quieten him, agreed to have another supper at another place although he nearly picked a quarrel with a fellow there. At last managed to get him back to camp.

19 July 1918

Amongst yesterday's batch of prisoners was a man of the 3rd Marine Infantry Regiment – [from] the equivalent of our Naval Division … The way this man was taken was remarkable. It seems that fraternising – meeting in 'No Man's Land' and exchanging souvenirs – had been in vogue a couple of days ago at Beaumont Hamel (further south to us). This fellow thought he would go over and meet our man, who appeared without a tunic. They spoke a few words and our man asked Jerry to come into our lines and have some wine. Jerry refused and our man pulled out a revolver and said "If you don't, I shall shoot you" and so the man was taken prisoner.

20 July 1918

Tommy Kay and I have started calling on a certain *estaminet* after dinner where we are alone with the *demoiselles* and I must say, we have rare fun.

Tommy is a bit of a sleight-of-hand merchant and also a gymnast and his tricks make us roar.

22 July 1918

Went to the 'Corner Café' after dinner and I am getting very friendly with Mme Lucile. Although married, she had no objection to a mild flirtation.

24 July 1918

These days are fearfully quiet and boring, so when I heard Mme Lucile say that she was going to Doullens tomorrow, thought I would enjoy myself and meet her there. She is quite young and very smart and chic looking – nothing of the village type. She is a refugee from Lens but this does not prevent her from enjoying life. Her sister, though, is much rougher and nothing like as refined as Mme Lucile, but otherwise a very good sort.

25 July 1918

I spun the yarn to Charlie and got a pass out easily. Arrived at Doullens after the usual jumping on and off motors and, as agreed, met the sisters at noon. After a very great deal of compliment paying, we proceeded to a hotel they knew of and, 'midst much giggling and laughing, found ourselves alone in the *salle à manger.* They seemed both so glad to see me that, on finding ourselves alone, each gave me a very juicy kiss, which I most heartily reciprocated. Then out came the powder and rouge and as a punishment for teasing them, I had to submit to being powdered and rouged myself. More laughter. I had just wiped off the effects when the door opened and a couple of officers walked in. the truth dawned on me that we had strayed into an officers' dining room. Still, I determined to stick it out. Mme Lucile understood and showed this by chatting in a most pleasant and sensible manner. The other fool of a sister understood too and showed this by loud guffaws of laughter, making me feel far from 'comfy'. So I turned to Mme Lucile who backed me up and we kept the conversation going. Officers came in, one after the other. Whether any could speak or understand French, I don't know. Anyhow, we didn't care much what we said and in fact I was really enjoying myself (it would have been perfect had 'the other sister' not shown her appreciation of the good meal by continuous and violent lip-smacking) when a Frenchman came in – a civilian and presumably a man of some standing. He evidently saw Mme Lucile, for she became most reticent and during all the time, the officers hardly opened their mouths, except to eat. Meanwhile, I worked hard at talking, on tenterhooks lest the 'other sister' would say something *mal à propos* and go off into loud bursts of laughter at her own joke. Halfway through the meal she suddenly remembered that she had brought a serviette with her, so out came a yard-square napkin with blood-curdling crimson borders. Such a serviette at any time would have caught the eye, but now, fished out of a ladies' bag, obviously specially brought for the occasion, it caught the eye doubly. A little later, as if she had not attracted enough attention, this 'other sister', in her anxiety to fill our wine glasses, must knock the bottle over and pour the contents over the meat. First a shriek, then hysterical laughter, till I proposed her health (after the crimson serviette had mopped up the spilt wine) when, in order to drink, she had to shut up though I was in a ghastly state of fear lest she should choke and begin at once to explain why she was choking. Well, after various spasms of fears and periods on tenterhooks, we finished our meal and found ourselves in the main road. The sister still had shopping to do. The first place was a shoe shop. The 'other sister' spent nearly half an hour choosing a pair of shoes (perhaps it was to give an exhibition of her rather shapely ankle) and I had the task of fitting the shoes on. With every shoe I put on she would burst out giggling and say I tickled her. The next shop was a draper's. I tried to keep in the background when I saw what they were buying, but no good. With the most matter-of-fact candour as if I had spent all my life doing so, I was asked my advice on corsets and skirts and more intimate articles of female attire. So for another half hour we discussed corsets and skirts and underwear until the choice was made. This virtually brought an end to the day's outing, as soon after they had to catch their train and I had to return by road. If only the 'other sister' had not been so boisterous at table, thereby keeping me in a perpetual state of "what's going to happen next?" the affair would have been a huge lark at the time.

27 July 1918

Most of my spare time I spend at Mme Lucile's although just at present, Jerries keep trickling in so I am kept fairly busy. After tea went to see a three-act farce *Passed to you, please* by the IV Corps Concert Party. Sat down, with others, in officers' seats but later on we were cleared out but got good seats on the balcony. Quite a good show, the chief man being one of Fred Karno's[198] leading men.

198 The famous musical hall comedian and impresario.

28 July 1918
I had dinner at Mme Lucile's today. It was far and away more pleasant than the one at Doullens on Thursday last. After the 'other sister' had informed me of the price of the fowl, I ate with as much apparent appreciation as I could decently show and I think she was satisfied with my demonstration of appreciation. Must say, it was a thoroughly enjoyable afternoon, as whereas the 'other sister' is continually bubbling over with *joie de vivre* and good humour, Mme Lucile is really a charming girl and is the easiest person to talk to I've met out here. We passed two hours thus, chatting and eating … [Later] Captain Squires gave me a note from Captain Sykes, Intelligence, Army HQ, to the effect that I was to be ready to return to Signals. It's a rotten feeling, after four months of paradise, to learn suddenly that one has to return to the line again. So spent the evening with Charlie, going to the pictures and later having eggs and chips at Mme Julianne's, perhaps for the last time. After closing hours, went to say goodbye to Mme Lucile, but an officer was there and so had to postpone the farewell until tomorrow.

29 July 1918
Paid a most affectionate farewell to Mme Lucile as I really thought that today I should leave, but nobody came and the day passed uneventfully.

30 July 1918
'Major' White relieved me this morning. After he had had a wash and tea, I took him to Mme Lucile's – the temptation to see her again was too strong to resist – and told him all there was to be told of the work. I then once more said goodbye to Mme Lucile who gave me her photo and then returned to camp, rather 'down in the dumps'.

31 July 1918
Was very lucky in getting a lift on a lorry … On the way we passed a 'Russian Labour Company' – rather an unexpected sight.[199] Were all dressed and looked exactly like our men. At Noyelle-Vion [Corps HQ] once more got into the hateful blue and white Signals atmosphere. How I hate it! The one consolation is seeing Bill again and from him heard that 'Dirty Dick' Lederer, who arrived here yesterday, will probably

199 For the Russian Expeditionary Force in France and their employment after disturbances in the summer of 1917, see Jamie Cockfield, *With Snow on their Boots: The Tragic Odyssey of the Russian Expeditionary Force in France during World War I* (London: Macmillan, 1998), 213–20.

accompany us when we go up the line to lay out a new Station at the end of the week, with 'Dad' Edwards in charge.

1 August 1918

New boots, pinching badly, do not improve my humour. This waiting to go up the line is rotten … Have to attend a Parade at 8 am but after that I am free. The overcast sky prevented a repetition of recent bombing raids. The one last night knocked out an aerodrome, blew up an ammunition dump and a bomb dropped very close to this village.

3 August 1918

We had loaded all the paraphernalia on to the boxcar … Made the journey in most atrocious weather, rain pouring down – a most miserable beginning to trench life. The boxcar ran along a road leading to [Adinfer Wood] where we unloaded and had dinner of bully beef whilst 'Dad' got his bearings. These found, I remained to look after the stores which the others could not take up with them. After always being used to waiting at some dump, or in a ruined village or just anywhere out in the open, it was quite strange waiting in a wood. We carted the equipment and stores to our dug-out in three journeys. It was very hard work and we were all done in by the end of the last trip.

4 August 1918

Last night a couple of earths enabled us to start on the instrument … After dinner, went with 'Dad' and [others] laying wires. We got as far as the support trenches and then chucked it, we were so hot and thirsty. We had to indulge in walking over the top, walking along sunken roads, through wire filled trenches and under barbed wire and concertina wire in order to lay out this wire. Returned to dug-out very ready for tea.

This place is capable of great developments though at the moment everything is in a very primitive state. We sleep down below in a corridor and spent nearly an hour sweeping chalk lumps off the wooden floor … When the crowd were relieved, we bagged and reserved the upstairs 'room' for ourselves. It will do excellently as a cookhouse and 'dining room'.

5 August 1918

After four months of comfort, this rough-and-ready life takes some getting used to. The crown of my head is quite sore with hitting against the dug-out roof. Then sleeping on the damp wooden floor makes one realise or appreciate a good bed, especially as black beetles here are very fond of running all over one. Last night I caught one in the act of running up my bare leg after I had turned in. Spiders are a nuisance, too.

6 August 1918

Felt very fit after the night's sleep and ready to meet the next batch of troubles which soon cropped up. After returning from wire laying right up to the front line, Bill told us that an artillery Major had blown in and claimed the dug-out as his own, including the room above and that he would take over that night, together with 12 men. Bill answered that a letter of authority was necessary, but suggested waiting until the Sergeant returned. So Sergeant Edwards later told us this Major that in taking over, he could not turn us out and that he, Edwards, would have to report the matter. Nevertheless, these artillery men came in and 'Dad' at once wrote to Captain Schönland, our present OC. Matters became worse when three guns were moved into position 20 to 30 yards away from our dug-out entrance. So Bill and I had to cart our kit down to the damp and cold gallery below again.

7 August 1918

On meeting boxcar with rations, Mr Lane told me that Captain Schönland was leaving. 'Dad' Edwards … went out to a new Station … leaving me in charge. Two petrol tins eased our shortage and the fitting up of a water tap not 200 yards away is a God-send. Thus slowly we are seeing our way through the wood. But our living quarters upstairs are miserable and I am only waiting the decision as to whether these RFA men are to go or stay in order to return to the partition and the room again if they go, or to turn to and thoroughly clean up the place if we are huddled together in now, if they stay. For one thing, the office is now respectable, after 1½ hours of cleaning up and fitting up with a table, chair and shelves etc. and now we can afford the luxury of writing in comfort and, when on duty, sit at ease and not cramped up like a snail in its shell.

8 August 1918

Meat turned bad but Bill made quite a good meal of fried bully and chips, onions and cheese, but as yet our cooking utensils leave much to be desired. Somehow, we don't feel to have settled down; there is heaps to be done in the place, improvements on every side could be effected, but these RFA men – very nice fellows – take up all the room and in consequence we don't like making improvements for men who, through no fault of their own, we look upon as having ousted us from our lawful possession. But today already, the first news simmers through in the shape of a Brigadier-General who comes along and asks "Why the deuce should these guns be laid so close to the dug-out when the Division know quite well for what purpose the dug-out is used?" And then he rapped out "These guns must be moved!" And if the men move out too, our cup of delight will be full to overflowing. I shall really look forward to settling down properly then.

11 August 1918

This glorious spell of fine weather suits us very well and every spare moment we spend outside in the field, basking in the sun, chatting with the artillery fellows who share the dug-out or chatting just amongst ourselves. We miss up-to-date news, though. At times, odd fragments filter through – reports have come in of a breakthrough at Montdidier.[200] Another report of a whole Bavarian divisional staff having been captured, but official news items are few and far between.

12 August 1918

Dick and Bill got into an argument on the origin of the War – a topic that by now seems to have been almost forgotten, so swallowed up in the many events of the War itself.

14 August 1918

Quite a lot of excitement was caused today by the news that the Germans are retiring on our right and that his retirement may extend to opposite our front. I had a wire from Brigade to report every six hours about the Hun traffic on our wires, particularly when it should cease.

15 August 1918

Three of our lines went 'dis' and [we] went up … at 5.30 am to repair them. Just opposite us, it seems that the Hun has not retired far and we still hear his signals on our instrument.

16 August 1918

We expect to be relieved tomorrow and as news has filtered through that this Station is to move up to the front line, I shall not be sorry to be away

200 Since 8 August, to the south of British Fourth Army at Amiens, French First Army had been attacking successfully in this area: Elizabeth Greenhalgh, *Foch in Command: The Forging of a First World War General* (Cambridge: Cambridge University Press, 2011), 420–5.

when this move takes place. Further, a Major of artillery has been nosing around for more gun emplacements and fixed on one uncomfortably close to our dug-out, so really the sooner we clear out the better.

17 August 1918

I don't think anything like a period up the line makes one realise the beauty of civilisation. Although only away a fortnight, yet we were all in the wildest spirits as the boxcar ran through one pretty village after another, singing *I Snap my Fingers, ha, ha, ha, ha* – the rage now – blowing kisses to the girls and generally kicking up such a row that our own men turned round to see who was making such a din. At Gouy, found our quarters quite decent, double tier of bunks in a barn, whitewashed walls and not over draughty. Spent the day, after a good wash and general clean-up, toddling round the village with Bill and Dick, feeling quite glad at being able to spend money again.

18 August 1918

We interpreters are rather curious about a certain 'proposal' according to which those that wish to, may, in due course (heaven only knows when) transfer to Intelligence, thus leaving Wireless and Signals in general, altogether. As the Signals are most distasteful to me, I asked for a transfer, as also did Bill and Dick, the former probably to Corps HQ, owing to previous steps taken through Major AK Evans.

20 August 1918

Sudden orders to report to … Gouy Prisoner-of-War Cage that night, Bill to go to Corps … I reported at Corps and promptly had to help load up a lorry with POW Cage stores. Then we learnt that our destination was Humbercamps, which we reached about midnight and after unloading, were told to report to Captain Barrow, the Intelligence Officer. We found him and had a few hours sleep in a barn. The opening bombardment woke us up and we were all dressed by 7 am. I then got orders to proceed to Bac-du-Sud for the interrogation of wounded prisoners at the Corps Main Dressing Station.[201]

Third Army launched an offensive across its front.

201 John Singer Sargent's famous painting *Gassed* (1919) depicts what he saw at the Corps Dressing Station, Bac-du-Sud in August 1918: Label, IWM ART1460.

21 August 1918

After a very hot journey, partly on foot, partly by lorry, reached the Dressing Station during the morning. I hadn't been there long before the first wounded arrived and once they did, they never seemed to end. But what a difference in 'morale' to those dark days in March! Now everybody was cheerful, our attack was going fine and everything promised well. German wounded came in too and I was kept busy all day, extracting quite good information from same.

22 August 1918

There was a bit of a lull today and I was able to take things a bit easier. I mess with the Sergeants as before and fare quite well. The RAMC are a nice crowd, help me where they can and after tea went with a few of them to Gouy for a drink … I had a narrow escape today. At 5 pm I had to send in a return of wounded Germans admitted, by wire. The nearest Signals Office is in Gouy and there being no despatch rider who went there, I borrowed a motorcycle. I had just arrived there and was slowing up when the handlebar broke off and it was just pure luck that I was able to keep on and not fall off.

23 August 1918

Owing to the large amount of documents and the re-opening of the attack, I asked for help and Dick Lederer turned up. Today was by far the busiest … All day long men came in and this place was not large enough to cope with the numbers. In consequence, by night, every ward, hut and available shelter was crowded out and large numbers had to remain out in the open. Wounded Germans came in galore and as Dick had not slept for two nights, I let him sleep and kept up until 4 am when the rush slowed down and I was able to classify the various regiments and men, which at one time looked like being too much.

24 August 1918

Lots of Germans are being brought in who have been two days in shell holes without being able to move and I must say, it's a sad sight seeing some of them. Amongst the crowd of wounded and sick one sees everywhere, there is one pathetic character. He is a typical middle aged, bespectacled, rather nervous German, a Red Cross man, unwounded, who got here, heaven knows how. At any rate, he has been extremely good on stretcher carrying, helping our men as well as his, pottering round with cups of water, cups of tea, always at it, extremely willing to oblige, painfully eager to help and known by everybody as 'old Fritz'.

25 August 1918

Not knowing how long we shall remain here, I fixed up a kind of office in the Reception Hut, but during the day was only able to see one Hun, a stretcher case, amongst whose documents I found a map of the defences of Fontaine … The Guards [Division] have left and this place is now taken over by a London crowd.

26 August 1918

These new men are not as easy to get on with as the Guards. The Sergeants' Mess etiquette would be very strict but borders on the ridiculous. The super-polite way the two waiters address one make me long to knock their heads together … We got our orders to move to Ransart and Ayette, I to the former, Dick to the latter.

27 August 1918

We moved to our respective villages and I found the Guards Dressing Station in the ruins of what was once a big farmhouse and chateau in the village … Spent the day up to 6 pm messing around, finding the Signals Office, arranging with the RAMC men here what to do when any Germans come in, discovering that German wounded arrive at a railway stopping place down the road, and making arrangements for a runner to call me should any come in and to detain them at night until morning.

30 August 1918

Once again packed up my goods and chattels and after the usual half lorry drive, half march procedure, reached [3rd Divisional Dressing Station at] Hamelincourt. I am now well within the area recaptured during the recent fighting and the devastation on all sides is awful. Many Nissen huts burnt, destroyed or blown up by shell fire add to the general atmosphere of waste and desolation. But on all sides men are working, repairing roads, clearing away rubbish, building shelters and the fields are covered with camps, tents, 'bivvies', horse-lines, lorries and vehicles of all kinds. The redeeming feature of this desolation is the bee-like industry in endeavouring to rebuild and make the most of the ruins. Men working and lorries running are everywhere.

Arrived at this Dressing Station, I was busy at once with some Huns. This ever moving life is getting quite a feature. One of my first jobs on arrival is to fix up an office, 'scrounging' some boxes for a table and chair and placing them in some convenient corner. I then get out my stationery, light my pipe and look important. I have found it is policy to be well in with the Quarter-Master and the cooks, a simple matter, by giving away postcards and other odd things as 'souvenirs', taken off the Huns, thus I don't easily go without food. Today, I have a real table and box as a chair out in the open and expect to sleep in one of the marquees. After I had scrounged these, I borrowed a cycle and scoured the neighbourhood for 'phone which I ran to earth in the 3rd Divisional POW Cage, meeting there a Mr La Touche, an Intelligence Officer. This search sounds simple, but it meant an hour's riding over broken roads, tracks, paths, enquiring times without number, being misdirected, re-misdirected, being nearly run over, covered in dust and generally working off a great deal of surplus energy.

31 August 1918

This Dressing Station is just a little camp of four marquees, about a dozen tents and a few huts. I slept in the corner of one of the marquees, surrounded by moaning and groaning wounded. Several times during the night I had to get up and interrogate Huns brought in and to add to the whole show, German planes came over and bombed not far away. Thus interrogating a man with perhaps an arm or leg blown off at, say, 2 in the morning, with overcoat just thrown over shirt and pants, to accompaniment of *divers* bombs dropping, is no easy job. During the day I am continually on the move, going from one tent to another, until 4 pm, when I borrow a cycle and cycle over to 'phone my report through at the 3rd Divisional HQ, there exchanging summaries of reports with Mr La Touche.

2 September 1918

As if I had not already enough to do, received orders to work another Dressing Station between Hamelincourt and the Arras–Bapaume road. Luckily met a Sergeant who used to be at 43rd CCS and who promised to help me. So I have to practically rush from here to the new place, then to the POW Cage and compare notes with Mr La Touche, then cycle back to the 8th Dressing Station (my present official one), have dinner, interrogate those come in during my absence, then cycle to the new place, interrogate those there, make out a 24-hourly report and rush off to the Cage to 'phone through to Corps Intelligence and in between, whenever possible, examine documents. Also I am liable to be called up during the night every time a wounded German is brought in. Rather a tiring business.

3 September 1918

Our advance seems to be going fine ... Suddenly the news that this Dressing Station is closing down and taking no further wounded in and that the Guards Dressing Station between Ervillers and Mory are taking the wounded. After dinner I left [here] ... (not sorry, very unsettled, rotten grub, too much to do) and got a lorry lift almost to Ervillers. Once again I found myself on the old Arras–Bapaume road, but marked by hastily covered up shell holes, remains of equipment, steel helmets, machine-gun parts and the whole time one noticed the stench of dead men.

I reached the Guards Dressing Station alright and had a most busy time until 4 pm, then got a lift to Advanced Corps HQ, found the telephone lines still being laid, so had to return later during the evening and found things in the same state, impossible to 'phone my report through. Wounded kept coming in and I was up to 3 am before being able to turn in and then I could not sleep through the moaning and the sad wailing, British and German. One poor fellow, hurt in the abdomen, in particular kept crying out for water, but with a wound such as his, it would have killed him. With some of the wounded one sees, one would think a bullet through the head would have been the most merciful thing.

4 September 1918

Went again to Corps [HQ] who have moved to Ervillers and gave in my report, also saw Bill, very excited in the midst of tables, chairs, maps and general office stationery – just unloading from a lorry. Slack day and actually managed to write home. But then came orders for another move and so once again ... packed up and made the journey to Lagnicourt in an ambulance ... Being rather close to the fighting and within the shelled zone, we had to 'kip down' in dug-outs, built by the Germans, about 500 yards from camp. My dug-out, or better said, 'funkhole', was just built for me, had straw laid down over square shell baskets and was quite comfortable. Being tired out, I turned in at 8 pm and slept right through to 7 am.

6 September 1918

The Germans started to shell the ridge, close by which lies my 'Jerry' bivvy and thinking he may be registering for 'future attention', I decided to shift into the valley. So I borrowed a wheelbarrow and stripping this Jerry 'bivvy' of its corrugated iron roof, wheeled it down to the site selected for my new abode and spent the evening fitting it up but owing to lack of time, it was only a very ramshackle affair. I had just got some bread and cheese and was settling down nicely to a feed and read by candlelight, when the alarm went for 'Lights out' owing to threatened bombing planes. I hadn't made my bed and in the darkness I upset the bread and cheese which got hopelessly mixed up with the blankets.

7 September 1918

As no Jerries came in, I spent the whole day properly fixing up my bivvy, the first thing being to deepen the cabin, making it about 4 feet deep. I then had a walk round the neighbourhood and found a German saw and pickaxe. With the help of these, I made a wooden staircase and three shelves – very rough unfinished articles, but serviceable. Three semi-circular corrugated iron sheets formed the roof, together with plenty of earth and by teatime I had knocked together a fairly waterproof compact little cabin. After tea had great luck in finding two large canvas bags. These I 'sewed' together with strips of wire and hung them in front of the entrance, making a good curtain without any candlelight being visible, that is, from the outside. In fact I enjoyed a good long read, with tea and rum, during which old Jerry came over and bombed the horse lines just the other side of the ridge here and then cleared off after the usual hullabaloo of 'Archies', explosions, detonations and machine-gun rattle and flashing of searchlights and other lights. This cabin is not bombproof by a long straw but it would keep out shrapnel splinters and at least is very cosy and comfortable.

8 September 1918

Cut up some coloured camouflage canvas and hung it on the walls, thus hiding the bare earth. Later I shall hang some pictures from the *Bystander*. After tea went into Lagnicourt and bought some chocolate from the Guards Canteen – a rare treat nowadays. Wasn't it a treat, lying in 'bed', eating chocolate, all on my own, nobody to disturb me!

10 September 1918

There is no doubt that being with a crack, the crack Division of the British Army, the Guards, has many advantages. For one thing the men are very decent, for another, everything is done with plenty of system and then the Guards, thanks to their prestige, can run a Canteen where others cannot, can obtain beer and rum and altogether make the best of things. They are a fine set of men, big and broad and to watch their drill in the morning on the fields round here, is a treat. Talk about machine-like precision and smartness. The officers, being Guards, all have pump breeches similar to those worn by golfers and one can see that a disciplinarian CO forbids any excess of dress or style.

11 September 1918

'Dad' Edwards called me from the road and I found him with face bandaged, bespattered with blood. It seems a shell dropped clean on to their tea hut.

12 September 1918

A wounded prisoner of the (German) Guards Reserve Regiment was brought in and gave me certain information which I took to Captain Barrow who is at the newly constructed Corps POW Cage about 1 kilometre down the road. Later on during the day, just after sending off my 24-hourly report at Vaulx-Vraucourt, Major Evans, OC Intelligence at Corps, passed me in his car, then stopped and gave me a lift. On the way I gave him what details I knew – just a repetition of my report. At any rate I took care that he learnt that the news emanated from an interrogation I had made and not from anybody else.

14 September 1918

Had a good bath at the Guards Divisional Baths in [Lagnicourt-Marcel], a good, big, airy place, shower baths, change of washing – I wanted it too. But the Guards Division stick very much to themselves and had I not made out a chit with 'Intelligence and attached to Guards Division' written in large letters, I doubt very much if I would have been let in. But 'Intelligence' is a remarkable 'open sesame' and attracts me to many who want to know 'what is what'. They seem to consider me the 'central news agency' and one man actually approached me by saying "You know the news you give us is reliable and authoritative" – I had to smile. As a matter of fact, I don't hear much more than they, but I get interesting extra details from the Wireless, from the Prisoner Cage and occasionally from persons here and there and just add them on to the general news; but reliable and authoritative?! Then several endeavour to be nice to me in the hope of getting souvenirs off Huns through me. I may say that on the whole they don't get much, certainly nothing of value. One man … in the hope of receiving future souvenirs, had given me a lovely pair of winter pants, whilst as for getting extra bread, cheese, jam, butter or tea, items such as these are thrust into my hands before I have finished asking for them!

15 September 1918

A stirring incident at night. Eight of our searchlights picked out and fastened on to a huge bombing plane of theirs, just overhead. Of course, it was the target of every anti-aircraft gun and machine-gun of the district but it only showed how close a shell can burst without doing vital harm. Then, from nowhere, one of our planes, invisible in the dark, started firing. The tracer bullets hit the *Gotha*, making sparks fly. For a moment we thought the *Gotha* had eluded the searchlights, then they picked her up again. Our machine then simply poured machine-gun bullets into the bomber and, to a loud round of cheering, she caught fire. The outlines first became visible in flames, then the tank caught fire and a moment later the whole, descending to earth one mass of flame, sparks and smoke. On the way down the red and green rockets caught fire and added to the lurid colouring of the whole scene, a sight not easily forgotten.

16 September 1918

I went to the Cage close by here to which Wilkie is attached. He told me the *Gotha* brought down last night had a complement of 8 men. 6 were burnt to death, one was wounded and one, *Ober Leutnant* von Wohlgemuth, came down unhurt in his parachute. He stated that he had brought down 22 of our airmen, so was a man worth capturing. Wilkie also gave me the rather astonishing news that he and Bill were to be trained as Observation Balloon observers – a job he was not at all keen on tackling – considering the number being brought down at present. Bill is away on leave and blissfully unaware of this treat in store for him, if it comes off, of which I am extremely sceptical.

21 September 1918

Got the idea of building a fireplace in this cabin, with a chimney through the roof. So started straight away, dug a half round hole in the side of the wall near the entrance, bored a hole from above which more by luck than calculation struck the roof of the fireplace just where I wanted. Then fitted a chimney which I was also most lucky in finding. I then went to Lagnicourt rather doubtful of obtaining a pipe to fit … Nosing around an RE dump … I selected a piece I wanted and returned, fitted it through the roof, then made a grate out of some handy wire netting and at last, just when the evening began to come over chilly, I started the fire – a success in every way!

24 September 1918

There is no doubt that things are now coming to a point and that very soon another big attack will take place. The 28th is the day most reckoned on ... Met Bill at the Wireless Station. Very enthusiastic about his leave, spent at Biarritz and certainly was far brighter than after his last leave. He told me many interesting things about the near future.

25 September 1918

From information received, I knew that nothing would come off today so snapped up a chance of a joy ride to Doullens and Frévent ... Darkness had fallen when we reached Frévent. I spent all the time with Mme Clara who was rather excited over a row she had had with some woman or other. Anyhow, it seemed to have done her good as after a most vivid and excitable account of the affair, she ended by being in excellent spirits and gave me a good supper. The journey back seemed short as the driver talked of touring on the Continent in a very interesting manner and it transpired he was chauffeur to the Duke of Leinster who spent 3 to 6 months abroad every year.

26 September 1918

My peaceful three weeks at Lagnicourt came to an end today. I left my cabin with great regret. So once more packed up and, with petrol tin of water and basin, rode on one of the Ambulance cars to Beaumetz-lès-Cambrai. I was glad of the petrol tin with water, this latter commodity being scarce. I found myself with the same lot as at Bac-du-Sud and at once spent a very jolly evening in the Sergeants' Mess, where I was remarkably well received – almost surprised me! They had pure English beer in and were sampling it before our 'Push' started though by the time we turned in, there was no more to sample!

Third Army launched its offensive against the Hindenburg Line.

27 September 1918

There is a 3rd Divisional Field Ambulance across the road and having no interpreter, I act as interpreter for both this one to which I am officially attached and [to them]. This means I am, to say the least, rushed off my feet. In fact, I seemed to see only dark huts, crowded out with wounded, all very weary, tired and dirty, unkempt and unshaven, all with fags alight, sitting, standing, lying as best they could, some talking, others trying to sleep, whilst others again were quite merry. Then, through the crowd, an

RAMC orderly's voice would be heard, saying hoarsely "Corporal, some Jerries over here for you". Gingerly picking my way through the crowd, I would find a group of grey uniformed Jerries in a corner, looking most lonesome and miserable. They would brighten up a bit on my talking to them and on my leaving them, would relapse into their previous state of apathy. Then I should have to cross the Field Ambulance grounds to the stretcher cases. Here one saw forms covered with blankets, lying motionless on the whole. Here and there a man, less seriously hurt would be chatting with his neighbour, exchanging their experiences. As soon and as quick as men were carried into the dressing room, other stretcher cases would be brought in and so this incoming and outgoing of wounded continues, day and night.

28 September 1918

Things are going very well and every time I go to the Cage to report to Captain Barrow, the Cage is filled with new batches. 5,000 odd have passed through here alone.

29 September 1918

One disadvantage to things going well is that one is liable always to move at a moment's notice. This happened to me today. So once more goodbye to a comfortable billet and decent quarters. Luck again favoured me and I was able to travel by ambulance car to my new destination, No. 3 Field Ambulance – a strange crowd. The ride was highly interesting, being through quite recently captured territory … Again, on every side one saw feverish bustle and work, road repairing, railway building and ceaseless traffic. The run along the Canal du Nord was splendid, just like a racing track or like a road running along a railway track minus lines with a high brick embankment towering up on both sides. One entered by a track or sloping bridge built in record time, then along the bed for a couple of miles. The embankment was punctured by numerous shell holes, one passed 4 or 5 bridges, some iron, some wood, destroyed by our shell fire or bombs. Here and there gaps showed where trenches cut through the ground above and at one place our engineers had already half constructed a huge trestle bridge. The bed of this canal was as broad as New Street [in Birmingham] and it was up to here that the Guards and other divisions advanced the beginning of this month and the width of the canal prevented further progress. Then [on 27 September], after due artillery preparation, another attack was made which, up to now, we have got as far as, if not completely, into Cambrai. I saw still the 12 to 15 feet high scaling ladders used to climb the embankment … The Field Ambulance was pitched out in the open, about a mile north of Havrincourt. I was busy with wounded at once, but they were an uninteresting crowd.

30 September 1918

Found time to have a walk … to the top of a ridge separating us from Flesquières. From the top, a better view of Cambrai was obtained but it was enveloped in many puffs of shell bursts and clouds of smoke, presumably from fires. All this country is strewn with intersecting trenches, barbed wire, rifles and equipment, helmets, English and German, dead bodies here and there, whilst a tank from a distance still retaining its old shape, close to very knocked about – stands on the brow of the ridge, looking straight towards Cambrai. I thought how mad the officer must have been in being put *hors de combat* just with Cambrai in view. It is a relic of the famous November 1917 'push' which so nearly succeeded, when tanks were used for the first time in numbers. One can just discern 'G31' on this tank.[202]

2 October 1918

The usual Huns found after 2 or 3 days spent lying wounded in shell holes coming in. Seems impossible that human beings can remain alive under the present cold conditions. They present sad pictures … Walked into Havrincourt and gathered mushrooms. It struck me as incongruous, picking mushrooms 'midst almost perfect peace, whereas only a few days ago – less than a week – this village must have been a veritable inferno, judging by the wreckage on all sides. Still, it is not so utterly levelled as other villages, but somehow the sight of one blown up, shell-torn house after the other, with all the timber lying about in most grotesque shapes and forms, makes one realise the wreckage more vividly than where just a patch of overgrown bricks and iron meet the eye. Another remarkable sight, yet somehow in keeping with the surroundings, was the carrying of a piano through one of the main streets by a party of men who had discovered it amongst the ruins. How it remained untouched and unhurt is a marvel. Whenever this party halted for a rest, one of them started to play and the others danced around like so many street urchins. The sight of this piano being played in the middle of the street, these men dancing round and the ruins around was a very striking picture which yet seemed

202 Named 'Galatea', the tank had formed part of 20th Company, G Battalion, Tank Corps and was attached to 62nd Division during the November 1917 attack; information supplied by Tank Museum.

to be quite the natural order of things where, at present, the unnatural has become the natural. We got back to our camp and seeing a red glow in the sky, continued up the ridge from which Cambrai was distinctly seen burning in two places. Being dark by now, the red glow of the flames made a picture reminiscent of the Black Country [of the West Midlands] at night.

5 October 1918

Although, with the exception of a few, I do not like the men here as much as the other Field Ambulances, yet I must say the food is excellent considering the exposed cooking conditions. We have porridge and bacon every morning and always rice or some pastry as 'pudden' after. It is a marvel how the men do it. The Sergeants Mess is a shelter composed of a few stakes and crossbeams covered by a kind of tarpaulin which does not fit in parts and lets through a biting draught. The cookhouse consists of four cookers or ovens and a couple of improvised ranges, bricks and iron railings; no shelter and an incessant wind howling. And yet these cooks turn out roasts, stews and pastry and pudding!

6 October 1918

In order to see about whether my rank as Corporal was confirmed or not, went to Wireless HQ … [at] Marcoing … Transacted my business and returned on a lorry via Flesquières. Traffic immense, both sides of road. Round 8 pm the sky cleared and stars came out. At 11.30 pm, a German bombing plane dropped four bombs on the Field Ambulance, killing an officer, a Staff Sergeant and two other ranks, besides wounding five … My tent-mate had a narrow squeak, a small piece of shrapnel penetrating the tent and hitting his head. When he exclaimed "I'm hit", I thought he was joking and said "Get away with you" although the deafening crashes just outside had given me a nice shock. However, when I saw he was serious, I jumped off my stretcher, looked at the wound – a very slight one – and told him to go and have it dressed. He did so and came back with the news of the above-mentioned dead and wounded. Luckily all the wounded had been evacuated. During his absence whilst being dressed, I thought again what a narrow squeak we had had and how easily it might have been me with a more serious wound.

7 October 1918

After last night's catastrophe, everybody started making dug-outs and bivvies, including, of course, ourselves. We selected a portion of trench close by and practically spent the day widening it and covering it with wooden beams and corrugated iron sheets, scrounged from Havrincourt.

8 October 1918

Our guns opened out and by the time we arrived [at Noyelle-Vion], the noise was deafening. The guns lined the roadway, every bank, ditch or cover. The artillerymen, in any serviceable turnout as long as it was warm, moving about like monkeys and being a biting cold morning, they seemed to revel in the exercise … Found the Field Ambulance in what remained of a sugar factory, all knocked to pieces, of course, and all the dressing of wounded took place in the cellars. I was soon busy, but pleasantly so – not the rush I have had on other occasions. Old Jerry got busy too and during the morning answered our barrage in grand style, his shells bursting in and over the whole village.

9 October 1918

Was awakened by a fellow asking whether I wanted to interrogate a German trench mortar man who had driven into our lines, with trench mortar wagon and horses complete! … Arrived at the Guards Field Ambulance [in Masnières] … We had one or two useful Huns in and from one got the actual confession that the withdrawal was to be a considerable distance, also about where to. He overheard two officers talking about it when laying in their dressing station after having his wound dressed. That night, officers and personnel did withdraw, leaving the wounded behind who in time were captured by us. I had a ride to Hermies and gave in this report. There heard officially that we had surrounded Cambrai and then taken it. The traffic en route was stupendous, one long procession for miles and miles, of troops, limbers, lorries, wagons etc. all moving up, infantry, New Zealanders, artillery, also even cavalry.

10 October 1918

Slept in a dug-out close by, an old German one, of course, lined with wallpaper. Only one wounded German came in who gave quite interesting information, stating the line to which the Germans intended to withdraw, the Solesmes–[Le Cateau-Cambrésis] line. Our advance continues fast, so fast in fact that a map I got from Corps yesterday, today is almost out-of-date. No. 3 (Guards) Dressing Station were to open up … but have orders to wait and see where the advance is held up and then open up their Field Ambulance. A Corps HQ is supposed to be in Cambrai and the broad-gauge railway already runs into the town.

Marvellous rapid construction. Otherwise things very quiet, chiefly spent document reading.

11 October 1918

Yesterday we were in the land of desolation, destruction on every side. Today we crossed the destroyed area and entered once again into the land of untouched villages, whole houses, trees with leaves just turning red, bushes lining gardens, in fact, everything intact with only one thing missing, the actual villagers who had to clear out six weeks ago. The ride in front of the ambulance was hugely interesting and the sudden change to untouched habitations, striking. [On 7 October] all this was in German hands, then followed his mysterious retirement and now we occupy country held by him for over four years. As one walks through the streets of this village (Carnières), one's feelings are peculiar. A mixture of delight at being in a village so long in German hands, of pride in being able to participate in this extraordinary advance and of being able to see everything at so first-hand and lastly of pleasure at having at last gained villages offering a roof for a billet. Everybody seems to feel this.[203] The contrast is so great, one has to experience it to realise it. On all sides fellows are singing, here and there pianos left behind by the Germans are being lustily hammered upon by our fellows and in spite of the raw, wet weather which has set in, everybody is smiling. Each house had its fire, smoke coming out of the chimney, not out of rainwater pipes pushed through a cellar grating hole. Beds, chairs, tables etc. add to the feeling of comfort – in many windows I even saw flower boxes. I visited the Church and in it listened to one of our fellows playing Handel's *Largo* on the organ. I must say, it brought tears to my eyes, what for, I don't know. But it sounded magnificent. The Church itself was untouched, all the chairs standing in rows. As far as I could make out, only the chandeliers had been removed. I wished Linder Robinson had been with me. Today, the return to signs of civilisation, 'the other side', has been a strikingly impressive day.

13 October 1918

Sergeant Cox, of the Ambulance Convoy and I visited the Church although the service was the Roman Catholic mass, of which we neither of us understood a word. We both believed the chance of a good organ to be played upon would have permitted of music, but to our disappointment, the monotonous droning and murmuring of the Padre

203 For soldiers' satisfaction at participating in the liberation of occupied territory, see Gibson, *Behind the Front*, 370.

was all we heard, the ringing of a bell here and there startling us through its unexpectedness, but of singing and chanting there was none … My old friend, Sergeant Francke of the Intelligence Police [arrived] … Heard all about the old Arras friends … Also heard of the astounding state of affairs in Arras "only 450 inhabitants, with vice and morals raging amongst themselves". What astonished me was the news that my old friend Mme Magniez had been accused of theft, which accounted for her departure from Arras.

15 October 1918

After tea strolled round to Francke's place and stayed for supper, to which their 'chief' sat down with us and without ceremony at all. Francke's job and that of his men is rather a risky one just now as 'getting in touch' with civilians means pushing ahead of the infantry in places. The first man into Caudry was an Intelligence Police fellow and as usual with the Intelligence, they are on their own, in case of trouble, nobody owning them.

16 October 1918

I am reading a damn good book, *The Man with the Clubfoot*[204] – one of the best yarns I've read for a long time. Rain has been falling these last few days and mud abounds, splashing one from top to bottom when a lorry passes (which happens about every few seconds). This dull rainy weather is very cheerless and somehow is taking the edge off the feeling that we are in good quarters, under a roof etc.

17 October 1918

Whether it was the rotten wine [in the Sergeants' Mess] last night or a cold I've caught, or what, I don't know but I felt out of sorts today. Meredith and I had a stroll to the Guards Canteen but a Sergeant appeared and hearing we were only attached to the Guards Division would not let us be served. Outside the HQ is a large map showing the progress which continues to be fine.

18 October 1918

During our usual walk to [Divisional HQ] saw from the map that we had taken Ostende, Lille and Douai and a later report stated also Bruges. At last we are seeing the collapse so often talked about, the taking of one

204 Valentine Williams, *The Man with the Clubfoot* (1918).

town after another, at a speed never anticipated. It is all happening so fast, one is scarce able to take it all in. Who would have thought at the end of March that before 8 months had passed we should be in possession of Ostende and Lille?!

19 October 1918

Another 'Push' is coming off here tomorrow … As usual, the day before an attack, there is the feeling of suppressed excitement, confidential whisperings of some items of news 'from someone in the know' and the ceaseless clatter of horses, traffic and men moving up the road. Heavy tractors pulling guns make the building tremble.

Third Army attacked across the River Selle.

20 October 1918

Towards evening an old Frenchman, wounded by the blowing up of a bridge, came in. He was in gay spirits. Said that when he heard our drumfire, he put on his best clothes to greet our troops. He seemed very upset about the loss of a special bottle of wine he intended drinking with the first British soldier at liberty to do so. He had kept this bottle hidden … for this occasion and was just getting it out, thinking the Germans had left, when one unfortunately came down the cellar steps for cover from our fire, saw it, took it and drank it. The one consolation he had was that the fellow got drunk and was taken prisoner, being too far gone to clear off when he had the chance.

21 October 1918

I had a mysterious call to report to OC Signals and there was told that Lederer and I were being permanently withdrawn from our duties and were being sent down to Base. Nothing further, no reason why, nothing. A certain enquiry I had to attend a few days ago gave me a clue. Signals not being able to tell me anything, I asked to see Major Evans, my Corps Intelligence OC. He could give me no further particulars except that it had to do with the enquiry mentioned. I asked him whether it was through any lack of confidence in me or fault in my work. He at least consoled me by saying that they, at Corps Intelligence HQ, had always had full confidence in me and my work had been quite satisfactory and he even thanked me for what I had done. But he said that the instructions for my recall had come from Base and in consequence all power of acting for me was taken out of his hands.

Later I had a long chat with Bill and I must say that if ever a fellow showed practical sympathy, he did, telling me all he knew of the matter (thereby certainly complicating the possibilities of our future fate) arranging with me a plan by which I was to inform him of what should befall us and otherwise doing and saying all he could to cheer me up. He certainly felt for me most deeply and I realised that in spite of his often outwardly cold attitude, yet he had real feelings of friendship for me. The private nature of this enquiry prevents me from explaining why he should have shown his feelings so openly on this occasion. It was a revelation to me but at the same time, a great consolation.

22 October 1918

A good night made me feel refreshed. Dick and I had to catch a 3 pm train from Cambrai this afternoon for Abbeville – that is all we know. Never before have I felt so uneasy about the future. It is hard to realise that after 2½ years, since June 1916, we are being sent away, away from all the scenes so familiar, the faces so well known, both of which one has almost learnt to love, in spite of the many hard times … Dick and I made our farewell bow to the Corps HQ and by lorry jumping reached Cambrai in a nasty downpour of rain. I must give Dick credit for obtaining tea and putting me on the track of rations. I myself seemed to be under a cloud. We got on a train supposed to be bound for Abbeville, the usual goods-truck troop train … The journey was hideously slow from Cambrai to Bapaume, the reason being that many time fuse mines, left by the Huns, are going off and blowing away stretches of railway. In consequence, traffic gets distinctly dislocated. After 12 hours we were only at Marcoing, 6 miles from Cambrai and only reached Bapaume at dawn – 16 hours to do 18 miles!

23 October 1918

After Bapaume, with daylight, we got on better and reached Achiet early. Here we had to change … Dick and I managed to fry some bacon and meat in one of the tumbledown station huts, ending with a wash … Passing through the Ancre valley we saw what must be one of the most barren, bleak and shell-shattered districts along the whole front. Hardly a square yard that was not touched by a shell hole. Later we re-entered civilisation proper and the sun shining on the villages and the ploughed ground made a pretty picture. We reached Candas at 4 pm. We are supposed to continue by the 7 pm train to Abbeville but instead are playing truant and having a day off by catching tomorrow's 7 pm train. We arranged to spend the night at Mme Julianne's at whose house I often used to have eggs and chips ... The main attraction elsewhere was Lucile, as I call her now, and I found her as delicious as before. We stayed there until late, chatting, and enjoying ourselves after the nature peculiar to the house, which is never quiet. To celebrate our turning up, both Clementine and Lucile had their share of wine and in consequence we were lively, to say the least. This wild evening, our return to civilisation, will long remain in my mind.

24 October 1918

Slept like a top. Mme Julianne made our breakfast and afterwards we spent an hour at Lucile's ... Dick and I scrounged round for our dinner and a fellow in Lucile's café saying the Quartermaster at the station might have a Macconachie, we went round, interviewed him, the result being we got a loaf of bread, cheese and fresh meat, enough for four of us. Mme Julianne made a fine roast out of this, Dick declaring it was the best meal he had had for months. After a final chat and drink at Lucile's, we packed up and caught the 7 pm to Abbeville. We travelled in a horse truck with straw and droppings still in though we cleared some of it away, but the stench made sleep impossible. Reached Abbeville about midnight and kipped down in the rest camp, composed of good large huts, treble bunk beds and fairly warm – anyway, a great improvement on the horse truck.

25 October 1918

This place, Abbeville, has the reputation of being one of the most regimental and well-disciplined centres in France. I had my first reminder of this when asking a Sergeant for a lift in his lorry to the Signals Depot. The man looked at me as if I were mad and it was only with the greatest difficulty that I prevailed upon him to take our blankets. So we trudged along on foot and I saw for the first time the much spoken of WAACs, VAD motorcycle drivers etc. It was nice seeing English girls again. At the Signals Depot we soon had our wind put up us with the numerous parades, orders, this 'strictly prohibited', that 'strictly prohibited'. We had to parade to see the CO, again to see the OC Wireless, again for giving in our paybooks. On all occasions one must behave in an extremely smart, soldierly fashion, always mightily poshed up, dazzling boots and buttons. Everybody is most unsociable and curt and dry and, oh, how many times I thought of the glorious 'Hail fellow well met' atmosphere of the units and men nearer the line. Dick and I consoled ourselves as best we could with a walk through the town and a feed, but although under different circumstances I would have been in the height of good spirits, yet at present I have a most peculiar fear – not physical – of the unknown future.

26 October 1918

We sleep on home-made beds in huts lit with electric light. Breakfast is at 7 am and we have to Parade again at 8.30 am. During the day I tried, through interviews, to get to know for what reason we are down here. There seem to be two distinct parties, one the private reason I'm not going to mention as yet here, the other the recall of interpreters, each of which belongs to a different kind of department and apparently each is working in its secret silent manner to retain us without the other's knowledge. But there is no definite reason to be got as yet, so Dick and I, still hoping against hope that we shall not be shoved into a new Wireless Course starting and that we shall be able to wriggle our way through to Intelligence again, can only hang on and hope for the best.

28 October 1918

Pending further developments of the enquiry concerning Dick and myself, we were put on the rather humiliating job of supervising German prisoners disentangling mixed-up coils of wire. We feel we must grin and bear it, but thinking of the freedom we enjoyed in the past, the interesting work we were engaged in, and now this, it makes one mad. The camp itself is a huge concern, well laid out and well organised. The majority of the men are from the line, down here for a course of instruction, wireless, signalling etc.; there is an NCO School and NCOs' cadet class. The Corporals' Mess alone is over 50 strong. On the other side of the hill is the WAACs' camp of which only the huts are visible. The dividing line between the two camps is a road, very strongly watched by police. In our camp, work is over at 4.30 pm and we can go out.

29 October 1918

I sent in a formal application for a transfer to the Intelligence though I have little hopes of its coming through. Dick and I went to one of Lena Ashwell's concerts in the 'Old Theatre' and had a good laugh.[205] Dorothy Day and a Miss Ainsley were two of the four girls. The theatre itself was packed with our own men, conspicuous by the blue and white armlet on

205 The famous actress had helped to establish entertainments for the troops, including at Abbeville: L.J. Collins, *Theatre at War, 1914–18* (London: Macmillan, 1998), 149–50; Margaret Leask, *Lena Ashwell: Actress, Patriot, Pioneer* (Hatfield: University of Hertfordshire Press for the Society for Theatre Research, 2012), 139–44.

each man's sleeve, also by Australians and the proceedings were enlivened by numerous WAACs and VADs amongst the audience. It was a great treat. At supper I sat opposite a rather pretty *demi-mondaine* who kept up an amusingly suggestive conversation with me – I won't go into details – which I answered in a somewhat mockingly polite fashion, but which gave us mutual amusement. At least, she paid me the compliment at the end of saying she hoped to meet me again just for the sake of a chat and "for no other motive". Thought I to myself "perhaps?"

30 October 1918

Dick and I are really beginning not to care a damn what will happen to us. The old feeling of bitterness is leaving and the philosophical feeling of 'enjoy the present whilst you can' is taking its place. We feel we have done what we could and can now only await events. Abbeville is a nice little place, with cafés and restaurants galore, also theatres, concerts, cinemas etc., so we ask ourselves "why worry?" The War will be over soon now too. The latest news is that Austria has accepted President Wilson's terms and now asks for the armistice conditions. Everything points to matters coming to an end soon.

31 October to 2 November

The days are so similar that there is no need to write up each day separately. Dick and I with the other interpreters are engaged on the same job, guarding and superintending German prisoners disentangling wire, fearfully monotonous, and the hours drag. Dick was posted once as sentry and on complaining of the long hours, was promptly put under arrest for impudence, being improperly dressed (having one button undone) and for being dirty. "I'll make you bloody interpreters liven your ideas up a bit before I've finished with you" said the Corporal of the Guard. However, Dick, being no fool, spoke straight out when up before the Colonel and was dismissed with an admonition. But how they love us interpreters! Then again, we interpreters received a talking to for allowing the Germans to slack, according to the report of some officer nosing round, whom we never saw – a most unfounded report. Everybody agreed as to the injustice of this and Sergeant Johnson, who is in charge of the Cable Shed, spoke to the OC and this somewhat mended matters. But, like at the Wireless at VI Corps, the interpreters are looked upon as odd men out, to blame for everything and are disliked by all. Thank heaven for my stripes being confirmed. I should have been reduced to the ranks long ago had I been but an Acting Corporal.

4 to 6 November 1918

We got orders to report to an Intelligence Officer at the POW Cage, a gigantic barracks, to which all prisoners taken on our front eventually are brought and divided up into POW companies.[206] We reported and were examined individually and with the experience we have had, passed easily. This Intelligence officer then 'phoned through to the Adjutant of the Signals Depot asking whether we could be spared at once. Reply was "Yes, tomorrow morning if no special work arises" … [But then] was told "To continue work in the Cable Shed until instructions come for you from the Adjutant-General" … [On 6 November] I went to see this officer again, who returned with me to the Signal Camp to see the Adjutant – who, however was out. So instead he pumped the Orderly Room concerning us and our case is as follows: Signals may not lend us to Intelligence until definite orders are received from the Deputy Adjutant-General at GHQ. These orders will only be given on receipt of a certificate from the Intelligence that we had been examined and found fluent enough in German for intelligence purposes. Until then we should have to remain at the Depot. This would sound promising to anyone unacquainted with Army red tape. But we can see that days and weeks will go by before any Intelligence Section asks for us, things work so slowly. Then again, further evidence in the shape of the arrival of a fellow called Long (similar placed as Dick and myself), also Nienhaus[207] (a friend of Bill's whom I met … in December 1916) point to the fact that we are 'marked' (but not as we should have liked!).

7 to 9 November 1918

After the raising of our hopes and consequent dashing to ground, our life continues its weary hum-drum course. The work is punctuated by ½ hour's break during the morning, during which we can get the post in the Corporals' Mess, the dinner break follows and after that in the afternoon's spell, broken by the arrival of the Continental edition of the *Daily Mail*, for which there is an enormous rush just now. News is fierce, one gigantic event after another. During our stay here, just over a fortnight, Austria and Turkey have chucked up the sponge, the German Army is being rolled back from the Scheldt and as I write, the German armistice answer is being hourly expected … The Jerries are almost as delighted at the

206 Since 1916 the British had retained German prisoners on the Western Front to work in labour companies: Heather Jones, *Violence against Prisoners of War in the First World War: Britain, France and Germany, 1914–1920* (Cambridge: Cambridge University Press, 2011), 137.

207 108152 Corporal Bernard Nienhaus RE.

prospect of peace as we are. The Kaiser would hardly feel complimented with the things some of these prisoners say about him. But they are a very quiet lot, semi-starved into apathy, no spirit or 'go' in them at all, just reeling and disentangling wire all the working day, with their, by now, very shabby field-grey uniforms marked with their POW Company number on their back, sometimes with a circle of coloured cloth attached to the overcoat back. They strike one as walking in a dream and who knows, some of them might be doing just that … I am so disgusted and dissatisfied with the work I am forced to do in this Depot, that I can easily understand and almost feel like sympathising with the man who, overburdened with troubles and discontent, tries to drown his sorrows in drink, although personally, thank heaven, I am nowhere approaching that stage.

11 November 1918

This day, the 11th day of the 11th month at 11 am, the armistice was signed[208] … I had to translate certain armistice amendments received by Wireless … At 10.55 am, we had to Parade, the whole Depot. At 11 am, the Union Jack, French and US flags were run up the mast staff and *God Save the King*, the *Marseillaise* and the US national anthem were played by the Signals Depot Band. The Adjutant then said a few words, saying also that our troops had entered Mons at 4.30 am this morning. The Padre continued the theme and said that it was more than a coincidence, it was an absolutely visible act of God that the end of the War for the British Army should be in triumph on the spot where our first retreat started in 1914. With bare heads we sung the national anthem and a hymn of thanksgiving.

I myself consciously made myself realise that I was witnessing part of a ceremony on one of the greatest days of history. I photographed the scene in my mind, the assembled men with bandoliers over overcoats, facing the Orderly Room in six double lines. Behind, the Union Jack, French flag and the US flags flopping at the head of the high mast staff and below, a solitary thick-set little figure with a bushy white moustache, the Adjutant, speaking to us; to the right, the Padre, pale, thin and nervous looking. On his left, the Band, whilst on all sides the men, either listening to the words being spoken to them or singing or praying bareheaded, or with caps in hand, giving Foch, Haig etc. rousing cheers. Certainly it was a picture to be remembered. The Abbeville churches' bells are ringing as I write.

208 The armistice had been signed at 0510 but did not come into effect until 1100.

After dinner, all men, 'except those engaged with prisoners' to have the afternoon off, was the announcement which would have kept me in, so I took the afternoon off on my own, strolled into Abbeville and found the town delirious with rejoicings. Flags of all Allies hung out of windows, everybody wore a ribbon or flag or some bunting and everybody was smiling, singing and shouting. In the main square, an Australian band played national anthems punctuated by loud cheers. Two-step music followed, officers and men dancing in the circle formed by the band. Old men, young men, old women, young women, each caught hold of whoever was nearest and danced some kind of dance. A fatigue party of six German prisoners appeared with one English guard. Guard and prisoners were 'roped in' and joined the mad dancing round. The whole time singing and shouting, cheers and laughter never ceased and the streets were thronged with a crowd seemingly half bereft of reason, male and females alike. I would not have missed the scene for worlds.

In November Vince was sent to another prisoner-of-war camp for registration work. In December he went home on leave. Before returning to France he arranged to be designated as an individual 'pivotal' to the economy and was therefore demobilised on 13 January 1919. Some administrative confusion resulted in a February visit from the police seeking him as a deserter, but this was soon resolved.

Appendix

SS.165, 'Listening Set Posts', May 1917[1]

Secret.
Not to be taken beyond Brigade Headquarters.

Organisation and Working.

The successful work of a Listening Post will depend entirely upon:

(a) Constant Supervision.
(b) Constant Experiment.
(c) Close co-operation between the Officer i/c of the Set and the Signal Offices of the units in the vicinity of the post, as well as with the Corps Intelligence.

I. PERSONNEL OF THE LISTENING SET POST.

1. The Listening Post Sub-Section of the Wireless section belonging to the Corps Signal Company provides the personnel for two Listening Set Posts. This Sub-Section consists of one Sergeant, nine Interpreter Operators, five Field Linesmen and four Wireless Operators.

1 AWM27/311/69, AWM.

2. In mobile warfare, and in certain portions of the front in trench warfare, there is little scope for the use of Listening Set Posts. In such circumstances the Listening Sub-Section may be employed on Wireless duties, but the sanction of the General Staff should be obtained if it is proposed to employ the sub-section for a prolonged period on such duties.
3. In cases where it is desired to employ more than two Listening Posts in one Corps Area, it will be necessary temporarily to transfer a Listening Sub-Section from another Corps.
4. *Relief of Personnel.* Although the personnel and equipment of one Listening Sub-Section per Corps is sufficient to establish two Listening Sets, it must be remembered that varying in degree with local conditions, the working of a Listening Set is very arduous, and the Corps concerned must allow for adequate relief and withdrawal for rest from the front line, of the personnel employed on each Listening Set Post. This can best be effected by having three Interpreter Operators on duty at each of the Listening Set Posts, and placing the other three in rest. One week's rest in three for each Interpreter Operator is thus provided.

   A similar arrangement can be made for the Wireless Operators so that they may have one week's rest in a month.

   The Linesmen's duties are the most arduous on the Post, and if it be desired to keep two Posts in action in the Corps, application may, if necessary, be made to AD Signals of the Corps for one additional Linesman, in order that the Linesmen of each Post may have sufficient relief, namely, one week's rest in three.

II. USES OF LISTENING SET POSTS.

1. Listening Set Posts are employed for two purposes:

(a) Intelligence with regard to the enemy.
To overhear enemy telephone conversations; telegraphic buzzer messages and power buzzer messages.
The information obtainable by these means embraces a wide field, and includes such information as identifications of units, reliefs, enemy artillery fire observation, warning of our attacks, raids, bombardment of special positions etc.

(b) Policing our own lines.
To police our own lines, that is, to ascertain whether information which might be of value to the enemy is passing across our front line, and whether all circuits are metallic and properly maintained.

2. Dangerous Circuits.

A conversation that can be overheard on a Listening Set with earths near the front line may also be overheard by the enemy. If conversation on a particular circuit can be clearly heard, that circuit is faulty, requires repair, and should be closed down until the fault is remedied.

It must be borne in mind that the lines running from a Listening set may, to a certain extent, carry towards the enemy signals induced in them from our own systems. Areas in which a Listening Set is installed are therefore doubly dangerous, and must be watched with the greatest care.

Listening Posts will not be used for purposes of communication from power buzzers; but any messages, other than practice messages, picked up from power buzzers must be forwarded at once to the nearest Headquarters.

III. SELECTION OF SITE AND LAY-OUT OF CIRCUITS.

The site for a Listening set will be selected by the Staff of the Corps. The following considerations should be borne in mind:

1. As far as possible a site should be chosen which is opposite a known enemy telephone system, and in the disposition of the earths, location of the loops, etc., due consideration should be given to the direction in which the enemy's cable trenches run, that is, whether they run parallel, diagonally or at right angles to the front.
2. Before deciding on the disposition of the earths or loop, all available information should be obtained from the Intelligence of the Corps as to the enemy's telephone system. The Corps are often able to obtain from the interrogation of prisoners much information of value to the Officer i/c Listening Set Posts on that front.
3. Much assistance may also be obtained from the study of aeroplane photographs, which show enemy cable trenches, and furnish in some cases indications as to the communication trenches through which wires are likely to run after they have left the cable trench.

4. Many of these photographs also show the up-to-date condition of our own trenches, and indicate clearly which portions of our trenches are specially to be avoided owing to bombardment. This information, combined with a knowledge of the locality, may suggest the expediency of laying out circuits across the open, and they may thus escape damage and interruption to which they would be subjected if installed in a trench liable to bombardment by enemy trench mortars or field guns.
5. *Tests for leakage from power or lighting wires.* After it has been decided which portion of the front is to be employed, and before any further steps are taken, it is essential that tests should be made to find out whether the portion selected is subject to leakage from power or lighting wires …
6. *Local soil conditions.* The condition of the surface soil and subsoil will also to a certain extent affect the results obtainable. This, however, should not govern the decision as to the selection of a site, as it is impossible to lay down any precise rules, and the exact disposition of the substrata is rarely known.

   As far as has been ascertained, soil is favourable and unfavourable respectively in the undermentioned circumstances:

   (a) *Favourable.* Ordinary ground of the type of arable or pasture land without water directly under the surface; Light surface soil with a depth of 10 to 20 feet over chalk; Thin stratum of clayey or heavy surface soil over rock or chalk.

   (b) *Unfavourable.* Surface soil which is so shallow that the chalk appears on the surface; Ground with water close to the surface.

IV. DUG-OUT – SITUATION AND CONDITION.

A matter of great importance is the selection of a dug-out or cellar for the accommodation of the Set and personnel.

This dug-out must be reserved exclusively for the use of the Set and personnel, and it is of first importance that it should have sufficient head-cover to withstand anything except a direct hit from a gun of 105mm or over. Under no circumstances should it be in such a position as to come under the observation of the enemy, even from a great distance.

The dug-out must be dry, and to ensure this, arrangements should be made for heating and ventilation. The instrument cannot work satisfactorily in a damp condition.

The station should be as quiet and private as possible, and if a cellar is used, it should not be situated on a road along which heavy transport frequently passes during the night.

In choosing the location, it must be remembered that while it is important to establish the station as far forward as possible in order to avoid interference from our line and the necessity for maintaining a long lead to the instrument, it must not be situated so far forward as to be in danger of capture or destruction in the event of an enemy raid.

It should not be situated too close to an Exchange or a locality where many signal wires exist.

It should not be within 300 yards of a Trench Wireless Station.

A reasonable degree of comfort must be provided for the personnel. Bunks for sleeping in, benches and a sufficiently large table to accommodate the instrument and enable the Interpreter or Operator to write unhindered.

Satisfactory lighting arrangements must be provided.

The porterage of the accumulators should be taken into consideration, since if great distances have to be covered, they put a considerable extra strain on the personnel.

V. DISPOSAL OF RESULTS.

1. The NCO i/c Listening Set Post is directly responsible for the secrecy of all messages and information passing through and received at the Post. These are not to be discussed outside, or communicated to anyone except in accordance with instructions at the head of the Daily Reports Sheets.
2. All results will be taken on AF W3412 (see Appendix A).
3. *Fullerphone to Brigade for disposal of Urgent Matter.* In order to communicate the results of importance, which in the opinion of the NCO i/c of the Post require immediate action, a Fullerphone should always be installed in the Listening Set Post dug-out and connected to Brigade or Battalion Headquarters, preferably the former, if not situated at too great a distance from the Post.

   The line for this instrument should be maintained by the area Signal unit and not by the personnel of the Listening Set Post.

4. Reports will be despatched at least twice in 24 hours in an envelope addressed in accordance with the instructions of the Daily Report Sheet and marked SECRET outside. The hours of despatch will be arranged to suit the [despatch rider] post from the Headquarters of the formation to which the Listening Post is attached.
5. (a) All buzzer calls, etc., will be written down exactly as they are heard.
   (b) Intercepted speech, whether English or German, will be written down as far as possible as in the conversation, and a fresh line should be commenced for each speaker.
   (c) English translation of interceptions will be recorded in parallel columns.
6. The officer in command of the nearest formation or the formation that is in telegraphic communication with the Post, will be responsible for the personnel in the event of an attack taking place which might endanger the Listening Set Post.

VI. INSTALLATION OF LINES.

1. *Class of Wire.* Unless the Post is situated in a very forward position and very short earth wires are used, field cables should be avoided, as the resistance is too high. If it is not possible to procure more suitable wire, D5 cable may be used for short lines.
2. When a number of lines are carried forward from the dug-out towards the front or support trenches through the same communications trenches, or by the same route, steel armoured quad cables are [the] most suitable type.
3. If single wires pass by different routes, endeavours should be made to obtain a low resistance cable of sufficient strength and insulation.
4. *Loops.* For the purpose of these instructions, a loop is a roughly rectangular metallic circuit, conforming with the trenches that have been selected.

   In practice, it has been found that loops having a front face of not less than 250 yards and not more than 1,000 are the most suitable.

   The back of the loop should not be too close to the front, and generally the depth of the loop should not be less than a quarter to one-third of its front.

   With a loop having a front of 700 yards and a low resistance cable, it had been found that results will improve by laying up to 6 loops in series. Results obtained with a greater number of loops do not justify the additional maintenance required.

5. *Number of Separate Loops per Set.* Unless additional assistance is received from the personnel of another Set or from the area Signal unit, it is inadvisable to install more than one loop, as the maintenance will be more than the personnel can cope with ...
6. The wiring of the loop should, generally speaking, be run between ankle and knee high in the trenches.

   If, however, owing to wet weather, the trenches are continually falling in and the locality is not subject to frequent bombardment, it may be found that less maintenance is required if the wires are run on the top and outside the trench, but just within arm's reach. This, however, does not remove the necessity of leaving the wires stapled down at frequent intervals.
7. *Junction Box.* A junction box is provided for installing at the junction of the loop and lead to the Set (see Appendix B).
8. *Use of Mine Galleries.* In order to reduce maintenance, mine galleries, infantry communications tunnels etc., should be utilized, if possible, for one face or more of the loop. These, however, can seldom be used if electric lighting or power wires exist in these galleries, as the induction from these wires causes such noises in the amplifier as to drown all other signals.
9. *Installation of Loops dependent on local conditions.* The double commutator switch supplied with the instrument (see Appendix C) provides for 3 loops. Each of these loops may be series loops in any number of turns up to 6. It is, however, [a] waste of material and labour to install more than one loop when enemy bombardment or the condition of our trenches does not admit of a good prospect of maintenance.

VII. EARTHS.

1. A system of earths should always be laid out in addition to the loop.
2. *Earth Base.* An earth base is an imaginary straight line joining two earth contacts, irrespective of the path of the lead.
3. *Position of Earths.* Earth contacts should not be simply placed along the front line, but arranged so as to obtain combinations of earth bases, diagonally and at right angles, as well as parallel to the enemy front line.

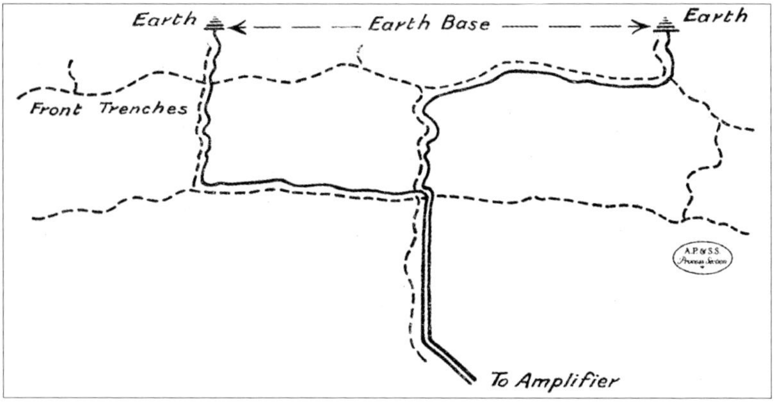

Where the direction of the enemy wires is definitely known, an earth base can be arranged at a definite angle, so as to obtain the best results from leakage on that line. To do this, it is necessary either to get the earth base of loop front as near as possible *parallel and opposite* to the enemy line.

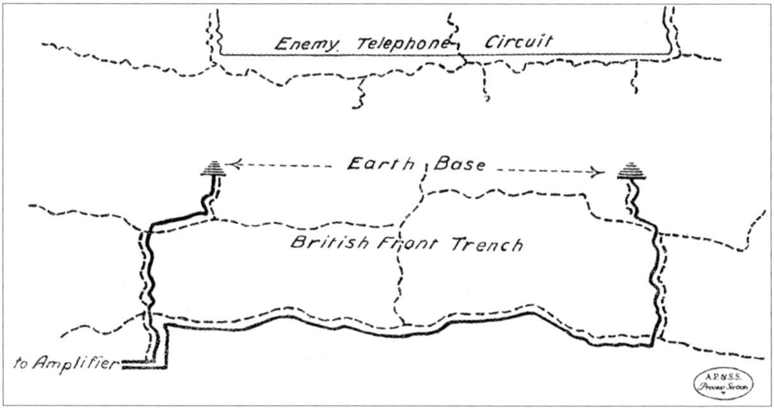

Should it not be possible to get the earth base parallel and opposite, endeavours should be made to arrange it as *a direct continuation* of the enemy line. If the enemy circuit to be intercepted runs approximately at right angles to our front, no difficulties should arise, and two earth contacts should be placed as a direct continuation of the enemy circuits with, say, the forward earth in No Man's Land (the wire having previously been painted so as to be invisible to the enemy, and stapled down so that patrols may not trip over it), and the other earth in either our front or support line. If, however, the latter earth is brought too far back, it may become subject to interference from our own lines.

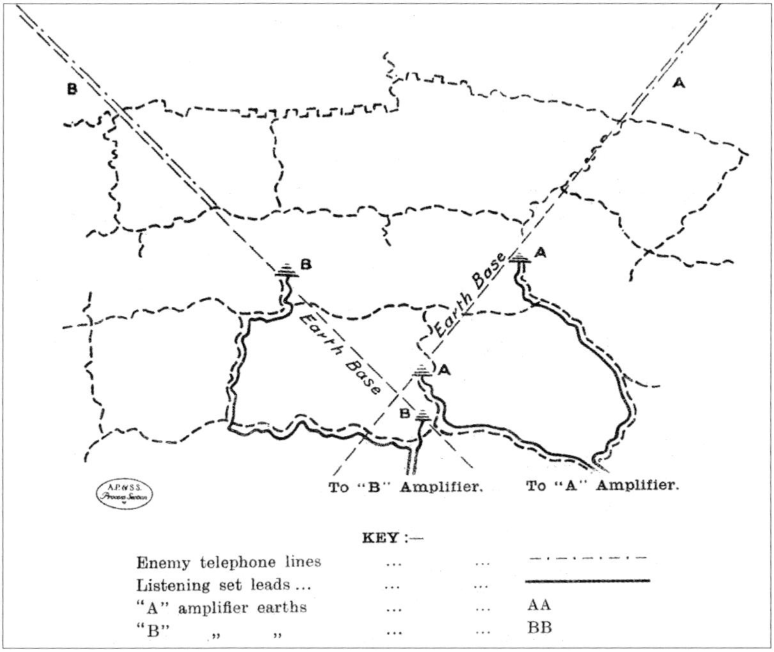

The condition of the enemy lines continually changes on account of bombardment, traffic and other causes common on electrical circuits, and consequently the position and degree of earth leakages on which interception is largely dependent will vary from day to day. The results of listening, therefore, will depend on systematic trial and experiment, which must continue during the whole existence of the Post.

4. *Length of Earth Base.* The length of the intercepting base which will give the best results cannot be laid down, as it depends on the trace of the enemy circuit and the point at which the leakages occur; but generally it is not convenient to cover more than 1,500 yards of front with one Listening Set Post.

5. *Commutator.* The commutator supplied with the Set allows for 8 earth circuits and is so arranged that any combination of these earths can be used (see Appendix C).

6. The necessity for a large number of different earths for each Listening Set is demonstrated clearly by the following diagram, which shows the lines of flow of current between two points of leakage on a telephone circuit and the equipotential lines emanating from these leakage points.

It should be noted that:

(i) Hardly anything will be heard on the pair of earths E4–E6 though both are very close to one of the earth faults on the enemy line, nor on the pair E3–E7, though in this case the base is enormous.

(ii) Either E4 in conjunction with a local earth E0 should give fair results, but equal only to the results on the pair E8–E4.

(iii) Combinations of E6 and E7 with other earths will give disappointing results.

(iv) The pairs E5–E2 and E5–E1 will give the best results – of these the latter is the better.

Owing to the impossibility of knowing at what point the leaks on the enemy line are, and the varied results obtained from different earths, a very complete system of earths at each Listening Set Post is obviously necessary.

7. *Nature of Earth Contacts.* It is of first importance that really good earth contacts be made. For this purpose, earth mats are supplied, which should invariably be used. They are generally superior to bayonets, flattened out tins, or shell cases. These mats should be dug in or well covered over with earth, stamped down sprinkled with copper sulphate and watered.

It has proved an advantage to bury two, three or even four mats at a distance of 5 to 10 yards apart and connected together.

Where there is a layer of soil over chalk, the earth mat should not be deeper than the soil, as it is the soil that mainly carries the current, and the earth is best placed where the surface soil has not been broken up by shell craters.

8. In leading earth lines forward, trenches containing many of our own wires are always to be avoided, as these will cause induction and interference on the line.

9. *Laying Lines.* It is of the utmost importance that when wires are being stapled on to the sides of trenches, the staples should not be driven in so as to injure the insulation of the wire.

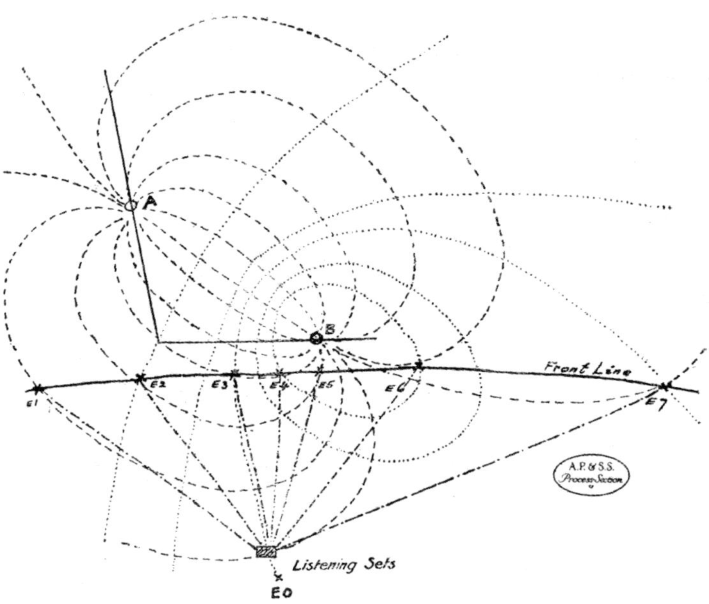

KEY :—

Listening Set Leads	— · — · — · — · — ·
Earths	×
Front line	——— (heavy line)
Enemy telephone circuit, with two earth faults, A and B	——— (thin line)
Lines of flow of earth-leak currents ...	- - - - - - - - - - -
Equipotential lines, cutting above at right angles	·················

NOTE.—An amplifier can overhear nothing from two earths, placed on the same equipotential line.

All lines should be properly labelled every few yards, and in every way follow the recognised practice for the proper installation and maintenance of signal lines.

Testing of lines, other than that described in Appendices B and C, follows the usual Signal practice. In the case of loops, endeavours should be made to maintain the insulation in such condition that the insulation does not fall below 10,000 ohms.

VIII. USE OF MINES AND COMMUNICATION TUNNELS

1. As pointed out [above], to minimise maintenance, use should be made, as far as possible, of mines and communications tunnels, and for this purpose it is essential that the Officer i/c of the Listening Set Posts should keep in close touch with the Officers Commanding the Tunnelling Companies operating in that locality.
2. *Loops in Mines.* It is sometimes possible to lay a loop in a lateral defensive gallery having only one face exposed in the trenches, that is to say, the back of the loop is in our front trenches, the sides of the loop run down two shafts, and the front of the loop is in a lateral defensive gallery. This arrangement, which saves maintenance, had been tried with good results.
3. *Russian Saps.* Russian Saps or shallow mines running out into the enemy's lines have produced excellent results.
4. *Mines in Chalk.* If operations are carried out in chalk when using mines, the earths should be made as far as possible where damp clay pockets exist in the chalk, where the chalk is porous and water percolates through, or where the sap runs into an old crater and the chalk is rubbly, with water coming directly through from the surface. Hard, dry chalk does not give good results. It has been possible, however, on certain occasions, to get so close to the enemy circuits when using mine galleries that good results have been obtained with the earth mat buried in practically dry chalk, but this practice is not likely to give results for a distance of over 60 to 100 feet.

IX. MANIPULATION AND MAINTENANCE OF APPARATUS

1. Instructions relating to the use of the French Valve Telephone Amplifier are contained in Appendix D.
2. To obtain satisfactory working it is of great importance that the instrument should be kept scrupulously clean. No dust should be allowed to accumulate on any part of it.
3. The French instrument and the English Mark II, which is an exact copy of the French instrument, require the greatest care and most delicate manipulation if the best results are to be obtained. When in operation both instruments are liable to howl violently if the

operator, other person, or some object in the dug-out is too close to the instrument. These sounds can often be reduced by careful manipulation of the valve rheostats and the transformer switch. If these fail, the following experiments may be tried:

(a) The operator should be insulated entirely from the ground. This can be done by placing the legs of the chair in the bottom of broken bottles or jam pots, and forming a foot-rest with a piece of board on two glass bottles laid on their side.

(b) Connect the band of the telephone headpiece to Terminals E1 or E2. It will sometimes be found that one terminal will increase the sound and the other reduce it.

(c) Connect the negative terminal of the 4-volt battery to E1 or E2.

(d) Change the order of the valves, or change the valves altogether.

4. It is most important that both the high voltage and low voltage batteries should be in an accessible position and insulated from the ground, that the insulation of leads from the batteries to the instrument should be as perfect as possible, and that all leads should be kept separated.
5. It is important to separate carefully the split contacts of the valve in order to ensure a perfect contact. The valve should not rock when in its holder, but should grip firmly.
6. During thunderstorms the instrument should be disconnected and the line earthed.
7. *Breakdown.* If the instrument ceases to operate, and the fault cannot be located externally, under no circumstances should be the instrument be opened up and repairs attempted in the dug-out. The batteries should be disconnected and a report sent to OC Wireless Section, Corps Signal Company.
8. *Accumulators.* Owing to the rapidly falling voltage curve of the Edison Battery, it has been found that even with the best charge, this battery will not last satisfactorily on a 3-valve Amplifier more than 30 hours. Allowing for normal conditions, such as low charging rate, loss of electrolyte during transport, etc., it can be taken that it is more satisfactory to use the battery for 24 hours only.

   Five batteries are issued with each set (see Appendix D). This allows for two on charge and three in the dug-out. The accumulators have therefore to be changed every two days, the third accumulator being connected to the instrument when the two discharged accumulators are being taken to the transport.

9. Instructions relating to the care and charging of batteries are contained in Appendix E.

Appendix A: Main Points to be observed in entering up Listening Set Forms.

Confidential.

On no account must this document be allowed to fall into the hands of the enemy.

1. The Number of the Listening Set will be entered on each sheet.
2. *Date*. Each sheet to show only the date on which the intercept was taken; thus, Jan 10th and not Jan 10/11th.
3. Each sheet to be numbered in block letters in the top right hand corner of the sheet; thus, Page 1, Page 2, etc. As soon as a 12 or 24 hour shift is finished, a new report will commence with Page 1 again.
4. All times to be expressed in the Continental fashion [24-hour clock] ...
5. At midnight, a fresh sheet with the new date will be started.
6. All German code calls, in addition to being written down as UA, FT, etc., must have their Morse equivalents written underneath.
7. Every conversation should be written down in conversational form, and, wherever possible, a separate line and number given to each speaker.
8. German conversations will be entered up only in the column provided for same. English conversations, on the other hand, will be written across the columns for German and English.
9. All Morse messages will be entered up in block letters, so that they stand out clearly in comparison with ordinary conversation.
10. If any light can be thrown on the nature of the instrument used for sending Morse, if it is out of the ordinary,

remarks will be made in the 'remarks' column, thus: 'German buzzer with a powerful note, much louder than any English buzzers.'

11. All action taken on conversations to be carefully noted in the 'action taken' column. The person to whom the information was conveyed, the means by which the information is conveyed, and the time at which the information was conveyed, should be carefully noted. If no action is taken on a conversation, the word 'nil' should be inserted in the 'action taken' column.
12. The loop or earth on which each conversation is intercepted must be entered up in the 'remarks' column.
13. The signature and rank of the Listener must be appended to each conversation, and at the bottom of the page, the column provided for that purpose only being used. In the event of two Listeners taking down the same conversation, the signature of both will be appended to that conversation.
14. When 'figure' ciphers are being intercepted, a remark should be made in the 'remarks' column as to how the figures were spoken, thus:
    2960. "Neun und zwanzig sechsig" or "Zwei tausend neun hundert und sechsig"
15. Cipher messages should be written out horizontally like an ordinary message and not in tabular form.
16. In the event of any enemy messages, cipher or otherwise, being jammed, as certain portions missing, great care must be taken to show clearly where the missing portions of the message occur. The cause of the interference should also be noted in the 'remarks' column.
17. When using any conventional sign to indicate portions of messages missed, these conventional signs should be clearly explained in the 'remarks' column.
18. If reports are made out and sent to any unit, other than those printed on the form, the name of the unit to whom the report is sent should be clearly entered at the top of the sheet.
19. Handwriting should be firm, so that the carbon copies are clearly legible.

20. Draw a line across the page after each conversation.
21. When a listener is relieved, the time of the relief and the name of the Listener to whom handed over should be entered up on the form.
22. The buff form should normally be retained in the Listening Set dug-out, for record and reference, up to a period of one month.

Appendix B: The Junction Box …

Appendix C: Commutator for use with IT …

Appendix D, Part I: Instructions as to the use of the French Valve Telephone Amplifier …

Appendix D, Part II: Component Parts of Amplifier Low Frequency Valve …

Appendix E: The Edison Storage Battery …

Bibliography

Archival Sources

Australian War Memorial

AWM 27

Imperial War Museum

Oswald Croft interview (1979), Sound Archive 4440
D Manning memoir (1919), 80/1/1
Vince Shirley microfilm (PBS No. 125)

Military Intelligence Museum

Vince Shirley diary

National Archives

1911 Census
Army Lists
AIR 1
First World War Soldiers' Service Records
Foreign Office Lists
HO 144
Navy Lists
RG24
WO95, WO100, WO339, WO374, WO399
UK Incoming Passenger Lists, 1878–1960

Newspapers

Birmingham Gazette
Birmingham Mail
Birmingham Post

Printed Sources

Beach, Jim, *Haig's Intelligence: GHQ and the German Army, 1916–1918* (Cambridge: Cambridge University Press, 2013).

Becke, A.F., *Order of Battle of Divisions: Part 3a, New Army Divisions (9–26)* (Historical Section, Committee of Imperial Defence, 1938) reprinted Uckfield: Naval & Military Press, 2007.

Bourne, John and Bob Bushaway (eds), *Joffrey's War: A Sherwood Forester in the Great War* (Nottingham: Salient Books, 2011).

Bowater, William (ed.), *Birmingham City Battalions: Book of Honour* (London: Sherratt & Hughes, 1920). Digitised by Midlands Historical Data, 2005.

Breul, Karl, *A New German and English Dictionary* (London: Cassel, 1909).

Bryant, Mark, 'Bairnsfather, (Charles) Bruce (1887–1959)', in *Oxford Dictionary of National Biography*, www.oxforddnb.com.

Carter, Terry, *Birmingham Pals: 14th, 15th & 16th (Service) Battalions of the Royal Warwickshire Regiment* (Barnsley: Pen & Sword, 2011).

Cesarani, David, 'An Embattled Minority: The Jews in Britain during the First World War', *Immigrants & Minorities*, special issue (1989), 61–81.

Cockfield, Jamie, *With Snow on their Boots: The Tragic Odyssey of the Russian Expeditionary Force in France during World War I* (London: Macmillan, 1998).

Collins, L.J., *Theatre at War, 1914–18* (London: Macmillan, 1998).

Cooksey, Jon and David Griffith (eds), *Harry's War: The Great War Diary of Harry Drinkwater* (London: Ebury Press, 2013).

Cross, Wilbur, *Zeppelins of World War I* (London: I.B. Tauris, 1991).

Duffett, Rachel, *The Stomach for Fighting: Food and the Soldiers of the Great War* (Manchester: Manchester University Press, 2012).

Emsley, Clive, *Soldier, Sailor, Beggarman, Thief: Crime and the British Armed Services since 1914* (Oxford: Oxford University Press, 2013).

Endelman, Todd, *The Jews of Britain, 1656 to 2000* (Berkeley: University of California Press, 2002).

Englander, David, 'Discipline and Morale in the British Army, 1917–1918', in John Horne (ed.), *State, Society and Mobilization in Europe during the First World War* (Cambridge: Cambridge University Press, 1997).

Ewing, John, *The History of the Ninth (Scottish) Division, 1914–1919* (London: John Murray, 1921).

Falls, Cyril, *Military Operations, France and Belgium, 1917*, Vol. 1 (London: HMSO, 1940).

Ferris, John (ed.), *The British Army and Signals Intelligence during the First World War* (Stroud: Alan Sutton for the Army Records Society, 1992).

Fuller, J.G., *Troop Morale and Popular Culture in the British and Dominion Armies, 1914–1918* (Oxford: Clarendon Press, 1990).

Gibson, Craig, 'Sex and Soldiering in France and Flanders: The British Expeditionary Force along the Western Front', *International History Review*, 23 (2001), 505–756.

—— *Behind the Front: British Soldiers and French Civilians, 1914–1918* (Cambridge: Cambridge University Press, 2014).

Greenhalgh, Elizabeth, *Foch in Command: The Forging of a First World War General* (Cambridge: Cambridge University Press, 2011).

Gunby, David, 'Ball, Albert (1896–1917)', in *Oxford Dictionary of National Biography*, www.oxforddnb.com.

Haber, L.F., *The Poisonous Cloud: Chemical Warfare in the First World War* (Oxford: Clarendon Press, 1986).

Harrison, Mark, *The Medical War: British Military Medicine in the First World War* (Oxford: Oxford University Press, 2010).

Hartigan, John, 'Volunteering in the First World War: The Birmingham Experience, August 1914 – May 1915', *Midland History*, 24 (1999), 167–86.

Henshaw, Trevor, *The Sky Their Battlefield* (London: Grub Street, 1995).

Herzog, Dagmar, *Sexuality in Europe: A Twentieth-Century History* (Cambridge: Cambridge University Press, 2011).

Hill, Kimloan, 'Sacrifices, Sex, Race: Vietnamese Experiences in the First World War', in Santanu Das (ed.), *Race, Empire and First World War Writing* (Cambridge: Cambridge University Press, 2011).

Hinrichs, Ernest (ed.), *Listening In: Intercepting German Trench Communications in World War I* (Shippenburg, PA: White Mane Books, 1996).

Holmes, Colin, *Anti-Semitism in British Society, 1876–1939* (New York: Holmes & Meier, 1979).

Hughes, Clive, 'The New Armies', in Ian Beckett and Keith Simpson (eds), *A Nation in Arms: A Social Study of the British Army in the First World War* (London: Tom Donovan, 1990).

Hussey, A.H. and D.S. Inman, *The Fifth Division in the Great War* (London: Nisbet, 1921).

James, Gregory, *The Chinese Labour Corps (1916–1918)* (Hong Kong: Bayview, 2013).

Jones, Heather, *Violence against Prisoners of War in the First World War: Britain, France and Germany, 1914–1920* (Cambridge: Cambridge University Press, 2011).

Laugesen, Amanda, 'More than a Luxury: Australian Soldiers as Entertainers and Audiences in the First World War', *Journal of War & Culture Studies*, 6:3 (2013), 226–38.

Leask, Margaret, *Lena Ashwell: Actress, Patriot, Pioneer* (Hatfield: University of Hertfordshire Press for the Society for Theatre Research, 2012).

Lebzelter, Gisela, 'Henry Hamilton Beamish and the Britons: Champions of Anti-Semitism', in Kenneth Lunn and Richard Thurlow (eds), *British Fascism: Essays on the Radical Right in Interwar Britain* (London: Croom Helm, 1980).

Lloyd, David, *Battlefield Tourism: Pilgrimage and the Commemoration of the Great War in Britain, Australia and Canada, 1919–1939* (Oxford: Berg, 1998).

Lüdtke, Alf, 'What Is the History of Everyday Life and Who Are Its Practitioners?' in Alf Lüdtke (ed.), *The History of Everyday Life: Reconstructing Historical Experiences and Ways of Life* (Princeton, NJ: Princeton University Press, 1995).

Madigan, Edward, '"Sticking to a Hateful Task": Resilience, Humour, and British Understandings of Combatant Courage, 1914–1918', *War in History*, 20 (2013), 76–98.

Mason, Tony and Eliza Riedi, *Sport and the Military: The British Armed Forces, 1880–1960* (Cambridge: Cambridge University Press, 2010).

McCartney, Helen, *Citizen Soldiers: The Liverpool Territorials in the First World War* (Cambridge: Cambridge University Press, 2005).

—— 'The First World War Soldier and His Contemporary Image in Britain', *International Affairs*, 90 (2014), 299–315.

Meyer, Jessica, *Men of War: Masculinity and the First World War in Britain* (London: Palgrave Macmillan, 2009).

Palazzo, Albert, *Seeking Victory on the Western Front: The British Army and Chemical Warfare in World War I* (Lincoln: University of Nebraska Press, 2000).

Panayi, Panikos, *The Enemy in Our Midst: Germans in Britain during the First World War* (Oxford: Berg, 1991).

—— *German Immigrants in Britain during the Nineteenth Century, 1815–1914* (Oxford: Berg, 1995).

—— *Prisoners of Britain: German Civilian and Combatant Internees during the First World War* (Manchester: Manchester University Press, 2012).

Pennell, Catriona, *A Kingdom United: Popular Responses to the Outbreak of the First World War in Britain and Ireland* (Oxford: Oxford University Press, 2012).

Putkowski, Julian, *British Army Mutineers, 1914–1922* (London: Francis Boutle, 1998).

Rasmussen, Anne, 'The Spanish Flu', in Jay Winter (ed.), *The Cambridge History of the First World War*, Vol. 3 (Cambridge: Cambridge University Press, 2014).

Richter, Donald, *Chemical Soldiers: British Gas Warfare in World War I* (Lawrence: University Press of Kansas, 1992).

Sheffield, Gary, *The Redcaps: A History of the Royal Military Police and Its Antecedents from the Middle Ages to the Gulf War* (London: Brassey's, 1994).

—— *Leadership in the Trenches: Officer–Man Relations, Morale and Discipline in the British Army in the Era of the First World War* (London: Macmillan, 2000).

Simkins, Peter, *Kitchener's Army: The Raising of the New Armies, 1914–16* (Manchester: Manchester University Press, 1988).

—— 'The Four Armies, 1914–1918', in David Chandler and Ian Beckett (eds), *The Oxford Illustrated History of the British Army* (Oxford: Oxford University Press, 1994).

Snape, Michael, *God and the British Soldier: Religion and the British Army in the First and Second World Wars* (Abingdon: Routledge, 2006).

—— (ed.), *The Back Parts of War: The YMCA Memoirs and Letters of Barclay Baron, 1915 to 1919* (Woodbridge: Boydell Press for the Church of England Record Society, 2009).

Stanley, Peter, *Bad Characters: Sex, Crime, Mutiny and Murder in the Australian Imperial Force* (Millers Point, NSW: Pier 9, 2010).

Starling, John and Ivor Lee, *No Labour, No Battle: Military Labour during the First World War* (Stroud: Spellmount, 2009).

Strachan, Hew, *The First World War*, Vol. 1: *To Arms* (Oxford: Oxford University Press, 2001).

Todman, Dan, *The Great War: Myth and Memory*, (London: Hambledon, 2005).

Trask, David, *The AEF and Coalition Warmaking, 1917–1918* (Lawrence: University Press of Kansas, 1993).

Turner, John, *British Politics and the Great War: Coalition and Conflict, 1915–1918* (New Haven, CT: Yale University Press, 1992).

Watson, Alexander, *Enduring the Great War: Combat, Morale and Collapse in the German and British Armies, 1914–1918* (Cambridge: Cambridge University Press, 2008).

Whitton, Frederick, *The History of the Prince of Wales's Leinster Regiment (Royal Canadians)*, Vol. 2 (Aldershot: Gale & Polden, 1926).

Winegard, Timothy, *Indigenous Peoples of the British Dominions and the First World War* (Cambridge: Cambridge University Press, 2012).

Xu Guoqi, *Strangers on the Western Front: Chinese Workers in the Great War* (Cambridge, MA: Harvard University Press, 2011).

Yockelson, Mitchell, *Borrowed Soldiers: Americans under British Command, 1918* (Norman: University of Oklahoma Press, 2008).

Zabecki, David, *The German 1918 Offensives: A Case Study in the Operational Level of War* (London: Routledge, 2006).

Theses

Cherry, David, 'Sex and Morale: The Sexual Life of the British Soldier on the Western Front, 1914–1918', PhD, University of Reading (2012).

Gibson, Craig, 'Relations between the British Army and the Civilian Populations on the Western Front, 1914–18', PhD, University of Leeds (1998).

Kang, Changboo, 'The British Infantry Officer on the Western Front in the First World War with special reference to the Royal Warwickshire Regiment', PhD, University of Birmingham (2007).

Index

alcohol, 21, 28–9, 39, 45, 48, 54, 59, 61, 63–5, 68, 70, 77, 97–8, 101, 107, 109–12, 115–34, 136, 138, 143, 146, 154, 159–60, 166, 169, 178, 181, 183, 187, 189, 195–6, 212, 214, 218–21, 223–4, 230, 233–5, 245, 247–8, 252–6, 258–9, 262, 264–6, 270–2, 278, 282, 285, 291–2, 294, 298
anti-German sentiment, 2–3
anti-Semitism, 73, 90–1; *see also* British soldiers: Lederer, Richard
aircraft, 20, 39–40, 50, 65, 94, 107, 150, 158, 166, 172–3, 181, 188, 204, 242, 244, 263, 266–7, 280, 282, 284, 288; see *also* British Army: RFC/RAF
anti-aircraft guns, 66, 172, 204, 263, 266–8, 284
artillery, 20, 54–5, 60–1, 66, 69, 71, 73, 75–6, 78, 83, 86, 92–3, 94–5, 104–5, 107–8, 117, 122, 126, 129, 140, 144, 149, 151, 153–6, 159–60, 171, 173, 184–5, 188, 192, 212, 223, 231, 237, 239–40, 243–4, 260, 269, 275–7, 286, 289; see *also* British Army: RFA, RGA
Australians, 110, 134
balloons, observation, 284
Barbados, 177
battles
  Arras, 163–7
  Caparetto, 216–17, 222–3
  Lys, 250
  Jutland, 107, 166
  Somme (1916), 14, 80, 93, 104, 106, 118, 120, 130, 158, 192
  Somme (1918), 83, 93, 240–7
  Verdun, 64
bombardments, *see* artillery, mortars
bombing, aircraft, 39–40, 85, 94, 96, 181, 183, 192, 234, 253, 257–8, 263, 266–8, 274, 280, 282, 284, 288
bombs, *see* grenades
Brazil, 185
Britain
  Alcester, 31
  Aston, 217
  Aysgarth, 38
  Birmingham, 1–3, 5, 9, 12–13, 15, 18, 21, 29–31, 66, 181, 217, 226–7, 259, 286
  Bournbrook, 181
  Cardiff, 130
  Codford St Mary, 15, 19, 39–44, 45, 48, 62, 135

Durham, 201
Exeter, 140
Fenny Stratford, 251
Glasgow, 48, 91
Hammersmith, 209
Hornsea, 39–40
Hull, 39, 201
Liverpool, 3, 118
London, 2–3, 40, 101, 160, 182, 227, 279
Malvern, 9, 15, 17, 21, 31–5, 37
Manchester, 3
Moseley, 13–17, 19–22, 24–32, 44
Redcar, 39
Richmond, 36
Salisbury Plain, 9, 15, 17, 40, 42
Small Heath, 217
Sutton Coldfield, 222
Welland, 33
Wensley, 9–10, 15, 17, 35–9
West Bromwich, 1
Wylye, 44
British Army:
Army Service Corps, 35, 46
Intelligence Corps, 4, 11, 93, 103, 133–4, 163–5, 180
Intelligence Police, 79, 90, 101, 103, 105, 108, 111, 113, 120, 124, 129, 131, 143, 148, 159, 169–70, 191, 259, 291
Military Police, 28, 38, 72, 79, 88, 103, 115, 117, 129, 169–70, 178, 180, 183, 215, 228, 259, 295, 299
New Armies, 9–12, 14, 17–19, 22–3, 36
RAMC, 164, 171, 199, 201, 205, 212, 215, 226, 227, 246, 257–8, 261, 278, 279, 286
RE, 54, 70, 103–5, 110, 122, 138, 141–3, 156, 162, 166, 213, 217, 284
RE (Signal Service), 1, 79–81, 83, 89, 100, 101–3, 111, 113–14, 138, 140, 145, 151–2, 169, 175–6, 178, 184, 186–7, 190, 193, 202, 204, 213, 221, 234, 242, 244–6, 251, 254, 259, 273, 277, 285, 288, 292, 294–9
RFA, 105, 113, 149, 275
RFC/RAF, 130, 135, 151, 263, 267
RGA, 130
WAAC, 294–6
British Army: armies
First, 102, 163, 173
Second, 182
Third, 47, 88–9, 102, 156, 163, 173, 194, 221, 240, 258, 261, 273, 277, 285, 292
Fourth, 276
Fifth, 173, 240
British Army: casualty clearing stations
19th, 261
43rd, 89, 246–62, 280
45th, 190
49th, 194
British Army: corps
IV, 272
VI, 79, 88–9, 93, 99, 101, 105, 107, 110, 114, 119, 123, 136, 161–3, 166, 169, 170, 172, 173, 178, 179, 184, 187–8, 190–3, 197–8, 200, 202–3, 212–13, 219–22, 228, 231, 238, 241, 245, 249, 254–5, 261, 273, 277, 280–1, 283, 289, 292–3, 296
XVII, 109
Tank, 287

British Army: divisions
Guards, 279, 282–3, 291
3rd, 89, 155, 160, 279–80, 285
5th, 9, 18, 23, 53, 72, 77, 103
9th, 140, 157–8
11th, 110
12th, 144, 155
14th, 107, 120, 122, 125
16th, 203, 212–13
21st, 200
32nd, 9, 17, 36
34th, 224, 238, 241
41st, 258
51st, 248
56th, 178
59th, 231, 241
62nd, 287
British Army: dressing stations
3rd Division, 89, 279–80
8th Division, 280
VI Corps, 277–8
Guards Division, 279, 281, 289
British Army: hospitals, 49, 63, 85, 87, 96, 129, 189, 194, 220, 226, 246, 267–8
No. 6, 254
No. 19, 257
British Army: infantry battalions
1st Birmingham City see 14/Warwicks
2nd Birmingham City *see* 15/Warwicks
3rd Birmingham City *see* 16/Warwicks
10/Argylls, 140
8/Black Watch, 140
1/Cheshires, 17, 51
5/Dorsets, 110
6/East Kents, 144
8/East Yorkshires, 155
13/Gloucesters
6/Gordons, 248
9/King's Own Yorkshires, 200
7/Leinsters, 213–15
1/Londons, 166
1/Munsters, 203, 212
1/Norfolks, 53
22/Northumberland Fusiliers, 241
1/NZ Entrenching, 248
5/Oxfordshire and Buckinghamshire, 107
19/Royal Welch Fusiliers, 231
5/Shropshires, 107
7/Suffolks, 155
2/Warwicks, 46
14/Warwicks, 12–13, 42, 266
15/Warwicks, 12–13, 45, 101
16/Warwicks, 9, 12–13, 14, 17–18, 20, 24–78, 86, 90, 92, 174, 231
British Army: infantry brigades
8th, 155
9th, 160
15th, 18, 53, 55, 59, 63
26th, 140
34th, 110
35th, 155
37th, 144
41st, 120, 122, 125–6
42nd, 107
43rd, 107–8
47th, 203, 212–14
64th, 200
95th, 17
102nd, 199, 238, 240–1, 243
119th, 231
152nd, 248
British Army: infantry regiments
Artists Rifles, 136

Durham Light Infantry, 103
East Yorkshire Regiment, 133
Norfolk Regiment, 129
Northumberland Fusiliers, 157
Queen's Regiment, 131
Rifle Brigade, 168
Royal Warwickshire Regiment, 107, 132, 136
Suffolk Regiment, 163
British Army: IT stations
No. 21, 143, 149, 151
No. 22, 79, 101, 152, 208
No. 24, 79, 130, 158, 166–7, 175, 180, 199, 210, 225
No. 26, 79, 81, 138, 167, 175–6, 187, 213, 216
see also signals intelligence
British nurses, 63, 129, 177, 189, 249
Dalrymple, Nora, 257
Laing, Mary, 257
VADs, 294, 296
British soldiers
Acton, E.L.L., 214
Auckenthaler, William, 91, 95, 97, 133, 135–7, 139–44, 147, 149, 151–4, 157–8, 161–3, 165–9, 173, 176–7, 179–80, 183, 187–8, 192–3, 195–9, 207, 209, 211–12, 216–18, 220–3, 230, 234–8, 240, 242, 244–7, 250, 267, 273, 275–7, 281, 284–5, 293, 297
Bairnsfather, Bruce, 163, 173
Ball, Albert, 130
Barrance, K.M., 148, 155, 157
Barrow, P.L., 245, 247, 277, 283, 286
Bayliss, E., 53
Bayliss, Sergeant, 270
Benoly, Herbert, 163, 171, 173, 179, 183–4, 187, 189, 200–1, 203–4, 207, 209–10, 216
Bernard, 121
Blackstaffe, Harold, 130
Bobagin, 121
Borham, Frederick, 60
Bowle-Evans, Wakefield, 82, 168–84, 186, 188, 191–2, 198, 220–1, 223
Boyce, 149, 151
Bradgate, Lionel, 245
Breakey, Walter, 130, 167, 202, 205, 207–8, 212–13, 215–16, 231–2
Broomhall, Sergeant, 61
Brydon, Sydney, 102, 106–9
Buckley, G.A.M., 214
Bury, Edward, 82, 163–7
Campbell, W. Pitcairn, 29
Churchill, 'Winston', 137, 143, 145, 147, 153, 156–7, 159, 161
Class, Herbert, 136
Coke, Edward, 148
Corker, William, 201, 210, 217, 232, 240, 242, 244, 255
Cox, 290
Davis, 144, 149, 158, 202, 208–9, 217, 220
de Trafford, Alan, 18, 77
Dell, J.D., 73
Dench, R.A., 214
Denton, 189
Dingley, F., 63, 65, 68, 75–7
Diver, Thomas, 18, 33
Doust, Joseph, 124, 126
Drinkwater, Harry, 5
Dudgeon, Robert, 18, 77
Edwards, 'Dad'/'Daddy'/'Uncle', 208–9, 215–16,

218–19, 225–6, 230, 233, 235–6, 274–5, 283
Eoll, Joseph, 131
Ernie, 263, 265
Evans, Arthur, 188, 249, 277, 283, 292
Floyd, 233
Francke, Frederick, 103, 120–1, 127, 142, 146, 169, 174, 261, 291
Gauge, Joseph, 135
Gilkes, Jack, 101, 103–4, 107–8, 112–13, 115, 118–19, 123–6, 132, 135
Glover, 257
Gosney, Charles, 237
Gosney, Staff Sergeant, 233, 235
Graham, 184
Grassett, Arthur, 105, 107–8, 113, 116
Greenwood, Bertram, 44, 61, 68
Griffin, Sydney, 133, 135–8
Griffiths, 130
Grimes, 255
Hadley, G.H., 67
Haig, Douglas, 135, 194, 298
Haines, Cyril, 201–2, 206–7, 210, 212–13, 224, 229, 236, 239, 241–2, 255
Haldane, Alymer, 179, 255
Harrison, Neville, 44
Harvey, H., 53, 57, 77
Heaven, George, 45–6, 58, 60
Hicken, Charles, 201, 203–4, 207, 210–11, 213, 215–17, 220, 229, 236, 238–40
Hogg, 261–3, 269–70
Horne, Charlie, 262–5, 271, 273
Hutt, Robert, 120, 148
Jack, 266
Jacques, 133–4
Johnson, 296
Jones, D.E., 59
Jones, J.S., 59
Kay, Tommy, 267, 270–1
Kiff, 147, 153, 157–8
La Touche, 280
Lane, 212–13, 235, 275
Lederer, Richard, 84, 90–1, 166–7, 175, 184, 196–7, 208–9, 216–17, 225, 240, 263, 268, 273, 276–9, 292–7
Lewis, David, 18
Lewis, J.W., 58
Lillis, George, 101, 103–4, 109, 113, 115, 117–18, 120, 123, 125–6, 129
Loch, Lord, 179
Magahy, C.H., 214
Manser, F.B., 258
Marsh, E.V., 82, 94, 145, 147–8, 150, 152, 153, 156–62, 166, 176, 179, 197–8, 200, 202, 205–6
Martin, M.J., 49, 63, 175
Mason, 'Blitz'/'Berlitz', 124
Mason, 133
Meredith, 227, 291
Moore, G., 57
Morgan, Peter, 47, 49, 54
Myers, Ronald, 180–1
Newey, F.A., 77
Newton, 'Skipper', 152, 158–9
Nienhaus, Bernard, 84, 297
Noble, 232
Oldham, Richard, 51
Ormerod, 210
Page, J.C., 144
Parkes, Dr, 129
Partridge, 175, 179–81, 183, 187
Paxton, Alexander, 114–15, 117–18

Potter, Herbert, 160
Quinn, 154
Rathbone, William, 118, 144, 148
Redgrave, Harry, 82–3, 88, 97, 102, 108–11, 113–19, 121–4, 126, 128, 132, 136, 138, 143–6, 150, 156–7, 160–1, 176, 187, 189–90, 192–3, 196–7, 200–1, 204–10, 213, 220, 223–6, 229, 237–9, 241–5, 251, 255, 264
Reynolds, 120–1, 146, 219
Richardson, H., 47, 53, 58–9, 61, 63, 72, 77
Roberts, William, 101–3, 105, 107–8, 110–11, 113–26, 132, 135, 154, 156–7, 161, 172, 174, 186, 188, 191, 196, 202–3, 209, 211–13, 215–18, 220–1, 230, 240, 242, 244–5, 255, 284
Robertson, Jock, 101–4, 107, 110, 132
Robinson, Linder, 4, 10, 14–17, 19–20, 22, 30, 37, 39, 42, 43, 45–6, 49, 56, 61, 74, 77, 175, 177, 180–1, 290
Routledge, Edgar, 60
Ryan, J., 214
Sampson, P., 261
Schönland, Basil, 262, 275
Shepherd, 131, 145–6, 199, 218, 226, 242
Simpson, 177
Skinner, Percy, 125–6
Squires, 262, 264, 266, 273
Stallworthy, Cecil, 139–41, 143, 148–9, 152–3, 156, 158, 175, 226–8, 235, 267
Staples, W., 46, 76
Stolzle, Gustav, 133
Sykes, 187, 194, 261, 273
Taffy, 101–2, 109–10, 113, 115, 118, 120–1, 126, 131, 140, 143, 147, 158
Thompson, F.V., 162
Titterton, Philip, 16, 22, 42, 47, 53–4, 56, 58, 63, 65–6, 74, 111–12
Tucker, 185, 196, 198–9, 202, 227, 236–8, 242, 244, 255
Vine, Arthur, 113, 118, 126, 133
Walters, G.E., 48, 65
Watson, Bob, 208–9
Watts, 113, 118, 121, 126
Weaver, H.J., 54, 75
Webb, H., 34
White, 'Major', 135, 143, 148–9, 153, 155–6, 161, 196, 202, 219, 273
Whittingham, A.E., 54–5, 63, 65
Wolridge, Jimmy, 263–4
Woodhouse, E. de C., 165
Woodward, H.T., 54

Cameroons, 130
Canada, 40, 133–4, 172, 177, 252–4, 256, 259, 267
casualties, 11–12, 14, 19, 52, 54, 59, 104, 200, 214, 247, 261
cavalry, 104, 289
Chinese workers, 255–6
Church Army, 111, 114, 119, 158, 188, 190–1, 223, 228, 234
church, *see* religion
cinema, 6, 40, 96, 111, 114, 116, 130, 158, 162, 191, 195–6, 219, 229, 235, 251, 253, 257, 265, 273, 296
civilians, 6, 15–17, 20–1, 30–1, 34–5, 37–40, 44–9, 61–3, 65, 77, 89, 94–5, 97–9, 109–12, 114,

116–17, 119–25, 127–9, 131, 133, 135, 138, 142–3, 146–8, 158, 165, 167, 169, 179–83, 188–90, 193–4, 196–9, 208, 218–19, 222–4, 229, 235, 247–8, 250–62, 266–73, 277, 285, 291–2, 294–5, 299
Ainsley, Miss, 295
Ashwell, Lena, 295
Asquith, Herbert Henry, 226
Birmingham, Lord Mayor of, 30
Candas, Mme, 179
Carmen, 138
Carpentier, M., 183
Claire, 120, 122, 125, 128, 131, 208, 219, 221–3, 234
Colette, 127
Crainket, M., 183
D, Mrs, 31
Day, Dorothy, 295
Degonne, Mme, 260–1
Denise, 127
François, M., 169
Hortense, 116
Ivonne, Mme/Mlle, 49, 124, 127–9, 131
Jeanne, Mme, 253–4
Julianne, 258, 273, 294
Karno, Fred, 272
Kerensky, Alexander, 194
L, Mrs, 15, 30
Luce, 120, 122, 129
Lucianne/Lucy, 252–7
Lucile, Mme, 98, 271–3, 294
Lulu (Amiens), 199, 229
Madeleine, 22, 46
Magniez, Mme, Ivonne and Jeanne, 143, 146, 148, 169, 219, 235, 291
Maria, 117, 123
Martel, M., 182
Mathiny, Mlle, 120
Poole, Rev. E.M. and Mrs, 34
Povey, Rev W.J., 34
Pruvost, Mme, 95, 142, 158, 181–3, 219, 235
Robinson, Mrs, 15, 37
Rosa, Mme, 123–4, 128
Smith, Gipsy, 147
Susanne, 111–12, 114
Suzanne, 218, 229
Williams, Mr, 30
Wilson, President, 226, 296
Colombia, 2
concerts, 20, 30, 39–40, 74, 96, 111, 125, 129, 148, 151, 157–8, 175, 177–8, 224, 229, 234, 250–1, 256, 258–9, 272, 295–6
cooking, *see* food and drink
Cuba, 2

dentists, 129–30, 132, 228, 258
doctors, 75, 135, 181–2, 204, 212, 233, 258

engineers, 45, 72, 99, 102, 124, 148, 191, 256, 286; *see also* British Army: RE, RE (Signal Service)

food and drink, 19–20, 24–7, 29, 31–5, 37–40, 42, 44–50, 52, 54, 56–7, 59, 61–5, 67–72, 74, 76–7, 84, 88, 90–1, 94–5, 97–8, 102–4, 106–17, 119–30, 132–4, 136, 140, 142–4, 148–56, 159–60, 162–3, 165–7, 169, 176, 181–8, 191, 194–6, 198, 200–11, 214–30, 232–7, 239–40, 246–51, 254–6, 258, 261, 263–4, 267, 270–5,

280–1, 282–3, 288, 291, 293–4, 296; *see also* alcohol
France and Belgium
Abbeville, 79, 84, 89, 91, 95, 293–9
Achicourt, 101, 103–4, 107–8, 179
Achiet-le-Grand, 190, 195, 207, 293
Agniez lès Duisans, 68, 74, 77
Albert, 104, 106, 192–3, 218, 250, 269
Amiens, 22, 62–3, 98, 190, 192–3, 196–8, 208, 218, 229, 253, 276
Ancre, 293
Armentières, 250
Arras, 9, 16, 66, 68, 71–2, 75, 78–80, 87–90, 92, 95–8, 101, 103, 105, 107, 111, 113, 115, 119, 123–4, 127, 129, 131, 138, 142–3, 148–50, 152, 156, 158, 160–1, 162, 166–8, 172, 177, 189, 199, 219, 235, 269, 280–1, 291
Avesnes-le-Comte, 111–12, 114, 116–17, 123, 129–30, 159, 162, 247, 249, 262
Ayette, 279
Bac-du-Sud, 247, 277, 285
Bapaume, 125, 190, 193, 245, 280–1, 293
Barly, 119
Beaumont Hamel, 270
Beaumetz-lès-Cambrai, 285
Beaurains, 189
Béhagnies, 190, 192, 229
Belloy-sur-Somme, 64
Bernaville, 118, 121, 123, 127–30, 264
Bihucourt, 190, 194
Boisleux-au-Mont, 220, 221, 224, 228, 234, 245
Boulogne, 44, 118, 219, 226
Bourlon Wood, 222
Boyelles, 207, 209–10, 213, 215–18, 224, 227, 233, 238, 239, 242, 244
Bray-sur-Somme, 50, 52, 55, 58, 60
Brétencourt, 221, 234, 245
Bruges, 291
Bullecourt, 198, 204–5, 208, 227, 241
Cambrai, 221, 285–9, 293
Canal du Nord, 286
Candas, 64, 89, 98, 179, 261–3, 293
Carnières, 290
Caudry, 291
Corbie, 61
Coullemont, 65
Courcelette, 192
Croiselles, 79, 199–201, 203–5, 207–10, 223, 225, 228–30, 232–3, 236, 240–2
Dainville, 88–9, 127, 129, 162, 165, 170, 199
Delville Wood, 120
Douai, 291
Doullens, 64–5, 98, 194, 262–3, 271–3, 285
Duisans, 68, 188
Écoust-Saint-Mein, 205–6, 209–10, 213, 216, 223, 227, 241
Ervillers, 281
Étaples, 267
Étinehem, 49, 52, 54
Étrun, 198
Flesquières, 287–8

Frévent, 89, 247–9, 251, 256, 258–62, 285
Gézaincourt, 263, 266, 268
Gouy-en-Artois, 119, 246, 277–8
Hamelincourt, 279–80
Harbarcq, 68
Hauteville, 65
Havrincourt, 287, 289
Hermies, 289
Hesdin, 79, 88, 91, 98, 132–3, 136–7, 256
Humbercamps, 277
Kemmel, 253
Lagnicourt-Marcel, 281–5
Le Cateau-Cambrésis, 289
Lens, 98, 251, 271
Le Sars, 192
Ligny-sur-Canche, 250–1, 259–60
Lille, 291–2
Longpré, 45
Longueval, 112
Lys, 250, 253
Marcoing, 288, 293
Masnières, 289
Mercatel, 126
Messines, 182, 267
Molliens-Vidame, 62
Monchy-le-Preux, 204
Montdidier, 276
Montreuil, 135
Mory, 281
Mouflers, 46
Neuville-Saint-Vaast, 180
Neuville-Vitasse, 254, 267
Noyelle-Vion, 110, 113–14, 123, 130, 162, 251, 254, 262, 273, 289
Ostende, 246, 291–2
Paris, 119, 171, 245
Péronne, 156, 245
Pont Noyelles, 47
Poulanville, 62
Pozières, 110, 192
Ransart, 279
Riencourt, 208
Rivière, 110, 112, 114–15, 117–18, 120, 122, 125
Roclincourt, 174
Saint Catherine, 172
Saint Nicholas, 68, 70
Saint-Léger, 210–11, 215, 218–20, 230–3, 238, 240–2
Saint-Pol-sur-Ternoise, 124, 129, 161
Saint Riquier, 45
Saint Sauveur, 161, 174
Scheldt, 297
Selle, 292
Solesmes, 289
Somme, 9, 14, 16, 80, 93, 104, 106, 118, 120, 151, 158, 192, 240
Thiepval, 120
Vaux-sur-Somme, 48
Vimy, 118
Vignacourt, 47
Wailly, 109, 111, 117
Warlus, 111, 114, 117–19, 121, 123–4, 126–31, 138, 161, 166
Wyschaete, 182
Ypres, 118, 182, 195
French army, 61, 64–5, 69, 80, 92, 186–8, 190, 196, 199, 251, 276
First Army, 276
Foreign Legion, 91
graves, 72
French soldiers
Demey, Paul, 181
Georges, 223
Indo-Chinese, 190–1, 224
Masquelin, 182

games
  cards, 24, 44, 49, 61, 74, 96–7, 116, 120, 122, 128, 130–1, 159, 201, 203, 215, 217–18, 231–3
  Crown and Anchor, 52, 76, 267
German army:
  airmen, 85, 244, 262, 284
  Alsatians, 133, 171, 174, 186
  Lorrainers, 198
  Poles, 173, 180, 261, 263, 269
  withdrawal to Hindenburg Line, 151, 156
German army infantry regiments:
  Guards Reserve, 283
  76th, 185
  119th, 178
  121st, 171
German documents, 85, 95, 162, 185, 191, 193, 221, 223, 269, 290
German economy, 89, 193, 218
German prisoners, 84, 88–9, 93, 112, 116–17, 163, 168, 184, 191–2, 194, 212–14, 221, 232, 245–6, 249, 261, 263–4, 267–8, 270, 277, 283, 292, 295–9
German soldiers
  Brandenbourg, 186–7
  Hentze, 185
  Wachsmann, 185
  von Wohlgemuth, 284
German U-boats, 85, 228, 232
German wireless press, 207, 217
Germany
  Alsace-Lorraine, 85, 223, 237
  Cologne, 103
  Hamburg, 103
  Hildesheim, 2, 145, 185
  Stuttgart, 101
  Westphalia, 1
  Württemburg, 171
grenades, 52, 74, 122, 143, 214; *see also* rifle grenades

horses, 35, 41, 49, 77–8, 174, 181, 190, 229, 279, 282, 289, 292, 294

infantry, 1–2, 5–7, 9–78, 80–2, 85–6, 88, 90, 92–7, 99–100, 102–4, 113–14, 120, 133, 138, 173, 183, 209, 211, 213, 215, 231, 238–9, 243, 266, 289, 291; *see also* British Army: infantry battalions; British Army: infantry regiments
Intelligence B *see* British Army: Intelligence Police
intelligence, military, 1–2, 4–6, 11, 34, 79–101, 111, 146, 159, 162, 167, 172, 175, 188, 190–1, 198, 203, 222, 224, 248, 259, 261, 273, 277, 280, 283, 292, 295, 297; *see also* British Army: Intelligence Corps, Intelligence Police

Kaiser Wilhelm II, 145, 298

Lusitania, 3

machine-guns, 53, 94, 106, 120, 122, 149, 171–4, 185, 205, 210, 213, 241–2, 244, 267, 281–2, 284
mail, 200, 234, 297; *see also* parcels
medical services, *see* British Army: casualty clearing stations; British Army: dressing stations; British Army: hospitals; British Army: RAMC; dentists, doctors
Mexico, 2–3

mortars, 51, 53, 55, 59–60, 66, 70, 72, 93, 104, 113, 122, 140, 144, 146, 150, 156, 170, 200–1, 289

newspapers and magazines, 30, 32, 48, 85, 153, 193, 259
Berliner Tageblatt, 153
Birmingham Gazette, 2–3
Birmingham Mail, 3
Birmingham Post, 3, 9, 12–13, 18, 24, 29
Blighty, 112
Bystander, 282
Daily Mail, 112, 136, 142, 156, 251, 297
Frankfurter Zeitung, 181–2
Leipziger Neuerste Nachrichten, 153
London Gazette, 1–2
Nash's, 110, 112
Petit Parisien, 136, 142
La Vie Parisienne, 153, 157
New Zealanders, 72, 76, 148, 248, 257, 289

Old Timers' Club, 11, 45, 138

parcels, 20, 37, 56, 58, 65, 74, 108, 195, 217, 227
policing, *see* British Army: Military Police
post, *see* mail

reading, 6, 20, 30, 39, 42, 44, 49, 52, 64, 67, 69, 71, 73, 76, 85, 96, 98, 103, 106, 110, 112, 114, 116, 118–20, 122, 125, 136, 150, 152, 177, 188–9, 193, 198–9, 202, 208, 218, 226, 228, 230–2, 235, 251, 258, 268, 282, 291
religion, 20, 28, 34, 38, 40, 49–50, 61, 63–4, 78, 95, 103, 116, 127, 136–7, 192, 222, 224, 255, 290, 298–9; *see also* Church Army; Salvation Army; YMCA
rifle grenades, 70, 76
rifles, 10, 14, 17, 19, 27–9, 34, 36, 39, 41–2, 45, 51–2, 60–1, 65–7, 73, 76–7, 94, 108, 112, 122, 132–3, 213, 231, 241, 243, 287
royal visit, 247–8

Salvation Army, 30, 40
Schürhoff, Vince
attitude towards enemy, 13
commission applications, 11–12, 21, 57–9, 63, 77, 81, 259, 264
danger, 18–19, 93–4
diary, 4–6, 16, 38
education in Germany, 1–2, 145
everyday life, 16–22, 91–9
father, 1–3, 13, 51, 45, 83, 106, 113, 120, 121, 135, 217, 230
first time in trenches, 17, 50–2
French language skills, 2, 10, 20, 45–6, 72, 79, 128, 162, 177, 198, 252, 254, 258
friendships, 16, 23
Gas NCO, 9, 11, 68, 70–1, 73–4, 76–7
German language skills, 2, 71–2, 77, 79, 81, 84, 125, 133–4, 213–15, 258, 297
initial training, 17, 24–44
injured, 47–8, 57, 75–6
joins 16/Warwicks, 12–13, 24
leadership style, 81–2
military motivation, 12–14, 84–7
MM, 1, 3, 80, 83, 251, 254–5, 257, 264

name change to Shirley, 1, 262
promotions, 1, 10, 31, 80, 97, 217–18, 288, 296
settings, 14–16, 87–91
sexuality, 16, 21–2, 63, 98–9, 136, 171, 193, 196
status, 9–12, 80–4
transfer to intelligence, 1–2, 4, 16, 79, 101
transfer to RE, 1, 80–1, 111, 122, 138
uncle, 2–3
to Western Front, 17–18, 44
scouts, 10, 31, 33–4, 37, 49
sex, *see* Schürhoff, Vince: sexuality
Shirley, Vince, *see* Schürhoff, Vince
signalling, 49, 71, 80–1, 87–8, 90, 92, 106, 119, 128, 135, 143, 146, 149, 160, 162, 166, 201, 203, 224, 227–8, 231, 237–8, 241, 243, 263, 278–9; *see also* British Army: RE (Signal Service)
signals intelligence, 5, 79–83, 86–7, 90–5, 96–7, 100–61, 175–6, 187, 193, 197, 199–243, 255, 274–7, 301–16; *see also* British Army: IT stations
smoking, 20–1, 26–7, 29, 35, 42, 45, 54, 57, 65, 67, 69, 76, 106, 108, 121, 142, 147, 153, 158, 160, 169, 183, 197, 202–3, 214, 218, 225–6, 231, 247, 251, 258, 279
snipers, 13, 49, 55, 58, 61, 66, 77, 106
sports, 20–1, 97
athletics, 21, 34, 74–5
fishing, 250–1
football, 21, 35, 63, 97, 128, 135, 137, 189, 208
horse racing, 77
physical training, 61, 97, 179–80
swimming, 97, 191
tennis, 21, 25, 34, 97, 188, 195, 197, 199

tanks, 192, 220–1, 287; *see also* British Army: corps, Tank
trench systems
cellars, 66, 74–5, 88, 101–2, 138, 140–50, 152, 154–5, 157, 159–61, 167–8, 176, 209, 289–90, 292
digging, 31, 54–5, 72, 86, 157, 168, 189, 195, 203, 209, 253
dug-outs, 14, 41, 50–1, 53–6, 58–61, 66–7, 69–73, 75–7, 85, 88, 97, 109, 114, 121–2, 125–6, 157, 176, 187–8, 192, 199–201, 203–4, 206–8, 210–11, 214, 225–7, 230–3, 235–44, 267, 274–7, 281, 288–9
listening posts, 69, 73, 171
saps, 52, 57, 60, 66, 72, 76, 140, 171
trenches, 12, 14–15, 17–22, 40–2, 49–61, 66–8, 70–2, 74–5, 78, 80–2, 86–8, 90–6, 98–100, 109–11, 113–16, 121, 125–6, 133, 140, 144, 149–50, 156–7, 164, 171, 174, 176, 188, 199–201, 207–10, 214, 225, 231, 236, 238, 241–3, 257, 274, 286–9
tunnels, 148, 154, 156–7, 159, 161, 214, 236, 239
tobacco, *see* smoking

wireless, *see* British Army: RE (Signal Service); signalling

YMCA, 15, 29–30, 40, 95, 113, 146–7, 171, 190, 191, 208, 211, 228, 230–1, 259, 265
Zanzibar, 103
Zeppelins, 39–40, 166